FROM JAZZ FUNK & FUSION TO ACID JAZZ
THE HISTORY OF THE UK JAZZ DANCE SCENE

To my wife Sarah and our two rascals Jessie and Lillie

London Jazz Dancers IDJ circa 1986 . Photo bu Nick White

AuthorHouse™ UK
1663 Liberty Drive
Bloomington, IN 47403 USA
www.authorhouse.co.uk
Phone: UK TFN: 0800 0148641 (Toll Free inside the UK)
*   UK Local: 02036 956322 (+44 20 3695 6322 from outside the UK)*

First published by Chaser Publications and AuthorHouse 08/07/2020

ISBN: 978-1-4389-7360-9 (sc)

Print information available on the last page.

FROM JAZZ FUNK & FUSION TO ACID JAZZ

THE HISTORY OF THE UK JAZZ DANCE SCENE

BY MARK 'SNOWBOY' COTGROVE

authorHOUSE

Design by Swifty

CONTENTS

Rhythm Doc, Linford 'Fanny' Taylor, Eric X, The Fusion Few (by Stretch and Lizard), Fire and Robert Johnson, Spectrum, Mahogany/Jazz 5 (by Big John and Rico), Smiler and Bruce Q.

149. THE DANCERS -

Talking to the original dancers that inspired the innovators of the London 'Fusion' Style – Travis Edwards, Leon Herbert, Dez Parkes, Trevor Shakes, Paul Anderson, Michael Brown and Kevin 'The Penguin' Haynes.

Talking to members of the barrier-breaking Fusion Jazz Dance troupe – I.D.J., Gary and Seymour Nurse, Perry Louis of Bubble And Squeak (and currently, leader of the Jazzcotech troupe) and members of the equally barrier-breaking Swing/Be Bop troupe – Brothers In Jazz.

FOREWORD

In the summer of 1999 I came across Snowboy's Mambo Rage CD. I got excited. I had not heard such rich and thrilling Mambos since early Perez Prado or mature Tito Puente. Snowboy and his jazz-mambo messengers ('The Latin Section') were taking the music several degrees forward and I could not wait to hear them live. So I flew over and grabbed a cab to the Jazz Cafe in Camden Town in North London. It was one of Snowboy's Sunday night Hi-Hat sessions. He was DJing in a corner, challenging the dancers with Coltrane, Palmieri, chants to the Orisha of the Yoruba, and his own hard-swinging Mambos. On other evenings he was on stage with his mighty band and when he took several solos I could easily see why he is considered the best Brit conguero of them all. Responding to all this: young men and women on the floor unleashed lightning-fast footwork. One danced up the wall like Donald O'Connor. Several broke to the floor a la Bronx. Two came down in splits like the Nicholas Brothers. In other words, there was a lot of what we might call motion erudition flaunted on the floor. They were aware of jazz steps and where they all came from. But, at the same time, they were not copying Black America but minting something new. This was jazz dance passed through new minds and strong bodies. It was energy blessed with promise and direction.

The jazz dancers were rewriting the geography of the United Kingdom. Leeds and Manchester and Liverpool and London were now more than just towns. They were alive each with it's own compact style of jazz dance. And as if that weren't complicated enough jazz dancing ran in tandem with another British scene, called Northern Soul, which as Snowboy tells us, has "a specific, very gymnastic style of dancing." In the process, the dancers of Britain proved that you can dance to modern jazz, that bop did not totally abandon dancehalls but came back as bop-flavored mambo. If Bird played mambo, and he did, it's therefore not strange to see young blacks dancing to bebop in Mura Dehn's classic film. But nowhere has jazz been danced to as ingeniously over the past thirty years as in the UK. The need for comprehending this world-class achievement is immense.

Now, with Mark 'Snowboy' Cotgrove, the field has found its Homer. In his book there is everything you could possibly want, a history of UK Jazz Dance, an assessment of UK Jazz Dance styles, plus a history of Fusion music and Fusion dance. The text is well-armed with copious interviews, reminding us of the rewriting of the artistic geography of England and Scotland in the fact that we listen to informed voices from Scotland to Kent and back again, There is a section devoted to interviews with the dancers, the original dancers who inspired the rise of the great London Fusion style.

The writing is direct, free of affectation or pretense. Cotgrove talks to us in his own level voice, drawing us in, DJing points. Shakespeare himself, who once poked fun at Norman over-elegance in favor of direct Anglo-Saxon, would have been proud of this lad. In sum, the cultural significance of this text is immense. It is a classic in the field of dance and music.

Robert Farris Thompson

ACKNOWLEDGEMENTS

I'd been doing this book on and off for so long now that I'd lost track of how many years I'd been chipping away at it, and then realized that the first interview (Bob Jones) was done over 9 years ago!

As a professional musician, I've literally lost thousands of hours of quality practice and song-writing time doing this. In some ways, that side of my career has almost been on hold for the last few years. It's been a lone quest to get this book done - driving the most abstract amount of miles (I'm talking thousands) and receiving punishing phone bills, so I hope you think it's all worth it.

As thorough as this book is, there are still people that I couldn't get to or couldn't track down or have missed out by mistake (I'm sure), so I apologize in advance for that. And of course there were the few people that just wouldn't be interviewed or never turned up at arranged meeting places (on one occasion I drove 250 miles each way to Leeds and back for that to happen!). These are all the reasons that I will never, ever write a book again (even though there still needs to be more books written on our Jazz Funk, Rare Groove, Jungle/Drum and Bass and UK Garage movements). I've befriended hundreds of people from this scene through this project and finally put 'faces to names', but if I'd known how long it would've taken and how extremely unhelpful, selfish and inhospitable a few people would've been I wouldn't have done it, but it's finally finished and I'm very happy. It needed doing.

I'd like to thank all of you that sorted me out with the phone numbers of the most elusive people or getting interviews arranged for me - especially Sarah Foote @ Favouritizm for initiating the Pete Tong interview; Bruce Qureshi for the sheer amount of contacts in Birmingham that he gave me; Fitzroy The Buzzboy for convincing George Power that I, rightly, wouldn't stitch him up (George now has finally got his rightful place in British club history) and Lincoln Wood for liaising the Japanese interviews; to Colin Curtis, Chris Hill and Bob Jones (without these innovative DJ's there wouldn't have been a book to write in the first place); to the UK's unique and varied Jazz Dancers whose creative and innovative steps have always inspired me in many ways - from Huddersfield to Oldham; from Newcastle to Devon; from Norwich to Glasgow - I just physically couldn't get to you all, but this book is for you; thanks also to all of you that offered me photos and various memorabilia (even if some of you never actually gave them to me! - at least you offered); the legendary photographers Peter Williams, Ian Tilton, Kevin Cummins, Nick White and Eric Watson for being so generous with their photos; thanks to everyone that I interviewed, of course, and to Gary Dennis for the loan of his Blues and Souls; Keith Griffin for his Black Echoes; Ralph Tee for the Groove Weeklys; Phil Levene for his Black Music and Jazz Reviews; Keb Darge for giving me his place to host many interviews; Roger Armstrong, Carol Fawcett, Dean Rudland and all at Ace Records for the eight days going through Billboard magazines in the warehouse (without lunch-breaks); Swifty for his amazing artwork, and his partner Janine Neye for sharing her important 'Dingwalls' personal memorabilia and photographs; Seymour Nurse: one of the few other people I know who's just as bothered about UK Jazz Dance history as I am (www.thebottomend.co.uk) - as our massive phone bills show; Perry Louis - who tirelessly promotes our dance-style; thanks to everyone else that also encouraged me, and in particular Mike Chadwick, Mark Webster, Adrian Gibson, Peter Haigh, the publisher and historian Mike Ritson whose book The In Crowd was an ongoing source of inspiration, the great dance historian Terry Monaghan and lastly, my dear friend Professor Robert Farris Thompson of Yale University whose many visits to the UK just to experience my band, my DJ-ing, the Jazz Dance scene and (ultimately) the amazing dancers, would have been inspiration enough to want to have done this book alone. Thank you for that fantastic 'foreward' too Bob. I couldn't have wished for more.

Special thanks go to my family - and finally my wife Sarah, who typed it out for me (and just wanted me to finish the book!).

I did this book because I thought it was about time that our unique Jazz Dance scene and all the DJ's and incredibly talented dancers within it are recognized properly for the first time. For such an enormous scene, Jazz Dance - and its predecessor Jazz Funk - continues to either not get mentioned or barely acknowledged in other music-history books, so now I've re-addressed the situation.

Mark 'Snowboy' Cotgrove

PREFACE

I have a life-long love of Doo Wop, Rockabilly, Rock And Roll, Blues, Rhythm And Blues and all other permutations thereof (like Cajun, Zydeco, French Hot Jazz, Hillbilly etc) which was sparked off from the soundtrack album of the British 1950's-based film That'll Be The Day in 1973 - which my brother Paul (as a second generation Teddy Boy) played constantly. The interest galvanized a year later with the release of Francis Ford Coppola's incredible, life-affirming film American Graffiti - with its Doo Wop-heavy soundtrack. With the odd exception of an occasional flirtation with a Glam Rock record, this was the soundtrack to my youth.

It all changed in 1978, when, as a 17 year old, I went to Southend College Of Technology to study graphic design. I'd stopped going to Rockabilly clubs by then because of the escalating violence in them, so I had no social life, but luckily an old childhood friend of mine, Paul Webb, started trying to convert me to his taste in music. At that age, already an incredible bass player and multi-instrumentalist, he would smother me with Jazz Fusion records by Weather Report, Return To Forever, Brand X and - I remember - the George Benson album Breezin' (it was an alien sound to someone who was brought up on the twelve-bar Blues of Crazy Cavan And The Rhythm Rockers!). In September of that year he encouraged me to go to a disco on Canvey Island three miles away called The Goldmine, and I relented. With he and his friends from the fashion college, we went there and (without being too emphatic about this) on entering, the atmosphere hit me like a ton of bricks - the DJ (Chris Hill), the music, the fashion, the dancing (Mark White, Elvis Da Costa, Laurence and Stewart Dunn, Mick 'Ralph' Ricks, Rob West, 'Remould'....) - I'd never seen or heard anything like it in my life; and that was IT. I'm very proud to tell you that Paul went on to be one of the founder members of the band Talk Talk - one of the most important bands of the 1980's, and thanks to him (I now realize), that first night out at The Goldmine (and his insistence on pushing his Jazz Fusion collection on me) set me off on a love affair of all forms of Jazz, and Black music in general, that has seen me follow a path where I firstly became a DJ, and then a Latin Percussionist and Recording Artist, and eventually it lead me to writing this book that you are now reading.

INTRODUCTION

Let's get a few things straightened out before I start: Firstly, for you British readers - this is NOT a book about the UK Jazz Funk movement of the late 70's. I mention this now because there are loads of DJ's from the 1970's that you'll probably be looking for in here that I haven't interviewed. Of course, their contributions to that particular scene would have been integral, but I'm just dealing with the ones who put Jazz on the dancefloors of the countries discoteques then. Like any movement, despite many, many DJ's playing Jazz (actually - Jazz Fusion), it took just a few innovative ones to create the environment in the first place to make it possible to do it. Naturally, I have heavily gone through the Jazz Funk movement to get to the Jazz Dance one of the 1980's, so it's all here. Like the many books that there already are on our Northern Soul scene, there still needs to be one just done on its neighbouring, enormous, national Jazz Funk movement too.

Secondly, as I mention later - the 'Jazz Dance' that is the subject of this book is not the 'Jazz Dance' of the 1930's in the US. It is a scene that was created here in the UK by innovative DJ's daring to play Jazz Fusion next to the Disco, Funk, Soul and Jazz Funk releases of the time - inspired (and probably cajoled, in some instances) to play harder grooves and faster tempos by the dancers. From just initially freestyle dancing, the dancers were developing steps to particularly take-on the increasingly challenging music - which, in-turn made the DJ's dig up even more records to taunt and tempt them with. Although some dancers later, in the 1980's, admittedly, did eventually take steps from the classic 'Hoofers' from the Harlem Cotton Club era - like The Nicholas Brothers and The Berry Brothers, initially it was all straight out of the discoteques of the UK.

I'm glad that all this has been documented at last. Jazz Dance steadily grew for nearly twenty years until the Acid Jazz movement had virtually killed it off by 1992, but prior to that it had been a very large and inspirational movement that had not been properly documented. Every scene feels that they're playing maverick music, but we were playing John Coltrane, Art Blakey and Chick Corea in discoteques! Now that's maverick! This was a soundtrack to the most vicious and intense dance battles on the dancefloor, where the dancers would spend many of their waking hours preparing moves for the next battle - in most cases, for the reputation of their area.

   One of the things that this book uncovers was the essential, but uneasy, relationship between the DJ and the dancer. The DJ was happy to welcome the heavy dancers in to their club because it would give them a busy floor early in the evening and it would be something impressive for the punters to see as they come in, but it would be the same dancers that would later destroy the dancefloor at peak-time by dispersing it by creating a battle-circle. Also, of the thousands of people that liked dancing to Jazz of all tempos, they didn't like being forced off of the floor when challenges happened either. I was absolutely surprised how many high-profile DJ's candidly moaned to me about the dancers, and I was equally surprised, in contrast, at the amount of dancers that believed the DJ's or Clubs couldn't do without them. At the end of the day, what DJ wants to see their busy dancefloor ruined?

   Personally, I have great interest in the dancers (and their unique styles) and felt that it's just as important to put their stories and opinions across as the DJ's. As for the dancers in this book: I mainly interviewed various members from all the main professional or semi-professional Jazz Dance troupes (as opposed to crews) around the country (from areas that had a significant scene), as I found that these troupes were made up of all their areas best dancers anyway. It is right that they finally get a chance to speak.

Another thing that had always been present in this scene was the North/South divide. It wasn't really until the 1980's that DJ's started to travel all over, but before then DJ's only knew what was being played elsewhere by reading the charts in magazines like Blues And Soul or hearsay. The North/South divide wasn't really helped that much by Northern music journalist Frank Elson, who had a page or two in every edition of Blues And Soul then. He would never miss an opportunity to make barbed comments about Southerners. With all of todays technology, I was still shocked at the naivety of the DJ's and punters alike of what they perceived went on elsewhere: I've spoken to Londoners that didn't realize much went on outside of the capital, in the same way that I've had many Northerners boldly stating: "this started here", or "that started here", without any hard facts to back their opinions up other than basing them on area pride.

I've traveled hard and far to make sure that the whole countries of England and Scotland are represented because, at the end of the day, yes there IS area pride at stake here, and so I've been meticulous about detail. If I'm wrong about anything it's because I'd been told the information wrong by my sources; despite trying to cross-reference everything. After all, most of the people I've interviewed had never been before and were quite nervous.

As balanced and impartial as I've tried to be (and believe me, I am very sensitive to this), the London section has ended up unintentionally enormous. I couldn't ignore the fact that so much more happened there than anywhere else (by far) just to appease other areas. That's just the way it is. In actual fact, a big proportion interviewed about London were from different parts of the country anyway, they just lived and worked there.

In writing this book, I was very inspired by the only book written on the life of Tito Puente - *The King of Latin Music* by Steven Loza. The book basically consists of loads of different interviews about him and the environment around him, so put into a logical order it is a fantastic read because the story just unfolds bit-by-bit. And that is just what the main part of this book is - interviews. Covering area-by-area and the majority of all the main players, the story unfolds here too (finishing in London, where the scene continued on way after it was virtually finished elsewhere). I've started, though, with a basic, detailed time-lined history, so that when you get to the interviews you'll have an idea of who and what people are talking about.

THE HISTORY
OF U.K. JAZZ DANCE
A short, time-lined version

As reported in the leading US music-industry magazine 'Billboard,' in a column on June 6th 1970 headed, "Rock-Flavoured Jazz Opens New Vistas For Musicianship." It reports: "Jazz and Rock are fusing new musical relationships. *John Klemmer; Miles Davis; Jerry Hahn; The Fourth Way* and now, *Gabor Szabo* are examples of Jazz's new face." *Miles Davis' Bitches Brew* album (possibly the first example of Jazz Rock?) had already charted for seven weeks previously, and the *Freddie Hubbard - Red Clay* album on the CTI record label followed on quite quickly (CTI - producer, Creed Taylor's label - unknowingly was about to become one of the most important labels in this market). The question is asked: "Is Miles Davis the latest pop discovery? He is the new sound in Jazz." And so it begins.....

The hatred for this fresh new music hybrid by the conservative (so-called) Jazz purists was beyond belief, and yet it was also generally accepted that Jazz had become stale to the point of grinding to a halt. To say Jazz was dying, as I'd read many times, was, perhaps, a gross exaggeration, but the fact is: Jazz wasn't selling. Whether the puritans liked it or not, thanks to these artists, a whole new generation of young people of all colours of skin started to take an interest in Jazz through it's merging with Rock styles: "The young, good, Rock musicians of today are really playing a form of Jazz when they solo. They are constantly searching for new techniques and sources of inspiration from *John Coltrane* and *Rahsaan Roland Kirk* for example, and through this, the audience is now becoming aware of Jazz."

Jazz has always given and taken influences from around itself of course. The Blue Note and Prestige jazz labels, amongst others, had already been experimenting for a decade previously with 'Soul Jazz' - a merging of Jazz and Rhythm and Blues - with artists such as *Big John Patton, Trudy Pitts, Jimmy McGriff* and, first and foremost, *Jimmy Smith*, so it was quite a surprise to see the reaction in 1972 to the newly refreshed *Jazz Crusaders* with their album *Crusaders1* and *Grover Washington's Inner City Blues*. Despite the criticisms of watering down the Jazz, this new music was selling. Both albums went high in the Jazz AND Soul charts. The Jazz Crusaders dropped the word 'Jazz' from the front of the band name, because they wanted their listeners to judge their music without the hindrance of the term 'Jazz' to distract them. It was reported that: "Today, the Jazz musician who is the largest commercial success is one who plays Jazz music in front of a Rhythm and Blues rhythm section. This is the new sound in Jazz which the people can dance to." and, following a fifteen page article documenting 'The New Jazz Explosion,' it said: "There is an interest in Jazz today by a growing number of new ears. Sonny Lester of the Groove Merchant record label said that he hears a Pop and R&B sound mixed together to form a commercial Jazz sound: "You have to handle the production like a Pop date." The media began to term this new, exciting music as 'Crossover Jazz' (meaning, 'crossing over' into the Pop market). Meanwhile, the new Jazz Rock super group Weather Report were said to also have had a 90% young audience.

By 1973 things were beginning to snowball with yet again, two more landmark albums - *Donald Byrd - Blackbyrd* - with the production debut of two of Byrds ex-students from Howard University in Washington: Larry and Fonce Mizell, giving us the whole epic landscape and cosmic production that has touched so many Jazz artists, whom, from then on, became the staple diet of the best dancefloors in the UK (of more later), and secondly: jazz pianist *Herbie Hancock's Headhunter* album, with his until then unheard experimentation of electronic keyboards mixed with Funk and Rock - the first single release from it - *'Chameleon'* - being a huge chart record worldwide. Hancock had always (and still does) lead the way with new developments in Jazz and there's been none more important than this album. CTI, and it's funkier sister-label, Kudu, continued to have chart hit after chart hit with their releases by artists such as *Freddie Hubbard, Hank Crawford, Esther Phillips, Deodato* and *Grover Washington Jr*. They always recorded at legendary Jazz producer Rudy Van Gelder's studio at Englewood Cliffs, New Jersey, with, invariably, the same musicians: Ron Carter (Bass), Richie Tee (Keys) Bernard Purdie (Drums) Hank Crawford (Sax) and Eric Gale on guitar - all of whom became recording artists in their own right in this genre that we'd termed Funk Jazz here in the UK.

By 1974, Jazz Rock was officially termed 'Fusion' or 'Jazz Fusion' (although I saw one or two references to the name as early as 1970) and so it seemed that there now wasn't any element of contemporary Afro American music that wasn't being affected by Jazz - including Disco.

I was panicking, in my research, to find where the Jazz elements came into Disco around this period, especially in the productions of the classic Soul label Philadelphia International, and yet it was right there in front of me. It was a question that didn't really need answering: the current trend (Jazz) had merged as easily, naturally, and commercially as it had done with the Funk and the Rock. Basically, there was a whole new, young crowd buying Jazz without realizing it, with 15% of the content of the Soul chart being 'Crossover Jazz.'

It's hard to gauge what the dance floor reaction in the clubs in the US would've been to all of this. All of the music was charting with massive record sales, and getting huge radio exposure, plus these artists were doing massive tours too, and yet it's popularity didn't seem to crossover into the Discos. The Disco Chart's that I saw had no representation of jazz-based music in them at all (although that's not to say that it wasn't getting played somewhere). Billboard reported that the "US is not grasping the importance of the discoteque. It's use has not been properly developed. England is ten years ahead - there are hundreds in London and the provinces," and yet there was an estimated 150 Disco's in Manhattan alone. Discos were the latest craze, and the market in 1974 was growing 10% each month.

Whether or not Funk Jazz was accepted on the dancefloors of the US, one thing is for sure: by 1974/75 in the UK, it certainly was, and was growing in momentum rapidly. This exciting new music - now termed 'Jazz Funk' by Blues And Soul magazine - was featured at the more funkier underground club's around the country such as Maximes in Bristol; Pantiles in Bagshot, Surrey with Chris Brown; The Goldmine, Canvey Island with Chris Hill, and Dee Jays, Chelmsford with Bob Jones - both in Essex; many London west-end club's such as Upstairs At Ronnie Scotts, Crackers with Mark Roman and the many residencies of George Power; Les Spaine and Terry Lennaine's various gig's in Merseyside such as The Pun and Timepiece; Mike Shaft's various clubs in Manchester; The Highland Room at The Mecca, Blackpool with Colin Curtis and over to Leeds at Primos with Paul Schofield. I'm just scratching the surface here, but it was a minority sound with a solid following being played alongside the import Soul and Funk of the time. These club's were also attracting the high-fashion crowd, so in them there would be people a year ahead with fashion, dancing to the greatest new underground Black music - like the barrier-breaking *Gil Scott-Heron - The Bottle* on Strata East, for instance; massive both North and South of the country.

1975 was an important year, more than anything, for the release of the song *Expansions* by jazz keyboard player *Lonnie Liston-Smith* (Flying Dutchman records). Some feel that this is 'where it all began' regarding the UK Jazz Dance movement; certainly thing's were never the same. Expansions is fast, glorious Funky Jazz Fusion with a soaring vocal and the kind of epic production that transports you to some majestic, cosmic dreamscape that one gets totally lost in, and never want to end. You know, from the beginning - with the large complex funky-fusion bass line by Cecil McBee and the ensuing barrage of percussion, that you're in for something special. I do wonder sometimes if there is a better record than this? There was certainly nothing at all ever recorded like this before its release. How it must have been perceived as a new release, I do not know. Initially it made a little impact in the North of England but was played to death down South on 7 inch single, prior to it's full album release, I've been told many times. The record was certainly no small-label obscure release - it was number 1 in the Jazz charts in the US, reaching 79 in the Soul charts as a single as well. It didn't appear in any club charts there, although Lonnie Liston-Smith - in an interview in the UK magazine Black Music - said that it was played in the discos, which conflicts with when he was taken to an all-nighter event at Flicks nightclub in Dartford, Kent in late 1979 where he said that this was the first time he'd ever seen people dancing to Expansions. He said that he'd never made it as a dance record. It is possible that it was indeed played in the US. It was reported: "The strangest twist to musical acceptance in Discos concerns

Jazz." The CTI jazz label said: "We make great dance records that are great jazz records. Jazz plays no real part in the disco acceptance, it's just the fact that CTI make great dance records." Either way, here in the UK, Jazz was well underway on the dancefloor.

If 1975 was a fantastic year, '76 was an absolute classic. The year kicks off with the *Gears* album by *Johnny Hammond* on the Fantasy record label subsidiary Milestone - and yet another production by the Mizell brothers geniuses. It is such a strong album, with many classic cuts, but I have to highlight *Los Conquistadores Chocolates* - a piece of fast keyboard-led Jazz Funk that was like nothing before on the dancefloor, and in isolation, actually made the top 10 in the New York club chart too. I say 'in isolation' because I saw nothing similar in those charts before or after that song, ever; with the exception of the strange hard, fast Jazzy Disco track *New York City* by *Miroslav Vitous*, that also came out in that year. Technically, it's Disco but, no, it's not. It's a tense acid-trip carpet-ride of monstrous proportions, verging on Jazz Fusion. I can't think of any other record to compare it to. I do know, however, that it was so popular in the UK that it got a domestic release on Warner Brothers on 12 inch. File this alongside another new release - the pile-driving *Evolution* by *Roy Ayers* - and there was a style of killer up-tempo tracks starting to develop next to Expansions, giving the challenging DJ's a new avenue to discover; a new sound to champion. The more demanding of dancers in the best clubs would have certainly fuelled the DJ's imagination as well. These dancers would want more of the same - the heavier the better. Not every club would have got away with this, but the dancers began to form a circuit throughout the country of where to hear this music and have burn-ups with the local dancers too.

By now, the Jazz-influence was everywhere: from the heavy Disco Funk of United Artist recording artists *Brass Construction* to *Kool And The Gang* on Delite; the Mizell brothers were giving us so much more of their special brand of cerebral cosmic Jazz Funk productions and, as mentioned before: it was there too, in the Soul sound of the Philadelphia International label and, infact, it was generally common to hear jazz solos in the contemporary Black dance music of the time. Other than CTI/Kudu, Blue Note, Groove Merchant, and Strata East, there were many other labels coming aboard with this new Jazz Funk sound too - Fantasy and Capitol, for example.

Still in '76, two DJ's out in Essex were making important changes and taking it all one step further:

CHRIS HILL AND BOB JONES

Bob Jones was a Soul and Blues fanatic throughout the 1960's, and was experimenting with a little DJ-ing by '67, but he didn't start his first big residency until 1971 at Dee Jays in Chelmsford, Essex on Friday nights. Initially he was standing in for someone else and playing a majority of the chart music of the time, but by '74 it was a totally 100% Black music policy with people queuing way before the doors opened.

"A birthday present from my Dad in 1970 was *Jimmy Smith - Back At The Chicken Shack*, and this was typical of the type of R&B that was getting a lot of play at Dee Jays. Despite this and the jazz-influenced Disco and Funk that was being played there, at this point, there was no intention of playing jazz as such. By 1976 of course, you had the Jazz Funk stuff like *Jack McDuff - Sophisticated Funk* and the *Eddie Russ* albums on Monument etc and then I started to introduce Fusion."

As with so many great innovaters, Bob discovered Jazz Fusion by chance: a Dee Jays regular and rated Essex dancer by the name of Mac brought along a copy of the album *Chick Corea - Return To Forever* (Enja) and, as Bob often started the evening off with the jazzier sounds of the day, Mac asked him whether he would play a track from it so he could dance to it. The track was *You're Everything*, with Flora Purim on vocals. "Watching Mac dancing to it, I could draw comparisons to the sound that I was already playing but it was in a direction that I didn't know much about, and that was the turnaround. I went searching for that style after that," Bob told me.

Chris Hill's story is different. Originally a Blues collector (and I know this because a friend of mine, Dave Tobin, used to swap Blues records with him at the Ford's factory in Dagenham in Essex in 1960), Chris lived the Jazz life of Soho throughout the 60's, and as you will read in his interview, jazz was everywhere: it was in the chart's (*Dave Brubeck - Take 5; Buddy Morrow - the 'Johnny Staccato'* theme etc); it was on juke boxes; it was on film soundtracks (*Alfie - Sonny Rollins*); the Soho bands such as Georgie Fame would be doing Big John Patton covers; you would hear albums like *Miles Davis - Sketches Of Spain* or *Charlie Mingus - Oh Yeah* at parties, so he didn't really see what the fuss was about people dancing to jazz in the late-70's.

Although Chris started to DJ in the mid-60's, and even used Miles Davis - Milestones as his opening record at his long running residency at The Orsett Cock in Grays, Essex in 1969, it was in 1973 that Chris started at his most famous club - The Goldmine, Canvey Island. Canvey (which is the last place you hit on the left as you follow the River Thames east 35 miles out of London), was an unlikely place to play. It was miles from anywhere and with a close, tight, quite insular population, it didn't really welcome outsiders. Chris got poison-pen letters from Islanders saying: "Why are you bringing these coons on to the island?" Ironically then, the Goldmine went on to be voted the Souths - sometimes the country's - number 1 club for 12 years, as voted by readers of Blues And Soul magazine. Chris always saw Funk and Jazz together and had the collection, so having a Jazz edge was just natural. By accident, in late '75, Chris had started a 40's Swing revival. What had started as just playing a few *Joe Turner*, *Glenn Miller* or *Benny Goodman* records ended up as a focal point which grew out of proportion. The media latched on to it and TV and Newspaper Journalists were coming from all over the world to see people dressing in 40's fashion and Jiving; Swing Compilation albums came out: *Glenn Miller - In The Mood* went in to the Top 10 in the national singles chart; coaches were coming from all over the country - as Fashion and Arts journalist, club owner and musician Chris Sullivan said, "We got a coach to the Goldmine from Wales in '75 for Chris Hill's Swing night. We were all into Roxy Music and were dressed in these 40's clothes." Chris was in the media spotlight anyway for his two recent 'Top 10' novelty chart hits ('Renta Santa' and 'Bionic Santa'), so he'd had enough. He didn't even recognize the regulars at The 'Mine anymore, so it was time to go. He'd lost his way a bit, so friend and respected music journalist James Hamilton - who he'd known since James was resident DJ at The Scene, Ham Yard in Soho in the mid-60's - suggested, "Go back to your roots and start again - the 50's/60's Blue Note Soul Jazz etc." Chris put those intentions on hold for a couple of years though, because he went straight from The Goldmine to The Lacy Lady, Seven kings, Ilford in 1976. It was at least a 50% Black crowd who demanded the newest, underground Black music. It was full of heavy-weight dancers - as you will read in the dancers interviews, later in the book.

"When I moved down to London, I went to The Lacy Lady and I noticed that it was more of the 'Mecca-style' that I was used to but none of the Northern Soul. I noticed the dancing was very jazzy. I was overawed by it. A very Black crowd, they were down and dirty. Musically it was very jazzy, where as at the Mecca it was mixed.

Did anything disappoint you about The Lacy Lady?

The people weren't so friendly. They seemed unapproachable. I'd never seen dancing like it before though. Up-North I'd always be on the floor but there I was a wallflower. Such a standard."

Peter Duncan – a respected knowledge from the North-east

"We got changed in the bus-shelter in Seven Kings High Road and drove down to the club. When we got there, there were skinhead-types in the queue, but with colour-flashes in their hair and mohair jumpers and red or green painters jeans with winkle-picker shoes. When we got inside, the dancing was incredible, like ballet-dancing you know – spinning and all that. Chris Hill was a larger-than-life character, shouting down the microphone with echo on it. To the side of him was the Lacy Lady top ten chart and we'd never heard of any of them at the time: songs like *Bob James - Westchester Lady, Freddie*

Hubbard - Windjammer, Donald Byrd - Change, Miroslav Vitous - New York
*City ....*The music was superb. You would never hear music like it anywhere else. We went every single week and it was part of our lives."

DJ Paul Clark from Brighton

SOUL BOYS - THE ORIGINAL PUNKS

Although nothing to do with Jazz on the dancefloor, it must be noted that the whole Punky Soul-boy look started at The Lacy Lady in 1976. It was a fashion that spread all over the country - and without doubt, was first taken up North by the dancer and fashion guru from Leeds called Oki (as his interview will tell you, later). The original Punks from Bromley in Kent: Susie Ballion (Siouxsie), Steve Severin, Billy Broad (Billy Idol) and the others were regulars there, so was John Lydon (Johnny Rotten), various members that became The Clash (including the manager Bernie Rhodes) and various future Subway Sect members, plus art and fashion students from St Martins in London and Southend-On-Sea College. The spitting, pogo-ing Punks that came later would hate to think that it all came from the Soul clubs and was 'high-fashion'. One only has to look at where all the original Punk clothing was coming from: Vivienne Westwood and Malcolm McLarens Kings Road shop 'Sex,' 'Acme Attractions' and 'Seditionairies' - all expensive designer-wear shops. Heavyweight dancers such as Tommy Mac, Trevor Shakes, Leon Herbert and Travis Edwards would be seen dancing in all of that outrageous clothing. Chris Sullivan again, "I had lime green pegs, a yellow mohair jumper, green plastic sandals with a green striped 'acme' shirt with a wedge hair cut - a classic. It spread all over the country." In an interview with Kris Needs in the New Musical Express in 1993 Rotten said, "I'd spend more time down the Lacy Lady than the Roxy or any of the Punk clubs. I was much happier with Soul clubs. That's my musical roots".

Still in 1976 (I told you it was an important year!) Robbie Vincent's radio show on BBC Radio London, that he'd started in 1973 as a 'Talk Show' (the UK's first), had finally come-of-age with his two hour Saturday lunchtime essential mix of Jazz, Funk, Disco and Soul. In the South it became the 'voice of the people.' With the main importer of the time - Tony Monson - delivering directly to his house from the airport (as he did Chris Hill too), one knew that you were not going to get more up-front than that. Much-pirated cassette-tapes of his shows appeared all over the country, and it is said that his was the most copied radio show in history - although, how can that be monitored? I would've thought, perhaps, that, of anyone, John Peel's late evening under-ground music show on Radio 1 would've been. It would be nice to think Robbie's show was though; I certainly taped it, and everyone I knew did too! Because of the timing of his show, all Southern Soul import shops would be mainly empty while his show was on, and minutes after it finished they would be full of DJ's and punters alike trying to buy what they'd just heard. Fact. Also, in London, loved and revered was Greg Edwards 'Soul Spectrum' show on Capital Radio - although, to be fair, a very commercial show - and lastly, let's not forget the important Soul pirate-station Radio Invicta, that had been running since 1970. The following year would also see Dave Simmons' Soul 77 show on Radio London too. Around the country, equally beloved, would be Terry Lennaine's long running Monday night show 'Keep On Truckin' on BBC Radio Merseyside and Mike Shaft's 'TCOB' show on Manchester's Piccadilly Radio - Mike, very much being the North's equivalent of Robbie in so many ways. These were all helping to inform this steadily, but quickly growing movement.

COLIN CURTIS

By now, in the North, the legendary teaming of two of the most powerful and respected Soul DJ's up there - Colin Curtis and Ian Levine - were continuing to tear up the rule-book weekly in the 300 capacity Highland Room at The Blackpool Mecca, mixing up rare modern soul records and up-to-the-minute imports of Disco, Jazz Funk and Soul to a very progressive, forward-thinking and knowledgable crowd - drawing crowds from all over the midlands and the North. I hate the idea of a North-South divide, but certainly there was then. The Northern Soul scene had been such a domineering influence up there, focusing, initially, on the rarest-of-rare obscure 60's rare soul, breeding beyond-belief collections, un-surpassed knowledge of this subject and a massive, loyal following. It took maverick DJ's from that scene, such as Curtis and Levine, to have the courage to go with what they felt - musically - and play new releases of what they felt was relevant to where they wanted to go. Of course, some of the crowd didn't move with it but the majority did. Ian Levine concentrated much more on the Disco-thing, and so it is Colin Curtis who is concentrated on in this book. He was playing odd-ball Black music records that defy description that no-one dared play, along with the CTI/Kudu sound and the Mizell brothers quality production-line of recording artists - in tandem with the South - and an advanced selection of the latest imports. A few people have given me examples of odd jazz-based tracks that were played there over the years, but I firmly believe that those three or four records that I've heard of just fitted the bill 'tempo and feel'-wise, rather than turned people on to Jazz. Although they may of helped (who knows? Let's face it: Hill and Jones had also been dropping odd jazzy tracks previously too), I'm sticking to the major musical progression of the new Jazz-based Black music of the US which definitely led us to our eventual Jazz Dance scene.

Down to the midlands and Birmingham, important notorious Northern Soul collector / discoverer / DJ, record importer and shop owner Graham Warr opened the club Chaplins in Fiveways. He was sick of seeing so-called DJ's 'passing' on fantastic records in his shop, so he wanted a night to play them himself. There was so many amazing records coming through that he'd play almost a different set every week, and, like The Highland Room and The Central, he had so many excellent dancers there that he could get away with the heavy fast Jazz Funk tunes such as *Eddie Russ - Zaius* (Monument records). Chaplins was tiny and always packed solid. There was hardly anywhere to sit so you had no option but to dance anyway. Graham has actually had to turn away unscheduled coach-loads of people. "I literally can't physically fit you in. Have you seen the size of this place?" he'd say!

Into 1977 and over to the North-east in Leeds, again, there was the classic pairing of noted Northern Soul DJ Ian 'Frank' Dewhirst and Paul Schofield from Primos. Ian had become a recent convert to Jazz Funk after hearing it all the time on the car radio whilst out in Los Angeles searching for records, and, on return, would hear Paul playing this kind of music. They started a night at a club called The Central in Central Road, which Ian had remembered from DJ-ing Soul nights there. It was an immediate success, and, like The Highland Room, they were playing all the music covered so far. This club boasted the aforementioned dancer and fashion-guru - Oki, and his crowd. "Oki had a huge contingent of women following him around. The Central was as much about his crowd as the music. They were seen as the fashion go-getters of Leeds. He's a sophisticated guy. I like to think that The Central was instrumental in him getting into all that music," Ian Dewhirst said. The influence of that crowd of Oki's spread right across the North.

The US Jazz Charts in 1977 were starting to look like the play-lists of the more adventurous clubs here in the UK (and there were many). Literally, of the 100 in the chart, I could think of at least one track off of most of the albums that had gotten played here on the dancefloor at some point - not that the artists would have made them with a dancefloor in mind - and it continued like this throughout the rest of the decade.

ALL-DAYERS

The idea of all-night discoteques came about in London in the mid -1960's and then spread up-North. The Northern Soul scene invented the idea of the all-dayer - often midday to midnight or 2pm until 2am - which spread back down South. In the South, the first was promoted by Pete Mathews at Reading, Berkshire in The Top Rank Suite on August the 30th 1976. The main ballroom played Northern Soul whilst the smaller upstairs club - The Night Owl - played Jazz Funk and Soul. These were huge events that were on every bank holiday Monday, and by the sixth one (January the 2nd 1978) this event was attracting 4,000 people and now it was just all Jazz Funk and was advertised as 'The National Soul Festival.' DJ Chris Brown had been involved since the third event and by the fifth one, he'd brought in Chris Hill. The sixth one had the aforementioned two, plus radio DJ's Robbie Vincent and Greg Edwards. Thing's were now starting to explode and so the promoter started looking for even bigger venues. He found Tiffanys in Purley, Surrey - which was owned by the Mecca organisation and was called The Orchid Ballroom. It held 4,000 plus. It continued on seamlessly on the next bank holiday Monday (March the 27th) and had the same line-up, with the addition of DJ Sean French from Bognor Regis in Sussex, who had a very

FORTHCOMING HoESC EVENTS

Kicking off with the BIG ONE...

THE NATION'S No. 1 All-DAYER

BLACKPOOL MECCA
SOUL FESTIVAL

Bank Holiday Monday, May 29th — Noon-11pm

Featuring live on stage the World's No. 1 Disco Band

Blaze
Construction

+ *Britain's very own* **ROKOTTO**

Plus Top Disco/Funk DJ's Colin Curtis, Neil Rushton, Ian Levine, Ian Dewhurst,
Paul Schofield and Guests

*Spinning 100% Hot Soul Disco — Funk — Jazz + Dancing Competition. 1st prize
£100 of albums* **PLUS** *Northern Soul returns to the Highland Room ALL-DAY!! with
DJ's Richard Searling, Dave Evision, Pat Brady, "Ginger", Brian Rae.*

....

Brilliant PA System! — Freebies — Prizes — Films — Record Bars — Food & Licensed Bars — on **2** Floors
Never mind *"Saturday Night Fever"* — This is for REAL! Join 4,000 Soul Freaks at Britain's BEST EVER All-Dayer!!

Reduced price on advance tickets available **NOW:** *Send immediately to HoESC (Festival), 37 Lichfield St., Walsall, West Midlands
Tel: 0922 31363*
Prices HoESC & Highland Connection Members £2.25 (please state membership No) + SAE. **Non-Members £2.50** *(+ SAE)
Discounts for coach parties. Tel: 0922 31363 or Burntwood 3022 for details.*

GET YOURSELF TOGETHER "WE'RE MOVING ON" (AND MOONIN')

successful residency at Dantes nightclub there. The second Purley All-Dayer on May the 5th, again, had the same lineup, but this time the DJ's Froggy (the UK's first mixing DJ), Tom Holland and Jeff Young were also added on to the team. It was shortly after that this team was dubbed 'The Funk Mafia,' and Chris Hill was The Godfather! These events had become so powerful that the DJ's had enough power to break a record there which would reflect in it's national chart positioning! This book is not a blow-by-blow account of the Jazz Funk and Soul scene - that should be a whole book of it's own - but for the record, there were six more of these events with varying DJ line-up's. The Purley All-Dayers finally finished on January the 1st 1980.

Anyway, now things had gone absolutely berserk. The scene had exploded with the influence of Robbie, Greg and Dave's radio show's (not forgetting the Soul pirate-station- Radio Invicta); both Blues And Soul and Black Music And Jazz Review magazine; the Black Echoes newspaper and James Hamilton's ridiculously important and informative Disco page in the Record Mirror newspaper (it is worth mentioning that his page was read by ALL DJ's. James single-handedly had the power to break a track with his reviews, such was the respect shown for his opinion). At the same period as down South, thing's were about to absolutely blow-up in the North of England.

Noted DJ and promoter, Neil Rushton - through his endeavours with successful all-dayers in the midlands (amongst other events), got offered the huge Manchester Ritz venue in Upper Whitworth Street. "We didn't take any prisoners. We had the best of everyone: Colin Curtis, Ian Levine, Ian Dewhirst, Richard Searling and John Manship playing Northern 60's to contemporary new releases," said Neil. It started with an attendance of 300 and by the end of the year, he was getting 1700. By '77/78, he was putting on Northern Soul and Jazz Funk all-dayers - which were the biggest events outside of the South of England. In 1978, he took note of the Purley All-Dayers at Tiffanys in Surrey - fifteen miles South of London, and felt that there would be enough interest to do an event as big as that in the North, if not bigger, so, on May the 19th he took over the Blackpool Mecca's cavernous ballroom - plus utilizing the 300 capacity Highland Room upstairs for Northern Soul - he got an attendance of 3,200. Called 'The Blackpool Mecca Soul Festival,' it had the power-house Disco-Jazz Funk US act Brass Construction playing live, with an unmatchable Northern DJ line-up of all the main players: himself; Colin Curtis; Ian Levine; Ian Dewhirst and Paul Schofield. So, again, with the support of the specialist radio shows, import shops and the aforementioned magazines and newspapers, the Jazz Funk scene went absolutely enormous all over the country. It is not surprising really: because of the vast amount of people at all-dayers and the commanding presence of the very best DJ's from the scene, one would witness the kind of communal mass-hysteria that could be seen at cup-final matches (the roar of the crowd was certainly similar) - over import Jazz Funk and Soul records! One would leave these events desperate to spread the word of this music and scene, and our idol's - the DJ's. When the records broke big, we almost felt, individually, that we were partly responsible (collectively, we were of course). In the South, the Funk Mafia DJ's even dubbed the crowd The Family. As well as the all-dayer explosion that reverberated in to the clubs as well, we mustn't forget the huge Disco explosion, erupting even more because of the film 'Saturday Night Fever' in 1977 either. This would have certainly have been another major contributing factor to the explosion. By now at all-dayers - and there were now many, spreading all over the country - the 'community' would be inventing mass routine 'line-dances' (ok, I tried to avoid using that expression!) to the big anthems created there; there would be spontaneous human pyramids - sometimes eight bodies high - and even a bit of good-natured silliness in the shape of baring arses - called 'mooning' - which became all the rage (you're all wondering what the hell this has all got to do with Jazz, I know. Bear with it!). Such was the DJ's power at these enormous events that DJ Ian Dewhirst got banned from a venue for getting four hundred people to moon all at the same time over the balcony overlooking the ballroom floor! Every area or club had it's own crowds of friends into the scene called Funkateers, and down South, again, the Funk Mafia dubbed them 'Tribes'. There were hundreds of Tribes ranging from four to, probably, one hundred members (the 'Brixton Front Line'? - it seemed like it), and they all had names - some dramatic and some silly. Again it gave you a sense of belonging and identity - much like street-gangs, I suppose - where you'd feel proud to be recognized as a member of a certain Tribe (I was in 'The Black Kidney' for instance) - especially if the Tribe was mentioned on the radio or by a DJ over the microphone in a club. Although I'm just scratching the surface, to give an example, here are the names of some of the Tribes. Is yours in here? :

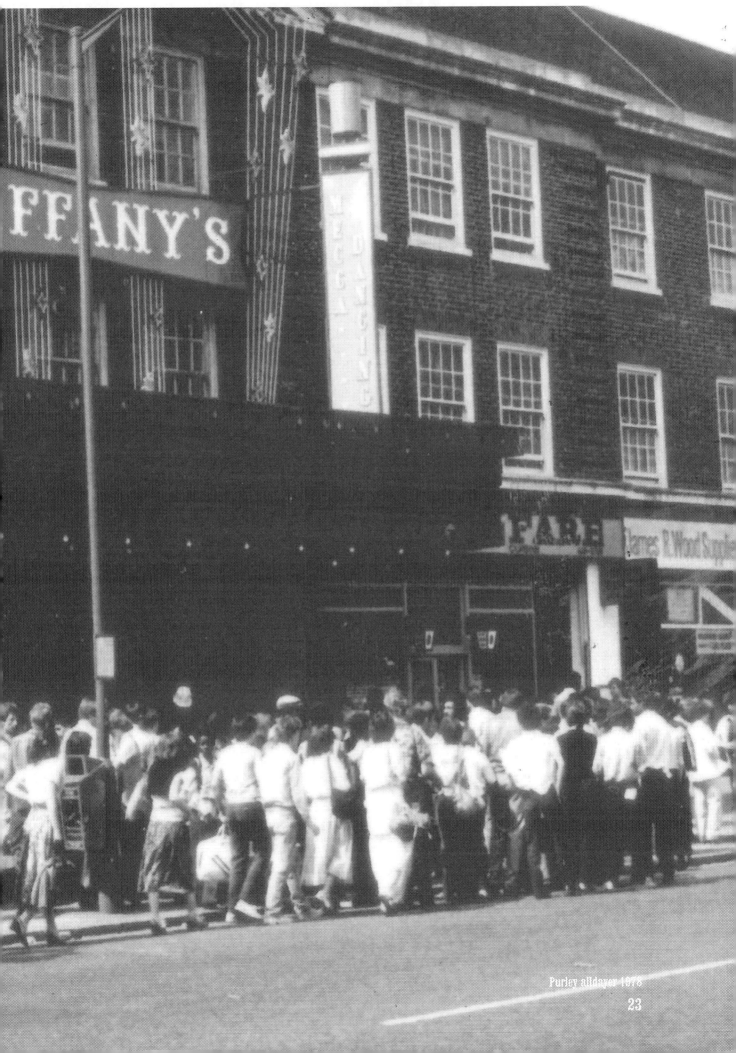

Pre-Clones, Brixton Front Line, The Black Kidney, Souldiers, Sidcup Slummers, Staines Fusion Few, The Funkmaster Generals, Magnum Force, The Rabble, The Privates, Jazz Conquistadors, Brewer's Troop, The Ovalteenys, Soulful Strollers, Rentacrowd, Sid Valley Jazzers, Plymouth Moocho Jazzers, The City Jazz Cruisers, The Desperadoes, The Jaffas, The West Coast Jazz Freezers, Yeovil Jazzatak, The Royston Travellers, Norwich Jazz Casuals, West Of Scotland Soul Clan, North Western Jazz Exiles, Mother Hens, Funky Chicks, Dimlos, Jazz Pilgrims, One Way, Northampton Nymphs, London Trotters, Dagenham Ladies, Stifford Sax Maniacs, The Bluenotes, Katford Cruisers, Funky Knights, Harrow Cubs, Central Posers, Harrow Breeders, Slickers, Sea Dogs, Rhythm Makers, The Bellamy Five, Sax Maniacs, The Nuffins, The Groovin' Gropers, Funk Union, Jazz Bandits, Enfield Breast Strokers, Watford F-Troop, The Medway Rain Forest Missionaries, Darlington Funk Force, Paddington Soul Partners, Loughton International Rescue, Darlington Jazz Force, Palmers Green Soul Patrol, Larkfield Loonies, Night Cruisers, Exeter Brainies, Milk Maids, Brighton Southern Atmosphere, Funk Fondlers, The Master Blasters, The Welwyn Wobblers, Dagenham Dynamite, Backwater Bruces, Gravesend Groovers, Hemel Crusaders, Bomb Squad, Reading Cruise Line, Tropicanas, Lady Boogateers, Eastbourne Earls, Crawley Leftovers, Southgate Soul Searchers, Jazz Inspectors, Hemel Lechers, Country Bumpkins, Great Yarmouth Funk Riders, Ugonauts, Sutton Soul Patrol, The Maltesers, Hemel Wreck Crew, Bedford Jazz Funk Pilgrims, Bexleyheath Sheep Shaggers, Racoons, Lambeth Infunktuation, Luton Dog Catchers, Ravels, Bury Funk Regiment, Liverpool Gnomes, Party Jerks, Newbury Girls, Maidstone Monkies, Royston Feline Funkers, Crusoe Funkers, The Toffs, Boasties Pirates........ad infinitum!

There were, of course, higher echelon Tribes that were respected for their knowledge and dress sense and behaviour who all the DJ's would rely on for support - of which they got complete loyalty in return (with them often holding banners or wearing badges and/or t-shirts with the DJ's name on at these events). The Tribes would have their collective-name on their t-shirts with pride and would think nothing of traveling anywhere to check out other clubs or events by the car or coach load. From the first Tribes starting to appear in late1978 it all escalated out of control and, by '81, got so ridiculous - with so many idiots jumping on the band-wagon - something had to give. It got too silly. Ominously, I'll come back to this subject shortly.

1978 was the year that serious Jazz Fusion on the dancefloor really started to take hold in a few clubs. The environment was already there musically - as I have already spoken of - and it was coming thick and fast; it was there with the dancers pressurizing the DJ's to find more adventurous music to feed them (of more later) and, of course, the punters had been so well educated and inspired by these DJ's that they were snapping on the heels, knowledge-wise, of the very people that taught them, causing the best DJ's to stay one step ahead (and some didn't, it has to be said).

From August the 26th Chris Hill was back at The Goldmine putting his Jazz-plan into action at last, that had been so 'rudely interrupted' by his moving to Lacy Lady (!), and was dropping a few Blue Note grooves and Fusion in amongst the new release imports etc; Bob Jones was still following the Jazz Fusion trail at Dee Jays after the dancer Mac's revelation of it to Jones back in '76, and a very similar story happened to Colin Curtis at his Sunday night residency with John Grant starting on June the 4th at Smartys, Cross Street in Manchester:

"At these times, nobody was doing a straight Jazz night, of course, but the turning point for me was: one night I was DJ-ing and who should turn up? The ex-England football player - Frank Worthington. He was dressed totally wrong for the club and looked out of place, but he stood by the DJ decks all night. I was playing basic Jazz/Funk Fusion and suddenly he asked me for the Jazz Saxophonist - *Art Pepper*. He'd made the link. This absolutely blew me

away! It got me thinking about how it fit's into the picture. This was a man 'ahead of his time' and who completely opened my eyes to the potential. If this guy responded like this then others would."

And so Colin went on the mission, as hundreds would after him, of searching out other albums by the artists featured in the record inner-sleeve adverts, and then check out albums by the other musicians on them (and of course squander vast amounts of money on albums that 'look promising,' only to find nothing on them - which we've all done). Colin was, and is, the kind of collector that has to have everything, and strikes like a cobra - he moves quickly - rapidly gleaning the knowledge and influencing everybody along the way, as only the very best do.

Interestingly enough, although I've been told that Graham Warr's night at Chaplins in Birmingham wasn't massively jazzy by some Jazz dancers, according to a playlist written down as it was being played, for the attendant journalist Frank Elson for his Blues And Soul column about Northern club-activity 'Check It Out' (21/11/78) - he played *Jeff Lorber Fusion - The Samba* (from 'Soft Space' on Inner City). Now, this is out-and-out fast Samba Fusion, and exactly what this book is about. This track became common on the dancefloors in 1979 when all the Jazz Funk DJ's - even the commercial ones - dabbled a little bit with Jazz Fusion, but certainly not in '78. I've seen other playlists from this period by him too which are also shockingly adventurous with tracks such as *Eddie Russ - Tea Leaves* (Monument) (6/6/78) - it must come from owning an import record shop; importing records himself and having the very best dancers in attendance as well!

Following hot on the heels of Jeff Lorber was *Chick Corea - Central Park* (from 'Secret Agent' on Polydor - Fickle Funk also got plays too). Again, this got play at the end of '78, but took off later in '79. This track is just powerhouse fast Samba Fusion. Definitely challenging. You must remember that these tracks were not put on the albums for the dancefloor. The artists are constantly shocked when they find out that their tracks are getting played in Discos. Here, DJ and presenter Mike Chadwick of the UK's Jazz FM radio station talks to Corea:

> **"Are you aware of the impact your music has had on the UK Jazz Dance scene?**
> Not at all.
> **'Central Park' is an anthem for the scene and is a big record in the clubs.**
> You mean as a remix?
> **No, no, the original track - people just go crazy to it!**
> No kidding. Boy, I'd love to see that.
> **'You're Everything' was the first Jazz Fusion record to be played in a club here in the UK and 'The Slide' is also danced to. You obviously aren't aware of this: what are your thoughts about that?**
> Well it makes me happy to hear that, because I always thought that my music is very danceable. I can dance to any of that music. I'm really happy to hear that the barriers are being broken down and other music is being used to dance to.
> **Central Park was issued in the US as a promotional 7" single for jukebox and radio play and a 12," do you know if the record company had any plans to try and cross that record over?**
> I had absolutely no idea, and it's practically a shock you telling me this."

.....and this is the story I heard time and again. Interestingly enough, Chick Corea is also guesting on that *Jeff Lorber* track 'The Samba' too! The Jazz wasn't all heavy that was being danced to, to be honest, Jazz of all styles and tempos were now getting played: from the break-neck speed Fusion Samba *Brazilia* by *John Klemmer* (ABC records) to the mid-tempo *Barbara Carroll - From The Beginning* (UA records) in 1979. Because it all seemed to fit neatly with all the new Jazz Funk and Soul getting played, one just accepted it as you would any other of these musics.

In1978, on the 1st of July, there had been an all-dayer at Alexandra Palace in London - with the

"The Kingswood Club" is Hornchurchs' Number ONE Soul Club, Because it is the only Soul Club in Hornchurch!

TUESDAY AT THE KINGSWOOD

WITH:

BOB JONES

PAUL GRATUE

PAUL MURPHY (NOT HIM AGAIN!)

AND A CAST OF THOU HUND DOZENS!

FROM 8.30 PM to 1.00 AM.

50p (BEFORE 10)
£1.00 (AFTER 10)

1P. THIS VOUCHER IS WORTH ONE PENNY OFF ENTRANCE TO: THE KINGSWOOD CLUB TUESDAY NIGHTS!

£1 THIS VOUCHER IS WORTH ONE POUND AND YOU COULD BUY £1'S WORTH OF FOOD AT THE FOOD BAR (IF WE HAD ONE!)

THIS VOUCHER IS WORTH NOTHING BUT ITS HANDY FOR FILLING THIS END BIT. KINGSWOOD — TUESDAY.

"GROOVERS" WAITING TO GET IN THE KINGSWOOD!

'Purley' team of Chris Hill; Chris Brown et al - that took these events to another level, with an attendance of 6,000. There were also two other important club sessions coming through; first of all, the young Kent DJ Pete Tong started to appear (who would, quite soon, get a reputation for being the hard-man of Jazz) with five DJ residencies in the Kent area alone - two of which: The Kings Lodge and, later, The Hilltop, West Kingsdown were absolute classics. He had such a large loyal crowd and some of the best dancers from the area, he could virtually play anything.

At the Lacy Lady in Ilford, there was a young man running coaches to other clubs called Paul Murphy. He was a face on the scene who everybody knew, and he called these organised coach trips 'The Exodus Club.' Paul decided to start a night just down the road in Hornchurch at The Kingswood Club next to the Bus Station (24/10/78), and he booked the DJ's Bob Jones and Paul Gratue to do it. It was a raging success. One week the snow was so bad that neither Bob or Paul could get there, so Paul took some of his own records there and did it. He decided that he enjoyed it and would DJ some more.

At the same time, you would also start to see smaller things beginning to happen, like Tony Hickmott - under the name of OBJ's - doing various clubs around London, playing 'the latest Jazz imports,' as it said on his adverts, and similarly with another London DJ Benny Wilson. I can't record all the DJ's and sessions that featured Jazz in their sets around the country because, by

1979, every single DJ that played Jazz Funk, Funk, Disco and Soul (and there was literally hundred's) were either featuring a little (or a lot) of Jazz, or trying to. As reported in Billboard March the 24th:

> "In the UK, the gay-influenced US disco style has been widely rejected by both dancers and DJ's. There is a fierce independence among the top trend-setting DJ's who are more likely to study the Billboard Jazz Chart than the Disco one." The magazine later reported: "A majority of the Disco product here is unsuited to the prevailing market there (the UK). The UK prefers to dance to the funkier and jazzier music."

By now, the term 'Jazz Funk' had become a blanket name for the whole scene rather than just a style of music, which got a little confusing: one could actually go to a 'Jazz Funk' night and not hear any (if you see what I mean), but it was an enormous movement that we jealously guarded and were all passionate about. It was beer-fuelled, it's true - unless you're a dancer: then it would be blackcurrant cordial and lemonade. Who'd heard of Class-A drugs? Everyone was high on the music, unlike the US Disco scene across the water - as graphically noted in the amazing book on the history of Disco: 'Turn The Beat Around' by Peter Shapiro (except that our movement - equally as big, if not bigger, than the House Music scene ever became - was not mentioned in it).

The Jazz Funk scenes of the North and South were quite different. Although there were club residencies in the North - like Colin Curtis and John Grant's many barrier-breaking sessions; Northern Soul legend Richard Searling's first foray into the Jazz Funk scene at Angels, Curzon Street in Burnley on Wednesdays; Peter Haigh and Frenchie taking care of Blackpool's surrounding areas in the North-east; Greg Wilson's pioneering session at Wigan Pier and Ian Dewhirst and Paul Schofield still taking care of business at The Central in Leeds - it had become much more about the all-dayer scene. There were at least one or two every weekend (more, if you include the all-nighters as well); generally enormous affairs with a similar line-up at each one. Although there were regular all-dayers, down South it was much more about clubs; and there were hundreds of them.

SCOTLAND

Elsewhere, Scotland's scene was booming - with a scene taking root as far back as John Snelling's Soul Ticket events in Aberdeen in 1975, and other club's around Ayrshire with Terry Quinn and co and Ned 'The Bottle' Jordan and Tony Cochrane in Dundee. The promoter and DJ Kenny MacLeod was starting to organize big events all over, utilizing Scotland's other two leaders of the scene: DJ's Bob Jefferies from around the Glasgow area and Billy Davidson from Aberdeen (but let's not forget Glasgow's true original: Segun - a non-Scottish Black DJ, resident in Glasgow around the late 70's). The feverishly-passionate crowd would travel North and South of the UK in search of the groove. The same can be said of Alex Lowes and Bill Swift in Newcastle in the North-east. Everything revolved around them and their many residencies - particularly Alex Lowes. As Scotland also did, they'd get DJ's up to guest from the North and the South, and travel as far as down to The Goldmine in Canvey Island (240 miles), or even further, west - down to Torquay in Devon (350 miles) to check out their growing scene. Bristol's scene was second to none too with DJ's such as Martin Starr; Dennis Richards; Super Fly; Doodlebug, and many others, in many essential clubs.

When I talk about 'North and South,' I am really talking about the North, and the South's 'home-counties' - excluding London. The Jazz Funk scene in the home-counties revolved around the DJ's clubs and tribes in areas such as Essex; Kent: Sussex; Surrey: Hampshire, even down to Bournemouth in Dorset and Devon; Oxfordshire; Bedfordshire (particularly Luton and the legendary club The California Ballroom in Dunstable). We're talking about DJ's such as Chris D Smith, Dave Howard, Chris Dinnis, Andrew Pinney, Robin Pele, Brother Louie; Allan Sullivan, Nick Wakefield, Duncan Uren, Black Velvet; Ian Reading; Owen Washington, Dwight Wizard, Bob Povey, Jon Coomer, John De Sade, Mick Clark, Paul Clark, Colin Hudd, Craig Royale, Chris Bangs, Friar Tuck, Gary Soul, John Douglas; Fergie; Kev Hill, Martin Collins, Steve Walsh, Kim Gold, Tom Felton and others, plus all the others already mentioned.

LONDON WAS A DIFFERENT STORY ALTOGETHER

Logic tells you that because of the sparse ethnic population in the home-counties, the scene was generally made up with a crowd of which the vast majority was White - not that it mattered one iota; that's statistics for you! In London however, just like any of the major cities around England, the scene was very Black and liked a different sound. London was much more into Funk, as well as the Jazz, and, although Capital Radio's Greg Edwards was a 'Funk Mafia' DJ and held rated residencies at The 100 Club (covering for the ill Ronnie L) in Oxford Street and The Dun Cow in Old Kent Road, South London - both sessions for the heaviest dancers, by the way - DJ George Power's rule was absolute. His main club out of all his many residencies in the city in early 1979 was, of course, Crackers in Wardour Street. George played a different selection than you would hear in a home-counties club and he kept a watchful eye on the dancers and encouraged them, gaining unswerving loyalty in return. Since 1976, his club had been attracting the higher-echelon of dancers from London like Trevor Shakes; Paul Anderson; Tommy Mac and many more (of more later), from The Lacy Lady out in Essex, Maggot and his crowd of dancers from Kent; Errol T and Rick and Ty Hassell (known as 'The Twins') from Birmingham; Bristol's number one - Clive Smith, and many more. The music was heavy-duty and funky, and George, although never claiming to be a Jazz DJ, gave the crowd plenty of it. Dancers went to Crackers previous to George when DJ Mark Roman was there in '75 - with, again, a very Jazzy policy - but as with most of London's central clubs at the time, the crowd was White. The racist-door policy of the time kept Blacks out of most of these clubs, but George used his power and influence to either walk out of where he was working or refuse to work anywhere that had that policy. He did much for breaking down these barriers and changing things.

What about Birmingham? Graham Warr had walked out of Chaplins over money and door policies (yes, the Black issue again) so thing's were looking bleak. Luckily, in March, quite soon after the closure, along came the DJ's Shaun Williams (also a rated dancer) and Dave Till at their influential Monday nights at The Rum Runner in Broad Street. Although they played all styles of upfront Black music, the accent was on Jazz, and again, like Chaplins, they could boast the very finest dancers and their night became an institution for many years. The dancers from Manchester that later became the famous professional Jazz Dance troupe (and later again, a band) The Jazz Defektors, used to travel down regularly just to check out the local dancers, as did many others from all over. 1979 also saw the famous Locarno all-dayers happen there in Hurst Street bi-monthly (April the 8th), with it's second room featuring Jazz, along with Funk and Disco.

While on the subject of all-dayers at that time: Neil Rushton, the promoter of the Blackpool Mecca Soul Festivals told me that, "We loved the Jazz Fusion. It was fantastic wasn't it? Everyone - except for Ian Levine, of course - went for the Jazzy side of things. Colin would go for something that was really heavy and really underground. It got adopted wholesale. There was a lot of Jazz Fusion played at the all-dayers - no compromise."

CAISTER SOUL WEEKENDER

On April the 20th 1979 things took yet another step forward. As well as treating us to his 'Fusion 40' each week on his radio show (forty minutes of Jazz Fusion), with the sheer amount of highly attended all-dayer's across the country, DJ Robbie Vincent came up with the idea of a whole 'weekend' instead of an all-dayer. It would run from Friday evening until Sunday evening. The weekender was promoted by 'Showstopper' who were behind the cavernous Royalty Ballroom in Southgate, Hertfordshire, where all the Funk Mafia DJ's worked - either as resident or as a guest. The 'weekender' idea wasn't a new one, in fact, previously there had already been Rock and Roll / Rockabilly weekenders by the same promoters and at the same venue: Ladbrokes Holiday Centre, Caister-On-Sea, Norfolk (on the East coast).

The venue is what we used to term in the UK as a 'Holiday Camp'. These are enormous places that are scattered all over the coast-lines of the UK (by the 100's), and can accommodate from 200 to 7000 residents. They are for family's who want to be fed and entertained all week, where they would stay in caravans, chalets or apartment blocks and be entertained in a main building which would give you bands, disco's, cabaret, bingo, instruction and games, or have competitions or sporting activity in the daytime in sports rooms or on a sports field. Holiday Camps (or

'Leisure Parks' as they are known now) have been an institution here since the 1930's (I believe they were very similar to the holiday resorts in the Catskills in New York, like Brown's Hotel Resort, Fallsview or Wolff's). These were normally only open from May until mid-September (and possibly Christmas), so doing a weekend event out of holiday season was quite original.

The weekender quickly sold out and was attended by 3000 people. It featured the Funk Mafia DJ's and the music was spread over three venues. As the weekenders developed, one of the venues (the smallest) became an alternative room where all the DJ's got a chance to play deeper Soul and Jazz than they would in the main ballroom - which would cater for the masses i.e. the big Jazz Funk, Soul and Disco anthems. Although some DJ's didn't like the term, the small room got known as 'The Jazz Room' as there was, to be fair, predominantly Jazz being played - and WHAT Jazz! There was also a restricted license or Pirate Radio Station introduced there too, where again, the resident DJ's and guests did shows. This was very important, as everybody would tape the shows. It helped to spread the music, and the tapes are highly sought after today.

Even though it wasn't noticeable at the time, cracks were starting to appear in different ways. Firstly: the high-fashion crowd who were around in the scene in 1975/76 - where some of them originated the British Punk look - had delved into the exciting world of the new developing Punk scene (not a Black scene, obviously, but new, fresh and exciting nonetheless). As soon as Punk took off, and people fell under the 'Rock 'n Roll Swindle' of 'do it yourself,' 'anyone can play three chords' and all that sloganeering; plus you had all the 'spitting' and the 'pogo-ing dancing' - a lot of the originals got out and came back into the still underground Jazz Funk movement. As the movement grew out of control in 1979, a lot of that crowd, it has to be said, wearing the most outrageous and outlandish fashions started moving out in droves to a new underground fashion-led movement in London, dubbed 'New Romantic' by the press. They now felt uncomfortable in the Jazz Funk clubs, where a whole new crowd had evolved:

Although playing the odd novelty record was nothing new to Chris Hill - look at the Swing explosion of 75/76, for example - he would often drop in the odd party record or even, maybe, the last half hour would occasionally be soley party dances or maybe there'd be a dance competition (which were still all the rage). They were good-natured, light-hearted fun which, at the end of the day, didn't detract from the seriousness of the rest of the music. Unfortunately this idea spread everywhere and many DJ's were doing party spots left, right and centre, and it was featured at all-dayers and weekenders too. It slowly started to attract a new clientele who weren't necessarily there for the music, and so the high fashion crowd (or Ultra-Trendies, as they were also known) started to distance themselves from these 'fools'. Secondly: we were starting to see the first breakaway Jazz sessions happening. When there is a splinter-off of a scene it is either because there is a minority that has got into one aspect of the 'picture' and wants to hear more of that, or they're discontented with what they're hearing and want it a little more heavier - remember, as I said earlier, all the Jazz Funk DJ's were playing a little or a lot of Jazz (actually, Fusion), so a big taste was developing. The first Jazz specialist night, although, not well attended, was at the Papillon at The Royal Albion Hotel, Old Steine in Brighton, Sussex, with DJ's Paul Clark and Mick Clark (not related by the way). This was on Thursdays starting on August the 18th. The following month on Tuesday September the 10th, Colin and Tricia Snow - who owned the Record Man import record shop in Rayleigh, Essex - started a Jazz night at the Zero 6 night club in Southend-On-Sea. This featured bands, and DJ's of the likes of Bob

ROYALTY SHOWSTOPPER PROMOTIONS present

1st NATIONAL

Soul

Weekender

FRIDAY EVENING 20th APRIL

TO

SUNDAY EVENING 22nd APRIL

AT

LADBROKES

Caister Holiday Centre

Great Yarmouth

Norfolk

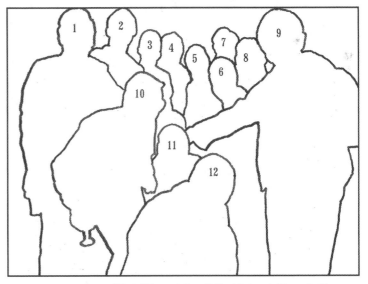

1. Chris Brown 2. Chris Hill 3. Jeff Young 4. Tom Holland 5. Lonnie Liston Smith
6. Brother Louie 7. Pete Tong 8. Froggy 9. John Grant 10. Robbie Vincent
11. Sean French 12. Greg Edwards

Jones. Actually, it was starting to get more common to see Jazz Funk and Jazz groups feature at weekend club nights now too. For whatever, these nights were - big or small - it was starting to show that a night was starting to be needed revolving around just Jazz on the dancefloor. Previously to that, it was generally featured country wide in what were know as 'Jazz breaks' - maybe two or three sets of fifteen to twenty minutes sections of Jazz of varying tempos and heaviness. It was now everywhere.

JAP JAZZ

Late 1979 was also the year of one of the big things to happen in the Jazz Funk movement, the introduction of Japanese Jazz Funk and Fusion by DJ and Record Distributor Tony Monson. Tony took over a record shop in Hammersmith, West London called 'Flyover which only sold Japanese imports - mainly Rock or 'picture discs' etc, but they had a little Jazz section. Tony discovered some gems and also used the contacts in Japan that Flyover already had to bring in more, and that was it - a countrywide phenomenon (see Tony Monson's interview for full story). 'Jap Jazz' - as it was known, became very collectable and 'elitist'. They were very expensive too. The quality and playing on these records was amazing (although a bit 'paint by numbers' if I have to be honest). There were crisp commercial or heavyweight Jazz Funk tracks and 'perfect for the floor' Samba Fusion tracks by the dozen. It was played everywhere. There were even 'Jap Jazz' specialist DJ's like Duncan Uren in Torquay, Devon and Malcolm James in Essex. For a couple of years there was, without doubt, a 'fever' around these records.

Talking about 'fevers', another thing that really made Jazz go berserk on the dancefloor was the appearance in record shops of 'cut-outs' These were deleted U.S Jazz, Soul or Funk albums that were discontinued, withdrawn, no longer available etc and had a little 'clip' taken off of the sleeve. Shops like Al in Glasgow; the countrywide 'Our Price' chain; Bluebird Records (the cut-out kings); Robinsons and Yanks in Manchester and many other import shops, were absolutely flooded with thousands upon thousands of these incredible known and predominantly unknown albums - some on tiny independent labels. They were cheap too: a half or a third of the price of a regular album. So many tracks were being uncovered for the dancefloor - literally by the hundreds. It was a breathtaking time. To make it even harder on the pocket, even regular record shops started selling them too, and even more cheaper! Until then, most DJ's that were dabbling in a little Jazz on the dancefloor were buying them as 'new imports' at their local specialist shop, but now all of a sudden hundreds of titles had flooded in to DJ's boxes thanks to cut-outs, and so the more committed DJ's were going deeper and more adventurous.

October the 10th saw the second Caister Soul weekender, but this time there were 5000 in attendance. The demand for tickets was so high that they organized another weekender at Perran Sands in Cornwall two weeks after, for the extra 2000 that couldn't get in to Caister. Caister weekenders still continue to date and are an institution, but at that Caister, the silliness had now gotten out of control (so I sought refuge in the Jazz room). Nothing to do with the weekender, but with the all-dayer explosions and the silly dances and fancy dress nights at the 'Jazz Funk' clubs all over the country overshadowing the music, it was starting to attract idiots. Some clubs were starting to make the last two hours of the night party dances even (and it is here that I have to admit my moment of shame too, though, and tell you that it was me that started the 'rowing dance' to *'Oops Upside Your Head'* by The Gap Band (or *'I Don't Believe You Want To Get Up And Dance (Oops),'* as it was originally called). I saw Chris Hill having the entire Goldmine rowing to *Anita Ward - Ring My Bell*, and so I revived it to *the Gap Band* at the Zero 6. I spoilt a brilliant P-Funk record there I'm afraid. I'm sorry!). What started out as a bit of a harmless fun spread like wildfire and nearly killed the scene. There were so many idiots and stupid Tribes attracted to the clubs that now there was a lot of drunken violence as reported in

Blues and Soul magazine at the end of year. This wasn't just a Southern problem: at Northern all-dayers there would be fancy-dress parties and attractions like 'The Phantom Flan-Flinger' from the 'Tiswas' children's programme and other novelties. Ian Dewhirst told me: "I think there was a bit of novelty introduced to break up the all-dayers. Because they were so long it gave a bit of variety - although I'd have been happy with it just being music. But all these all-dayers were huge events: I'd come on at eight o'clock to 3000 people and I'd be fucking pissed (drunk). It was so exhilarating. You felt you could do anything with the crowd. I stripped off once to my underwear and stood on a speaker conducting the crowd. You could get them to sit down en masse."

On the 26th May 1980, the unsurpassed event of our scene happened - 'The Knebworth Soul Festival' all-dayer in the grounds of Knebworth House, Hertfordshire. This event attracted 15,000 people, with the Funk Mafia DJ's plus Colin Curtis and John Grant from the North and with Lonnie Liston Smith and G.Q. playing live. It was a spectacular event. Again, there was violence, and even a riot in the massive food hall, where I witnessed chairs and tables flying everywhere. This beautiful, spectacular event in some ways was the book-marking point of the decline of the Jazz Funk scene. Despite the huge attendance there, numbers were absolutely plummeting all over the country. There'd been so many all-dayers attracting so many people that it was detracting from the clubs, and the numbers had desperately dropped off - it was predominantly the all-dayers as mentioned, but people were getting absolutely sick of the silliness too. The Jazz Fusion that was coming out was beginning to sound watered down and club music was starting to change too, moving toward a more electronic sound (e.g. *D-Train - You're The One For Me*) and lastly, of course, we'd just hit the biggest countrywide recession in modern times.

One thing that was fantastic in 1980 was the vast amount of new British Jazz Funk groups making records. It was quite common even, for them to only come out on a 'white label' 12 inch single. The music was dubbed 'Brit Funk' and it had a sound of it's own. Also interesting now was the real splintering of the scene, as documented earlier.

There was beginning to be a scene revolving around the deeper, more obscurer, independent Soul artists and now the Jazz and heavier Jazz Funk nights were really starting to appear too. It had to happen: there were so many so-called Jazz Funk DJ's playing a little Jazz that, through demand of the small new crowd of Jazz enthusiasts that had been nurtured through the scene, they were wanting it more harder and adventurous - which in most clubs became quite anti-social on the dancefloor, so a lot of DJ's then started dropping Jazz from their play-list's like hot cakes. Upon the release of *Tania Maria's* album *Piquant* (with the Jazz dance classic '*Yatra Ta*' on it) a famous local Jazz Funk DJ said to me: "What are you buying that for? No one plays that shit any more" - and that just went to show the true colours of him and loads of other band-wagon jumpers. What he and the others didn't know, was Jazz was just about to explode again, and turn into quite a different scene altogether.

Just as with all scenes, the knowledgeable punters were starting to transcend the majority of the DJ's. The DJ's initially instilled an interest in certain kinds of music to the crowd and there then became a situation where there were pockets of punters that started to know more than the DJ entertaining them did. There was a genuine thirst for music that they didn't know, or they were wanting it harder and faster. Jazz (Fusion) in general was becoming - on the most part - anti-social on the floor in most clubs.

As well as the passion for Jap Jazz and Cut-Outs, for a while there'd been an interest in the earlier real Jazz Funk from '75/76 - records that were known or not (cut-outs would have been partly to blame for the re-emergence of interest in this style of music too, due to the sheer amount of Jazz Funk surfacing that wouldn't have been know first time around). Chris Hill acknowledged the interest and listed a lot of titles to look out for in his column in Blues and Soul (12/2/80 and 11/3/80):

Sonny Stitt - Slick Eddie
Jack McDuff - Ju Ju
Charles Earland - Intergalactic Love Song/From My Heart To Yours
Johnny Hammond - Los Conquistadores Chocolates
Bobby Lyle - The Genie
Alphonso Johnson - Scapegoat
Lonnie Smith - Sizzle Stick/ Filet O' Soul
For The Coz Of Jazz - Flat Meat
Gary Bartz - Mother Nature
Jack McDuff - Blue Monsoon
Houston Pearson - Pure Pleasure
Joe Thomas - Funky Fever
Jimmy Smith - Can't Hide Love
John Handy - Hard Work
Johnny Hammond - Lady Smooth
Lee Ritenour - Fly By Night
Rueben Wilson - Got To Get Your Own
Donald Byrd - Dominoes (live)

Jazz was still being championed by two dozen or so DJ's in the country, and we were starting to see new names coming through like respected and knowledgeable Kerrso up in Glasgow and Pete Girtley with his whirlwind success at Dollars, Dixon Lane, Sheffield where at least a third of the night was Jazz (12/12/80). DJ Neil Neale in Derby, another one with a Jazz bias, would always travel across country to Sheffield to Dollars socially if he wasn't working - it was that good; Trevor M at The Place in Stoke-On-Trent, again, was committing to a lot of Jazz in his varied sets; future legend Hewan 'The Jazzman' Clarke was starting to make his first appearance at Fevers, Fennel Street in Manchester on Tuesdays with Russ Gray (21/10/80); Rob Willis in Leicester was playing it jazzy at Scamps; Chris Brown started his Fusion night 'Jazzin it' at Jacksons in Staines on Tuesday (21/10/80) and the legendary long-running sunday Jazz residency at The Belvedere, Ascot with the Jazz Fusion band I.C.Q. Although not just playing Jazz, Pete Tong was the man to see for the heavy stuff in Kent. The Caister Weekender continued to do big business and still feature a Jazz room (as it still does to date). The small amount of all-dayers that were left still continued, for the most part, to have Jazz rooms too. Most importantly, things started to change with the next venue: The Horseshoe, Tottenham Court Road, London W1. From a Southern perspective, this is where the division between the home-counties Jazz Dance scene and the London one happened. Ironically, the DJ responsible was an Essex man brought up in the home-counties Jazz Funk culture:

PAUL MURPHY

On the weekend starting Friday September the 5th 1980 you could have gone to either night at The Horseshoe - they were both for the Jazz fans: Friday night, after leaving Crackers, the innovative DJ and promoter George Power moved to The Horseshoe to start the first of his legendary 'Jazzifunk' nights. There was one main room, with George and Paul Anderson playing the upfront Funk and Soul imports, and he featured another room playing Jazz. The DJ's were two young Turkish lads by the names of Colin Parnell and Boo - who I've unfortunately been unable to trace for the purposes of this book. As with Crackers, the crowd were not solely, but a majority, Black, and the dancing was outstanding. Just starting briefly, I believe, on a Friday and moving quickly to Saturdays, a specialist mobile DJ by the name of Ray Reeves brought in a guest DJ to help him - Paul Murphy (Paul as you may remember earlier ran the Exodus Club from The Lacy Lady and promoted The Kingswood Club in Ilford with Bob Jones and Paul Gratue). I was told that Ray asked to borrow some of Paul's Jazz and Jazz Funk records to play and Paul said, "No, but I'll come down and play them for you." The billing, initially, was just 'Ray and Paul' and the night was eventually called JAFFAS (Jazz and Funk, Funk and Soul). The music was not heavy as it would go on to become at that point, but top quality all the same:

Barbara Carroll - From The Beginning
Ingram - Mi Sabrina Tequana
MFSB - Mysteries Of The World
Charles Earland - Cornbread
Cal Tjader - Shoshana / Rogers Samba
Fuse One - Double Steal / Grand Prix
Nobu Yagi - Mi Mi Africa
Victor Feldman - Rio
Dom Um Romao - Kitchen
Charlie Rouse - Waiting On The Corner
Patrick Williams - Come On And Shine

At that point, initially the Jazz music would have perhaps been a bit heavier on Colin and Boo's night on the Friday (judging by their charts), but Paul Murphy was now making his impression. From a Southern perspective with this book, everything that happened historically - jazz-wise - leads up to Murphy, and it was never the same after.

Their back...
"JAFFA'S"
return to the Horseshoe
(Tottenham Court Road, London W1)
Every SATURDAY
from
SATURDAY FEBRUARY 28th
Hard Jazz — Funk — Latin
with DJ's
RAY and PAUL
Admission: Members £1.50 Non-Members £2 — 8.30 'til 2.00

Pete Tong guested at The Horseshoe, as the current young upstart of Jazz, and was asked to permanently be involved, which he declined: "I never wanted to be tied down to one style of music, I always like to keep an eye on what's ahead and move on," he told me.

Whichever way you wanted it, you were getting Jazz at The Horseshoe on Fridays and Saturdays. Paul and Ray briefly left there in late '80 and started at The Green Man in Euston Road, London on Fridays for a few months, which, I'm told, started to attract a lot of dancers (dancer and DJ Andy Ward of Dagenham, Essex recognized a lot of the dancers there from The Lacy Lady, The Royalty and, importantly, the saturday under-18's Jazz Funk disco at Ilford Town Hall with the Funk Mafia DJ Froggy. He had an enormous Black following). When Paul and Ray returned to The Horseshoe on Saturday the 24th of February 1981 they started to feature live Jazz and Jazz Funk, booking the best of British like *Morrissey - Mullen* and *The Breakfast Band*. DJ-wise, through demand, the music played was now getting harder and very adventurous.

Although, as already mentioned, the general club scene was in a terrible slump (Chris Hill - as someone still packing out clubs then - even did a big free DJ tour later that year to try and attract people back into the clubs), things were looking great country-wide for Jazz. Greg Wilson started the Wigan Pier Jazz night in 1980 on Tuesdays. Murphy, again, had another killer on Fridays, at the St Louis Club, Finborough Road in Earls Court, London. This was with DJ Chris Bangs, and musically it was Fusion and heavy Jazz Funk. This lasted for six months. At the same time, Jazz specialist Neil Neale was doing Sundays at the Blue Note in Derby and, as of the 20th of June, Colin Curtis fully dedicated to a 100% Jazz night at Rufus in Manchester on Thursdays. Journalist Frank Elson reported in Blues and Soul: "Although Jazz is on the wane to the masses, the Rufus crowd want loads of it." September was an important month for the Jazz Dance scene for so many reasons: Bob Jones started a Jazz-only session on Wednesdays at The Countryman in Chelmsford, Essex; Sean French started a Fusion-only night on Saturdays at Wheelers, Henley-On-Thames; the pirate radio station JFM launched on 94.2 - which featured a lot of Jazz, and the doors opened at Fusions Records, Exmouth Market, London. Owned by Paul Murphy (and later, with a partner - Dean Hulme), this was the shop that changed everything.

MURPHY'S RECORD SHOP 'FUSIONS' AND 'THE ELECTRIC BALLROOM'

Paul was importing directly from the US from warehouses advertising in the Billboard and Cashbox magazines initially. The records were deletions and because the records were so cheap, he was taking chances on hundreds of titles. He was also buying up hundreds of obscure Scandinavian Fusion records too. The stock was unique, because, as he was taking chances on most of the titles - despite some not being very good - suddenly there were tons of new Jazz

Fusion records being discovered for our scene, and only available there at the shop. Generally, a vast majority of the Jazz being played until then was regular new Jazz releases from the import shops (with Jap Jazz still going strong too), and from the incredible amount of cut-outs that had started to come through, but the stock at Fusions was unique to the shop. No DJ that specialized in Jazz could afford to miss shopping there - North or South. Murphy would take a sales box up-North as far as Scotland when he DJ'd or, a little later, the Midlands Jazz DJ Baz Fe Jazz would take up records to the midlands and the North (when he worked part time at Fusions, whilst at dance college in London). The home-counties DJ's (including me) had to shop there because there was so much competition they could not afford to miss out; there were only a few copies of some of these records after all. DJ's would panic in case they missed something. These fresh new titles introduced so many new tracks onto the dancefloor that it generated a huge buzz. Possibly, the only other person doing this - and the only serious competition to Fusions - was Tony's Imports of Clacton. Tony Ashby sold Jazz Fusion and Soul on a market stall in Clacton, and set the stall up at various clubs too, such as The Embassy Rooms, Colchester; The Bull in Royston and The Countryman, Chelmsford. He took his chances, like Paul and Dean, on titles from the US. Without doubt though, the discoveries coming through Fusions entirely changed the face of the Jazz dance scene.

Historically, equally as important as the opening of Fusions in September was an event on Friday September the 19th: George Power seamlessly moved from The Horseshoe to the cavernous Electric Ballroom in Camden Town, London - still retaining the name of 'Jazzifunk' and the same line up of George and Paul Anderson playing Soul, Funk and Boogie, and upstairs the Jazz room with Colin Parnell and Boo. It was the beginning of the most important club night in this scene's history. Like The Horseshoe, The Ballroom's attendance was almost entirely Black and the playlist of Parnell and Boo was out of this world - as you would expect, playing to a room full of expectant, fevered dancers. Quite soon, their playlist, like many other DJ's, reflected what was for sale at Fusions. Murphy's influence was everywhere now. They shared more or less the same dancers as Paul Murphy too, as they did previously at The Horseshoe - as remembered by dancer Dean Lima-Moore.

Considering that there were now five or six dedicated Jazz dance nights in Essex; Manchester; London; Surrey etc; and Jazz rooms at the newly re-appearing all-dayers around the North like The Locarno, Birmingham; Romeo and Juliets in Sheffield and Clouds in Preston - plus Jazz still being featured as Jazz breaks all over the UK, it was strange to read in the end of year summary in Blues and Soul (15/12/81) that: "1981 saw the need for obscure Jazz fly out of the window - although Paul Murphy's session at the Horseshoe went mad." It was true that a lot of the 'Jazz Funk' DJ's had stopped playing Jazz because the demand for fast tempos and lesser known tracks were becoming anti-social to a commercial dancefloor, but the scene was not dwindling, it was growing - and quickly!

As mentioned earlier, the scene had certainly split into two factions: the home-counties predominantly White scene and a very Black scene revolving mainly around the circuit of Jazz rooms at the all-dayers and The Horseshoe and The Electric Ballroom. It was all about the dance challenge - the battles and area-pride. Of course it was about the music, but the music had to be, on the whole, hard and heavy. There was a whole new generation that had just come through that were not from the 70's Jazz Funk scene and had different priorities. Meanwhile, the home-counties Jazz Dance crowd liked the fast stuff too (remember all the DJ's were buying from Murphy's too) but liked their Jazz at all tempos - they had gone through two Chris Hill-led club movements of Blue Note R&B and a Bossa Nova revival even - the Bossa one being big enough to make Verve records reissue *Astrud Gilberto - Girl From Ipanema* and *Take Me To Aruanda* (*there* is an all-time Goldmine anthem for you). Bob Jones had introduced the Caister Jazz room to *John Coltrane - Mr P.C* - which, although unsure at first, the crowd went mad to by the time the solo kicked in. After that weekend, the Southern Jazz specialist DJ's and punters were out searching for anything 'Be Bop' and remotely danceable; remember me saying earlier about elements of the crowd being almost as, or more, knowledgable than the DJ playing to them? Such was the thirst for knowledge. Just like the Northern clubs, the home-counties scene liked a variety of tempos, and was big enough to exist outside of what was starting to happen in London and the countrywide all-dayer Jazz rooms. Many different Northern dancers and DJ's told me that, all of a sudden it was hard for DJ's to play a variety of tempos because this young new crowd - who were

the majority - wanted it hard and fast.

Meanwhile, in 1982, Paul Murphy continued on at The Horseshoe, occasionally putting on international Jazz acts such as the *Heath Brothers; Alphonse Mouson; Jay Hoggard* and, later, *Tania Maria* too - plus doing a few different residencies in Surrey with the late legendary collector and reluctant DJ Tarun Sen Gupta at Alladins in Wallington and Jesters, Kingston (12/3/82). For six or seven weeks Paul Murphy started a Friday residency at Devils, Earls Court Road (5/3/82) with Benny Wilson. Benny's name cropped up time and time again from the late 70's onwards as a Jazz-based DJ. This was a very rough club full of unsavoury characters. Bob Jones guested there and told me that he couldn't wait to get out. A tribe from Chelmsford - The Pre Clones - went down there too, and as dancer Clive 'Jah Burger' Smith told me, "It felt aggressive in there. We'd never go back." Even after it's short run, for those regulars that were there, it was considered one of the first of the hard core sessions.

On August the 17th, George Power's 'Jazzifunk' night at The Electric Ballroom moved from Saturdays to Fridays. Colin Parnell and Boo were out and Paul Murphy was in (why they went, nobody remembers). And now the most important phase of this club and the Jazz Dance scene begins. A lot has been written about this session. It was certainly, without a doubt the focal point for the Black scene. The dark, heavy and hard Fusion that Murphy was playing, plus with the dancing and fashion unique to that room, it was virtually a scene of it's own. Of course you had dancers there that had been around since the 70's but you had a whole new crowd of youngsters (mainly underage) that were in there to dance. That room was all about dancing, but to be more precise - battling. I was told, jokingly, from Lizard - a major dancer from Birmingham - that the room was so small and full of dancers that you could turn the wrong way and find yourself in a challenge. A dance style became noticeable at The Horseshoe and developed to further extremes at The Ballroom, and it was named Fusion. It was never termed that in the club but it was a term used around the country to differentiate between the other dominant styles of Jazz dancing: "I'm more 'Ballet' style, he's more 'Fusion'."

'Electric Ballroom' dancers and their fashion. L to R - Morris, Mark, Melvin, Marshall and Simon. Photo Eric Watson

BRITISH JAZZ DANCE STYLES, AND THE HISTORY OF FUSION DANCING

The 70's was a great time for dance innovations of course: we had the Disco explosion and all that went with it, with thepartnered dance The Hustle; there was The Bump, The Freaky Deaky etc; there were many troupes forming too due to the success of Arlene Phillips' 'Hot Gossip' - who were on television all the time; we had the Northern Soul scene (which came from the 60's) with it's own steps and extreme spinning - plus acrobatics taken from the Teddy Boy dance 'The Bop' (not to be confused with the US dance of the same name). Of course, of major interest to this book was the free-style dancing done to Disco, Soul, Funk, Jazz Funk and Jazz Fusion.

Dancing is unique to an individual, of course, but like in all forms of music there were distinct styles of dancing formed naturally within our scene. One or two dancers have told me that they were influenced by Northern Soul dancing, and quite a few have said they were influenced by the veteran tap-dancers The Nicholas Brothers. I don't, and can't dispute it, but if they were influenced by The Nicholas Brothers, it would have been from a fleeting glance of an appearance on a Saturday-afternoon film-showing on television, as no one had video players in the 70's. It has always rankled me a little anyway, when lazy journalists have tried to make out that our Jazz Dance scene is a continuation of the US one from the 1930's Cotton Club era. Young fifteen and sixteen year olds dancing to sophisticated new-release Jazz Funk and Jazz Fusion in the late 70's in a discoteque wouldn't have looked at what they were doing as a continuation of the 30's Jazz scene - in fact London dancer and DJ Seymour Nurse told me that they he and his brother Gary thought the Nicholas brothers style of dancing was funny, and would call it 'Charlie Chaplin' dancing. They saw no comparisons. It meant nothing to them. It is true to say, however, that in the 80's the influence of the Nicholas Brothers; Berry Brothers and Fred Astaire had become very apparent and cannot be denied. But to re-iterate- our Jazz Dance scene came from the dance-floors of the K Jazz Funk scene in discoteques, not from Harlem in the 30's. Our Jazz Dancing is not related to the stage-dancing term 'Jazz' (although some dancers did take steps from Bob Fosse-type shows) - the terminology is a coincidence - or 'Street Jazz' - as taught in sport-centres and leisure halls around the world either.

Of all the influences there has been on our Jazz Dancing, it was intriguing to see influences coming through from the Martial Arts films. Dancers from the 1970's as well as the 80's have told me, from all over the country, how they'd taken moves from those films. I know dancers that would travel to all-night Kung Fu films in Handsworth, Birmingham and then go on to a Jazz Funk all-dayer straight after, all fired up with new ideas. There were all night Martial Arts films showing in London too - like in Soho for instance. One of the key dancers in Sheffield - known as 'Berni'- still has a whole wall of Martial Arts films. Why Martial Arts? Because there are so many combination moves and knee-spins that could be directly used or adapted to dancing, linking different moves.

Jazz Dance as a scene didn't happen until the early 80's so what styles were around in the 70's?

BALLET/CONTEMPORARY

Of course, the best freestyle dancers in the clubs then, countrywide, would strive to look as professional as possible and take their influences, even, from ballet and certainly stage dancing - whether it would be state of the art modern contemporary dance or the classic Bob Fosse-style of stage dancing, as exemplified in shows and films such as Guys And Dolls, Seven Brides For Seven Brothers, and certainly the king of them all - West Side Story. Professional Manchester dance crew The Jazz Defektors were the greatest example of what could be done with that. It was all about interpreting the music. I'm sticking my neck out here but one could almost call the freestyle disco dancing in the U.K of the 70's 'Jazz Dance' in a way. Certainly a lot, if not most, of the best-rated dancers would have entered disco dancing competitions. Don't discount this opinion. When you see the freestyle Disco dancers (And I mean 'freestyle') they look trained and you can see contemporary and ballet in there - and Funk (we'll come to that in a second).
Ballet or Contemporary style is often mistakenly called the 'Northern' style of Jazz, when in fact pre-the London style of Fusion in the early 80's (we'll come to that in a second too), that was the dominant style all over the country - as told to me by dancers from Essex, Kent and Bristol. The one thing about Jazz Dancing in the North, however - whatever style - was that in a challenge, the dancers would agree on 'contact or no contact'. If one agreed 'no contact' and there was, that could cause trouble, and has done.

The other dominant style in the 70's was of course....

FUNK

I'll keep this in simple terms (mainly because it's a hard one to put into words): for the best example of Funk dancing, look at old footage of *The Jackson Five* or footage from the old US television show 'Soul Train'. The body is twisting, turning and contorting to the rhythm - the groove - of the song. Jazz Funk dancing was certainly a continuation on from that.

Without trying to sit on the fence, of course individual freestyle dancers would have mixed up all these styles then. A Contemporary/Ballet dancer would certainly have danced, and loved dancing, to Jazz Funk just as much as a funkier dancer, but I'm sure we're all agreed that there are two distinctly different styles.

Into the 1980's, Contemporary/Ballet continued as one of the major styles of Jazz Dance, and the other was the heavily Funk influenced Fusion.

FUSION

As Contemporary/Ballet interprets the melody, Fusion interprets the rhythm.

This is our very own homegrown UK style and it came from London. More specifically it came from the dancers from The Horseshoe and later, The Electric Ballroom. Some people feel that Fusion is just the Funk dancing sped up to Jazz, and there is a lot of truth in that: to watch it, it certainly looks like it. Remember, that when the first few Jazz Fusion tracks started to get played next to the Jazz Funk, people would have danced the same to either without distinguishing between the two musics.

Fusion is a very distinct style - easily recognized. It had been known around the country as Footing, Tappers, Tap-Style, or Steppers. Just previously to Fusion it was quite common to see fast side-to-side shuffling feet with all the movement coming from the waist down with not much upper body movement. There was a 'look' of a Fusion dancer too: they would have had their arms tight by their sides (almost like traditional Irish dancing if you like) and that came from Kevin 'The Penguin' Haynes at The Horseshoe. Initially a funk step that was previously common at Crackers, the classic basic Fusion step - known as Cockroach Stomping or Crushing - arrived at the Horsehoe via Michael Brown. Just as a paradiddle is the basic snare-drum rudiment and a time-step is the basic rudiment of tap dancing, such is the cockroach crushing/stomping with Fusion. Imagine the motion of extinguishing a cigarette with the ball of your right foot moving to your left foot and repeating - there you go. Almost everyone says that is cockroach crushing/stomping but one or two have said that it was just 'a slapping of the sole of the foot on the ground'. There were many other innovators like Richard Baker (the younger cousin of legendary Crackers dancer Hoyle Baker), Steve 'Afro' Edwards, Jerry Barry - later known as Jerry IDJ and too many others to mention. There were so many dancers then that people's steps were getting copied left, right and centre (not only in Fusion-style. Any main dancer will tell you the same story, whatever area). So the dance style was developing quickly. As is traditional in all Black styles of dance, challenges (aka burn-ups, cutting or battling) were more common then. Quite often there would be two dancers battling it out from one to six records, and dancers would work on their moves all week in order to have fresh moves for the following week as part of their ammunition. Of course, there would be combinations of fast footwork, but the floorwork was coming to the fore now - knee spins etc (floorwork moves were also known as 'Cuts' in Birmingham and 'Drilling' in Leeds).

Fusion spread all over the country initially, by a group of dancers from Birmingham led by Stretch and Lizard. After they saw it, it changed the dance-style forever. Stretch told me: "We teefed the moves, teefed the style, did it our way and took it round the country." After a while you started to see small areas doing Fusion. "It was like a virus that was spreading," Lizard said. It caused a lot of resentment initially. The older balletic/contemporary dancers didn't like it - "That's not dancing" was a common objection - but there was a whole new wave of very young (many underage) predominantly Black dancers coming through in their hundreds and they wanted the music fast and rough (mainly Jazz Fusion) to dance their rough battling dance to. It became hard for Jazz based DJ's not to cater for these dancers as they were now the majority country-wide. The contemporary dancers couldn't do their style to the fast tempos so, all of a sudden, it was a matter of changing their style to Fusion or waiting in hope for the DJ to drop a couple of 'social tempos' in - as many a dancer told me. The major exponents of Fusion were the IDJ dancers of London - a crew that totally came straight out of the heart of the Electric Ballroom scene.

FUSIONS

JAZZ CHART

BY PAUL MURPHY

1) TERUMASA HINO-Merry Go Round.
2) VALI SCOBELLI-The Tune
3) DAVID FRIEDMAN-Rachels Samba
4) BARRY MILES-Magic Theatre (a real Cockroach crusher!)
5) AZAR LAWRENCE-Forces Of Nature
6) ALPHONSE MOUZON-Antonia
7) NORMAN WILLIAMS-Billy's Ballet
8) MACHITO ORCH-Macho
9) ANDY NARELL-7 Steps To Heaven
10) JERRY GONZALES-Evidence

This, the 'Electric' Cockroach Crusher chart, is compiled in no particular order by Paul Murphy.

WHERE DID FUSION COME FROM?

When I Interviewed the key innovators of Fusion dancing, they mentioned other dancers names that influenced them, and of all the many dancers mentioned these two names: Trevor Shakes and Paul Anderson (the London one) came up time and time again; in fact, the dance greats like Errol T - The Godfather and Rick and Ty Hassell from Birmingham, Chris Sullivan from Wales and Clive Smith from Bristol all mentioned them too. Trevor Shakes insisted that in order to understand where he comes from I had to interview his influences: Travis Edwards, Leon Herbert and Dez Parkes. and so their full interviews are later in the book. The one thing that Paul; Trevor; Travis; Leon and Dez mention is the Jamaican dance done to Ska, and later, Reggae - shuffling. This was also mentioned by London DJ Ed Stokes, of The Brixton Front Line too. There would often be big battles between 'Shufflers' in clubs (often ending in serious violence, it has to be said). The dancing would involve fast footwork and a vibrating of the legs. A dancer would throw a handkerchief into the circle to challenge - the handkerchief would also be flipped in the air by sliding a foot under it, used to mock shoe-polishing or thrown over the head and caught. This is interesting because the use of handkerchiefs have been used in traditional dances across the caribbean islands and Africa for centuries (also in English Morris dancing too actually - and there is a link), and is also used in Funk dancing.

I try to observe rather than comment because it is a history book, but having seen 'shuffling' I can't really see the influence in Fusion - which after all, comes from Funk - but I will record these observations; after all, it makes sense: the vast majority of the Black population here then would have been from Jamaican parentage, as pointed out by Dez Parkes: "Being Afro Caribbean, music is our life. It's around from day one." And it's true: friends and relations would see or swap moves at parties in the house, community or church halls and there would have been an explosion of Black dancers in the clubs in London around 1975 where they were finally getting admitted. It's mentioned in interviews later by Chris Sullivan, Maggot and Paul Anderson that, until then, the majority of the main dancers were White - simply, the Blacks couldn't get in! Historically it is also worth mentioning that countrywide, it was quite dangerous being Black and into Soul or Funk in a Black area because the majority - The Reggae lovers - would call you a 'Soul Head' - which although not sounding abusive, would be meant antagonistically - almost as if one were a traitor. It would, and could, cause trouble.

I make no apologies for spending more time over the history of Fusion dancing, and risk over analyzing it, because, although there are many, many incredible individual dancers and styles out there, love it or loathe it, Fusion was the first, truly uniquely British Jazz Dance form in the UK.

SWING OR BE BOP

This was a style innovated by the London-based Northern dancers: The Brothers In Jazz. They developed their own form of fast-footwork to take out the fast fusion that was being played in the South which bore similarities to the Nicholas Brothers and the Berry Brothers - the veteran US tap-dance acts - which they didn't realize until London Black social-dance expert Simon Salman pointed it out to them. He showed them videos to make the point. They were not tap-dancing of course, but were just as fleet-of-foot, and held themselves in that same elegant manner. The Brothers mixed in some 'Mambo' style that had been popular at Colin Curtis' club Berlin (also as danced by The Jazz Defektors there) and expressive hand movements - (something Fusion had never had) - and bingo - Swing style. Their style is now known as 'Be Bop' in Japan and remains the dominant style in that country's burgeoning Jazz dance scene.

'OSCARS' STYLE

What the hell am I talking about? The Bristol dancer, by the name of Paul 'Oscar' Anderson (not the London dancer of the same name), has such a unique and influential style, that you can always tell a dancer from within a forty mile radius of Bristol because of Oscars influence.

For you dance-historians: I'm sorry, I can't explain his style. It is best to be experienced. It has a kind of tap-feel about it and, again, like The Brothers In Jazz, is very elegant, plus, added to that is a smattering of Fusion - much like his professional Jazz Dance crew The Floor Technicians - a pure cross of Fusion and Swing.

Oscars style is definitely a legitimately influential one and must be set apart and highlighted along with the others. So to recap, the four main distinct Jazz dance styles of the 1980's were: Fusion; Ballet/Contemporary; Swing and, er... Oscar!

JAZZ HOUSE

The Foot Patrol Jazz Dance troupe from Mancester are the reluctant innovators of this style. I haven't listed 'Jazz House' as a distinct style of it's own as it is basically slowed down Fusion, and the dancers almost have a 'bounce' in their step to the bass heavy electronic, but soulful, mutant Disco from Chicago popular in 1986 onwards. Members of Foot Patrol told me that they didn't consider themselves 'House dancers,' they danced to it because there was nothing else ('owt or nowt') - Jazz had died on the dancefloors in the North by then, in 1986. Other professional Northern Jazz Dance troupes, such as Fusion Beat from Manchester, Elite from Leeds and Bamboozle and The Unknown Troopers from the North-east - as well as many other Jazz dancers - dabbled in dancing to House too. Various dancers told me that it was good dancing Fusion to House music: because it was slower, one had a chance to work on, and sharpen up, the moves so that, when inevitable battles took place they were ready and also warmed-up.

SO WHERE DID THE PROFESSIONAL JAZZ DANCE TROUPES COME FROM?

There were a lot of professional or semi-professional dance groups (or troupes) around in the 1970's of course, made up from the prime freestyle dancers in the area, and fuelled, in the most part by the Disco boom. In London there was 'Hot Gossip' - who were national celebrities on television for years with their sexy multicultural troupe of punky-looking muscular men and beautiful women - a perfect antidote to middle of the road sterile dance troupes such as Pans People on the Top Of the Pops television show or Dougie Squires Second Generation. These were dancers everyone could relate to and aspire to.

Even if none of the other troupes wanted to look like them, it showed that there was a demand for it. Pre-Hot Gossip, you had Trevor Shakes troupe Torso (the original? Probably) and then you had Carribean Showboat; Expansions in Birmingham, Mahogany and Switch in Bristol and countless others. Of course you also had many, many crews around that had names (or not) - many just representing their area, like the hundreds of tribes or crews of Funkateers did. For example, you had The Westereners in Manchester from the Western Pub in Moss Side and The Scorpions; XR4's, Zebra and Shanti of Sheffield; The Meanwood Posse from Leeds or The Smethwick Spades and The Convicts in Birmingham, and I could go on. There were also crews of Jazz Funk dancers such as The Tuxedos and The Firm in Leeds; and The Mirror Squad, 10-4, Renegades, Minor League and The Sweat Hogs in Bristol, and also many DJ's had their own dance troupes too such as London DJ's George Power and Kelly (Kellys Force).

The first recorded true Jazz Dance performance by a semi-professional troupe was at Smartys in Manchester in either late '78 or early '79 by the troupe Expansions from Birmingham. Colin Curtis saw them in Graham Warr's club Chaplins and wanted to show Manchester 'Jazz dancing' so he invited them up. They caused a big stir running on with stockings over their faces - although this 'militant statement' was actually nothing other than to cover their faces out of embarrassment!

In 1981,the first troupe representing the London Jazz dance style was The Untouchable Force Dancers - also known as TUF. This trio of dancers - comprising of Richard Baker, Richard Green and another - did their first performance at The Horseshoe dancing to *Fuse One - In Celebration Of The Human Spirit* and *Toki And The Samba Friends - Aquarela Do Brasil*. They were dressed in rolled-up commando hats, trainers and beige army khakis. Key dancer Jerry Barry, aka Jerry IDJ, also remembers them as dancing to Jazz Funk too. Late 1982 saw the formation of the future super group from the main dancers of Manchester - The Jazz Defektors. Not Fusion in anyway, their own style of contemporary; Bob Fosse-influenced stage dancing; influences of some of the Birmingham originals such as Rick and Ty Hassell mixed with a little Mambo, Fred Astaire and Gene Kelly made another unique impact on the scene. As you will read later on in the interviews, they became international recording artists too, fronting their band singing and dancing like a Jazz version of the Funk based London band The Pasadenas (of which dancers Michael and Geoff Brown were a part of). Following shortly after, also in Manchester, was the birth of another troupe called JAB - Jazz At It's Best, formed by dancer Godfrey Pemberton - later of The Foot Patrol.

Early 1984 saw another representation from Birmingham. When the two rival crews: The Smethwick Spades and The Convicts joined together, a troupe emerged made up from dancers that had been going to The Horseshoe in London like Stretch and Lizard - who brought back the Fusion style of dancing, as mentioned earlier. They were called The Fusion Few - named after an advert for Paul Murphy's record shop 'Fusions'. They made a big impression on their debut performance at The Hummingbird all-dayer.

Following on shortly after, a troupe formed in London of the higher echelon of dancers called IDJ - I DANCE JAZZ. There is not much that you can say about IDJ - their influence was felt all over the country, and they became a reference point and inspiration to the many Jazz Dance troupes that formed after. Later that year in London another Fusion Jazz Dance troupe appeared called A Fuego Vivo who were a quartet of dancers by the name of Michael Knott (later of IDJ), Coach, Simon De Montfort and another. It is believed that they only did a few performances before splitting up from arguments. It is said that they were excellent.

Suitably impressed by a performance by IDJ, London based dancers from Leeds: Irven Lewis and Wayne James decided to form Brothers In Jazz. Finding performing routines exhausting just with two persons, they got Bolton dancer Trevor Miller involved, who was studying ballet in London, thus making the line-up complete. Every troupe that appeared after Brothers In Jazz were either influenced by them (they made serious impact when they came onto the scene) or IDJ, with their explosive representation of Fusion.

Many more troupes followed of course, most of whom are covered in in-depth interviews later, but here is a list of all known professional or semi-professional Jazz Dance troupes throughout the 1980's. I'm sorry if I've missed any out:

A Fuego Vivo
Brothers In Jazz
Bamboozle
Bubble And Squeak
Back Street Kids
Dynamic Steps
Elite
Expansions
Floor Technicians
Foot Patrol
Fusion Beat
Fusion Few
Groove Merchants
IDJ
Jazz Defektors
JAB - Jazz At It's Best
Mahogany (aka The Jazz Five)
Spectrum
Step Brothers
TUF - The Untouchable Force
Two Of A Kind
Unknown Troopers

By the late 1980's it was much easier to recognize what area a dancer was from, by their variations of the main styles of Fusion or Swing. By then, the dominant style in the UK was Fusion and was used for battling. Whereas in the South a Fusion dancer would do footwork and floorwork, in some areas - such as Sheffield, Leeds and the North-east - you'd have dancers that would specialize in either footwork or drilling (floorwork). In a battle, if a man was drilling, the opposition would send their key driller in. This is all covered in the dancers interviews later - as is the battle-grounds of the dancefloors of the country, where area-pride was seriously fought for.

BACK TO THE STORY......

I can speak, as someone totally involved in the Southern Jazz Dance scene then, that out in the suburbs we just thought of Paul Murphy starting at The Electric Ballroom as 'just another residency'. Every serious DJ anywhere that played some Jazz bought from his record shop, and was well aware of what he was up to. It was also well-documented in Ralph Tee's essential Groove Weekly magazine - which, although based in London, was essentially mainly 'home counties' and Funk Mafia DJ based. What we took for granted (The Electric Ballroom) was, without us knowing, in actual fact, the clean break away from the safer home-counties Jazz Dance scene. This was the logical conclusion of what had been building slowly through The Horseshoe.

The attendance in both the cavernous main ballroom with George Power and Paul Anderson playing Soul, Funk and Boogie and Murphys tiny upstairs Jazz room was virtually all Black. It wasn't a pleasant atmosphere, I've been told - you'd have gangs hanging around the stairs up to the dimly lit Jazz room. Murphy's room was full of dancers dancing on the sticky floor where the carpet had been pulled up, and it was very competitive. This was the home of the new breed. Dance innovators such as Paul Anderson, Michael Brown and Kevin 'The Penguin' Haynes all mentioned in their interviews that there was too much challenging, tension and violence in there and it was true. To most, it was all about the battling, although there were dancers such as Jerry (IDJ) Barry and Steve 'Afro' Edwards that didn't entertain them. Of the many that did, there was a new kid coming through - probably 14 or 15 years old - that quickly became 'The Ballroom King' - Milton McAlpine. Of the Fusion style that came about at The Horseshoe, Milton took it on to outstanding levels that have never been surpassed since. Much of Milton has been written about in this book and of the many other dancers from West London that were starting to domineer and influence that room.

Much has also been written of the fashions that were unique to that room too - with it's mixture of post - New Romantic and Punk outrageousness mixed with stretch 'Pepe' jeans (frayed at the bottom) with different unique footwear like the 30's spats; leather riding boots; the New Romantic 'tucker boots', karate slippers (an old 70's favourite, along with the thin soled black school-plimsoles); Crown carpet slippers and black-patent dress shoes with (or without) small ribbon bows at the front (sounds awful, looked amazing) plus many, many other styles. Fashion writer and dancer Chris Sullivan thought the style was absolutely awful though, and Paul Anderson said that he'd seen a similar look at the Paradise Garage in New York at that time. It certainly didn't exist outside of the Jazz room in London until other dancers (like the Birmingham ones) took that style with them. Dancers there wore that style to other clubs too, and one could always recognize who went to The Ballroom in the home-counties clubs - with their rolled up woolen-hats, sleeveless t-shirts, stretch jeans leg-warmers and individualized footwear ("they're the Jazz men," people would say).

What about the music? Paul Murphy was, by then, taking it to extremes. Other than Jazz rooms at all-dayers no-one was ever going to get away with a whole night of music like this. He would play the toughest, darkest, rarest Fusion - keeping it up-tempo for an hour and a half, drop it down for a few and go up again - Murphy told me. As already said, he was importing this stuff and you were hearing it there first. A night as anti-social as this shouldn't have worked but it did, and drew dancers from all over the country desperate to make a reputation. The battling went to unprecedented levels there and reverberated in all the Jazz rooms at all dayers all over the country up as far as Scotland. Leading Glasgow DJ and dancer Kerrso told me - as a 'Ballroom' regular - that Murphy played just as hard in the Jazz rooms in Glasgow as in London; as verified by DJ Bob Jeffries (it was Bob who suggested a Jazz room at the massive Scottish all-dayer scene after seeing it work at the Caister weekender). Music promoter and DJ Kenny MacLeod was very keen to push the Jazz to the Scottish crowd too - and was just about to start his 100% Jazz session at Le Club De France in Coatbridge in January '83.

In the North of England of course, Colin Curtis' rule was absolute. But generally then, in the clubs, it was getting harder to get away with the Jazz. At Legends in Manchester DJ Greg Wilson was now pioneering Electro Funk to a crowded club and Jazz breaks were played of course, but sitting awkwardly next to these big modern electronic productions. Although most DJ's had dropped Jazz altogether in their clubs, it was very, very strong in the Jazz rooms at the almost weekly all-dayers happening all over the North and midlands. So, it was by no means dying, it had just changed location.

FACTORY RECORDS

There was another jazz scene developing in Manchester based around the alternative and electronic music label Factory Records owned by maverick Anthony Wilson. Much to the confusion of the label - who after all, had acts such as *Joy Division, New Order* etc... two of their acts had Jazz influences and were getting Black music publication interest: *A Certain Ratio* and *Swamp Children* (later, *Kalima*). The alternative music scene was only just coming to terms with the whole Bristol-based Punk Jazz movement that had started the previous year with the march release of the 7-inch single *Papas Got A Brand New Pig Bag* by *Pig Bag*. Many bands followed from there - most notably Rip, Rig And Panic, who debuted in '82.

ACR (*A Certain Ratio*) and The Swamp Children were checking out Colin Curtis' clubs (and others) with interest, and it was them going to support DJ Hewan 'Jazz Man' Clarke at Fevers in Fennel Street that introduced them to the newly formed Jazz Defektors dance troupe. They were mesmerised by the dancing of this troupe made up of Manchester's finest. The Jazz Defektors and Hewan Clarke quickly became 'part of the crowd' with these two bands.

The JD's first professional performances were dancing for ACR many times that year, confusing the 'rain-coat brigade' alternative music followers, and this was the beginning of a whole different Jazz movement in Manchester to the one revolving around the all-dayer type scene.

Factory records opened the world-famous Hacienda night club that year too, with Hewan playing Futurist (as they called 'alternative' music) and Funk six nights a week.

There were now a lot of other out-and-out Jazz DJ's coming through all over the country that were young and represented this new scene. You had the aforementioned Baz Fe Jazz and Chris ' Rhythm Doc' Long from Coventry; Eric X and Chris Reid from Birmingham; the Asian super-sound system from West London - Distinc-shun; Errol Davis, Pablo and Eric Miller from Nottingham; Simon Mansell from the North west; Sylvester in London; myself, as Mad Marx, out in Essex; Dave Angol from Preston (also a highly rated Jazz dancer), a young Gilles Peterson - who'd written a letter to Groove Weekly (May the 15th) informing everybody of his new pirate station; and there was Andy Jackson, whose show on the pirate station Radio Invicta is thought to have been the first all-Jazz Dance show that represented our scene - reflecting the product on sale from Fusions records. Meanwhile, there were older DJ's such as Jonathon from Nottingham; Chris Bangs from Surrey; Trevor M and Neil Neale from Stoke (although Neil was established in Derby) and Alex Lowes from Newcastle that were getting big reputations for their Jazz sets now along with the Soul and Funk, as well as the continuing mission of Hill, Brown, Jones and French, in the South, Curtis and Wilson in the North, Dinnis, Uren, Lewis, Coomer and Wakefield in the west and MacLeod, Davidson, Kerrso, Jefferies, Hendy et al in Scotland, among numerous others.

BREAK DANCING

By late 1982 a new development had happened in the British dance music culture - Break Dancing. Until the public was exclusively introduced to the video of the song Buffalo Gals by ex-Sex Pistols guru Malcolm McLaren on the maverick Channel 4 Friday night programme The Tube, the only reference to break dancing had been from New York club reports in the UK style magazine The Face. One would've assumed that they were using artistic license when they spoke about kids spinning on their elbows and their heads, but then there it was at last, for us all to see. With this new phenomenon *Buffalo Gals* was quickly followed up with records by break dancers *The Rock Steady Crew* and Pop/Rap outfit *Break Machine*. Club goers were still confused by the recent release of *Planet Rock* by the *Soul Sonic Force* - with its odd-ball, jerky electronic rhythm, and now, at last, it was all coming together. This new Black electronic music - Electro - and break dancing, came in with a massive force and there were new break dancing crews forming left, right and centre. Everyone wanted to know how to do it. It became the national obsession of the youth.

1983 was an interesting year, because at the Electric Ballroom Electro had now taken over as the main music in the main area, so you had break dancing on one floor and Jazz dancing on the other. It was becoming common for some dancers to spend time in both rooms. There was also the first Electro Funk and Jazz Fusion all-dayer at Birmingham's Powerhouse too. DJ Greg Wilson had already been pioneering Electro for sometime at Legends in Manchester, and this club became the home of break dancers in the North. Greg would still play some Jazz too though. Later in '84 there appeared Wildstyle at the west-indian centre The Checkpoint in Bradford, Yorkshire over a year or two period. It was interesting - with the two floor principle too - the Jazz room upstairs introduced us to the future legendary Jazz DJ Lubi Jovanovic. It was interesting to see the amount of Jazz dancers that left the scene to get involved with the breaking, and then many that left breaking to get into Fusion - they were both 'battle' dance-styles after all. Another interesting thing was that you wouldn't see Fusion dancers from a breaking background pull Breaking moves in Jazz battles - one would just switch styles. Unlike any other country, you would have break dance crews - like the famous SMAC 19 - who would have dancers that would break off to take on the Fusion dancers, covering all bases. The equally famous Broken Glass breakers from Manchester were made up of Fusion dancers too, and of course, the number one Fusion dancer of all time - Milton McAlpine was a member of the London All-Star breakers. Although I've gone slightly ahead here, it is best to tell you in one go rather than keep breaking off from other subjects. This is all fully covered in detail later in the interviews.

BERLIN

In Blues and Soul 3/2/83 the Jazz Dance scene was officially represented regularly by Bob Jones with his column called Dr Jazz. Ralph Tee's now defunct Groove Weekly magazine had done so much to champion it, so there was an important twice-monthly column to replace it. Not bad for a scene that was supposed to have finished in '81!

Of enormous importance though was the beginning of one of Colin Curtis' finest moments, and historically the Norths equivalent of Paul Murphy's Jazz room at The Ballroom. The club was called Berlin and was to be found on King Street West and Bridge Street. Already, famously known as an alternative 'Futurist' club, Hewan Clarke came across it and secured a Tuesday night there weekly (19/4/83). Hewan would start the evening off with Jazz, and the dancers would get there early to practice their moves (including Hewan - a rated dancer), leaving the bulk of the night to the main man. The night wasn't all Jazz, it was a unique merging of Jazz and Soul of all tempos and permutations played in long sections - an hour and a half of Jazz, then Soul for 45 minutes, then Jazz etc... This session became the focal point for the scene in the North, attracting people from all parts of the country. It became a home for the Jazz Defektors, ACR and The Swamp Children, and one would see members of the pop-jazz band *Carmel* and the future *Simply Red* superstar *Mick Hucknell*, amongst others. In the midlands, yet another regular all-dayer started to appear, at The Hummingbird in Birmingham.

BERLIN
38 King Street West, Manchester.

1985
SPECIAL BIRTHDAY EDITION
Tuesday 29th January
9 till 2

COLIN CURTIS & HEWAN CLARKE
Present
THE BEST

Jazz & Soul
Accept No Substitute
EVERY TUESDAY

FREE ADMISSION BEFORE 11PM
£1 AFTER 11PM

GILLES PETERSON, AND 'THE WAG'

The DJ Gilles Peterson was now starting to appear in clubs, having started to make a name for himself on Pirate Radio such as Radio Invicta etc. They weren't clubs as such, they were what were called 'wine bars' and there were hundreds (no, thousands) all over the country. These glamorous pubs with DJ systems were the backbone of this, and many other Black music scenes in the UK, along with the back rooms of pubs. Peterson was busy. He was also a regular guest on rotation at the hard core Jazz Dance session Jazz Junction at Marco

Polo Hotel, Bayswater London on Saturday lunchtimes with DJ partners Darren Johnson, David Stokes, Mark Hawkswell and Frank Johnson (and later, Darren continued it at Spats in Oxford Street). Living on the Surrey side of London, Gilles soon made contact with Chris Bangs and began supporting him (initially at The Rio, Didcot), and this was the beginning of an important partnership.

Somewhere that Gilles had been supporting was Bob Jones' session at a new venue in Tooley Street, Bermondsey called The Swan And Sugarloaf. The DJ and promoter Nicky Holloway was bringing in the home-counties DJ's Bob Jones; Sean French; Pete Tong and Jeff Young on rotation every Friday, giving that scene a London base. Nicky Holloway's promotions are absolutely integral to this book as you will later read.

Style journalist and Jazz collector Robert Elms had started to take great interest in the endeavors of Paul Murphy. Elms - like Chris Sullivan and Mark Webster - had been around since the mid 70's and seen it all develop as an active punter - living it. He was enthusiastic about every aspect of the Jazz room at The Electric Ballroom, which he attended with his Jazz-based pop-star girlfriend *Sade*, and would be the first journalist to really document the scene in an international magazine. He was introduced to it all through *Simon Booth* (real name Emmerson), who had a track popular there: *The View From Her Room* by his band *Weekend*. Two members of Sade's band - Andy Hale and Stuart Matthewman - decided to put on a weekly session with Paul Murphy in Brighton (26/11/83) at The Jazz Room, Churchill Palace Hotel, and it was a total success. Murphy asked London DJ Ed Stokes to support him. Ed was someone who's knowledge Paul respected.

He'd been around since the early 70's and was a key member of the Brixton Front Line tribe, a face on the scene and an enthusiastic customer at Fusions records. He guested at the Ballroom a few times to excellent response, and it was one night when Paul was checking Ed out at his weekly residency at Flappers in East London that he asked him to get involved - the ultimate compliment. And so the residency on the South coast began. Paul would play typically 'Ballroom' Jazz to this eager White fashion and student crowd, but he'd also be dropping some Salsa too, and Ed would do the same. There would be Be Bop played too, which was gaining popularity. This shift away from the typical 'Electric Ballroom' set was evidence that he wanted a change. He was feeling restricted playing a certain sound in Camden every week when there was so much more that he wanted to play. Paul was approached by promoter Chris Sullivan, who had taken on the legendary 60's Soho club The Whiskey A Go Go in Wardour Street and renamed it The Wag. Chris, as already mention so many times already, had been a key dancer and punter in the mid 70's traveling all over the country from his native Merthyr Tydfil in Wales to experience everything, and from the Soul and Funk scene (including the Northern Soul one) into Punk, New Romantic and illegal warehouse parties, he'd been

at the forefront of everything - and, with his influential friends, lead the way in club and street fashions. Chris was also a member of the band *Blue Rondo A La Turk*, which had both an Alternative and Soul Boy/Jazz Boy following - which wouldn't normally mix; even though *Spandau Ballet* and *Duran Duran* were from a Jazz Funk background too. Blue Rondo made a huge impression - with their 40's Zoot Suit appearance (starting, again, another street fashion), and Funk and Latin Jazz sound. By '83, Blue Rondo break-offs *Matt Bianco* had chart success and there was talk of a Pop Salsa movement too, which happened - but unfortunately *Modern Romance* came in and ruined it all with their 'middle of the road' *Everybody Salsa*. All this because of the impact of Blue Rondo.

Chris had already done some key promotions, and now The Wag was his. He and Paul Murphy discussed music policy - as Chris told me - and so Paul Murphys new weekly night started on Monday 9th January 1984. Playing live were *Onward International* - a band who had the honour of being the first release on Paul and Dean's label 'Paladin' the previous October, with the incredible *'Foot In The Door'* EP (featuring the classic *Samba Doo Bonnay*). I was there, and I remember a lot of Salsa and mid-tempo Blue Note Be Bop being played. It was packed solid, with a very fashionable majority White crowd. Paul was still briefly continuing at The Electric Ballroom, where he'd been dropping some fast Bop into the mix recently, and some lighter stuff too, signaling the new direction. As of the 21st of April Paul finally handed that Friday night session over to Gilles Peterson - to the disappointment of up coming DJ's Tim Morris and Sheldon Willox, who were hoping to have got it.

Gilles struggled there for the first couple of months (as he and others have told me). He'd only been there once before and wasn't prepared for it. This was a room full of competitive young Black jazz dancers who were used to the sound and selection of Paul Murphy and were not getting it. He was lucky, because a lot of the key dancers followed Murphy to his new residency at The Titanic but weren't allowed in so they came back. This crowd, and the enviroment that revolved around them, took some understanding. This wasn't the Caister Jazz Room home-counties-style Jazz Dance scene, it was a whole different one altogether - with it's own style, sound and rules and regulations.

By August, Paul Murphy had closed down his record shop and he'd personally sold Gilles the key records that were integral to The Ballroom crowd - such as a mysterious white-label oddity known as *The Bottom End*. Originally discovered by Chris Bangs for 10p at Notting Hill's 'Record And Tape Exchange' this was a fast (but not too fast) and tough, quartet jazz-jam with drums high in the mix, with a female vocalist unexpectedly coming in with the song right at the end eight minutes in. Peculiarly, on the other side of the record was what sounded like Church Organ music. It was issued to demonstrate the bottom-end on Ken Kreisel's M&K hi-fi speakers. I remember people telling me about this record, and also my friend and jazz collector Darren Gale saying: "Murphy's got this weird one-off white-label record that's massive. Ask him to play it for you next time you go in the shop - he keeps it behind the counter." Such mystique! The secret has been uncovered now by DJ and dancer Seymour Nurse, and we now know it to be called *Get Off The Ground* by *Don Baaska and Valli Scavelli* (www.thebottomend.co.uk).

Through perseverance, Gilles won-over The Ballroom and the dancers had their key records back at last, too. It is, unfortunately, a leveller to the DJ's when dancers say (as many key ones have), that the scene there in that tiny dark room was all about the records and dancers, not the DJ's. The dancers were never that interested in who the DJ was - they were 'Ninjas', as Jerry IDJ told me - they were invisible. Certain records meant certain things to certain dancers. Most dancers had their special record that they would battle to - and that room was a 'battle-ground' remember. Without those key records it wasn't the same. Contradicting this of course, I've also had dancers - such as Dean Lima Moore - who dispute that, and say that, for instance, Paul Murphy was so revered that the dancers would follow him anywhere. One witness at a Northern all-dayer told me that Murphy was actually cheered and applauded as he walked across the dancefloor to the DJ booth - such was the reverence for the man.

I DANCE JAZZ - THE COMING OF I.D.J.

Musically in 1984, the second release on Paladin was the disappointing *'Look Inside'* album by *Paz* - with a saving grace of an incredible new version of their Jazz Dance classic AC/DC. March saw the release of Manchester band *Kalima - The Shining Hour* and *Fly Away* on Factory Records. Kalima had changed their name from The Swamp Children - which they thought was no longer an appropriate name. *Fly Away* became an immediate Jazz dance monster country-wide.

The month of May saw the long awaited debut by *Working Week* on a joint label project Paladin / Virgin. This track was called *Venceremos* (flipped by a cover of the aforementioned Electric Ballroom monster - The Bottom End). This was the new band by ex-'Weekend' man Simon Booth and avant-garde saxophonist Larry Stabbins. It was inspired by, and tailor made for, the Fusion dancers at The Electric Ballroom. The video for *Venceremos* (made in regular length and a long versions for cinema) was directed by the young barrier-breaking film director Julien Temple and featured an early formation of Jazz Dance troupe IDJ - I DANCE JAZZ. They got together by request of Booth, to do a gig with the band at Camden Jazz Festival, and they then featured in the video. The video is amazing because it captures a moment in dance history. Quite soon after the video, the newly professional dance troupe whittled down to the first proper line up (as detailed in their interviews). Although not the first professional or semi-professional troupe (they were the 6th in fact, if you're counting) they were of paramount importance - they were the top dancers from the home of Fusion - The Electric Ballroom. They represented that whole Fusion scene and inspired many dancers and troupes, country-wide, for years to come. As much as The Ballroom was theirs, the Manchester troupe The Jazz Defektors believed that The Wag was theirs. They came down to do a show there with Kalima and tore the place apart. Their style of 50's suits and The Wags imagery suited them perfectly. Chris Sullivan loved them to come down as well, because their style was what he wanted at the club. There had very much become a 'Wag-look' - as documented, again, in The Face and other style and music magazines, and with DJ's such as Baz Fe Jazz, Andy McConnell and Sylvester dressing that way too, it could only enhance the look. Saltz - from The Jazz Defektors - told me that they were personally trying to create that ambience of The Wag at Colin Curtis' night at Berlin, and their style certainly took off in Manchester - everyone was into that 50's style. Anne Quigley of Kalima told me too, that they started a night at a club called the Tropicana which they'd hoped would become the North's Wag Club. The Tropicana nights were hard, because, again, you had the alternative crowd of hardened Factory music followers and the Jazz crowd that just didn't mix.

In many other ways though,1984 was quite uneventful: with the all-dayer scene in the midlands, North and Scotland running smoothly. Scotland's main promoter and higher-echelon DJ - Kenny MacLeod - started a promotion company called 'Just Jazz' because of the enthusiasm towards the growing Jazz Dance scene there, with it's plethora of knowledgable DJ's, collectors and punters.

By November, Gilles Peterson started a new weekly Sunday residence in Richmond at a pub called The Belvedere Arms in Sheen Road. Originally just down the road at The Black Horse (3/10/84), it lasted just one week where, although packed solid, it ended up with a big fight, so he moved to The Belvedere Arms. Why is it worth mentioning a pub residency? The Belvedere session became the most important Sunday night gathering, attracting DJ's and punters from all different scenes. Even representatives from record labels would attend, as would crowds from either side of the Jazz Dance scene, and it remained that way well into the next decade.

Earlier, in June of that year Nicky Holloway had started running new events on Thursdays at a huge pub/club down the road from The Swan And Sugarloaf in Tooley Street called The Royal Oak. Moving to a Monday night and, by February '85, settling on Fridays, these weekly events were named The Special Branch. Still with the staple diet of home-counties DJ's, there were other cutting-edge London DJ's from the 'warehouse parties' scene getting involved in this two-floor two club session venue too - such as Paul Oakenfold and Danny Rampling, plus Ed Stokes, Bob Jones, Sean French and Chris Brown. The Friday night was starting to become completely unmissable, with DJ's such as Pete Tong and Jeff Young guesting for Nicky Holloway downstairs, and Gilles Peterson and Chris Bangs and others guesting for Mark Webster and Dave Hucker upstairs. The pirate station KJAZZ had also gone on air by this time too, as of the 30th of April - which was started by Gilles, Jez Nelson and Chris Phillips.

A fairly successful couple of years was had by the Essex Jazz DJ partnership of Andy Ward and Andy McConnell from Dagenham - known as The A2 Connection - culminating with the success of a couple of Jazz all-dayers above Ronnie Scott's Jazz club in Frith Street, but Andy McConnell was now on his own and starting the first of his many road-block attendance Jazz 'warehouse parties' in Rotherhithe called Saturday Night Fish Fry. Illegal warehouse parties had been happening for a few years then (most famously - The Dirt Box, with it's mixture of Funk and Rockabilly), but this was the first Jazz one. It was getting midlands Jazz DJ Baz Fe Jazz to guest there that started their partnership called Take 5. Sylvester and Paul Murphy also guested there occasionally too, by the way.

THE SPECIAL BRANCH

The partnership of Chris Bangs and Gilles Peterson was ever growing stronger. Chris was already a spectacular promoter with his mega-successful Bournemouth and Boscombe Soul Weekenders (co promoted by Bob Masters) which had been taking place on bank holiday weekends since 1981. By late '85 these events were starting to represent the musically diverse line-up of Nicky Holloway's Royal Oak Special Branch nights, and were becoming essential and influential. Chris and Gilles started the first of many nights called Mambo Madness - originally at Jacksons in Staines (28/5/85) with Chris Brown and Bob Cosby too, which were enormous events. It was all about putting the 'fun back into Jazz,' as it had all become a bit serious (apparently). Fun tracks such as *Eydie Gorme - Blame It On The Bossa Nova* and *Earl Grant* or *Perry Como's* versions of *The House Of Bamboo* would pack the floor.

Gilles Peterson's interests were starting to turn more to the Special Branch on Fridays now. Musically, it was very stifling at The Electric Ballroom for him as it had been for Paul Murphy before him. Chris Hill once said, "Never let the punters dictate what you do," but they were there. Also, there was the all-embracing comfort of a home-counties feel at The Royal Oak, and, of course, women. Peterson was starting to leave The Ballroom early on Fridays (initially just monthly) leaving it to the back up DJ's Mark Higgins and Andy Dyer - The Mambo Cartel - and then it went from leaving there early to doing the session alternate weeks to Mark and Andy (where they still continued to back him on his own nights), and eventually and inevitably - he left. He had his own other residencies of his own as well as The Royal Oak and was doing special events with Chris Bangs, and by November he was also writing about Jazz in the Street Sounds record-label magazine spin off Street Scene - owned by music-entrepreneur Morgan Khan. Gilles put together the first of many Jazz compilation albums on Street Sounds, entitled *'Jazz Juice'* - which were representations of what was big on the dancefloor for him and other Jazz DJ friends such as Bob Jones and Chris Bangs. This was the first time the scene had properly been acknowledged on vinyl.

The film director Julien Temple, meanwhile, had been putting into production a film version of Colin McInnes book 'Absolute Beginners,' and the whole Jazz dance scene was expectant. Artists such as Sade and Working Week were involved, as were The Jazz Defektors and IDJ dancers and the higher-echelon, best dressed regulars from The Wag, but already the project was running into trouble, running way over schedule and out of money. We still wouldn't see its release until 1986. The Wag was just going from strength to strength, with its constant style-magazine coverage and celebrity patronage. Artists such as *Tommy Chase, Robin Jones* and *Slim Gaillard* had achieved cult status there - firebrand Jazz drummer Chase's hard core Be Bop quartet and quintet almost becoming a focal point of the Monday as much as Paul Murphy. For whatever Tommy had achieved previously, his time had come in a big way there.

As if enough hadn't already happened in '85, London witnessed the rise of the 'Rare Groove' scene. I'm not going to side-track this story to confuse matters with details of the Rare Groove movement, but it was like a breath of fresh air. Majority Black perhaps - but by no means totally - it all revolved around the revival and discovery of lesser-known bass-heavy Funk 45's and album tracks from the late 60's to mid 70's. A lot of the records that were being uncovered then were never played in the UK first time around. As this movement essentially came from Soul Sound Systems (think Reggae Sound Systems) the sound was very specific - with those melodic, heavy (almost Reggae) bass lines. Rare Groove records were starting to become incorporated into some areas of the Jazz Dance scene - especially at The Royal Oak.

Since Gilles Peterson's departure from The Ballroom, it had been continued by Mark and Andy, until it's closure in that November. It was perhaps fitting that the Jazz room culminated with them; they had been regulars when Paul Murphy was resident. They loved that club, and the crowd loved them. They lived and breathed it.

The battling on the dancefloor now, though, had gotten out of hand. Not only at The Ballroom, but in the Jazz rooms at the all-dayers all over the country. The competition was everywhere with many crews and troupes, and many coaches from all over would attend these many events. The best dancers would know who they would be battling in advance in a lot of cases, and both personal and area pride was at stake. Dancers would be putting in severe work on their footwork and 'cuts' in preparation, but there was starting to be a lot of violence at these events and Birmingham was getting blamed. Of course, no one likes to get humiliated, and the loser would get humiliated. Most of these Black dancers had nothing in life but pride, and losing face on the floor in a challenge would cause trouble sometimes, but the gang violence was becoming consistent and it was coming from Birmingham.

FOOTBALL HOOLIGANISM AND THE NEAR-END OF THE NORTHERN JAZZ DANCE SCENE

For a while in the clubs, the street fashion was what was known as 'Casual'. It was expensive Golf wear-type designer-wear with names like Pringle and Tacchini, and the problem with that was it was also the clothing of football hooligans. At football matches, police would be on the lookout for type-cast skinhead-looking thugs, so the epidemic of hooligans, nationally, started to fool the police by donning the 'casual' wear - looking like anybody else in the street. Whereas other areas would take a coach (or maybe two) to an all-dayer, it was quite normal for Birmingham to go with at least four, and a lot of them were from the Birmingham City FC multi-racial football hooligans called The Zulus. They weren't necessarily there for the music - they'd get drunk, womanise, and always finish the night with a punch up - sometimes (and often) on a massive scale. Of course they were proud of the dancers, but in no shape or form were they there to support them. The hooligans couldn't be banned from the coaches because they knew most of the people on them, and, anyway, everyone had to live peacefully through an average day in Birmingham. Also, if they weren't allowed to go on the coaches, they would've got to the all-dayers by train or car anyway - they knew where the events were, after all. The trouble was that the Birmingham dancers were having the finger pointed at them all over the country; their reputation was awful. As if the tension wasn't bad enough in the Jazz rooms already! All of a sudden, there were no more all-dayers. Why would promoters want to put on events knowing it would finish in violence? The end of the all-dayers was virtually the end of the entire midlands and Northern Jazz Dance scene. Another blow to the Northern Jazz dance-lover was Colin Curtis giving up DJ-ing through ill-health. This ripped the heart out of the scene. This leader had retired. In London, with the end of The Electric Ballroom, many of the greatest dancers left the scene too, never to be seen again. All those amazing moves lost forever.

In a nut-shell: With the death of The Electric Ballroom Jazz room, there were now two opposing Jazz scenes in the South: one with the 'Special Branch' crowd and one at The Wag. In the North and midlands it had almost disappeared. through football violence. Not pretty. Some people have the theory, that the sudden explosion in the clubs of the mutant - but - soulful, electronic music from Chicago known as 'House music' killed the Jazz Dance scene, but why would it have done? Anyway, the Fusion dancers loved it - especially in the North.

THE HACIENDA AND HOUSE MUSIC

Although the world-famous Manchester club The Hacienda was known for breaking House music, it was not going down well there originally. The Norths top Fusion troupe The Foot Patrol were given free passes to the Hacienda (which included free drinks), and they kept the floor going to House and other music. Other dancers and troupes such as: Fusion Beat; Elite; Bamboozle and Unknown Troopers would later dance to House as well as Jazz too. With the near-death of Jazz on the dancefloor in the North there was still a few places to go. In the North east there was Alex Lowes' massively popular session at MacMillans in Yarm on a Sunday night, which had already began in '85 (and continued until '92). Alex would play some Jazz breaks for the dancers, but they would dance to House as well, regardless. MacMillans became one of the most important 'battle grounds' of the North, with dancers traveling from everywhere - even from as far as Bristol. MacMillans is now the beautiful, massive country-club known as Tall Trees.

Although quite irregular, probably the biggest session in the North in late '85 and '86 was Jive Turkey. This session, at Sheffield City Hall, was run by the influential DJ's Winston Hazel and Parrot, playing a mixture of cutting-edge dance music. There was also a smaller second room playing Jazz by DJ and Bamboozle dancer Andy Bex. Again, this was incredibly popular.

Further North in Leeds things were quite unscathed by the closing of all-dayers and the dropping in popularity of Jazz on the dancefloor. DJ's Lubi Jovanovic and Chico and the Jazz DJ team The Educated Jazzmen from Bradford had discovered their new home - The Coconut Grove, Merrion Street. This was owned by Jazz fanatic and restrauteur Gip Dammone. It was a three level club, and on one floor he had amazing live Jazz acts, with Gip DJ-ing support - just playing Jazz. Gip was DJ-ing because he didn't know anyone played it out. He was shocked and inspired by seeing Jazz Dancers coming to his club, he didn't know people danced to Jazz. This club became the central point for the Jazz dance scene in Leeds for years to follow. It was a strong area. You still had the higher-echelon dancers such as Dovel Morten - who some consider one of the countrys all-time top dancers - there was the Jazz Dance troupe Elite; an influential Black dance company called the Phoenix (which started in '80) and a lot of musicians. With his passion for Jazz mixed with business-suss, Gip Dammone made a potent DJ partner of Lubi and Chico, pushing the Jazz scene to unscaled heights in Leeds.

In Essex, DJ Gary Dennis had quickly become a huge, influential force since coming back into the scene in '84 after a divorce. Now he was a DJ, and with his knowledge, contacts and knack of collecting he rose to the top and became a powerful and influential figure in the Rare Groove scene. He had already been putting on huge, monthly events at the Hadleigh Suite in Leigh-On-Sea, which greatly reflected that whole Special Branch scene in London. He featured guest DJ's such as Gilles Peterson and Chris Bangs too, and was also attracting 600 people every Sunday night to The Windmill, East Hanningfield. Chris Hill had long since left The Goldmine and it was also no longer owned by Stan and Jane Barrett. Gary was given The Miners Bar (which was connected to the main club and on the same level) on friday nights to do a weekly Jazz room, which was Gary's first (and only) all-Jazz session. It was immediately popular and a short while after the start in January, he brought in local Jazz expert and reluctant DJ Phil Levene to partner him. Down the road, Southend-On-Sea finally had a replacement for a home for serious Black music since the closing of The Goldmine: Scruples in Milton Road. It was, technically, a wine bar but it was huge, with a great sound system and a late license. Every night of the week were specialist nights playing Jazz, rare Soul, Boogie and Rare Groove - and - again Gary was DJ-ing there too. The venue was absolutely buzzing.

In April, after many, many setbacks Julien Temple's long-awaited film 'Absolute Beginners' was released. Even with a vast amount of publicity, the film was panned by the critics. It looked beautiful but was very disjointed and disappointing. There had been such a massive build-up for the film country-wide in the scene, that the anti-climax was awful. The bubble had burst, and all of these people going to Jazz Dance clubs because it was fashionable (especially The Wag) deserted it in their droves. Paul Murphy and the Jazz dance troupe the Jazz Defektors went to Japan to promote the film though, giving that country the first real taste of Jazz Dance.

Meanwhile, moving along obliviously to all this ballyhoo, Nicky Holloway arranged a Special Branch holiday event for two weeks in Ibiza (11/5/86). Staying in out-of-season 'Club 18-30' hotels, Nicky flew over the full Royal Oak team and crowd to have special events at what was quite a quiet balaeric Island. This was, without doubt, the first event leading to what eventually spiraled out of control in the early 2000's as the top worldwide destination for the 'rave' scene.

Gilles had now gone legitimate on the radio now as of August, with a show on Radio London called Mad On Jazz. He had to find outside finances to pay for the show though, so on 27th September he put on an enormous event at North Londons Town and Country Club called the Radio London Jazz Bop. It was an event that had 1,500 people attending with The Jazz Defektors and Tommy Chase headlining. It was the first of many.

THE MODS

So after nearly two years of fridays at the Sol Y Sombre, as of the 6th May 86' Paul Murphy started a whole new night at the Electric Ballroom. This time he took over the vast main ballroom, and Baz Fe Jazz and Andy McConnell as Take 5 - were playing Jump Jive, Big Band Swing and Mambo up in the Jazz room. Murphy's music policy was 60's Rhythm and Blues and Blue Note-style Bop, and he called the night The Purple Pit.

The night immediately started to attract a big crowd of the higher echelon from the Mod scene, who were so sick of that scene's insular and narrow minded attitude, that they were on the search for something different. Experimentation had already begun in the Mod scene with forward thinking DJ's starting to play tracks by Jazz organists - such as *Brother Jack McDuff*, *Jimmy McGriff* and, of course, *Jimmy Smith*, and out-and-out Jazz such as *Miles Davis - So What*, so Murphy's night was the logical conclusion. This was certainly the case with Russ Dewbury and Dean Rudland - who were soon to become big movers within the Jazz Dance world - and the 'ace face' Eddie Piller. Eddie was already a big name within the Mod scene as a DJ, promoter and

SPECIAL BRANCH

ibiza 86

DETAILS ON
01 853 1953

ONLY
£135

INCLDING INSURANCE
NO EXTRAS

MARTIN COLLINS
NICKY HOLLOWAY
CHRIS BROWN
TREVOR FUNG
GILLES PETERSON
CHRIS BANGS
PAUL CLARK
JOHNNIE WALKER

Luxury apartments (No hotel Porters
to get past)

Right In the middle of San Antonio
(No Taxi fares)

Deposit only £40 (A.S.A.P.)

Clubs & bars reserved for our
use Include

STAR CLUB, CAFE DEL MAR,

ES PARADISE, PROJECT,
IF & MORE

MAY 17 - 24

SPECIAL BRANCH
EXCLUSIVE

Confort Plaza Apartments

Set on the Plaza d'Espagne in the centre of town, these attractive modern apartments are not only close to the harbour, but also handy for San Antonio's most popular bars and nightspots. The Confort Plaza has its own small swimming pool and sun terrace plus a bar which serves snacks. Each of the apartments (for 2-4 people) has a balcony, private bathroom w.c. and kitchenette as well as a living room with sofa beds and an adjoining bedroom area which can be curtained off. Studios for 2 people are also available.

Historically, the evolution of the Ibiza 'Rave Scene' started from this event record-label owner (Re-Elect The President), and was also the manager of the major garage-Mod group The Prisoners. He and his influential friends from the Mod scene had discovered both The Purple Pit and the friday night 'Special Branch' events: "Nicky Holloways club had a jazz-room upstairs with Bob Cosby and the other DJ's like Kevin Beadle and Gilles Peterson, and there was great looking women in there! Other than that,musically, it was soul music from artists like *Tyrone Davis* to *Miles Davis* - what the Mod scene should be all about. Me and about ten friends stepped over into that scene". As of July, Russ Dewbury had been checking out The Wag on Mondays as well, with the DJ's Take 5, and particularly liked the 60's Jazz that they were playing (The Jazz Fusion meant nothing to him, of course). Eddie becoming comfortable within the social life revolving around Special Branch, soon became friends with all the movers-and-shakers and started to do DJ within that scene too.

DINGWALLS

Elsewhere in 1986, as well as Gilles Peterson putting on the London Jazz Bops to help finance his Radio London show 'Mad On Jazz', he, at some point that year (probably late autumn) had started to put on sporadic events at a venue in Camden Lock, North London called Dingwalls - a residency previously held by the Jazz drummer and Jazz Dance institution Tommy Chase. These, initially, irregular events - called Mad On Jazz - had DJ support from Bob Jones, Kevin Beadle and occasionally Sylvester plus a very young (under 18) heavyweight collector Joe Davis. Occasionally they would hold the fort if Gilles was away. His career had absolutely sky rocketed by then.

As earlier hinted, as of July the 14th that year Paul Murphy had suddenly left The Wag. It'd been over an argument about wages. The music policy at The Purple Pit was proof, anyway, that he was gradually, but rapidly, pulling away from the Jazz dance scene, so it was fitting perhaps then that he'd again, influenced yet another scene - The Mods - coaxing them toward ours.

Some people felt that when Murphy left The Electric Ballroom the first time that that was the end of the 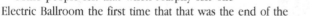 real Jazz dance movement (and certainly when it finally closed with Mark and Andy - The Mambo Cartel - at the reins), but DJ and journalist Mark Webster - who'd been a long time champion of the Jazz Dance movement - believes that when Murphy left The Wag, that was it: "Murphy disappeared and then the scene fell on its arse. From my perspective, when Murphy wasn't around anymore the big dream had died. It genuinely went underground." Baz and Andy struggled on Monday nights at the Wag. They had also put Gilles Peterson upstairs too, with his selection of Jazz and Rare Groove, which was turning out to be competition. His smaller room was becoming a bigger draw than the main room. If this was the way the scene was going, Andy McConnell didn't want any part of it and he left The Wag and the scene altogether. Things hadn't been the same there, since the disappointment of the Absolute Beginners film anyway, as mentioned earlier. Joe Davis replaced Andy.

JAZZ DANCE ON TELEVISION

Ironically, with the scene in a state of flux,1986 was a great year for exposure on film and television for Jazz Dancing. There hadn't been anything to expose it to the British public since seeing the early (original) formation of IDJ in the video of *Venceremos* by Working Week in June '84 or The Jazz Defektors video on Factory Records - *'Hanky Panky'*, but '86 kicked off with a huge televised event called 'Father Time'. It was a documentary of Art Blakey playing at The Shaw Theatre in London on March the 22nd and 23rd with IDJ, The Jazz Defektors from Manchester and The Jazz 5 (actually, they'd changed their name to Mahogany by then) from Birmingham. There was superb footage of the interaction with Blakey and the dancers, although unfortunately The Jazz 5 never got filmed. Jazz 5/ Mahogany dancer Rico told me that they had a great battle with IDJ on the first night (The Jazz Defektors were performing on the hip music, style and arts programme on Channel 4 - The Tube that night and couldn't perform. So there's even more Jazz Dancing on television!). As already mentioned: the film 'Absolute Beginners' came out in April - which featured a lot of Jazz Dance, and was followed by an excellent Jazz Dance special on a programme on a regional ITV television station (Anglia) called 'South Of Watford' - which featured IDJ, Tommy Chase, Paul Murphy, Baz Fe Jazz and Courtney Pine. Finishing the year off nicely, there was a documentary shown in October that year called 'Ten Days That Shook Soho' filmed at the Soho Jazz Festival in London.

Again, featuring most of the people from the Jazz Dance scene it has spectacular footage of The Jazz Defektors and Tommy Chase with IDJ.

Interestingly enough, although I have no information on who was behind it: towards the end of that year, CBS Records released a compilation album called 'Get Wise' — representing of a lot of the 'hipper' bands or solo artists in the general Modern Jazz scene at the time, like: *Team Ten; Expresso Seven; A Man Called Adam; Jazz Defektors; Courtney Pine, Steve Williamson* and *Phillip Bent* from *The Jazz Warriors*; and *Loose Tubes*, amongst others. It was an odd mixture of the 'legitimate' Jazz scene and 'what the Jazz Dance scene had become' (to a certain extent) but it was, at least, something and it was ours!

In '87 things were much the same in the North, with the Jazz dancers looking for a battle wherever they could get it - certainly at the usuals: the Hacienda in Manchester, Jive Turkey in Sheffield and MacMillans. Out in Leeds Gip, Chico and Lubi were steadily building and consolidating their strong scene, although, now as an alternative you had the five-man DJ crew known as Take 5 (not to be confused with the London one), consisting of Tony Jacobs, Aff Ahmed, Mike Walwyn, Joe Gatewood and Michael Richards, who were also starting to make a noise with their one-off parties playing Hard Jazz, Soul and Rare Groove.

THE FIRST NORTHERN WEEKENDER

Of tantamount importance was the appearance of the Norths very first Soul weekender. Organised by North east DJ legend and promoter Alex Lowes. It was at Berwick Holiday Centre, Berwick On Tweed - a beautiful location high up in the east coast, on the border of Scotland. It started on October 22nd and is still running today on the opposite coast of Southport. It featured a Jazz room, which at the time was not too well supported.

In the South, in London, Nicky Holloway's events continued with yet another two week Special Branch event away - this time in Corfu, and his six times a year events such as 'The Doos At The Zoo' at Regents Park (with an attendance of 2000) amongst others, and his Rockley Sands weekenders continued - all with Jazz rooms dominated by Chris Bangs, Gilles Peterson and Chris Brown. Bangs' Mambo Madness also continued 'putting the fun back into Jazz'

Out in Essex Gary Dennis was having the most successful night in the county every Friday with his influential night at Chesters in Southend On Sea High Street with the best guests from the Jazz and Rare Groove scenes, giving him queues down the road.

From June that year, Bob Jones, Phil Levene and myself started a Jazz-only monthly session called The Hi - Hat - initially at the function room of Southend United FC (called Shrimpers) and from there, moving down the road to The Moonraker in Westcliff On Sea. It was intended to be a hard core session musically somewhere between Murphy's session at The Electric Ballroom and The Wag - with guests such as Bangs, Peterson, Sylvester and Baz Fe Jazz. The night continued it's path through to 1995, moving to Southend venue Saks under the name 'Back to the

Tracks' with Phil and I. There was hardly any heavy Jazz being played in London anymore, and although we loved the predominantly organ-based Prestige label-type Funky Jazz being played at Dingwalls, we felt that there was overkill with it there so we adopted a 'No Funky Jazz' policy at The Hi - Hat.

The Dingwalls Sunday session had now been given the name 'Talkin Loud' and Patrick Forge had been brought in to start the proceedings with a heavy cerebral Jazz selection to take care of the almost-homeless dancers. Although not an experienced club DJ, Pat had built up a big following with his show as the Kiss FM pirate station, which Gilles thought would bring something new to the session.

By September, Gilles had taken over the Monday session at The Wag, with Chris Bangs and Bob Jones, playing more Funky Organ Jazz, Rare Groove, Bossas - such as *Willis Jackson - Nuthern Like Thuthern* and *Nancy Ames - Cacara* - and featuring, as always, a live band. Upstairs was Sylvester playing a harder-than-hard selection of Fusion, Be Bop and Afro Latin (like Mambos, for example) for the dancers such as the newly formed Brothers In Jazz troupe - who were making massive waves within the scene. After a few months Sylvester brought Essex DJ Phil Levene in to partner him up there in that battle ground!

ACID JAZZ

1988 was the big change. It was the beginning of the end for some, or purely, the beginning of a whole new era for others. Although Chicago 'House Music' had been getting hefty play country-wide since early '86 on an underground level, 1988 was the massive explosion to the masses. With heavily attended illegal raves happening left right and centre, the mass discovery of the drug 'ecstacy' and the huge rise of the drug-addled close relation of House Music - Acid House; with it's monotonus-yet-majestic, squelching analogue synthesizer basslines and melodies played over skeletal rhythm tracks - programmed on what sounds like cheap drum machines.

This year, was what was known as 'The Summer Of Love' and much has been written about it by far more authoratative persons than I (even though I was in the middle of it all) so I won't attempt it, other than to make you aware that it was happening.

These music styles were certainly a large part of what the Special Branch had become, as they'd always embraced the latest cutting-edge music. On February the 6th at one such event at the Watermans Arts Centre, High Street, Brentford, Middlesex, Nicky Holloway had had the room decked out in banners and with flashing lights and strobes. As usual Gilles Peterson was DJ-ing with his unofficial partner Chris Bangs and was playing a rather heavy *Art Blakey* and *Sabu* track - either *Message From Kenya* or *The Feast*. While the record was playing, the words 'Acid' kept flashing up on a screen behind him and he said to Chris: "What the hells all this about?" and Chris replied, as quick as a flash: "It's Acid Jazz, isn't it?" and they laughed. Gilles immediately picked up the microphone and said over the record: "Yes. Acid Jazz" and there we are: the beginning of the next chapter of our scene. There is an alternate story that Chris

The first night to mention 'Acid Jazz' in the advert

and Gilles were following Nicky Holloway playing Phuture-Acid Trax, and Chris came on with the Rare Groove classic *Iron Leg* by *Mickey And The Soul Generation*. The song begins with a stark, almost rocky, guitar with no backing, so Chris played it while pushing up the vari-speed up and down on the DJ deck making it 'wobble' and he said: "If that's Acid House then this is Acid Jazz" This must have happened later in the evening after the 'flashing acid' situation. Either way, the joke began that night. Spearheaded by Chris Bangs and his wicked sense of humour, it quickly became a big in-joke amongst their circle of friends such as Gilles, Nicky Holloway, Bob Jones, Simon Booth and Eddie Piller.

The Acid Jazz phenomenon went one step further the following month on March 26th at the first of many events initially at the impossible to find 'Cock Tavern' in the poultry market EC1 called 'Cock Happy!' Chris had taken the 'smiley face' badges that represented Acid House and given it crossed eyes, glasses, a tuft of hair and buck-teeth and made badges of this new logo and gave them out that night. This was the 'official logo' of Acid Jazz (a later adaption had the character drawn with a Dizzy Gillespie beret and goatee beard!). Of course, already, now people were saying: "What is Acid Jazz?" The music hadn't changed at the Jazz Dance gigs: it was wah wah-ed, Organ-led Funky Jazz; it was Art Blakey, it was the *Tito Puente*, it was *Sergio Mendes*, it was Rare Groove - but these were now called Acid Jazz gigs not Jazz Dance. Perhaps Jazz Dance was too narrow a term by then anyway, as there was so many other styles of music being played too. If the Special Branch events, and Friday nights at The Royal Oak; Chris' Bournemouth and Boscombe weekenders and his and Gilles' Cock Happy's were fuelling the fire and imagination, Talkin' Loud at Dingwalls was certainly the home of this movement. Dingwalls represented every aspect of the scene and was visited by many important DJ's, punters and media persons to help spread the word.

THE BIG SPLIT

By May the whole Special Branch scene had pulled itself apart. The second Ibiza trip had seen half of the DJ's and punters discover the drug Ecstacy and they went off to the main clubs extolling the virtues of Balaeric club music and House. Other such DJ's such as Simon Dunmore and Bob Jones distanced themselves from that crowd: "We don't need to take drugs to enjoy music" someone said, and they put on separate unscheduled events in bars that were nothing to do with Nicky Holloways organization; in fact, they were competing with his events that he'd booked those very DJ's to attend. On the flight home Nicky realised that there'd been a big split, musically, and he decided to stop the Special Branch events and go off in the House music direction.

The Acid Jazz bandwagon was rolling now: John Godfrey had done a big article on the 'Acid Jazz scam' in the influential fashion magazine I.D. interviewing all involved, and this really got people talking everywhere.

May saw the first release on the Acid Jazz record label. The label was co-owned by Eddie Piller and Gilles Peterson; Eddie already had experience with recording, record pressing and distribution from previously owning his 'Re-Elect The President' label and, earlier to that, working for Dave Robinson's Stiff Records. They basically got their friend Robert Gallagher - who was a social poet and close friend of Gilles - to do a kind of Rap/ narration over the top of *Pucho And The Latin Soul Brothers* version of *Freddie's Dead*. The track was called *Frederick Lies Still* and Gallagher had acquired the recording name of *Galliano*. It sold 2000 in the first week just in London alone, with no advertising. Galliano would feature quite heavily at Dingwalls - often performing his unique style of 'ranting rap' over records while Gilles was DJ-ing. For the past year Gilles had been running the ACE records reissue off-shoot label called BGP too, with fellow DJ Baz Fe Jazz, and they immediately did the first of many compilations of the Prestige record label organ-based Funky Jazz that was enormous at Dingwalls, simply called *Acid Jazz Volume 1*. Already known in what was 'The Jazz Dance scene' was the group *The James Taylor Quartet*. They'd already scored a club hit in 1987 with their 7 inch single *Blow Up* - which was championed by the British bastion of all good music - John Peel, on his five-nightly show on Radio 1. Managed by Eddie Piller, they were formed out of the ashes of The Prisoners and immediately brought their progressive Mod following with them to support them in their sell out shows wherever they played. James didn't really know what the hell was going on the first time he played at The Wag:

> "When I heard DJ's playing fast Be-Bop at The Wag, I wondered what the
> hell I was doing there, as we have nothing to do with that. I don't think that
> crowd liked us at first, but the gigs were packed anyway with our following.
> After a few more times, we got what they wanted. We were way too 'indie' at
> first."

The buzz was massive on them. The club-arm of Polydor / Urban - were having massive results by reissuing in-demand Funk tracks from their back catalogue on 12" because of the boom in the 'Rare Groove' scene; some of these 12"s even charted nationally. They were looking for something new to release, and as Eddie Piller was an advisor for Rare Groove music, for that label he recommended the James Taylor Quartet. The label manager John Williams was a fan of the band and they got signed.

Their debut album for Polydor *'Wait A Minute'* was a strong album, they thought, but it needed a strong single to come off of it, so around May/June the band went into the studio to record their version of the theme from the television series *'Starsky And Hutch'*- funky Film and TV soundtracks were popular both in the Rare Groove and the newly-termed 'Acid Jazz' scenes. The track was produced by Working Week's Simon Booth and featured two of *James Brown's* ex horn players, *Pee Wee Ellis* and *Fred Wesley*, and (fully bringing it into the Acid Jazz world) Galliano.

Through Eddie, Gilles Peterson and Simon Booth got into Polydor to do their concept album

representing this new scene with their compilation album of all the current musicians within it entitled 'Acid Jazz And Other Illicit Grooves'. Talkin' Loud at Dingwalls and the Cock Happy and Mambo Madness events had, by now, with this new Acid Jazz tag, gone beyond the regular confines of Jazz based music. With the new term 'The Freedom Principle' representing what this scene was all about, other music as well such as Rare Groove, House, instrumental B-sides of Hip Hop 12"s and 70's and 80's Soul were getting played too. These events were referred to as 'Raves' I've noticed, and even featured Beat Poetry a la Ginsberg etc too...

In the summer of '88, a magazine 'dedicated to the cause' came onto the market, called Straight No Chaser - "An attitude, a new magazine, a new time," and was "Commited to the Freedom Principle". Magazine owner Paul Bradshaw was so sick of his then current bosses attitude and dismissiveness towards Jazz Dance (Richard Cook - editor of The Wire magazine) that he started SNC. Paul said that he hung out with Paul Murphy, Baz Fe Jazz and Gilles Peterson and always knew what their future plans were. SNC wasn't all Jazz dance: it was "World Jazz Jive" as he called it - encompassing all the different avenues of world beat (or world music) too. This was always an important scene, running adjacent to Jazz Dance (and probably bigger actually), with the whole big Club Sandino sessions in London, Glasgow, Edinburgh etc... the Bongo Go sessions in Birmingham with Brian Parsons (Zuppe Inglese), Babatunde, et al, Rick Glanvill, in Newcastle and London and the DJ heavy hitters Dave Hucker, Tomek, Sue Steward and John Armstrong in London (not forgetting the newly formed Mambo Inn sessions in Brixton with Gerry Lyseight, Rita Ray and Matt Reinhardt). These DJ's were always incorporated into the Jazz pirate radio stations too. Bradshaw covered the Acid Jazz scene blow-by-blow in the magazine.

Let me re-cap, once again, and put all this in perspective for you, so you can appreciate the impact:

From the expression 'Acid Jazz' being born by Chris Bangs in February, and the initial scam article in ID, by July, a label had formed called 'Acid Jazz'; there was a James Taylor Quartet album ready to go; a compilation of all the current creative musicians from the scene on Polydor; a retrospective compilation on BGP; all of Chris Bangs and Gilles Peterson events were packed and with people wearing the aforementioned Acid Jazz badges; as of June, Peterson started writing a 'Mad On Jazz' page in Blues and Soul magazine heavily promoting this new scene: "Turn on, tune in, drop out- Acid Jazz is here! What is Acid Jazz? - Easy, Acid Jazz is the sound of esoteric noises over danceable jazz rhythms," and Gilles goes on to say: "It's mad, sure, but it's another way of subtley introducing John Coltrane to Jazz ignorants." Meanwhile he was still having the beloved Jazz Juice compilations released.

By September, the James Taylor Quartet single 'Starsky And Hutch' had charted nationally at number 68, and this was the first commercial breakthrough for the movement; in October, at a Dingwalls all-dayer, there was a massive Acid Jazz special featuring all the big artists from the scene. For something that has always been claimed to have just been 'Just a joke' it was now a serious proposition as a music scene. Kevin Beadle:

> "We all took it a bit serious. We made ourselves a bit aloof; I don't know
> why because it was a joke. We all got into the 'Beat' poetry and all that shit.
> I look back now and it's quite embarrassing."

Of course people were now really starting to ask: "What is Acid Jazz?" Well, what is it exactly anyway? In retrospect, one can see a massive problem immediately: there was all this progressive Jazz being mixed in with other styles of contemporary Black club music and yet the first compilation on BGP was called Acid Jazz - with it's retrospective funky-organ jazz, and (Galliano's rap aside) the James Taylor Quartet's music was just that too. By early '89 Chris Bangs had got out of the scene altogether. He'd had enough of where it was all going and wanted to concentrate on music production.

Outside of the Acid Jazz clique, elsewhere in London Tim Morris, Hugh Albert and, on occasion, Sheldon Wilcox, were making their presence felt with The Cutting Edge at Clowns in Frith Street, Soho, with their hard-nosed fad-free selection of Jazz of all tempos, and across the river uber-collector Rajan was running his Hi Note session at the Alexandra in Clapham Common featuring hard to obtain Latin Jazz. Paul Murphy had returned after a short break with his new sound of Rhythm and Blues, Jazz vocals and Afro Cuban music at his club The Happening in West London, and would go and do sessions at The 100 Club and (later) HQ's in Camden Lock (opposite Dingwalls) - which were more low key affairs, publicity wise.

Interestingly, down in the west in Bristol, to the DJ Tin Tin (Steve Symons), the mix of music under the name of Acid Jazz was nothing new to him: since 1988 he'd already been running his night with his DJ partner John Stapleton, playing that mixture at The Cooker at The Thekla to enormous effect anyway. They'd play anything from Blue Note Be Bop to House and had a lot of the heavy dancers in attendance too - such as The Floor Technicians troupe - and also had the luxury of being able to book all the bands from the scene there.

THE BRIGHTON JAZZ BOPS

In 1988 still, as the post-Special Branch Acid Jazz scene was gaining rapid momentum, there was something very important happening in the South in Brighton. DJ's Baz Fe Jazz and Russ Dewbury were starting to make a big impact in this lively, fashionable seaside town - Baz, of course, had probably always been the busiest Jazz dance DJ of all, with his hundreds of residencies. He never stopped trying, and he was without doubt the only competition to Gilles Peterson on that higher level. Baz's crowd was always more of a Time Out readers crowd as opposed to Peterson's home-counties Soul-boy one. Baz could see that Acid Jazz had diverted the attention away from the mother 'Jazz dance' and it was suddenly a struggle to make it work in London.

He'd been working a lot with Russ Dewbury on many residencies in Brighton for a while and had the opportunity to put Art Blakey on at the cavernous Top Rank Suite on Brighton seafront. The powers that be in the large Jazz scene in Brighton thought that they were mad to try it - and they certainly didn't understand that people actually danced to Jazz! On the 6th May they rammed the venue with over 2000 people. As an added bonus, IDJ were also on the bill dancing with Blakey too. Leaving their non-believers with their mouths open in shock, Russ and Baz decided to put on another event like this, so on October the 28th they put on a bill of the James Taylor Quartet, Tommy Chase and the Jazz Defektors amongst others, with Baz and Russ DJ-ing alongside Gilles Peterson and Bob Smith - one hell of a line up. They cheekily borrowed the name of Gilles Radio London Jazz Bop calling their events Brighton Jazz Bop and this, again, sold-out event just became the first of many, many essential Jazz Bops over the years (to this date), bringing over artists too numerous to mention such as *Big John Patton*, *Johnny Lytle*, *Charles Earland* and *Jon Lucien* - often exclusively, and in some cases reviving their career. The most important thing about the Jazz Bop is that they reflect all areas - old and new - of what made the Jazz dance scene amazing.

HIP HOP AND STREET SOUL

By early '89, within the musical circle surrounding Dingwalls, and led by Peterson, the Hip Hop influence was becoming very apparent on the dancefloor. The first time Gilles played *Public Enemy - Fight The Power* there it cleared the floor and he was met with jeering. He persisted with it and Hip Hop became the norm there. There was starting to become a Jazz flavour to some US Hip Hop anyway, with the Branford Marsalis sax instrumental of Fight the Power, *Stetsasonic's Talkin' All That Jazz* and The Jungle Brothers album utilizing Jazz samples (and with *Pharoah Sanders* playing sax on it too).

A largely undocumented Soul movement had recently started. Based in London, but equally as big in Birmingham, it was called 'Street Soul'. I'm guessing that Soul To Soul - Back To Life was the first record in that genre - raw, unpolished and funky but both contemporary and retro in equal measures. A progression from the Rare Groove movement, without a doubt. By '89 there was hundreds of 12" singles coming out on tiny independent labels, largely distributed by Jetstar - a Reggae specialist. The bass-lines were funky but had the weight of a Reggae one, and the vast majority of the singers were from the British 'Lovers Rock' Reggae scene as opposed to the Soul one. Street Soul later became known by the old Reggae term 'Drum And Bass' - which later became confusing because of the off-shoot of the furious paced Jungle music, also called Drum And Bass. Some Street Soul was played at Dingwalls too, so (other than the Jazz) along with that, Rare Groove, and Blue Note/Prestige-label Organ Funk, Hip Hop actually fitted in - they're all Funky in different permutations of course. As said earlier, some House music was also played.

Except for Leeds now, Jazz dancers in the North only had House music to dance to (and there were still many, many Jazz dancers around). They liked to battle to House. Home grown House music was starting to appear and the Fusion Beat dancers had already been touring to promote a project by Hacienda DJ Mike Pickering, Simon Topping from *A Certain Ratio* and Ritchie Close called *T-COY* with the club hit *Carino*, but later in '89 a House record called *Voodoo Ray* by A *Guy Called Gerald* surfaced. It had already been around since '88 but had now made a huge impact. The Jazz dancers in the North were proud because the record came from their own. Although credited to Gerald Simpson, it was also co-produced by Parrot from Sheffield, and dancer/producer Aniff Akimbola from Manchester, and, although not Jazzy, some feel that this record could only have come from the Jazz Dance scene. This was the sound and groove that the dancers liked, and it was nothing like what would have come from the home of House music - Chicago.

Starting on August of '88, there was a new late-night weekly ITV music television show going out live from various discos presented by pop-guru Pete Waterman and Michaela Strachan. It was called 'Hit Man And Her'. What was important about that show was that a lot of the predominantly Northern Jazz Dance troupes were regularly dancing on there to (mainly) House or Hip Hop. On the whole, it was the gig of Manchesters incredible Foot Patrol, but Fusion Beat, Elite from Leeds and Bamboozle and The Unknown Troopers from the North east also appeared on there too (as did The Floor Technicians from Bristol).

Probably though, some of the greatest (and most important) Jazz Dance footage ever was in a competition in a boxing ring between The Brothers In Jazz and 'IDJ break-away' troupe The Back Street Kids. It was from an idea by Jerry IDJ and was broadcast on a sports show on the national television station Channel 4 called '7 Sport' later in '88. The station took it away from Jerrys original idea of it being a staged performance (as detailed in his interview later) and it ended up as a proper battle. Although subjective, The Back Street Kids won and it caused a lot of bad feeling amongst the scene. Really, although great exposure (and it was), the scene was too fragile to handle such a controversial situation. The overall presentation was nothing short of pretentious as well, but, nevertheless, as a record of the incredible dancing in our scene, it was fantastic exposure.

THE FREEDOM PRINCIPLE?

By early '89, another album had emerged on Polydor/ Urban called *The Freedom Principle*. In so many ways, this album was way more progressive than *Acid Jazz And Other Illicit Grooves* and really encompassed all contemporary Black music - in fact the first single release off the album was by myself entitled *Snowboy's House Of Latin* - which was Jazzy House. Rather than it being an awkward listen, all the styles mixed together and worked so well. Despite the albums raging success, it seems that Polydor wasn't joining in on the idea of 'The Freedom Principle' - they were just scouting for talent, and signed up the vocalist *Cleveland Watkiss* and saxophonist Steve Williamson from the project. A promised follow up compilation never happened. Other Polydor signing the James Taylor Quartet, had become the first true stars of Acid Jazz. They were now commanding audiences of up to 2000 wherever they played and in fact played twelve monthly concerts at The Town and Country Club in that year, selling out eleven of the twelve gigs. At a capacity of 2,200, by my reckoning that makes a total of nearly 26,400 played to in London in 1989 alone.

Gilles Peterson felt that the Acid Jazz label was not representing where he felt the scene should be going:

> "The Mod thing came in from nowhere and took Acid Jazz away, and to where it went! Which is where I fucking got out and formed Talkin' Loud records in late '89, and made a progressive British Black music label."

By late '89 he'd been offered an opportunity to start a label at Phonogram and so he formed 'Talkin Loud' (named after his Dingwalls session): "The plan is to take the spirit of the scene as it's developed and take it forward," he said in SNC. He could now represent what he felt was where the scene was at, and so he signed his friend Galliano (who started to develop a band) and the Young Disciples. The recordings would be ready to be released in 1990.

A Dingwalls chart in Straight No Chaser issue 9 in Autumn 1990 was very Hip Hop based. Both this magazine and Peterson had dropped the Acid Jazz tag, but it was all too late: there were now hundreds of Acid Jazz nights springing up all over the country in bars, universities, colleges, clubs, back rooms of pubs and, along with the Acid Jazz label, the music of Talkin' Loud records was also played, and a major part. The tag of Acid Jazz was becoming too hard to distance from no matter how much effort was made. The Face magazine had picked up on the Mod look that had come through from Eddie Piller's side of things and, did a big and influential feature called 'Neuvo Mod' with the retro stylings of clothing manufacturer and shop Duffer Of St James amongst others. There was also the '70s funky look of the James Taylor Quartet and, new major Acid Jazz signing *The Brand New Heavies* (who'd been around since the 'Rare Groove' movement), and all these styles merged. There was, actually, a big element of the Mod scene that took the 'Neuvo Mod'- thing quite literal and mistakenly thought that this was a new direction for them - which must have been confusing for them with all the Hip Hop being played. Either way, the following of Acid Jazz was a melting pot of different styles, scenes and colours, and each individual would have their own interpretation of "what Acid Jazz is".

THE SPREAD OF JAZZ DANCE (OR IS THAT 'ACID JAZZ'?)

Without wishing to distract from the story, it's worth briefly mentioning at this point what (if anything) was going on elsewhere. Japan and Holland's scene definitely had it's roots in the UK's early to mid 80's hardcore Jazz Dance scene, whereas New York took the 'Dingwalls ethic' and did it their own way.

JAPAN

Japan had always kept a close eye on what had been happening in Jazz Dance (and in fact all new movements in club culture). In the 1980's DJ's Paul Murphy, Baz Fe Jazz and Gilles Peterson and the Jazz Defektors, IDJ and the Brothers In Jazz dancers, Working Week, Jazz Defektors (who'd notched up 60,000 sales there as a band) and myself had all performed there. A lot of this interest would have been due to interest from Moichi Kuwahara's promotion company Club King who took whatever was hot in London and New York and exported it directly to Japan (the endeavors of the promoter Mr Tanaka must not go undocumented either). Tokyo had their own Jazz DJ

heroes too, in the shape of French model Raphael Sebbag, Toshio Matsuura and Tadashi Yabe who reflected every Jazz Dance trend, so there'd been a solid base:

Raphael started DJ-ing Latin Jazz in many small clubs around 1983 and continued to amass a huge collection of Latin, Jazz and Brazilian music. In spring 1986, Toshio was in attendance at a fashion show of the designer Takeo Kikuchi. The 'Absolute Beginners' film had been released and was making a big impression and Paul Murphy and The Jazz Defektors were in Japan to promote the film. They were performing at this fashion show. When they danced to *Kenny Dorham - Afrodesia*, it made a big impression on Matsuura: "I felt the electricity in my body!"

He used to work in a Jazz club in Nishiazabu then, called 'Bohemia' where there would be bands and DJ's from the UK playing such as *The Jazz Renegades* (at the opening) and DJ's such as Baz Fe Jazz, Rhythm Doc and Tomek along with his future partners Raphael and Tadashi, who were working a lot for Club King. In 1990 they formed a DJ (and later - recording) partnership called *UFO*. They had legendary club sessions at clubs such as Gold, Yellow, Mix and The Cave called Jazzin' and are considered the first to be 'the symbol of the scene' (as Toshio puts it), and from them the scene spread all over the island: from Sendai, Tohoku, Sapporo, Nagoya, Kyoto, Osaka and Fukuoka spawning many DJ's, Bands and Producers. UFO were the first to put Jazz Dancers and DJ's together there, and the original dancer was an English guy known as Johnny: "He played an important role to us. We teamed up, and, having him, we had a chance to see the real Jazz Dance - not just a simulation," Toshio told me (there was also a Japanese dancer called 'Sam' too, at the time). Shortly after, Japan's original and very influential Jazz Dance troupe were formed called The Sound Cream Steppers.

Of equal importance to the early growth of Japan's Jazz Dance scene are Shuya and Yoshihiro Okino from Kyoto, who Toshio first met in 1988. Shuya encountered Jazz on a dancefloor for the first time at The Wag with Gilles Peterson in 1987; infact it was Gilles that gave them the idea for the name *Kyoto Jazz Massive*, after signing an autograph to the brothers with that very inscription in 1990.

Shuya was a graphic designer and eventually became the manager and in-house graphic designer of a club called Container and started Jazz events there in 1988. In 1990 he was managing artists such as *Mondo Grosso* (who were at the forefront of Japan's Acid Jazz movement) and female vocalist *Monday Michuru*. Kyoto Jazz Massive went on to achieve an incredible amount as recording artists and as club owners (The Room, in Tokyo) in time periods that are not covered here.

HOLLAND

The Dutch scene started with David 'Tin Tin' Zee - a dancer and DJ from Rotterdam. He discovered Jazz Dance by going to the Electric Ballroom in 1982 and was very much influenced by the IDJ dance style. From going out and practicing his newly-acquired Jazz steps in local clubs such as The Full Moon he met some great dancers and taught a few, but there were two exceptional ones by the names 'Raymond' and Bryan Van Der Kust. "Ray was a powerhouse with a unique style and the greatest spinner in the world. Bryan could do everything and was unstoppable after he lost his shyness to the dancers from London," Tin Tin said. His first Jazz Dance session was in The Hague doing a guest spot in a club called Peppijn in the summer of 1986 and from there he worked in the Rotterdam clubs and bars such as Jazzcafe Dizzy in Gravendijkwal and other parties too. Under the name of The Brotherhood Of Jazz, Tin Tin and his serious Soul and Jazz collector friend Hoeney Chen started their own Afro Cuban Jazz Dance Parties in Rotterdam called Tin Tin And Doctor Soul At The Wheels Of Steel. Other Jazz Dance DJ's started to appear there too like Dadi, Eric Denz and Eugene (Van Der Poel). Tin Tin also worked for nine years in what he considered to be "the best Jazz record shop in the world" - Jazz Center in The Hague, and was picking up at Platen Mannecke in Delft and Platenboef in Rotterdam too among many others.

The British Jazz Dance troupe IDJ first performed in Holland in 1986 and came over a lot after, but the first dancer to move there was Norville Small from Leicester in England. He's a fantastic dancer and very much in the more Balletic and Swing styles. Tin Tin remembers his first encounter with him: "We met in Amsterdam where I was DJ-ing and dancing at a party. He thought I was a London boy and wanted to start a dance group with me and some of his students like Adolf Lisand and Johnny 'Benitez' Uyleman." As a DJ, he's played all over Holland, Belgium, Italy, France, Germany, Ireland and England and big festivals like the North Sea Jazz Festival (where he was also a programmer for twenty years) and Drum Rhythm Festival and also clubs like Roxy and Paradiso in Amsterdam, Nightown in Rotterdam and also big concert halls doing gigs with *Ray Barretto, Africando, Nat Adderley* and *Red Holloway*.

Over in Amsterdam one of the main DJ's was an English DJ and mega-collector called Mark Taylor. Mark grew up on a diet of the Northern Colin Curtis-led Jazz Funk scene in 1978, and rediscovered collecting through the Rare Groove explosion in Holland in 1987 through ex-pat DJ Johnson and The Brand New Heavies first gig there (with support from the IDJ dancers and DJ Norman Jay) at The Roxy. The following year, another English DJ came to Amsterdam by the name of Graham B and started playing Rare Groove with his DJ partner Paul Jay as The Soho Connection at a club called The Richter. By 1989, Graham had been liaising with Russ Dewbury to do events based on the Brighton Jazz Bop and in 1990 he did, as Club 802 Jazz Bop at the cavernous Paradiso.

In 1991, an important session started called The Message at a club called Havana. The DJ's were Cassie 6 and KC The Funkaholic and, originally, the music policy was Rare Groove, Jazz Funk and Be Bop. After a few months, KC left and was replaced by Mark Taylor - who played Soul and Jazz initially. They had occasional guest DJ's too, such as Ismael Ibrahim, - who was a Fusion and Latin expert from Leiderdorp, amongst others.

Ever since 1987 IDJ had been coming over regularly, and by 1991 Jerry, Marshall, Gary and his brother Seymour and fellow dancers - David and Levi Graham, were coming over socially for at least a weekend a month and they started going to The Message. Because of this, the DJ's could start playing the heavy Jazz. Now that these dancers were going there it encouraged others to come in too, and within six months to a year there were Dutch dancers such as the aforementioned Adolf, Johnny, Raymond and Bryan and others such as: Abdul Fikri, Carlos Vigelandzoon, David Koop, Dominique Bertens, Eszteca Noya, Jean Charles (John) Agesilas, Jelly Germain, Jerry Glydesdale, Johan Van Look, Peter Kuyt Remyl and Urvin Vigelandzoon appearing and learning either from them or previously from Norville Small. Unusually for this scene, there were female dancers too such as: Anouk De Valk, Barbara Rouwendal, Ina Zelaya, Marike Hetjes, Maureen Schipper and Victorien Barendrecht. Seymour Nurse told me that The Message remains one of his all time favourite Jazz Dance sessions - which is a compliment indeed coming from him.

Tin Tin, Cassie and Mark have all played regularly at Graham B's immensely successful Jazz Bop's, and other than the aforementioned Rotterdam and Amsterdam DJ's at that time, you had the English DJ Desmond Antoine and a DJ from Utrecht too, called Frankie D - who ran his famous Hard Bop nights there.

Holland, at that point was the only country doing Jazz Dance the same (albeit much smaller) than the UK.

U.S.A.

Following a visit to Dingwalls in 1990 with Sue Steward at the height of Acid Jazz, former 'World Music' DJ Jonathan Rudnick decided to start a night at S.O.B'S, 200 Varick Street in Manhattan, New York - where he was the PR and Media and Special Events person and resident DJ. The night was called Giant Step.

Meeting his kindred spirit - Maurice Bernstein, in 1988, they both had similar ideas and (frustrations) about jazz and funk and the lack of it in NY at the time. Both of them being from other countries (Manchester, England and Johannesburg respectively) had - as they put it - naively thought that they were in the vital musical centre of it all with the musics they loved - which turned out to be not exactly true, Rudnick said, so, mainly for selfish reasons, they wanted to have live events and parties where they could go and dance and see the living legends. Dingwalls showed them that it was vital and did work, and there was a very healthy respect - plus a growing young and active support system in Straight No Chaser magazine and the vibrant early BGP/Acid Jazz-type labels. "Dingwalls blew me away. Seeing the Jazz Dancers full on, that early buzzing spirit of community and hearing Patrick and Gilles spin original jazz for dancing - exactly what I

could not find and that was missing in NYC; which was meant to be the jazz capital of the world," Jonathan told me. Very much with the support of the visionary owner of S.O.B'S - Larry Gold, Giant Step developed out of other events there called Groove Academy: "The Groove Academy - Dedicated to the Preservation of Funk' was our first entity created to showcase the overlooked legends of funk who were being heavily sampled and loved by the Hip Hop generation but who were not being exposed for who they were by name nor as the amazing live groups that they are. The first show we did was Leon Thomas meets The JB's," Rudnick says. Giant Step was to be the Jazz Dance side of Groove Academy, and to re-create and re-introduce jazz and dancing into NY. The idea was simple: to use DJ's playing classics and lost gems and see how a young crowd would react. They had conceived Giant Step to eventually be a playground of DJ's, dancers, musicians, poets, tap dancers (al la the Nicolas Brothers), street painters. "We were lucky to have bumped into a young wandering musician - *Richard Worth*, who we gave a flyer to. Being English, he understood what we were trying to do and asked if he could come and jam at the club, and so he came down and jammed with *DJ Smash* and our tiny crew of interested dancers and the curious at SOB's. *Nappy G* also ended up coming by to play timbales and percussion, and together with our 'tribute to the masters' visuals, imaging and slides of the legends like Miles Davis, John Coltrane, Herbie Hancock and all the great great photos, we were off to somewhat of an encouraging start."

The first two DJ's were Smash Hunter and *Jazzy Nice*, whom Maurice knew, and were told to bring out as many jazz and funk tunes as they had, and slowly over time the 'new' classics were born. A new label called 8 Ball Records came out of New York in 1991 with jazzy productions by DJ Smash which were Funky drum programmed loops with sample breaks and Jazz samples. There was a track called *Jazz Not Jazz*, which seemed to sum up the whole new sound. I wondered if the label was anything to do with Giant Step: "No not as a label, but since Smash was our first DJ he very wisely used Giant Steps dancefloor as a playground for creating and trying out jazzy grooves on a fresh audience, and then putting those tunes out on 8 Ball."

Much to the initial frustration of Jonathan and Maurice, they never got any Jazz Dancers (as they'd hoped) or got away with the Jazz that they would've liked to have done - that they heard at Dingwalls. Hip Hop was the overriding influence in New Yorks' streets and this was the domineering influence at Giant Step, as well as Acid Jazz. The dance styles that became established there were more about Break Dancing and street forms. The multi-faceted dancers from the Garage/House Music clubs - Paradise Garage and The Loft added their influence, as regulars to Giant Step, too.

Eventually, Giant Steps influence was felt, not only in the US, but all over the world. Unfortunately, a lot of the older Jazz artists that came to Giant Step to check it out (such as saxophonist *Tom Scott*) totally missed the point of the interaction with DJ's, rappers and musicians and, along with many others, just made half-arsed Jazz with funky drums thinking that they were making 'Acid Jazz' records (in turn, this made their public think that this sound was 'Acid Jazz' too).

Across the country, in San Francisco, it was always obvious that Acid Jazz was going to take off. I paid a visit there in 1988 and there was already a small Rare Groove/Jazz Funk scene happening where you would hear the UK DJ's Alan Riding and Simon Grace play such things as *Lonnie Liston Smith - Expansions* at the Brad 'BBQ Brad' Been-ran Nickies Bar And Grill in the Haight area, and fuelled by Michael and Jody McFadins record shop Rooky Ricardos among others (like Village Music, over the Golden Gate bridge in Mill Valley). Things were looking healthy there. Michael and Jody, of course went on to start the very well respected record shop Groove Merchant and their Luv 'N Haight, Ubiquity and Cu Bop record labels that continue to play a massive part today. The local scene was lovingly very well documented by journalist Wendy Kurman, who was then the partner of Alan Riding (who was also a Jazz record dealer, and sold in the cloakroom of Dingwalls, by the way. He introduced many important records to that clubs dancefloor, and the UK scene in general). She later took a high position at Peterson's Talkin' Loud record label in London.

ON WITH THE STORY...........
THE SOUTHPORT WEEKENDER

From it's original base at Berwick On Tweed, and on to Fleetwood on the North west coast, Alex Lowes' Soul Weekenders had at last settled 20 miles South down the coast from there at Southport at the Pontins Holiday Centre. This enormous twice-yearly event had a Jazz room there which was now revered and well attended from all over the country. Reminiscent of the classic Jazz rooms of the all-dayers that had abruptly stopped mid-eighties, there was, again, somewhere to seriously battle on the dancefloor. With music by DJ's such as Sylvester, Simon Mansell and Bob Jones (and later, me) - battle they did! The Caister weekender was also continuing twice yearly with it's Jazz room too. Considering that the heavier side of Jazz Dance was rapidly on the wane, it was surprising to see the vast amount of Troupes and Crews forming. In particular, snapping at the heels of IDJ and Brothers In Jazz were Bristols Floor Technicians, who'd been formed for a couple of years by then and were working heavily (and making the first of their few trips to Japan too). They're as good as any of the best ever was.

I don't know why Camber Sands, on the South coast, was chosen - maybe because it would pose no competition to Southport or Caister or perhaps they were hoping to get some of the crowd from the incredibly successful Brighton Jazz Bops - but the new Jazz radio station Jazz Fm organized a Jazz Weekender on 23rd to 25th November at the Pontins Holiday Centre representing what was happening in the Acid Jazz scene revolving around Dingwalls and Talkin' Loud records. I apologise for calling it an 'Acid Jazz' weekender - after all the efforts concerned to distance themselves from it - but what music would you call it? It wasn't Jazz Dance. The freezing cold weekender featured *A Tribe Called Quest, Roy Ayers, Pharoah Sanders, Galliano, Brand New Heavies, Working Week, Incognito* and myself playing live, and all the usual DJ's, but it was not well attended. Perhaps it was too soon to have done this? No. It was the right time: Acid Jazz was getting even bigger everywhere. This would be the only blip on the rise of the movement (with both the Talkin' Loud and Acid Jazz labels doing incredible business) - until March 1991.

It had been rumoured for a while that Dingwalls was closing down, and in March it did. It had been sold, and was to be gutted and refitted, and would re-open as a comedy club called Jongleurs. Gilles was devastated - it could have continued there probably even to date, but that was it: the end of an era and one of our greatest ever club sessions. Shortly after, Gilles and Patrick Forge tried to restart it at The Worlds End - which was very similar to the look and feel to Dingwalls and less than a quarter of a mile from there, but it didn't work. It wasn't the same. These things never are, are they?

Although, as I said, Dingwalls closing was the end of an era, Acid Jazz, as a supposed style of music, had become a runaway train, and certainly in the US. Through the introduction of Acid Jazz and the 'Freedom Principle' from New York's Giant Step to the rest of the country, the focus was very much on the Hip Hop side of the scene. Of course there had already been some great Jazz Rap-based (if you will) releases made there since *Stetasonic* used *Lonnie Liston Smith - Expansions* as the musical basis of their hit *Talkin' All That Jazz* in 1988 (Tommy Boy), and by 1992 we'd seen *Soho - Hot Music* (USOA-1990); *Dream Warriors - My Definition Of A Boombastic Jazz Style* (Fourth And Broadway -1990); *Gang Starr - Jazz Thing* CBS - 1990) *Jazz Not Jazz - Flip And Trip* and every release after on Eight Ball records from 1991,plus a lot of records on the new and influential New York label Nervous and Ninja Tunes in the UK from 1991 on, and there was even many Jazz House tracks as well like *Jazz Documents - Secret Code* (Nu Groove -1991). Occasionally there would be referencing to Gilles Peterson on a label or there would be an Acid Jazz remix, so this Jazz influence was certainly no coincidence. The majors were now picking up on what they thought was Acid Jazz too, with saxophonist *David Sanborn* leading the way with his album *Upfront* (WB 1992) - with its funky sax and Hip Hop drums, with *Art Porter* following suit quite soon after with the *Jeff Lorber* produced *Pocket City* album (Verve), and from there it was spreading like wildfire coast-to-coast in the US, and Acid Jazz was the buzzword amongst the excited major labels - "ahh, a new way to market Jazz".

Back in the UK: by now *Ronnie Jordan*; The James Taylor Quartet; The Brand New Heavies, *The Young Disciples*, Incognito and Galliano had become enormous, and *Corduroy*; *Mother Earth*; UFO and particularly *Jamiroquai* and *US 3* were just about to be. There were soon to become many other new labels joining Acid Jazz and Talkin' Loud too like: Mo' Wax; Marden Hill; Delicious Vinyl; Tongue And Groove; Dorado; Boogie Back etc. On writing this I suddenly realized something that a student once said to me around then. He spoke to me before a concert with my Latin Jazz group *Snowboy And The Latin Section* (who were on Acid Jazz records) and said something like: "Your music is Latin Jazz so what's that got to do with Acid Jazz?" and of course, that was it: that's the thing - Acid Jazz had become absolutely enormous (and would get even bigger) with literally a whole new generation. A whole new young crowd were buying, and supporting Acid Jazz and dressing like Galliano or The James Taylor Quartet - of which 95% of these people would never have heard of The Wag or Berlin and certainly not The Electric Ballroom. They'd come in through the buzz of these hip new labels - Acid Jazz and Talkin' Loud, and this endless amount of bands surrounding the labels. They loved all this music with the Funk and Hip Hop grooves and Jazz soloists and Rappers. The Jazz Dance scene didn't run alongside Acid Jazz, the Jazz Dance scene became the Acid Jazz scene and there were hundreds of new nights where Jazz Fusion, Be Bop and Latin Jazz would've meant nothing at all to this new young crowd. So much for the 'Freedom Principle'.

This new following wasn't just in the UK though, many, many other things were starting to happen worldwide then, to push this 'new scene' too: like Nicola Conte's Fez night in Bari, Italy; Brass in Los Angeles and the German clubs: The Beat Box in Wuppertal, Into Somethin' in Munich and Mojo in Hamburg and as I've just said: in the UK there were loads of new nights suddenly happening. The main ones were going from strength-to-strength: Baz Fe Jazz had retired from DJ-ing in late 1991 for religious reasons and so his partner - Russ Dewbury - continued on with the incredible Brighton Jazz Bops which continued to sell-out every time. He'd mix the new with the old - Hip Hop next to Salsa next to Be Bop - and the crowd were of all ages too. Russ' weekly 'across-the-board' Jazz Dance-based sessions at the Jazz Rooms, Ship Street, Brighton, continued to be packed. Gilles and Patrick Forge restarted Talkin' Loud at the cavernous Fridge in Brixton, London every Saturday from the 7th of September '91; Tin Tin and John Stapleton were still running their important Cooker nights at The Thekla, Bristol and The Dig Family - Gip, Chico and Lubi - also continued to dominate the North, at The Gallery in Leeds, with their enviable, packed-solid, sessions Dig and The Cooker - looking forward but remembering 'the roots' at all times.

Unfortunately though, other than the Jazz rooms at the Southport and Caister Weekenders, the un-occasional Jazz Dance competitions; the monthly Back To The Tracks at Saks, Southend On Sea with Phil Levene and myself or Gilles Peterson and Sylvester's Jazz 90 events, the unique and skilled Jazz Dancers were left homeless. Other than these few events across the entire country, the opportunity of playing or dancing to John Coltrane or Art Blakey in a club was now no longer a possibility.

TALKING LOUD & SAYING SOMETHING

The Final Hours!
SUN FEB 24th
JOHNNY
LYTLE   £5/4

SUN MARCH 3rd
INCOGNITO £4/3

SUN MARCH 10th
THE LAST
SESSION 12-8pm

GUEST ARTISTS AND DJS

DINGWALLS
Camden Lock, Chalk Farm Road, NW1.

Legendary line-up! L to R - Mark Webster, Billy Davidson, Kenny MacLeod, Paul Murphy and Bob Jones

THE INTERVIEWS

The full UK Jazz Dance history: from Soul Jazz and Jazz Funk to Acid Jazz. From area-to-area, it is told by the people that were there.

SCOTLAND

"I was booked to play in Glasgow – I'd already played up there a couple of times – and these three Scottish blokes turned up to The Electric Ballroom the night before I was playing there. One of them asked if I wanted a lift, so I loaded my records into their car. We got up to Leeds and the car broke down but they got it started again, and it was sick all the way to Glasgow. It took fifteen hours to get there and when we got to the DJ Nick Peacock's place, he wondered why I was late and how I'd got there, so I told him the story. Nick told me that they didn't have a car - they'd stolen one!

What kind of jazz did you play there?
The same as The Ballroom. They loved it as hard as it gets."

Paul Murphy

With a population of only just under 5 million (that is less than half of the entire population of London), and a tiny ethnic population, it is a little surprising that this country has any Black music club-culture at all. In fact, it was the opposite: they had a big, almost weekly, Jazz Funk all-dayer scene (as well as many clubs), along with an equally as huge Northern and Modern soul scene there. Through DJ and promoter Kenny MacLeod's **many events across Scotland, and events such as John Snelling's 'Soul Ticket' in Aberdeen, and many others, it created a big interest in every permutation of Soul and Jazz Funk music. There was not the North/South divide that existed in the scene in England in the 1970's; they got the very best DJ's from all over England and Scotland. From a Jazz Dance perspective, they liked it as hard as it could be given it to them from their many knowledgable and influential DJ's – such as** Bob Jefferies, Billy Davidson, Kerrso, **and later,** Nick Peacock **- and punters alike.**

KENNY MacLEOD

Scotlands major promoter (and one of the top DJ's) for Jazz Funk and Jazz in the late-70's to the mid-80's. MacLeod was there from the beginning.

I started going to the (Northern Soul club) Wigan Casino in 1974. It changed my life going there. It was a long way to go from just outside Glasgow to Wigan in Lancashire, but I loved it. I started DJing in 1979 playing Soul, Jazz Funk, Disco and Jazz. I was playing a lot of Jap Jazz.

Was there much of an invironment for it?
No. We had to create it. We worked very hard - especially me and Billy Davidson. I built a reputation over a couple of years.

You formed *The Scottish Soul Society.*
Yes. It was to do promotions and also to give us an identity.

I had a residency at a place called *The Crossroads* in Whitburn – my home town – and that had a great following. We had enough support to fill a couple of coaches to go to other clubs. I featured a lot of jazz there. They liked it a lot. I was organizing a lot of all-dayers and playing at them (and others) too; probably two a month. Bearing in mind the population of Scotland, we used to get between 600 and 1200 at each one - depending on venue size. Some of them in England you'd get 3,000. We started to have two rooms at the all-dayers like in the North of England; the main hall playing the big Jazz Funk, anthems and the smaller second room playing Jazz and Latin. I'd always play in both rooms.

There were a handful of you that were *really* influential in Scotland.

I would say that people watched what me and Billy Davidson played. We played the Soul and Jazz first and others followed. A lot of what I would play was jazz-tinged, and it was going down to see Paul Murphy's clubs and Colin Curtis at *Cassinellis* and seeing the Jazz that they were getting away with that made me think that we could do that up here, and that's what I tried to do.

What was your impression of Cassinellis?

I could not believe it. It was packed by 8pm and Colin would play all the latest Jazz stuff. There were dancers there that you would not believe. Colin had a massive following. I DJ'd at another club of his – *Rafters*. I took 100 people from Scotland with me. Same again – unbelievable. I would say that it was a 95% Black crowd and I remember seeing a lot of female Jazz-Dancers too.

I think everything changed when Murphy came on the scene with all this fast Latin and Fusion. He tipped everyone in to that. Promoters in the North saw that this style was taking off. Now, I wouldn't know how often he got booked in the North but we certainly booked him a lot in Scotland. I took Jazz in to the second room at our all-dayers. You could get away with it. I've never heard Murphy play a bad set. He was so far-ahead it was frightening. We even put him on in the main hall once and people loved him. Glasgow was always big for Jazz: at the Jazz All-Dayer at *Club De France* at Coatbridge, we had 6 or 700 people there. I had a Sunday residency at a place called *Joannas*. They loved jazz there too. That place held about 500. There was another place worth mentioning for the record which was upstairs at a club called *Paris,* in Silk Street, Paisley. I had a two year residency there with Bob Jefferies. You could get away with anything there.

> "I'll tell you something about the Scottish: they took their music seriously. They were very academic and appreciated what you played, so it made you feel good."
>
> *Baz Fe Jazz*

I booked Chris Hill and Jeff Young to come up to an all-dayer at Panama Jacks, but they couldn't make it. Chris apologized and sent me a cassette tape of a DJ set and I actually told the crowd what had happened and played it to the dance-floor - and they went mad to it!

That's weird - a DJ set but no DJ!

Yes, but it worked. They loved it. That was the first time that I heard *Fela Kuti – Roforofo Fight.*

In 1984, you started 'Just Jazz Promotions' where you were quoted as saying "For future events with hopefully all the best Jazz DJ's around".

The music wasn't flavour of the month but we wern't interested in fads anyway. I had my successes and my failures. I had a good twelve-year run at it.

BILLY DAVIDSON

From the Aberdeen area. Billy is one of Scotlands original DJ's in the scene and has remained at the top.

The scene started for us by going to The Wigan Casino and then The Blackpool Mecca - that was our first experience of Jazz/ Funk. There were these events in Aberdeen called *The Soul Ticket* - which was the first Thursday of every month. It was packed with 6 or 700 people all dancing to Soul and Jazz Funk. We started playing at Ruffles (The Silhouette Bar). Steve Aggasild used to play in there, playing hot imports and I was bringing stuff in as well that he didn't have. There were 90 people in there who progressed to the all-dayers. The Soul Ticket helped as well. With those two nights it kept our scene busy.

> "We formed the Centre City Soul Club in the Spring of 1977. The name came from a Fat Larry's Band song title. We were undoubtedly the first Soul club in Scotland. When we started the Soul Ticket, we got the 40 most dedicated punters and more or less made them buy ten tickets each, so if they sold all ten they made their money back. They didn't care. Everyone was into it."
>
> *John Snelling*

In 1978 there was an all-dayer set up in Dundee by Tony Cochrane which had Chris Hill in one room and Richard Searling in the other, and this is where we met loads of people into the same music as us. After that, we started holding events all over Scotland. You had Tony Cochrane and Ned Jordan from Dundee and Kenny MacLeod from central Scotland doing promotions, and we were setting up all-dayers in all these different towns - mainly function rooms in hotels. The Stonehaven *Commodore* was the top place. It died out there because of over saturation - other people started organizing all-dayers so it filtered down the numbers. John (Snelling) and I took over The Commodore and brought up John Grant and Alan Barr (from Glasgow) and we built it up again for a while.

By the early eighties a lot of the music was getting poor and there was over saturation of events again, so Kenny MacLeod and I started doing a night in Glasgow at a club called *Chippendales*, and this is where the Jazz started to get played. Because a lot of the new music was rubbish, we started to play older Soul and Jazz – mixing the two together. It took off in Glasgow; we had Paul Murphy up to DJ and he'd also bring records to sell too. We had lots of great stuff. Glasgow really took the scene to its heart; they adopted it.

As soon as the DJ Nick Peacock was playing it, it became monstrously popular; he was very influential. It was hip to be into it, I mean, it wasn't as big as the Jazz Funk scene though, like the Motherwell Civic Centre – the size of an aircraft hanger, and we had 7 or 800 people in there.

I also guested at *Rafters* in Manchester with Colin Curtis a few times and it was an amazing place. The doors opened at 9 and the doors were closed by10. They were a really open minded-crowd; you could play anything. There's a good example of the difference between the North and the South: On the *James Mason* album *Rhythm Of Life* down South they'd play *Sweet Power*, and up North we'd play *Free*. It was an enormous track (note: Free was huge in London, but not the home counties).

Jazz remained popular in Glasgow in the '80's. I remember even when 'House' music took off, you'd still have Jazz in the other room in club's, At this point I got more into Soul.

BOB JEFFERIES
Along with Kenny and Billy, Bob was one of the top three in Scotlands black music scene and has remained so to date.

I was doing all the Scottish all-dayers. There was one every weekend from late 70's onwards. Originally all-dayers here just had one room where you'd hear all types of music, but I went to a Caister Soul weekender in the early 80's and saw that there was a second room with DJ's like Bob Jones or Chris Brown just playing Jazz. It was about then that we'd have back rooms (or second rooms) that was all Jazz. By the early 80's we'd have guest DJ's coming up because the events got so big. We mirrored the Chris Hill scene really, with the 'tribes' and all that - the 'family' thing. It was more across the East of Scotland.

Kenny MacLeod arranged most of this
Kenny was a great organizer. He had the talent for it. I worked with him a lot. He was a little more commercial, but I'd really try and push the barriers with the Jazz.

Kerrso - a regular at The Electric Ballroom – said that the Jazz was equally as intense up here.
Yes it was. That's true. We had some great dancers in Glasgow and in Ayrshire, They were more ballet-style as opposed to all the fast footwork that you'd see in London. But there was amazing, expressive dancers like *Frankie Devine* and *John 'Jimpy' Simpson*.

You're a rated dancer.
I think that the best DJ's are dancers.

Did you travel much?
I never got booked further South than Leicester until about 1990. I regularly did the Clouds All-Dayers in Preston and play the Jazz room, and I'd guest in Newcastle. I'd go down to London occasionally searching for records, like going over to Paul Murphy's record shop and those Soho shops like *Hit Man*.

...and *Bluebird* with all the cut-outs, but then you had *Gordon A1* here in Scotland – he was the cut-out king!
I spent an absolute fortune with him. He had a shop that just had racks and racks of cut-outs,

and I'd come out with bundles of them. I'd just buy up everything by certain artists without listening to them because that's how you learned: reading the sleeves or talking to Kerrso or swapping tapes. Someone like Art Blakey - you'd buy everything and then buy everything by the musicians in the band. I got into Be Bop before Latin.

I played a lot at *the Sub Club* and at *Club Sandino*. I did that club in Glasgow and in Edinburgh. Although it was more 'world-musicy', we played the Jazz hard.

Why would that be, the population of Scotland is so small?

It's because there were small pockets everywhere so when they met up at all-dayers they went for it. There was someone like Kerrso in every major town.

It all revolved around you, Billy Davidson, Kenny MacLeod and Tony Cochrane.

Kenny and Tony were the main promoters. There were a few others but it never worked for them. They were just after the money.

Was there much happening in Edinburgh?

No. There was someone called Gary Young, who was as mad a jazz collector as me, but Edinburgh was really a Northern Soul city, and us and Aberdeen were Jazz Funk and Jazz. Paul Murphy was a regular up here. He'd come up here on the train with an extra box of records to sell, and it'd go back empty (laughs). The word would spread like wildfire when he'd come up.

Panama Jacks was an amazing club. That had a Jazz room. People would really travel for that. I organized a club called *Bobby Jones*, which was the same. We even had a couple of coaches from Birmingham come up which was great but strange - people in Scotland are not used to seeing Black people there, so seeing a hundred in a club was unusual!

By '85-86 I was playing in bigger clubs and playing a lot more mainstream, but because of clubs like Club Sandino I was still being booked to play Jazz until '95 when it tapered off, and I was also resident at The Sub Club for three years until 92.

KERRSO

Scotland's most major knowledge and collector. He is rightfully respected all over that country. He traveled the depth and breadth of the UK searching out clubs, DJ's and music.

There was a DJ called *Segun* who must be mentioned. He was at a pub called *City Limits* in 1977; the music was fantastic. We used to get coaches from there and travel all over the place, down to *Rafters* in Manchester to see *Colin Curtis,* and all over the place. There was thirty from the housing estate where I lived, called Castlemilk. We were all into our music. We went to Leeds *Central,* down to *The 100 Club, The Lacy Lady, The Goldmine* - that was my favourite club; a 10 hour drive! I would say that the music being played in Scotland was similar to Manchester.

Glasgow being the capital of Scotland was very similar to London. It led fashion and was far ahead with music. Glasgow was always very Jazzy as opposed to the east coast which was more Northern Soul. London loved the Jazz and hard Funk and so did we. We were no different than all the big Northern cities either.

Kenny MacLeod was the main promoter. He worked very hard and put on loads of gigs. Paul Murphy was up here all the time, so was Bob Jones. In about 1977 Kenny got me to DJ. I just started the evening off but I've never considered myself a DJ, I've done it, maybe 100 times.

> "Kerrso used to dress really outrageously. I remember at one all-dayer he turned up in this suit with 'plus-fours' and spats, and I thought I'd better get to know him! He was going to a lot of jazz festivals and had one of the best record collections I'd ever seen. I told him that he must DJ, but I felt but he was very shy. One day I convinced him to play at an all-dayer and before he went on he was vomiting. He's got an amazing ear for music."
>
> *Kenny MacLeod*

We must mention *The County Inn* in Cainber Lang. It was every Sunday night and ran from 1978 to 84/85. There'd be literally three to four hundred punters every week and, musically, it was very jazzy. The DJ Alan Barr did a fantastic job, and even I'd play there sometimes. And jazz-wise they'd play tracks like *Dandy's Dandy – Manteca* and *Cal Tjader- Primitivo* and a lot of other good hard jazz. The place is folklore. It was a very important place, so was *The Glen Ruth* in Rutherglen, - also South of Glasgow - on Saturdays. It was owned by the people that had The County Inn. People would come from all over the west of Scotland. This was '77/78. They played some good Jazz. It was rammed; a lock out. We all went there, all of us.

From 1977 to 1980 at our all-dayers they had two rooms - one was Northern Soul and the other was Funk/ Jazz Funk and by 1980 one room would be Hard Jazz

In 1983 there was a place called *Le Club De France* that played 100% Jazz every Friday. That was in Coatbridge. There was a small back room called *Frenchies*.

Was the music heavy?

Listen, it was Afro Cuban and Latin Jazz: *Sabu, Art Blakey, Gene Ammons- Jungle Strut, Airto, Dom um Romao*. It was well heavy. You could get away with murder. I used to go to The Electric Ballroom and it was a step up from that. That was the 'cockroach crushers' all night and this was 100 mile an hour Jazz all night, and the crowd loved it. The music was the same as The Ballroom. I used to shop at Paul Murphy's all the time. I was buying a lot then. The DJ Hendy played some great tunes as well, Gordon Watson should be mentioned - he played some right hard tunes. It was major here.

What was the standard of dancing like up here?

There was some great ones like Jimpy and Frankie Devine, but people danced though anyway.

Glasgow always had a big Jazz Dance scene. We had Club Sandino here and Edinburgh which I've done a dozen of, and got away with murder, I'd play stuff like *Maynard Ferguson – Mambo Le Mans, Jayne Cortez – I see Chano Pozo, Fela Kuti – Roforofo Fight* and other tunes by him. People found it to be a great night out. These were charity nights to raise money for women in Latin America whose husbands were locked up for no reason. You heard heavy tunes there, believe me, and that went for about 6 years. I don't mean to sound funny here, but the music here was on a par with London.

Why do you think Jazz took off here?

The music was militant here. Down to its raw form. The jazz was played hard. Glasgow was a big jazz city before our scene: Coltrane played here, George Coleman... there'd been a jazz festival since the early 60's. As the Jazz Funk got more commercial, we started to look back. There'd been certain individuals such as me, Kenny MacLeod, Nick Peacock, Gordon Watson, Hendy... kept it going and strong. How did it get big? - and it was big - we had *Murphy, Baz FeJazz, Sylvester, Bob Jones*...they all came. Murphy would play here exactly what he was playing at The Ballroom. *Exactly*. I knew because I went there quite a few times. He was well known here and he got away with murder. He was relentless, but that's what we wanted.

Where were you buying your records from in Glasgow?

A1 Records – which had an incredible amount of cut-outs, and there was a record stall at a place called *Paddys Market*. He always had good records; the most amazing stuff. *Soundtrack* on the Southside was an import shop that we used to buy our stuff from - they had everything, and by 1979 they were also selling cut-outs too.

There was this DJ in Edinburgh Gary Young who had this excellent collection but he never said where he was buying it all from, so I got him drunk one night and found out the name: The shop was called the *Gramaphone Emporium* and sold 78's to collectors. They didn't sell by rarity, they sold by condition and so I was coming out with these £30 albums for £3 each, I took about 80 albums back to Glasgow with me, and I met up with Gordon for a pint, and he wanted to know where I'd got all these records from but I wouldn't tell him. He said "The Gramaphone Emporium?" and I asked him how he knew, and he said that the 'shop name' was printed on the bags! He went there the next day and spent £200. Unfortunately he told the guy what they were worth and that we were DJing with them too, and the owner was horrified, so 'that was that'!

What else was happening?

There was ton's of stuff happening. *The Volcano* was fantastic on a Monday '89-'95 - *Nick Peacock's* residency. He played hard jazz. You could've got away with murder there because all the right heads were there. He had three to four hundred people in there. Nick really did a lot in our scene. Of course, his sessions at *The Sub Club* were very jazzy. I DJ'd there quite a bit for him there.

NICK PEACOCK

A barrier-breaking Glaswegian DJ. One of the second wave that came in to the Jazz Dance scene in the early 80's. By the end of the 80's he'd become Glasgows major cutting-edge DJ.

Me and my pals were going through town off our faces on Acid and we saw this huge queue outside of a club called Joannas on a Sunday night. Shakatak were playing live. We were 'Indie' kids with 'A Certain Ratio' haircuts - angry young men fucked up on drugs. We got in but we were so out of place, but when I looked around the club I thought: "This is what I've been looking for." That was it: I used to tape Mr Super Bad's show on Radio Clyde every Saturday from midnight till 2 and listen to it solid all week and try and buy the records.

I worked in Virgin records. You could listen to loads of music without buying it. That's when I got into DJing. We had so many cut-outs in there to listen to. We stocked loads of them. The manager, Gordon Al – now owner of record shop chain *Fopp* - was known as the cut-out king. He was a great Jazz man and into Miles Davis. I'd go up to his house and he'd play me loads of stuff and I'd hear records that I'd eventually buy which got me discovering my own records in that style.

Were you DJing at the Scottish alldayers?
Yes, well I went all over and got to know all these DJ's like Kerrso and of course, Kenny MacCleod – who was the main DJ here. I did DJ at these events later. I was a diverse DJ but I was known more for Jazz. I'd fill the gap there, because I came into the scene later. I wasn't really into the Fusion Jazz, I was into the *Blue Note* sound and Afro Cuban and Hard Bop. We had the DJ Sylvester up here quite a few times and he influenced us with his Mambo and Afro Jazz music. I remember Colin Curtis coming up here and playing five versions of Mas Que Nada in a row and we only knew the Sergio Mendes version!

Kerrso says that the Scottish jazz dance scene was the equivalent of the English.
Yes, well there was a lot being played up here. *Billy Davidson* would always play a few Fusion tracks and *Bob Jefferies* was one of my favourite DJ's. He'd always play a lot of Jazz. We didn't have *Jazz Dancers* but we did have a lot of excellent dancers – the kind that danced really fast. I think in the 80's here, it was quite acceptable and normal to hear Jazz in the clubs.

Chippendales was when Paul Murphy started to come to DJ for us, on the all-dayer scene. It was a long bar that opened out into a club. My brother brought Paul round to where I was DJing for 8 years - *The Sub Club*. I was playing West End club music and I said to Paul "Go and get your records" and he came on and played *Carmen McCrea - Take Five* and after a while the place went berserk. It wasn't a sound they knew but it was the sound that they'd been looking for. After a while at that club I could get away with anything. *Horace Silver – Filthy McNasty* was a fucking classic there. It would blow the roof off.

THE NORTH EAST

There'd always been a small but very strong and dedicated following for underground Black music originally in the 70's and 80's in the North east, from Newcastle Upon Tyne going South to Sunderland, Darlington, Stockton On Tees, Chester Le Street, Newton Le Willows, Yarm etc and was mainly fuelled by the endeavours of DJ's Alex Lowes and Bill Swift. Alex went on to run enormous Black music promotions (including the barrier-breaking twice-yearly Southport Dance Weekenders) and is single-handedly responsible for putting that area on the map. The North east was also home to some of the UK's most rated dancers and troupes too, such as: Bamboozle and The Unknown Troopers.

ALEX LOWES

What's your background?
Northern Soul. I used to go to *Va Va's* in Bolton; that's where I learnt my trade, I used to go to The Blackpool Mecca with my friend Michael (Powney). I got bored of all that Northern Soul scene - it had to move on like the way The Mecca moved on in the Highland Room with Colin Curtis and Ian Levene, and that's where the Jazz thing came in for us originally.

What were your early residencies?

Julie's, Buddys (Stockton), *MacMillans*(Yarm), *The Gretna Green* - all legendary places - and the Jazz was a part of them. It was Soul, Funk, Jazz…

Was it Colin changing the style at The Mecca that influenced you to play that music?

Aye. Thinking about it, it must have been. We used to get coaches to The Mecca, and later we used to travel to see Colin at *Cassinellis*. I didn't like the Manchester clubs though - they were too rough. There was always trouble.

Tell me about The Gretna Green. I was told that you played really un-safe stuff there.

I played the Jazz there, and the Jap Jazz (and at Julies). It was great. Packed to the rafters every week.

Where were you picking your jazz up from?

There used to be that really good shop in Newcastle called *Callers*. It was very upfront, and I'd travel down to London to *City Sounds* and *Rays Jazz* shop.

I used to push things to the limit. If people weren't showing much interest I'd push it until there was.

Did people travel much outside the North East or was it quite insular?

Quite insular, but there was a certain lot of us that would travel. I took two coach loads to The Goldmine (280 miles) – about 100 people, so there was people interested, but they had to be helped along the way.

You used to be one of just a few that would be a guest DJ in Scotland.

Their crowd was 100% into it.

It seems to me that there was quite an effort to shut Chris Hill out up in the North of England, and yet he appeared in the North East.

Oh aye. We had a great rapport with Chris. We had him here quite a few times in the 70's and 80's.

You're considered a taste maker in your area.

Michael Powney - You were a taste maker Alex, putting stuff on from Northern to Jazz-Funk when people here didn't know anything about it.

Alex - People were relying on us. I guess we *were* trend-setting.

How did you play jazz in an evening?

A few here and there or a couple of Jazz breaks in the evening.

Jazz Breaks. Yes, that's what we called them as well.

I didn't realize they were doing them down South like that. A couple of 15-20 minute Jazz breaks per evening. We were teaching people.

There was a period in the early 80's when a lot of DJ's stopped playing Jazz because of the fast tempos were getting too anti-social: did you stop?

No, no. I played Jazz right up until I stopped DJ-ing. I got too busy with the weekenders.

Yes, Berwick-On-Tweed (which later progressed to the world-famous Southport Weekender)

Yes, and there was jazz there (and still is). The same as any of my events: If there was room, jazz was in there. *Simon Mansell* looked after the Jazz side of things. We had Gilles Peterson there, Sylvester; I used to do a set…..

Michael why do you think Alex stood out from the others? I know from my experience down South that there were a lot of DJ's with reputations, but really they were playing the same as everyone else…

Alex was a fanatic. His sets had an edge. He'd always take it to the limit.

GARY ROBSON

A respected knowledge and friend of Alex Lowes.

Julies was on the Quayside and it was dead around there. It had the fashionable crowd. It was a good groovy little club. The DJ there before Alex was Tony Clarke, and he used to run a record department on the third floor of a furniture shop in Northumberland Street called Callers. Everyone would go in on a Saturday afternoon. The shelves were stocked with Northern Soul and Jazz Funk. It was an incredible selection. So he was playing great stuff at Julies.

You've known Alex Lowes from the beginning of of all this.

Yes. Alex started in about '78. He and Michael Powney went down to Torquay (Devon) and heard all this Jazz Funk at a club called *Sindys*, which, along with the Highland Room at Blackpool Mecca, turned him on to that music. He started playing Jazzy stuff - you know, the Disco Jazz. He was also guesting all over the place.

About 1984 at the Sunday nights at MacMillans in Yarm, people were traveling from everywhere - all over the North – and that continued for years, but it was'85/86 in *Walkers* was where proper Jazz dance took off. The owner, Billy, loved Black music and he and his brother Malcolm did more for Black music in our area than anyone. It was100% quality. There would be serious jazz played. It was played as 15 minute breaks and there were a lot of dancers there. It had two good years. Alex played some extreme jazz in there. Some hard-to-find stuff.

SIMON MANSELL
The North east's original Jazz specialist DJ.

About 1980 I started going to various clubs here, and one of them – *Gretna Green* (Newton-Le-Willows) had *Alex Lowes* and *Paul Cook* DJ-ing, and they were the only people I could think of playing jazz, and it was mainly Jazz Fusion stuff. The night lasted three hours and about an hour of that was jazz. Alex used to play a lot of Japanese jazz like *Genji Sawai and Bacon Egg – Foot And Mouth, Nobuo Yagi – Mi Mi Africa* and other US Fusion, like *David Larsen – Sudden Samba, Dave Benoit – Life Is Like A Samba, Richie Cole – New York Afternoon, Janet Lawson – Sunday Afternoon, Jeff Lorber-The Samba......* You must remember that in the North of England this would have been strange. It was a lot of 'pleasant-to-the-ear' type jazz. It was Alex that got me interested. He had another classic club called *Julies*. It was the same crowd.

What else was going on up here?
We had all-dayers but they didn't work. They were too long and not enough people to fill them. Around 1984, we started traveling down to the Nottingham all-dayers, which were amazing. You'd get these dancers walking in with those steel 'photographers cases' where they'd rip out the foam and carry a spare pair of shoes and t-shirts and things, so at all-dayers then, there were hundreds of these cases. If you were a jazz-dancer you had one (note: these were the dancers from Sheffield).

Were there many jazz-dancers in your area?
No. About ten or twelve, although there was a club nearby in Stockton called *Buddys* which Alex and *Nigel Wanless* DJ'd at. That held 180 and about fifty were jazz-dancers. Musically, it was the softer side of jazz. In Manchester or Nottingham there'd be one or two hundred in one room!

When did you become a DJ?
Technically 1979, but that was just at parties. My first major club was in Middlesborough at *Mandys* in the middle of 1983. It was more of a mainstream club. They gave me fifteen or twenty minutes in the middle of the session. It was more Jazz-Funky, but the thirty or so dancers would come on to the floor. The resident DJ wouldn't let me do longer. I think that was because my sets went down so well. I started doing Monday nights there and I started playing a bit of jazz, which didn't go down amazingly, but I started doing other bars and clubs as well. I was working with a DJ called Funky Nigel who was into the lighter Jazz, but he loved the dancers and the scene. We did about ten clubs in two years and he gave me a lot of breaks in what were pretty big clubs. Nigel used to book a lot of DJ's from the midlands and they'd always bring dancers with them, which meant that I could get away with some heavy stuff like *Dom Um Romao - Braun Blek Blu*, which was unheard of. I got quite popular with the Manchester dancers because they knew they'd get something good. By this point Alex Lowes was playing less jazz.

But he started his weekenders at Berwick-On-Tweed around then, didn't he ?
Yes.1986. The weekender was a total success with about four or five hundred people there, and they had a jazz room - but I don't think I ever saw more than fifteen people in there.

In my area, I was about the only one playing jazz, and that was always to the same twenty people. I couldn't create a scene, but I tried hard. I was getting my fix from going to weekenders like Berwick and *Caister*, but I was coming back disillusioned after seeing two hundred jazz-dancers there and coming home to twenty - and it was hard to get those twenty to a gig. The Jazz Room that they had at Caister was excellent. *Bob Jones* and *Sean French* played the best stuff. Bob was the *King* at the time. We worshipped him, and you could talk to him. He was approachable.

I saw you on some bills for all-dayers.

Yes. I pestered the promoters and always brought loads of people. I was very persistant. There were lots of great jazz DJ's at the all-dayers that were never mentioned on the bills. Obviously, Colin Curtis' reputation was untouchable – although not my favourite, and Jonathon played the proper stuff, but I felt the unmentioned guys played some of the best music.

I'd tried a hundred bars in my area and so I moved to London in 1987, as I wanted to be where the music was. The Wag was heaven. I worshipped Sylvester. Gilles' sessions at The Belvedere and Dingwalls were essential, although later on, when he was playing more Acid Jazzy kind of stuff, I once went up to him and said " Do you sleep well at nights? Because you shouldn't after playing a set like that," and our relationship has never been the same since (laughs). Actually, I guested once at The Belvedere and The Wag, so I must've been forgiven.

BAMBOOZLE

The North easts major Jazz Dance troupe.

Bobby Johnstone – I used to go to a night with Andy called 'Across The Tracks' at Walkers in Newcastle around '86. We'd met on a Saturday night: he was dancing in a Northern Soul-style but with some fast footwork, and I recognized it immediately. I went straight over to him and started dancing with him. This night played all kinds of music: Jazz, House, Hip Hop, Funk - it's where we met Tony Bains.

Tony Bains - We started *Bamboozle* there. I'd seen Bobby dancing with another crowd and the same with Andy Bex. I'd never seen his type of dancing before, with all the fast footwork. We became friends and started traveling out of town to nights in Sheffield that Andy was telling us about, like *Jive Turkey* and *The Kitten Klub* and we traveled out to Manchester and other places. At *Jive Turkey* I saw people battling for the first time there in the Jazz room, which moved us on to another level. I suppose we started to become a crew because of just seeing so many others – mainly Jazz ones. It seemed the natural thing to do. We practiced together and started doing routines too.

Bobby - We went anywhere. Once, we went to *The Mall* in Stockton where they had this Jazz Dance competition and three coaches came from Manchester with the Foot Patrol and Fusion Beat. They wanted the crew *The Unknown Troopers*. They battled and the Troopers were getting defeated so I went in with Andy to help out but I could see there was friction. We decided to leave.

Andy says that a lot of Jazz dancers came out of the House scene.

Andy - In my opinion, most of the Jazz Dancers up here *were* House dancers that danced jazz. I think the Jazz Dancers came from House. They cut their teeth to the slower tempo and moved on to jazz.

Tony B - I was more into the House side of it than the Jazz. I think that in a tight circle, floor-work shows more. I preferred the floor work side of the dancing to the footwork.

So there were three of you in Bamboozle.

Bobby – Originally. There were other regular dancers like Mans and Dave Turnbull and other people came in and out of the group: Jeff Ford, Kevin Topping and Sarah Day. We got the rated dancers in the area.

Tony B – We came across Rob and Tony at a club called *Liberties*.

Rob Hylton – I jumped in front of them. I had about three moves but I was hungry. I went home and practiced. I got a 'Jazz Juice Volume 3' album and wore that out. I wanted to go head-to-head. I thought they were twats (laughs).

Bobby – There was loads of friction between us, I suppose because he was up and coming and I was established. I wouldn't have him fronting me, so I'd get stuck into him.

How did you Hylton brothers get into all this?

Tony Hylton -We left school in '86 and went to Soul gigs. You'd always get one or two Jazz tracks and see some dancers. Because me and Rob are from a break dance background we'd get involved. We'd buy the BGP or 'Jazz Juice' compilations and get into it through that. We'd go to Liberties or the Southport Weekender and hear the Jazz there. Within six months of seeing it we were totally involved. We knew it was for us.

Rob – It was a case of "If you can't beat 'em, join 'em" with Bamboozle - we'd annoy a lot of people taking up a lot of space, so we gravitated towards each other. They were better than us because they'd been around and knew the scene. The competition between all of us was tough though. We'd push each other in a circle.

What places did you go to dance?

Tony B - *Chambers* in Sunderland on a Wednesday with the DJ's Steve Smith and Ian Wright. It was one you didn't want to miss. They'd always play maybe an hour of Jazz at the end of the night, so you'd always get battles. People would travel from all over the North east.

Tony H – It was heavy.

Rob - We'd be upstairs at Walkers dancing to House and challenging, and downstairs you'd have the Jazz with *Rob Bogie*. The best of both worlds. Rob really kept the Jazz going there.

Tony H – Walkers remained a big home for us.

Bobby – But wherever we went, whatever the music policy, if we went there they'd play jazz for us. The DJ's would feed off us.

Andy - The only place in the North East you had to *really* dance later was Alex Lowes' session at *MacMillans* in Yarm. That's where we did all our challenging. That's where the big battles were. Musically, it was House and a little Jazz. What made it exceptional was 'who was there.' It was the most important session for the North.

Tony H – We traveled all over though, so we didn't get stale dancing to the same old records. Because the Southport Weekender was (and is) every six months, you had to keep on top of it and keep it fresh. It was heavy. It was Jazz all night. That was the gathering of the top dancers from everywhere. It was intense.

Rob – There was a lot of sparring sessions before the big battles, but they could be just as intense. They were relentless. The circles were aggressive.

Not that that bothered Andy.

Tony H – No. Bobby was the spirit of Bamboozle but Andy taught us to get straight in the middle and get on with it.

What style was Bamboozle?

Bobby – We'd take influences from whoever we saw.

Andy - Bamboozle were predominantly House dancers, but with Rob Hylton in it, it gave us depth

Tony H - We were *not* House dancers! You could do floorwork and footing to it, so it was a good warm up and practice, so when the Jazz came in you were ready.

Rob – We were Fusion really. IDJ were a big influence. We did a lot of floorwork. We were strong on that. I started to switch when I saw the *Brothers In Jazz*. Andy was hard Fusion 'kamikaze-style' but liked to do a bit of rough ballet too, to dance to the more lyrical jazz.

Andy - Also, it's worth pointing out that the difference between our Northern style of *Fusion* and the South was that: in the South, a dancer will be on his feet and doing floor work in equal amounts – up, down, up, down - but the North is: a bit of pre-emptive footwork and then get down and stay down. They don't get up. 80 to 90% of the set would be floorwork.

Bobby – We did floorwork together, not in a routine, but we'd be bouncing off each other or one would be under the other etc. We were the only crew that did that. We used it as a tool in battle: one of us would go in, and then the other, and we'd work together.

Andy - If I have to be honest, the dancers were my proteges. We danced very violently in Newcastle, we were very aggressive. We did it because we could: we would do drop kicks and bounce off each other and do 'scissors.' We'd practice hard, but this was only amongst ourselves; if we'd done that to another crew they'd have literally killed us.

Tony B - In clubs, Andy would always be the first on the floor because he wasn't scared of anyone. He loved challenges. He would always start by messing around on the floor, and when the challenges came, he'd turn on the juice and surprise them – this great big bald muscley White guy with the fast footwork. He'd throw me and Bobby in afterwards like cannon fodder to pick them off around the edges.

Tony H – Andy DJ'd too, and always had a bag of records with him when he went to clubs. He'd say "You got any Jazz? No? Well you have now"- tracks like *Mark Murphy – Red Clay* and *Dom Um Romao – Braun Blek Blu*. Those records were a signal. They'd start, and people came from nowhere to get 'at it.'

You did a lot of professional work.

Andy – The majority of the work was mainly me, Rob and Mans.

Bobby – We were starting to get very well known and getting offered gig's. Actually, our first one was dancing at the first rave for the famous 'Resurrection'- but dancing Jazz. We got t-shirts done, and went on from there. That was 1988. We got some great work like at the Theatre Royal along-side the Phoenix Contemporary from Leeds and Ballet Rombert...

Tony – ...and '89-91 was The Gateshead Garden Festival for a week; two shows a day.

What happened to Bamboozle?

Bobby – We never officially stopped, it was just by the early 90's people went off in different directions and had commitments.

Rob - I was lucky really after Bamboozle because I started at dance college in Leeds and there was still a scene there with *Gip, Chico* and *Lubi* which were the only Jazz sessions left in the North. I would knock heads with *Chris Hibbert* and *Derek Tauk*, and of course you had the Leeds dancers like *Miller (The Driller)* and *Mad Max.*

THE UNKNOWN TROOPERS
Rated Jazz Dance troupe from Darlington.

Zia Basit – The first time me and my friend Manjit Singh, saw Jazz dancing was at MacMillans. Dancers came from all areas. We started hanging around with two Black dancers called *Wayne Farquarsen* and *Winston Williams*- who were from a Breakdance background - and became The Unknown Troopers. We started having dance-offs against each other – Jazz dancing. Winston would still do some break moves and we'd say: "Don't do that, it's dead. It's history." We didn't have the balls to go to the dance-off at MacMillans, we'd just watch and learn. Manjit went to a club in Newcastle called *Liberties* and had a dance off with *Andy Bex.*

Wrong move.

(laughs) It *was* a wrong move. He got blown away but went away and practiced. He wouldn't be able to beat Andy, but got good enough to hold his ground. Manjit came to us with all these new (Fusion) moves and that's when we started getting better and better. Then we saw IDJ in the *Working Week -Venceremos* video which inspired us, and films with the Nicholas Brothers in, and we started ripping off their moves. We became quite good. It all came to a crunch at a club called *The Mall* (In Darlington): Graeme Park and Mike Pickering from the Hacienda were the DJ's. We were dancing – you know, nothing flash - and we got surrounded by two dancers from Coventry, two from Huddersfield and two from Manchester – maybe from *Fusion Beat*. Winston went in and started breakdancing and one of these guys threw a penny at him. Manjit slid in and did a spin, grabbed the penny and threw it out and did a few more moves, and those dancers, all of a sudden, were fighting to get in the circle. This was our first real confrontation. It was tough going because it was just me and Manjit against six but we went one-in one-out. We felt that we 'took' them that night.

That's all down to opinion though.

Yes. Well, we got a lot of respect in the area for it - all around town. There was another event three weeks later organized by *Alex Lowes*. and we could feel the tension. We knew Manchester were coming back down. The week before, I'd broken my toe so I wouldn't be dancing, but me and Manjit went - none of the other Troopers came down. We found out that three coaches were coming from Manchester and then they turned up, in their trench coats. When they walked in, the atmosphere changed, and they were going round the club looking for 'Unknown Troopers.' We went upstairs in the chill out area out of the way and about halfway through the night the DJ Graeme Park announced a dance competition between The Foot Patrol, Fusion Beat and The Unknown Troopers and we're thinking: 'What the fuck is going on here?' and then a spotlight came on us and we jumped under the table. We ended up walking downstairs toward the circle, but I just couldn't dance because of my toe. We saw Andy and Bobby from *Bamboozle* and they said that they'd help us out, but they weren't let in the circle. It went on for about an hour and Manjit stood his ground on his own. It was just him against the rest and he looked good. Toward the end, Andy and Bobby managed to jump in, but then disappeared after. Manchester claim they won but who knows? Trouble started to brew and we got out. We heard that there was a massive flare up and it went outside with the Manchester coaches fighting the police for an hour (note: This was nothing to do with Foot Patrol; who'd also left). Out of that night we got asked to dance on 'Hit Man And Her' on TV. We did other shows like fashion ones and we did one with Wayne

Sleep too. We became like legends in the Asian scene here. No matter what clubs we went to in the country, the Asians knew who we were.

When did The Unknown Trooper finish?

It never stopped officially, it just gradually stopped happening.

MANCHESTER

Although many areas had very strong Jazz Dance scenes (Birmingham's being the biggest, by far, outside of London), Manchester's had an entirely different flavour than London's. Of the many influential DJ's there (such as Greg Wilson at The Wigan Pier and Legends, and Hewan Clarke), there was none bigger than Colin Curtis. Through the association of the band Kalima (nee Swamp Children) and the Jazz Dance troupe The Jazz Defektors, Tony Wilsons 'alternative' music label *Factory* were the reluctant and unknowing leaders of a parallel Jazz Dance scene to Curtis' there, which stepped in and out of both Colins one (based around his club *Berlin* – one of the most important Jazz Dance-based sessions in the country), the London scene and the culture revolving around the worlds first super-club – based in Manchester *The Hacienda* (also owned by Tony Wilson). Following on from The Jazz Defektors world-wide success, the Foot Patrol and Fusion Beat troupes came through to make massive impact in the North

COLIN CURTIS

As a DJ, Colin Curtis is second to none. He is one of the most important Black music taste-makers there has ever been in the UK, and will be. His achievements in the Soul and Jazz Funk scene are well documented, but now it is time to tell how he instigated the Jazz Dance scene in the North.

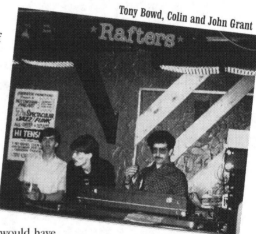
Tony Bowd, Colin and John Grant

I became a DJ in the 60's. I got into Black music when I was 10 or 11 years old through my best friends sister listening to Motown before she went out, and that was it. I was listening to pirate radio as well.

I had the first set of double decks up here; they were built in Staffordshire. I did weddings and childrens parties and all that. I was at grammar school and to DJ would have been unacceptable, I would have been expelled, so I changed my name. My real name is Colin Dimond. So I went through the phone directory and chose Kurtis (as opposed to Curtis). I developed a style that worked for me, for what I wanted to get across.

One of Colin's early clubs was The Magic Roundabout in 1969 and it was an all-nighter but not Northern Soul. It was 60's Soul, Motown, bands like American Poets, James and Bobby Purify, early R&B guys, Beach Boys, Marvin Gaye, The Equals. It was a top collectors club.

In the early 70's there were parallels here in the North to what was happening down South. Magazines such as Blues and Soul, and later, Black Echoes, helped bring the two scenes together (the North's Northern Soul and South's Import Funk and Soul new releases). You'd read about what was going on. Chris Hill was very critical of the structure of the Northern Soul scene but I don't believe, looking back at it, it was any different to the structure of what he was doing. I mean, we'd say "James Brown? What's he playing that for? Everyone in the U.S is playing that." People were going to London from here and going to the clubs as well. We had the Funk edge as well, it was there all the time. It may not have been perceived in the clubs but people were collecting it.

How do you think the Jazz Dance scene started up North?

It probably started in Birmingham, although nobody realized it was starting. There were a lot of mainly Black guys that were freestyle dancers, although there were Whites involved as well. The style was similar to the Jazz expression dancing that came later. They would dance to those long seven or eight minute Disco tracks and the odd Jazz instrumental: the kind of songs that wouldn't get played in a major club. The tracks would get played at a Birmingham club called *Chaplins*. It was a small club, with a great dance floor, which enabled you to experiment. The DJ was *Graham Warr*. Whether it was intentional or not, it meant a lot to the dancers. I've spoken to them individually, and experimenting was important to them. There was a great club in Manchester on Sundays called *Smartys* that I was doing with John Grant and I asked some of the great dancers if they'd come up from Birmingham and they turned up in a minibus. They came out to the dancefloor with black tights over their heads and frightened the shit out of everybody. They were doing organized routines and freestyling and they'd obviously worked hard at it.

People were experimenting with the music in the mid 70's, from the Soul scene to the break-away Jazz Funk scene; experimenting with Blue Note, C.T.I, George Benson, Johnny Hammond; stuff like this. The audience was intelligent enough to understand the music by these artists, and the 'game' was to look at the pictures on the Blue Note and C.T.I. inner sleeves of all of their catalogue and search them out. All of a sudden, through their own curiosity, some DJ's were starting to open up areas of music that would have been totally lost, had it not been for these one or two tracks that filtered through onto the club scene, and people started looking for other tracks by these artists, and the labels catalogue.

I started going to the Goldmine in 1978 and found my collection veering off, quite quickly to the Jazz. I couldn't pinpoint the transition of the Jazz Funk to Fusion, although, perhaps it's not a heavy record, I would say George Benson – The World Is A Ghetto would certainly have been one of those transitional tracks.

Exactly. Now there's a *Blackpool Mecca* track. A big, big tune; *Miroslav Vituous – New York City* – this big Disco track that has nothing to do with Disco - it's to do with Jazz. The Benson thing was a lot more poignant because before then you had the 'Superbad' album (with *Supership* on there, a big Northern Soul track).

You had Contempo record shop, in London (owned by Blues and Soul) pushing the 7's of Grover Washington on Kudu and Benson on C.T.I. I'd go down to the shop looking, essentially for Northern Soul, but I'd go in; I wanted all the knowledge, and I'd say to myself, "What do they hear in this?" and I'd come away with '*No Tears In The End*' on Grover Washington's *Kings Horses* album and I played it at *The Torch* and got this incredible response.

Instrumentals were very much a part of the 70's Northern scene: even *K- Gee by the Niteliters*, Psychedelic Soul - that's rooted in Jazz. Big record. So that helped me see the bigger picture. The odd 'odd ball' track used to come along and excite me more than the traditional stuff like The Zoo by The Commodores. I liked to play it and see 1,000 people dancing to it.

We got to the stage at The Blackpool Mecca when Ian Levine and me thought that Northern Soul was at an end. The Disco thing, for him, was big, but I wanted to go the Fusion and Soul route. We thought that we could no longer claim that The Blackpool Mecca was the epicenter for what was required, so I spent a few months visiting different club's in Manchester with a guy called Kev Edwards from Spin Inn Records (Manchester).

We started a residency at a club there called *Rafters* (September '78). There was a lot of seriously over the top music we got away with, with the Jazz Funk thing. We played music that would be totally unacceptable anywhere else. I would defy anyone – Blues And Soul magazine, or whoever – to have come up with a parallel.

I was doing all-dayers, playing to 1,500 to 2,000 people, and the small clubs, but, I believe it's the small club's where the general quality of music got better and better. People's expectations were higher. Feedback was important – good or bad – to keep you thinking; to give you new ideas.

At these times, nobody was doing a straight Jazz night, of course, but the turning point for me was: one night I was DJ-ing at Smartys and who should turn up? The ex-England football player Frank Worthington. He was dressed totally wrong for the club and looked out of place, but he stood by the DJ decks all night. I was playing basic Jazz/Funk Fusion and suddenly he asked me for the Jazz Saxophonist - Art Pepper. This absolutely blew me away! It got me thinking about how it fit's into the picture. This was a man ahead of his time and completely opened my eyes to the potential. If this guy responded like this then others would.

Eventually, as the Manchester scene grew, we decided to experiment with a 'Jazz-Only' night.

This was at *Rufus* in Fennel Street (June 81). We started with about twenty people and soon it got packed with a hundred and fifty. They started getting turned on to the bigger picture – to what you could get away with. We'd have people in from [what was to become] The Jazz Defektors dance group to Hewan Clarke.

Where were you buying your Jazz records from?

All over. *Piccadilly Records* – one of the few surviving ones from the sixties; *Robinsons* – which was essentially a cut-out-shop - where I discovered *Quartette Tres Bien – Boss Tres Bien*. I went back and bought the other eight albums by them. In the shop they'd have thick cardboard dividers with the 'band and titles' with 'date of arrival'; everything stock checked. There was *Jazz And Swing* and *The Diskery* in Birmingham. You'd go in with a few ideas and they (the owners and assistants) would help. These guys were fifty or sixty year's old, but they had ideas beyond anything that you could put in yourself. They used to bring out these 45's of 50's and 60's Jazz – it was crazy. I used to shop at Spin Inn – as I said earlier – and there was this big Jazz collector that used to go in there called Arthur. We used to have great conversations in there every Saturday morning, and I started to go to his house to look at his collection. The first time I went there I had no concept of what to expect: he pulled open these white wardrobe doors and I thought "Fucking Hell" – I nearly died. It was the best Jazz collection I'd ever seen in my life – not just from my perception, but anyone's. Original, pristine Blue Note's from 1958, all collected in sequence and in mint-condition. I learnt a hell of a lot from visiting and re-visiting and re-visiting. He had the respect for me through seeing me mentioned in Blues And Soul and he couldn't believe I was taking the time to visit him. I used to use his collection like a reference library, if you will. I never attempted to borrow any, but I thought: "Where am I going to find these records, let alone afford them?" These were original albums bought as new. To this day, it's the most phenomenal jazz collection I've ever seen.

Did you buy much stuff from Paul Murphy's shop *Fusions*?

Yes. I'd go to Paul's and I'd go to Mole Jazz in Grays Inn Road. When I got on the train to London, I knew I'd be coming back with something. Gilles Peterson used to drive me about looking for records and so did Pete Tong.

Brasilian was the toughest to find, but the DJ Hewan Clarke had a Brasilian friend who is a guitarist, and he'd say: "Colin, give me some Pounds", so I gave him £200, and he brought me back everything – *Ed Lincoln – Cochise*; you know, everything – and then I'd give him another £200.

Tell me about Hewan.

He is one of Manchester's own. He was one of the more important clients and one of the people whose opinion I would hold in high esteem. He developed his own Jazz thing.

Was he a headliner before you met him?

No. I don't think that Hewan had headlined in the way that he deserved to. He played some short sets at *Berlin* (April 83), but I almost always did it on my own.

What was different about Berlin?

I took the best of what happened before and repackaged it through there. It was special for me because I did the whole night. People accepted the different styles played, and danced to everything – the Soul one minute and the Latin and Jazz the next. The Jazz could even have been 'harder' than what would have been played at other's Jazz nights. The punters accepted the ride they were on – unlike The Blackpool Mecca (Highland Rooms) - "Oops. Here he goes again. Let's stand over here out of the way." (laughs)

How long did Berlin last?

Two years.

Birmingham was big for Jazz. The Jazz rooms at the all-dayers were second to none. *The Locarno* was the first place that we booked Paul Murphy (June 82).

Did Sheffield have much of a scene?

I would DJ there and John Grant, plus a guy called Neal Neale – who used to dabble with Jazz a bit. Sheffield had a big Black dance scene. The dancing was a sort of mixture between Freestyle (Ballet) and Steppers (Fusion) and that came out later as a pot-pourri at a club called *The Jive*

Turkey. Winston Hazel - the guy behind it – used to follow me around the club's of Manchester. Jive Turkey was the 'Hacienda' of Sheffield in it's day. The Jazz room was, musically, more Fusion and Vocal Jazz. I feel that Vocal Jazz was always more popular in the North than the South; very popular. We'd play forty five minutes worth sometimes.

You must be flattered to know that you achieved so much.

Historically, nothing can change – and I get a lot of comfort from that, as well as satisfaction. By 1986, I'd come to the end of my creative input, and then I became ill and went into semi-retirement. I had different considerations. Originally, though, there had been no specific music direction, but I stood there and made my feelings known and said "You must listen to 60's Soul", and then say "Hang on. What is this?" and then go in another direction .....The fact that I was allowed to operate in different scenes at what other people saw as high levels – yes, I'm very proud. I wouldn't change that for money.

NEIL RUSHTON

I haven't documented every Jazz Funk all-dayer, country-wide, that featured jazz, but, in the 70's, the Manchester Ritz and the Blackpool Mecca were so integral to the development of the Northern side of the Jazz Dance scene that their stories are more than worthy of inclusion. The midlands DJ Neil Rushton was the promoter of The Ritz and the equally huge all-dayers at The Mecca.

I DJ'd Northern Soul at The Catacombes in Wolverhampton, but I started off promoting in '75 in

TRENTHAM EXTRAVAGANZA

No. 1 ALL DAYER

SUNDAY 26th NOVEMBER, 1978
at TRENTHAM GARDENS, STOKE-ON-TRENT, STAFFS
12 noon - 11 p.m.

featuring the incredible DETROIT EMERALDS

WITH D.J.'s IN THE MAIN BALLROOM

From Stoke		Blackpool's No. 1		Birmingham's No. 1		Leeds No. 1
COLIN CURTIS	CHRIS BROWN	IAN LEVINE	KEV & ANDY	GRAHAM WARR	NEIL RUSHTON	IAN DEWHURST
Souths No. 1			Notts. No. 1		Walsall's No. 1	

In the Roman Bar with Gary and Tony playing the best in Jazz

A special attraction! SOUL at its best with OLDIES and NEWIES

with D.J.'s

SOUL SAM	CHRIS KING	PEP	KEITH MINISHULL	JOHN POOLE	ROB SMITH	BRIAN RAE	DAVE EVVISON

TRENTHAM, THE EVENT OF '78!   Advance Tickets £3.00
on the day £3.50

Queen Mary's ballroom at Dudley Zoo. It was Northern Soul, but we played new stuff too. It's not a retro scene like it is these days. From there I started doing all-dayers at *Tiffanys* in Coalville, which were very successful, and then I got *The Ritz* in Manchester - which was in Upper Whitworth Street – the same street as the famous *Twisted Wheel* club. It was amazing. I was only 21. I started with 300 people and by the end of the year I was getting 1700. The Blackpool Mecca 'Highland Room' with Colin Curtis and Ian Levine was the most influential, but it only held 300 and was weekly, but along with *Nottingham Palais, Cleethorpes Pier* and *Wigan Casino* we were the biggest event for Northern Soul in the North. We didn't take any prisoners, we had the best of everyone: *Colin Curtis, Ian Levine, Ian Dewhirst, Richard Searling* and *John Manship* playing Northern 60's to contemporary new releases.

I used to wholesale and distribute records from Tony Monson, and I started importing myself. I was getting test–pressings from wholesalers before the New York DJ's were getting them, plus I was the first staff writer at Black Echoes newspaper, and I ran the Northern Soul label 'Inferno,' so I had a lot of good connections

In '77/78 I started doing just 100% Northern Soul events and 100% Jazz Funk events, and the Jazz Funk ones went mega, on a massive scale. We put a lot of live acts on. It became the biggest Jazz Funk event North of London.

What was important about The Ritz was that, because it started as a Northern Soul venue, that crowd had a thirst for knowledge and it continued as a Jazz Funk venue. It was a great crowd. The music that was coming through was amazing. We did them every month; sometimes three weeks.

I saw in London that they were getting massive attendances at the *Purley all-dayers* (3,500) so, I thought, "Why couldn't we do that up here?" The scene was booming and I was well connected – now supplying eighty record shops in the North West alone, so I put on this all-dayer at The Blackpool Mecca and called it the 'Blackpool Mecca Soul Festival.' It was me, Colin Curtis and Ian Levine and whoever DJ-ing, with Brass Construction live in the ballroom with Northern Soul in the Highland room, and got 3,200 in. We followed future ones with live acts such as Players Association and Crown Heights Affair, and we did them until 1980, where the live act was Ronnie Laws. We had big trouble with a gang from Moss Side and at the Mecca in August a girl got stabbed getting out of the way of gang violence between a gang from Bradford and Moss Side. It spoilt the whole thing.

Were you aware of the whole Jazz thing coming through in the late 70's?

Yes, we encouraged it. We loved the Jazz Fusion, it was fantastic wasn't it? Everyone - except for Ian Levine, of course - went for the Jazzy side of things. Colin would go for something that was really heavy and really underground. It got adopted wholesale. There was a lot of Jazz Fusion played at the all-dayers – no compromise. It all fitted in together.

RICHARD SEARLING

Not a heavy session, but the legendary, barrier-breaking Soul DJ had his finest hour –Jazz Funk-wise – at Angels. The night has been much talked about by others and, so, is rightly included here.

Angels in Burnley started in '77. We did a specialist night on a wednesday. *Rafters* and *Rufus* were already doing well in Manchester so the formula was already established. I was the resident and had semi-regular guests and because I was working for RCA I could get great P.A's there. We had a dance competition and Bootsy Collins was one of the judges. Bootsy was spotted in a fish and chip shop in Accrington in his full gear! It was the middle of nowhere so there was no passing trade, so the people that were there were there for a reason. A lot of people traveled from everywhere.

I was buying a lot of 12"s from John Anderson at *Soul Bowl* who was getting stuff people didn't even know was on 12" and I was playing some of that, but it was a more commercial night than a Colin Curtis night.

John stayed at my house for four nights when we were producing the demos for *Joy Division* and I still couldn't get him to the club. That's John isn't it?

The night lasted for a couple of years and was totally successful. It was a nice change from all the Northern Soul gigs I was doing. I didn't know much about this scene like I did with Northern at the Wigan Casino but it was fresh. It was a memorable time in my life and very unique in my career.

"I used to go up to Angels in Richards car.
Was the Jazz quite heavy?
It was more of a Jazz Funk club really. But it was a very influential session.
Up alongside Colin Curtis sessions?
I wouldn't quite put it like that. Colin was out on his own. I'm sure Richard would agree that, in that scene, Colin was King."

PC – The Jazz Defektors

HEWAN CLARKE

In the North, there was Colin and then there was Hewan. In some-ways, he became the 'people's champion' in the 80's, and was known for his impeccable taste (as well as being a rated dancer). Not only was his finest-hour opening for Curtis at the legendary Berlin but he was also the original DJ at the famous Hacienda –

but that's another story.
I was always into Reggae and then I heard some Herbie Hancock somewhere….
In the clubs?
No. I wasn't going to those kinds of clubs, but I got into Jazz through him and just stopped listening to Reggae altogether. I was just collecting it to listen to at home. I didn't become a DJ until the early 80's. Some of the Jazz Defektors asked me to DJ at a party for them.
They just knew you had a great Jazz collection.
Yeah. I didn't know Colin (Curtis) or anything then.
You hadn't gone to any of his clubs at that point?
No, no. We used to go to Placemate 7 on the other side of town, we didn't know about *Rafters* at the time, and one day, these fantastic dancers came into the club and *wowed* the place spinning on the floor and all that. I said: "Where did you learn to dance like that?" and they said Rafters, so the following week we went down there and it was 'love at first sight': the music, the atmosphere, the great dancing.
I suppose you could relate to the music.
Totally. Straight away. In fact some of what was being played I had. That was how I met Colin: I'd go to the DJ box and say "Have you got so-and-so's version of this?" and he'd say "No" and I'd bring it the following week and we realized that we had a very similar taste. My crowd used to follow Colin everywhere - up to Stonehaven in Scotland, everywhere. We'd dance to every track.
You were too young to remember *The Reno*, in Moss Side.
The Reno? It's been demolished now but I used to sneak out when I was young and go there in the early 70's. I know the DJ Persian very well and his partner Cooley, It was an illegal club. It's been in Manchester since the 40's. When I went, it was run by an African guy called Phil. Persian would DJ on one deck and play entirely different stuff than you'd hear in town. They'd go for album tracks.

Colin Curtis told me he used to go to the Reno and stand by the deck all night just listening. He didn't know Persian and vice versa, and he used to think: "I've got that album but never thought of playing this track." He said it was a strange crowd, with pimps and pros-

THE
NEW RENO CLUB
208 Moss Lane East
(entrance Princess Road)
Manchester 14

MEMBER'S CARD

No.

Name

Expiry Date

Secretary

ANY MEMBER OR GUEST WHO CAUSES A DISTURBANCE OR USES VIOLENCE IN THE CLUB WILL HAVE THEIR MEMBERSHIP CANCELLED FORTHWITH

titutes and drunkards and gangsters

It was open from 11a.m. till 6 a.m, - sometimes it was open till the last person left – perhaps 9'oclock. The Reno had a deadly reputation. If you had any decency about you, you wouldn't be seen there (laughs). It was just a little club with a sound system. You'd get Irish labourers, criminals, prostitutes who'd finish work at 4am and wanting a drink, you'd get a lot of stars of stage and screen - people that you'd see on TV. Fights would go off. It was sweaty, hot, sticky and there was a little side room where they would gamble. Persian used to play Soulful Jazz like *Grover Washington - Inner City Blues*. You knew what you were going to get at Rafters but you didn't at The Reno!

This party that you did for the Jazz Defektors – were they called that then?

No, they were called The Prophets then.

Right, well was it a one off or did you do many nights?

I did it every week, playing Jazz. It was at *Rufus*. This was after Colin had stopped DJ-ing there. There wasn't that many people there. It was a mid - week thing. It was a turning point for me because there was a crowd in the corner smoking dope that used to come every week and they turned out to be a mixture of *Kalima* and *A Certain Ratio* and they took me on tour with them as a DJ support playing Jazz. Tony Wilson (Factory Records owner) was their manager, and he said to me that in two years he was going to open a club and he did - it was the Hacienda, and that's when it took off for me. I worked every night it opened (May '82). When the Hacienda got going I was able to slip in a few Jazz tracks, mid tempo Latin things: *Crickets Sing For Anamaria,* that kind

of thing. My whole idea was to get the women to dance because I hated the whole eliteness of the scene. It was just totally men. Going into Rafters and seeing the women take on the men, I was like "Wow, we need to spread this out", that was always my aim. I never really played for the men.

You never played mental stuff?

No, no, the fastest I ever played was *Listen Love* by *Jon Lucien*. I used to play really slow stuff.

How did *Berlin* come about (April 83)?

At the time it was a 'New Romantic' club and was the trendy club in Manchester until the Hacienda opened. The DJ there, Steve, said: "Can't you come and do a night?" and I only agreed if I could bring someone with me – because all I wanted to do was to listen to Colin play. All I did was provide the club for him. It took months before it worked and all of a sudden it just did.

It used to be called The Apartment.

That's right. It had one of the best sound systems. It sounded brilliant. I wanted to dance and there was only one man for me, and that was Colin. This club worked beautifully.

Was Berlin the main Jazz club for you?

Yes, because Rafters was a soul club that had a Jazz break but Berlin was a Jazz club that had a Soul break. It was a dancers club – specifically a dancers club. There wasn't much standing around! I got there at 9 o'clock and the dancers had it all to themselves and we'd practice our moves. I'd put a record on and go out and dance, practicing, and when people came into the club we'd show off. In those days the girls were into the dancers. If you couldn't dance you didn't stand a chance (laughs). It was a very mixed cross-cultural club and scene. There used to be a couple of White guys with the Jazz Defektors originally, but when the Birmingham dancers came up, they were all Black. Birmingham were the best.

Yes, In London it was predominantly Black but in Essex, where it started in the South, it was predominantly White, and the home counties.

No, there was none of that. It was totally mixed. We'd go to *The Rum Runner* in Birmingham and watch them. We'd all have a particular favourite whose style we'd copy and take back up to Manchester. You ask any one of the JD's where they got their style from and they'll name a particular person. There was a lot of that. I remember going to Rumrunners and seeing *Hot Gossip* (the famous famous TV dance group) and, not just for us, but the Birmingham guys too, this was where a lot of the new moves were coming from. They were brilliant. They were trained dancers and we were going 'Fuckin' Hell how did you do that?" From there we started watching 'Oklahoma' and 'Seven Brides For Seven Brothers' - all those old musicals - we'd get the moves from them. I remember, at Berlin, they didn't sell much drink at the bar because we'd drink water from the taps in the toilets so, once, the manager turned the taps off (laughs). Berlin was the perfect club. It started just at the right time.

When did it finish? Was there a big last night?

No. It was at the beginning of the gangster thing and they started coming so the numbers started to drop. Colin was ill at that time and had to put replacement DJ's in. We were very particular about the sounds there but the guests played it too commercial and it finished it really.

Mike Shaft was one of them.

He had a show on Piccadilly Radio and he'd get me in to play three Jazz tracks every week.

Do you remember any stories from any of the Northern all-dayers that you did?

I remember one all-dayer when it got tear-gassed and the takings stolen, but no.... it was a family. It was all excellent. There was none of this gangster violence, shooting or kniving, and fighting - that was done on the floor with feet! A lot of friendly rivalry.

GREG WILSON

Another pioneering DJ. Before he put his neck on the line for Electro and Electronic Black Dance music in the early 80's, his two most famous club's - The Wigan Pier and Legend had a big following with the Jazz Dancers from all over the North and midlands.

I'm from New Brighton, the other side of the river Mersey. The biggest fallacy about the North of England was that, musically, it was all Northern Soul, which wasn't the case in Liverpool. It never took off there. In 1979 it was more Disco and Jazz-Funk. My inspirations were Les Spaine, and a guy from Radio Merseyside called Terry Lenniane. The music they played filtered through to the other DJ's in Merseyside. I DJ'ed in a commercial club in my home town for four nights a week and I had them packed. I started being able to slip in Jazz Funk imports alongside Funk and Soul. You could only take it so far obviously.

In 1980, through a friend - Nicky Flavell, I got a residency at the club *The Wigan Pier*, in Wigan, doing Tuesday, Thursday, Friday and Saturdays. Tuesday night was Jazz Funk and it was already successful for Nicky when I took it over (he left to open a sister club down the road in Manchester called *Legend*).

There was no Black population in Wigan and yet you would get 500 Blacks from all over to come to the night. Because it was a big night, I started to be invited to DJ on the all-dayers, and eventually I became a headliner. By August of 1981 I was offered Wednesdays at Legends, which took off after a while. There were always jazz-spots played at both. They became dominant.

Jazz was being played everywhere. Obviously, Colin Curtis was a specialist; you couldn't compete with Colin on that level because he was an obsessive. He had to have everything. He was a connoisseur. As a Jazz DJ you couldn't go beyond Colin, although I like to think I was playing some of my own discoveries. I played all styles of Black music as a professional DJ, but was known for my jazz. It particularly domineered in 1980, and of course you had all those Japanese Jazz albums coming through. Because they were twice the price of a British album, not everybody could afford them, and it became a bit elitist. I think that by 1983, the Jazz Fusion dancing was having to make way for the Break dancing that was coming in. Both my clubs were the top in the North, and were Electro dominated, whereas Colin Curtis refused to play Electro. You would never hear anything like that at his night at Berlin. It was Soul and Jazz and, really, it was one of the last nights like that in the North. Jazz had gone in the North by 1984.

KERMIT

Real name Paul Leveridge, Kermit became famous in the early 90's as part of the famous UK Hip Hop outfit The Ruthless Rap Assassins, and shortly after co-fronting Black Grape - formed by ex-Happy Mondays leader Shaun Ryder. Way before his stardom though, he was rated as one of Manchesters hot young (16 years old) Jazz Fusion dancers. Always eager for a battle, he was also the most faithful of supporters of DJ Greg Wilson.

The best was a guy called *Tay Narna*. He had some moves. He was in a crew with me called The Scorpions. We used to live for the jazz-breaks. We'd polish our *patents* ready for them.

As you were a Fusion dancer, what did you feel about *The Jazz Defektors* style of dancing?

They're old school *jazz-ballet*. Fair play. Great stuff, but we'd dance on one side of the dancefloor and they'd be on the other.

Was there much inner-area competition?

Yes, you'd have other crews from South Manchester, Moss Side, Longseight, Old Trafford..... but when we went outside, we were all Mancunian. People would travel back then, to all-dayers all over the place. I'd get a train even if I didn't have money for the fare. Sometimes I'd get thrown off!

Did you go to Colin Curtis' clubs?

Yes. I went to Rufus and Rafters – even though I was too young – and later – Berlin. I used to like watching Carl Lloyd and Saltz and a crew called The Westerners dance. It made me want to practice, and then, the next thing is: you're tearing people up! You know what the music's like – sometimes you hear a tune and *lose* it! I used to follow the DJ *Greg Wilson* up and down the country because he used to play the tunes. His clubs Legends and Wigan Pier were excellent.

You know, I'd go to all-dayers especially to battle certain people that I'd hear about. Once, there was some guy from Nottingham telling everyone that he was going to beat me, so I went down there and mashed him up. I didn't always win though. That was the way it was. You'd even battle a man for the right of a girl!

You had to look good when you were challenging. I used to travel to London to get my *spats* from *Shelley*s in Oxford Street. I had some *puttees* as well, that I would wear over white shoes – poor mans spats, but I had a special pair for the weekend and I'd clean them with a toothbrush. If someone trod on your spats when you were dancing there'd be a fight!

PETER HAIGH

This respected DJ, Journalist, Radio Presenter and Black Music archivist over-saw it all – from the Northern side of things – so here are his recollections and own achievements.

The 'Mecca' effect is what I see as the birth of the Jazz Dance scene in the North west; unintentionally, and then it was developed at the all-dayers.

Some records I remember from the Mecca were *Soul Yogi – Freddie McCoy* – that was massive – *Soul Improvations – Van McCoy* that had a Jazz feel, but the one record I think started it off was *Zola – King Errisson*. That's just a piece of 7inch Jazz. The steps you had to throw to that were fast because it was an intricate record. You wanted to dance to it and you couldn't do the normal steps you would do to Northern Soul, you had to be light on your feet. There was the other stuff *The Nightlighters – K-Gee, Gil Scott Heron – The Bottle*..... It was all new then. The last hour there Colin played a lot of esoteric stuff. He'd played a lot of that *Donald Byrd* and *Mizell Brothers* productions stuff; *Gene Harris – Los Almitos Latinfunklovesong, Johnny Hammond – Los Conquistadores Chocolates* was massive. A lot of the disco was very Jazzy then. Ian Levine went more 'disco' and Colin Curtis moved to Manchester and the rest is history.

Around '78 you started to see dancers from Birmingham at *Rafters* that were different – quite funky but doing things like shadowing each other. They were very inspiring. The sounds started to get more eclectic: you started to get stuff like *Judy Roberts – Never Was Love* and *Jeff Lorber – Samba* type stuff.

1980-81 – Casinellis was a strange choice of venue. It was a club for diners. It had a stone floor and two floors. You started seeing this intense dancing from a Black-led crowd – mainly from the midlands. If you couldn't cut it, you didn't go on the floor. I didn't have the edge but I could hold my own. You started getting odd-ball Fusion records played, like *Roy Hayes – Vistalite* or *Janet Lawson - Dindi*. It was the first time I started to hear some proper *Blue Note* Jazz, and vocal Jazz as well. You never heard old records before, you see. I remember someone moaning "Oh they're going further and further back like the fucking Northern Soul scene. You can hear the crackles on the records." It started to drive some of the people off the scene. They thought it was getting too retro and esoteric. It was obvious that a specialist night was needed.

It was hard to play Jazz up here after 1984. *Berlin* was about the only place you could hear it. It just started sounding too odd hearing it in a mainstream club in the middle of the night next to the latest Electro–flavoured club music or the contemporary Soul of the time. To be honest, with horrendous Jazz records being made by *Shakatak, Mezzoforte* and *Rah Band*, I'd rather play a *D-Train* record anyway. The Black crowd went with the Electro. Berlin was a shit–hole and very bohemian. The Jazz that was played there was the seminal stuff that you later heard on the *Jazz Juice* and *Blue Note* compilations, amongst other stuff. When Colin had his bouts of illness, Hewan did the main spot and I came up to do the back-up for the last year; which I'm very proud of.

There was no influence up here from all that 'Soho – Absolute Beginners – Sade' scene down South. Factory Records in Manchester took a little interest with *Kalima* playing down there and I also knew Barney from *New Order* took an interest too, and wanted to know what that underground Jazz Dance scene was all about.

By '87, Jazz was finished up here. Colin was ill and there didn't seem to be anyone to play to. It was all about the man - Colin Curtis.

Where were you Dj'ing?

My main residencies were the last days of The Mecca (summer '80); Scarthwaite Hall at Lancaster - which ran from '79 to '85. A lot of Jazz got played there like *Chick Corea – The Slide* and *McCoy Tyner – Love Samba*. It had a loyal local following. It was a club that was spoken about. I also did *Man Fridays* in Blackpool and I was on the all-dayer circuit too.

KALIMA

Other than the DJ's, this band were one of the original and most important things – alongside The Jazz Defektors – to come out of the Northern side of the Jazz Dance movement. Even more interesting is, that they were on the Factory record label - one of the most important 'alternative music' labels ever, alongside band's like *Joy Division* and *A Certain Ratio*. I interviewed sister and brother Anne and Tony Quigley.

Anne - In the mid 70's we used to go to a club in Wythenshawe called *Mad Movies* and the DJ was a guy called Mike - who was an ice cream man, You had faces like *Donald Johnson* (From the band A Certain Ratio), *Leroy Richardson* – who went on to run *The Hacienda*, myself, and lots of others. Mike would play from Soul to Funk like Fatback Band, Ohio Players, Rufus, Manu Dibango..... it seemed hard core for a 13 year old.

Tony - The music had more of an edge. He DJ'd at Bagley Hall to a youth club in Withernshaw.

Anne - People would follow him around and worshipped him as a DJ, and now, jump a few years past Punk and we were all living in Hulme. Anyone that was an artist or musician seemed to live there, and on Fridays we would go round the corner to Royce Road to *The Russell Club* – which was managed or promoted by Alan Wise (who went on to manage *Nico*). It was a Reggae club which dropped the odd 'soul' track. *Factory* took over (Friday nights) which was run by Tony Wilson and Alan Erasmus with Rob Gretton.

Tony - As well as the typical 'Factory' music for the 'raincoat brigade' we were going to other clubs too. We weren't Soulboys as such, but we'd go to those nights. The father of our sax player John was a big Jazz fan and through him, we'd be listening to *Miles Davis – Bitches Brew* and *Herbie Hancock – Headhunters* and *Airto* – that was how we got into it.

Anne - Then *Legends* came along with Colin Curtis. He had a God -like aura about him. People were in awe of his name.

Tony - It was Greg Wilson's night.

Tell me about *The Swamp Children*.

Anne - We had a punk–like attitude. None of us could play at the time but got a band together. We said we'd give ourselves six months before we do our first gig. Our friends, *A Certain Ratio*, shared a rehearsal room called The Rialto with *Joy Division* so they said that when they weren't rehearsing we could use the room, so Ceri Evans (who later became a well known keyboard player in the Jazz, Acid Jazz, Drum & Bass and UK Garage scenes) came up from London and we formed the Swamp Children. We used to borrow the instruments. We went to Sheffield to do a recording at *Cabaret Voltaire's* studio and Simon Topping (from ACR) said he'd produce it. It was called *The Little Voices*. You could hear that we were listening to Miles and Herbie – in a Punk-like way. Factory didn't know what to make of us: we were getting write-ups in Blues & Soul and Black Echoes and this confused Factory – it wasn't their area. They didn't know the DJ's that we worshipped so it was strange, but they stuck with us. They couldn't work out what we were doing, but they gave us the benefit of the doubt at the time

We used to support ACR on their gig's as it was a way of getting to play, and we had *The Jazz Defektors* dancing as well. It was quite a different gig than what people were used to. People compared both of us and said that we sounded like ACR, but that's because we had the same record collections. Both bands together sounded like *all* the influences *all* at the same time. *Southern Freez* by *Freez* was a big influence on us - Jazzy Funky with a girl singer - and so was the whole Funkadelic thing.

We got to know The Jazz Defektors from seeing them at a club called Fevers and *Hewan Clarke* was the DJ. Us, ACR and Mikey Wilson and others would go and watch them on the dancefloor. It was beautiful, graceful and balletic. They looked and dressed immaculate. We used them on a gig with us and ACR at Heaven in London and we all became like a tight gang after that.

You were all regulars at Colin Curtis' night at *Berlin*. What did you think about it?
Anne - Berlin was amazing. Colin was given free reign and could probably take more chances there than perhaps some other places that he'd played at. It was sophisticated and inspiring. The music he played was quality, vintage wine, and it's as simple as that.

How did Kalima start?
Anne - We didn't think the name suited us any more so we changed it to Kalima - after an Elvin Jones album track. Factory records didn't understand, and we told Rob Gretton (the label manager) that we were going more Latin, and he said: "What's Latin?!" We did our first single, which was *Fly Away,* and then we did a Sarah Vaughan song called *Smiling Hour*, which had a couple of the Jazz Defektors on backing vocals. They came from singing lessons with me.

From playing all over the country, did you see much difference area-to-area?
Anne - The dance scene at The Wag was a different dance scene to a Colin Curtis night up here. You'd see people like *Slim Gaillard* there as a regular and *Jerry Dammers* and *Robert Elms* from The Face magazine. People would do a type of 'couples dance' – not a Jive, but that kind of thing.

That was a Wag thing, not typical of other Southern clubs.
Anne - The scene was bigger in London. We always felt welcome there. When we played here (In Manchester) we did get going what was happening there but on a different scale. We thought we'd put on our own gigs and we used a club called *The Tropicana* which had plastic palm trees and all that. We printed our own 'Blue Note' style posters and sold merchandise. We were trying to do what they were doing at The Wag. No one else did it, and everyone would come because it was different. It was great and everyone was stylish.

Tony - It was a huge venue and we'd advertise it as a gig with us and ACR with Hewan, and we'd got Paul Murphy up. It confused people because, obviously you'd get the 'Factory' records followers that wouldn't understand it and then the DJ's playing to some people standing around. It was a mish-mash.

Anne - It did annoy some people, but we thought "Why shouldn't we have nights like this?"
How many of these events did you put on?
Anne - Absolutely loads.

With our gang of us and ACR we didn't have any fear about whether you could or could not do anything musically or dance wise.

The Punk ethic.

Anne – Well actually, the first concert I ever went to was the *Sex Pistols* when I was 14. This boy on the bus that I used to drawings of David Bowie for – for 50p or fish and chips – had got a band together and asked me to come and support them – they were called *Slaughter And The Dogs*. They were supporting the Sex Pistols. I know it sounds like a cliché, but seeing them as your first gig gave you a feeling in your heart that anything was possible, and I think that whole thing – Swamp Children, ACR, Jazz Defektors, us - was all about that. There has to be more than just listening to Coltrane, Hancock, Davis to get you to take up the sax: its your friends. This attitude was all over the country, doing the same thing, the same influences, with different accents and faces.

Its funny that outside of the Colin Curtis scene, there was another one in Manchester that revolved around Factory records, and Tony Wilson probably didn't really want that, as it wasn't what 'Factory' was all about.

Anne - He stuck with it, which was great, but it was funny because, in the US for some reason, our records would be higher up the college radio charts than *New Order*, and Tony just couldn't work it out.

Tony - We were so influenced by so many different styles of music. We weren't purist. We weren't an out-and-out Jazz group, and I quite liked that. There was a lot of soul and energy.

Anne - We were in it for the fun and games more than anything else. Jazz wise, it was the media that categorized us. We just did what we fancied.

Tony - It was good when we were busy and the crowds were good and we had records but we needed a good manager, so we missed a lot of business opportunities.

What happened to Kalima?

Anne - In the late 1980's you didn't get a look in Manchester unless you were a boy band wearing baggy clothes – the whole 'Madchester' scene. It had all changed. In London it was great because you could play at The Bass Clef, The Wag or Dingwalls and get excellent reactions, but by the early 90's it was hard supporting eight band members. We weren't in it for the money but some of the band were grumbling about wages. It had run it's course. It wasn't like a gang anymore. I felt that I could, and would, come back to music, so I stopped and had a little girl.

THE JAZZ DEFEKTORS

One of the original crews that turned professional. Like all noted crews, the JD's comprised of the very best dancers in Manchester. From performing as a troupe they became a band and recording artists, and went on to achieve heights only dreamt of in our scene; crossing over in to the pop market too!

Saltz -I played football at a high level and all the players were fashionable and went to the right clubs . I picked up that knowledge of clothes and dance steps and I'd bring it back to people of my own age. If you go out with an older crowd, you think older, then you see who's doing what. I was about 15 years old then.

Who were the older rated dancers?

Saltz -There was groups of guys. *Medwin Bowry, Clifton Crawford, Essie* and a guy called *Billy*. You could even put P.C in there – who later joined us. Before those guy's, I remember two amazing girl Jazz dancers *Debbie* and *Kadria*, her partner *Lloyd* and *Sly Gooden*. People didn't know surnames back then, but they must be mentioned. They were very important. To be honest though, I didn't realize there was a superiority in dancing until I saw the Birmingham dancers: The *Twins* (Rick and Ty) and *Carl and Lance Lowe*. I thought: "I like that. I want to do that," and I decided to form my own 'firm.' I went around - like in the 'Magnificent 7' film - rounding up dancers, *Barrington, Mark Swaby, Wayne Metcalf* (who was White), and later, *Tony Blades* [who was also White]. I didn't mess about, I took the best dancers. P.C joined eventually and we traveled everywhere. We'd never dance at Birmingham though. It seemed almost sacrilegious. I was used to playing in teams and wanted it run like that. As the older dancers petered out it gave us free reign.

Tell me about this Northern dancefloor hierachy.

The Jazz Defektors. Photo by Kevin Cummins

Saltz - Well, I was already in the middle of the floor looking out, so, I don't know how it looked from the outside. There were loads that you had to go through to earn your place. It was unspoken but people just knew. If we ignored some challengers it was for their own good to save them embarrassment. If you get assassinated on the dancefloor, you can't recover. It was a serious game.

In Leeds challengers would say 'contact' or 'no contact' did you have that in Manchester?

Saltz -Yes we did. But if you're at a certain level, you just say: "We don't even acknowledge you. You're not at our level." The problem with 'contact' is that it would cross over to fisticuffs. Also, you're getting embarrassed in front of women, and men ridiculing you til your dying day until you come back stronger. It's fighting talk.

Mark Swaby -The first time we saw Jazz dancers was when a load came up to *Rafters* from Birmingham. They came in with their long leather coats and rolled up hats 'took the floor' and took the women (laughs)! They came up often. At the same time there was a lot of competition between the Manchester crews from Longsight, Wythenshawe, the Westerners from Moss Side...and we said "We want to be top dogs." I met Saltz at Rafters and we danced a lot together, then Barry came in and Tony Blades – a guy from Sheffield who moved up here, and a white guy called Wayne.

Barrington Wilks – We met Wayne when us four starting going to Birmingham, watch the dancing, come back and train and copy the moves. We saw this white guy who was great and got him to join up with us back home.

Mark – We nearly got into trouble because we wouldn't dance and me and Saltz had the reputation of being the best dancers. We were the pinnacle, so people wanted to take us on, so we thought, "Lets get to a position where they'd have one dance and never bother again because they'd know that we're too good for them," so that's when we started going to Birmingham – *The Locarno* all-dayers. There were people there from all over the country - I couldn't say where though, we never used to talk to anyone.

Barry – We were there just for one thing – to steal moves (laughs)!

Mark – We met Hewan Clarke and we used to go to his bed-sit and listen to all his Jazz. He had an amazing collection. We used to practice there. We told him of our ambition to form a band and for him to DJ so it was the full package. The only time he really played *just* Jazz things was at Berlin. Anyway, we went out and bought carpet jeans and jacket, brown suede boots and cutaway t shirts and rolled up hats and went to an all-dayer in Manchester – everyone was there – and we did our thing and killed it. They never bothered us again after that.

Barry – We didn't really welcome other dancers. The dance floor was a battleground and it took ages to be the masters of it so there was no way we were going to give it away. It was our territory.

Mark – Once you own it then you could bring people in

Barry – But we never did (laughs).

Saltz - Our first professional work was dancing with A Certain Ratio. We were dancing to a whole different crowd who knew nothing about our scene. We were friends with Kalima too. They were on our wavelength and loved their Jazz. Another influence was Chris Sullivan's band Blue Rondo A La Turk, Pig Bag, Rip Rig And Panic....

Those last two were 'Punk Jazz'.

Yeah, but it was all quintessentially English - plus the Jazz acts like *Paz* and *Onward International*. Blue Rondo were stylish.

Was that how you got into the 1950's look?

They played a role, plus those 50's musicals. My mum used to run a cinema and they'd show classic film musicals and I'd get them to run those privately and we'd check them out. Bernstein, Cole Porter...the music was very jazzy.

I was told that you were all influenced by those 50's musicals.

Mark – Guys And Dolls, Seven Brides and particularly West Side Story. It was a particular style - Bob Fosse, the choreographer.

Were you dancing on the floor like that?

Mark – Well we debate that. Some of us say the more balletic side of Gene Kelly, others say Fred Astaire. We got into the Nicholas Brothers but West Side Story had it all: the dancing, the music, everything – especially the 'school hall dance.' We ransacked that film! We liked the Latin music in it as well as the Jazz.

Mark – By now, we were at the forefront at Berlin. Colin influenced us but we also influenced Colin. Talking about it with him, he would try different things out on us. The band's Kalima and A Certain Ratio used to go there and they were on Factory and we got to know them and starting practicing at The Hacienda. The label and club were owned by the owner of factory records and TV presenter Tony Wilson and we danced on his show.

Saltz - As dancers, we were getting booked at all these trendy events by PR companies, getting in all the major fashion magazines and TV programmes like The Tube. It gave us kudos. We had this aura and mystique and moved as a 'massive.' What happened was we ended up too big for our environment. In fact no one could breathe - we'd transcended the scene leaving a gap for another to take over.

So when did you form the band?

Mark – We did backing vocals on the track *Shining Star* by Kalima. We did a pseudo – audition for it. Wayne realized he wasn't cutting it - we said we wanted to form a band but he didn't want to do it, he wanted to form another, but nothing came of it. Tony Blades moved up to Nottingham to be with his girlfriend and we got P.C in. He was the main dancer in Manchester then.

PC - I turned them down at first. There was a lot of rivalry on the dance floors; guys from North Manchester going down as a team, from the South, from Hulme, Moss Side, but I never affiliated myself to one particular one, I just wanted to be on my own. After a while, when the scene died down a bit, I decided to keep my hand in as I wasn't dancing much anymore, and joined the Jazz Defektors.

Mark -We got him to do this video called 'Hanky Panky' with us.

Saltz - I said to our manager Tony Wilson that I'd like to make this micro-musical like 'West Side Story'. Gang culture was taking off in Manchester, so I had this idea for a 'Moss Side Story', we used bits of Jazz tracks that Hewan had. I don't know how Factory got clearance for all those. This is when we started thinking about making our own music. The tracks that Colin Curtis or Hewan were playing that we'd like to dance to were so rare and obscure, there was no way that we'd be able to get hold of certain tracks to dance to, it was becoming a problem.

PC -We were dancing at The Hacienda one Saturday night to this track called *Bahia* by *Willie Bobo* and people thought that it was our track and we were miming to it, and our friend Nick said "Why don't you try and form a band?" which we'd never considered. None of us were musicians, and the next thing we knew, we'd been offered to support Sade at The Ritz in Manchester.

Mark -We felt confident we could do it because the backing vocals sounded good on the Kalima track.

PC - We only had a month, with no songs and no musicians! With help from A Certain Ratio, Kalima and a Fusion band called Isis, we, together, wrote half a dozen songs. We went down a storm at The Ritz, and through that we got some TV work..

Barry – It went amazing. We then did our first gig on our own. We 'hand did' the posters and fly posted. We thought ten people would turn up.

Mark – But it was choc-a-bloc. Jazz was a big thing in Manchester at the time.

PC – With the JD's, I had to change my style completely to a more 'Balletic' style, and I started going to *Berlin*. It was where I really got into Mambo. Colin played some obscure shit.

Mark – We did get influenced by all that. We started listening to Tito Puente, Machito, Chano Pozo, Eddie and Charlie Palmieri. The faster the Mambo the better.

Barry – We liked all that 1950's Cuban style of dress too, like you see in Guys And Dolls. We were influenced by all that heavily.

Was that just stage-wear?

Barry – No we were in it everyday. Anything that reflected Cuban 50's we liked. It all fitted in really: the music we listened to, the way we dressed; the way we danced.

That's why Chris Sullivan liked you and Brothers In Jazz to go to The Wag because you suited the environment that he had there.

Saltz – Well, the concept of The Wag was what we'd have liked to do, which is what we tried to cultivate at Berlin.

And Kalima did at The Tropicana.

Saltz - The first time we went to The Wag, we were there dancing with Kalima. We dressed like we were Wag regulars, and then a certain set of music came on and 'Bam.' I wouldn't like to have been another dancer in there.

"When Kalima played The Wag we got there anyway we could. I remember the Jazz Defektors scaring the fuck out of the London guys. It was a completely different style. They took the floor that night."

Dean Johnson

People came from nowhere - directors, producers, women. We'd definitely arrived. The Wag became our club like The Electric Ballroom was IDJ's. It was our lifestyle there. I went to The Electric Ballroom to watch. There was no stand-out's, but there was an overall style of dancing. If we'd lived in London it would have been all over.

Mark – Julien Temple was at The Wag that first night and that's how we ended up in the film. We got a call.

Barry – That film was meant to be the saviour of the British film industry - the big film of the Jazz scene. It was nothing to do with it. It was a brilliant experience though: I'd never done it before.

Mark – It didn't represent what was going on, but for four Black boys from the ghetto in Manchester doing a major film was exciting.

Saltz – Originally, we had a massive part in the film, but the US finances fell out and the concept of the film changed. We still got a great feature in the film.

You must have used the publicity to push the band

Barry – Yes, we did well out of it but when the film flopped we distanced ourselves from it!

Mark – People booked us because of it.

The Art Blakey documentary that you did – 'Father Time' - was shortly afterwards. That was around the gigs at the Shaw theatre.

Barry – Yes. There was a competitive edge because IDJ were in it too. He did 'Night in Tunisia' for us - that was our tune. He lost the time at one point though.

Mark – It was good for people to have seen both of our styles: we liked some of what IDJ did and I hoped they liked a little of what we did. The main thing was the audience seeing the worth in what we do.

Did you encounter IDJ much?

Saltz - Yes. Between us and IDJ, we were the clear winners. We had a battle plan. We were different styles, but we learnt Fusion, so that we could dance against them with their style and 'Bam' quickly switch to ours; I ran the Defektors like military. Unfortunately, we never battled them and yet we were often together. They never approached us. Perhaps they just didn't acknowledge us.

You made an album.

Barry – After Absolute Beginners we did a gig at the ICA in The Mall, as guests of Paul Weller and after and we got approached by a Japanese guy called Koichi. He wanted to do things for us out there. We went out in April '87 and promoted the film, and Paul Murphy was with us.

Saltz - We became tight with Paul Murphy. Up until then it was Colin Curtis with Hewan as his understudy, and then as soon as we became 'international' Paul Murphy was the main boy, with Baz Fe Jazz as his apprentice.

Barry – The company worked us hard. Koichi got us a deal out there and we made an album and it made the Top 10. It sold 60,000 copies. We went back to Japan a second time and did a massive tour. Back here, we'd have tons of gigs; every university in the U.K, The Shaw Theatre, all the major clubs, the Albany, The Scala, loads…

PC - We were in the video of 'Rock Me Amadeus' by the Austrian pop singer called Falco; we were in the video for 'Have You Ever Had It Blue?' by Paul Weller - Paul Weller produced some of our album; we did the video for 'What I Like About You Most Is Your Girlfriend' by Jerry Dammers (The Specials); we did stuff with Sade. When we got back from Japan we did TV performances on Night Network and The Tube promoting Absolute Beginners, and just before the band split up we played in Austria; Italy; at the Midem Festival in France, we played at Club Celeste in Barcelona; The Town And Country Club (now The Forum) at least three or four times, The Astoria, The Wag, Ronnie Scotts; we choreographed fashion shows….

You did the first 'Brighton Jazz Bop' with *Tommy Chase* and the *James Taylor Quartet*.

PC - That was one of our last gigs. That was in 1988.

Mark – The turning point for us was when we supported Grover Washington Junior at the Royal Albert Hall, We were blown away by their professionalism, and attention to detail. There was talk of doing a second album and we said that we wanted to take our time over it, to do it properly, great vocals, everything good…

Barry – …create what we were doing on stage. All the rest of the band just wanted to gig, gig, gig, endlessly and we were saying that it was a business now and we needed the end product – we're selling things now. They didn't see it that way. We said that it was this way or not at all, and that was it.

ANIFF AKIMBOLA

Not only a rated dancer, but Aniff was, and sill is, a DJ, Song Writer, Record Producer and Label Owner. He was one of the brains behind *A Guy Called Gerald - Voodoo Ray* – a House record that the Jazz Dancers went mad to, and *Chapter And The Verse – Black Whip*, which made such an important mark in the 'Acid Jazz' period.

I originally started going to Colin Curtis nights at *Smartys* and *Rafters*, around '80. Every club has a record it's famous for and at Rafters it was a track called *Pigmy* by *African Suite* (Electra records). I don't know why, but whenever it was played, loads of people would form a massive 'huddle' on the floor – it looked like a giant spider. They had amazing dancers there too and even had some top girl dancers. There was Angela Mullins and Kadria and Debra. We didn't know their surnames, we just knew people by first names or nicknames usually. After there was the club *Berlin*.

It started around the time of *The Wag* in London, but a lot of the Rafters crowd didn't go there; it was like they'd stopped clubbing and settled down. This was almost another era. I knew Gilles Peterson from there, who used to come up from London. Colin would always print play lists from Berlin and Gilles liked that. Berlin was all about discovering new things and there was amazing Jazz played in there. You'd get bands in there like the *Thompson Twins, Carmel* and of course *Kalima* and *A Certain Ratio*. I told them about Berlin. That club was a community and was very stylish. There was a lot of 50's clothes suits and all that. There was an antiques market nearby that was famous, so there was plenty of places to buy all that style of clothing. Dance wise you didn't see many of the steppers (fusion) in there.

That was at the all-dayers I suppose.

Yes. I met my musical partner there, Colin, and formed our first band *Slip*. We did a lot of writing and production, which is how I came across *Housemaster G* (aka Gerald Simpson). Gerald formed a project called *A Guy Called Gerald* that I chose various tracks to go with, and one was the track *Voodoo Ray*. He did the groove and I did the topline. We put it out on our Ram Records.

I was told that this (House music) track could only have come from the Jazz dance scene.

Well, it was from the ghetto. The steppers (fusion dancers) liked it. Gerald knew all the jazz tunes anyway. House wasn't going down too well for about 3 months at the Hacienda and the DJ Mike Pickering, gave a load of free passes to Jazz dancers *Samson* and *The Foot Patrol*, for free admission and drinks. They were eye candy. People would see them dancing and it'd hopefully encourage others. They were very important and responsible for breaking the music there. They were dancing Fusion to it.

Let's talk about *Chapter And The Verse*.

Well we did some other tracks like *All This And Heaven Too*, but we did this track called *Black Whip*, sampling the *Ivan Boogaloo Joe Jones* track of the same name. I took a riff from (jazz singer) *Eddie Jefferson*, which I sang a bit with some other stuff, and I did a rap about Margaret Thatcher and all that lot. We stuck it out on Ram. Gilles loved it and was interested in signing us. He said he was starting a new label (Talkin' Loud), and he came up here to sign us. We liked him, but the reason the deal never happened was because of a political line I put in about Margaret Thatcher. Gilles said he liked the track but we'd have to take the Thatcher line out. Her policies caused problems up here and I didn't want to remove the line so we just told Gilles we didn't want to do the deal. And he was fine about it. A few years later I met him and he asked why we never signed and I told him and he said that he was only joking! He thought that was the best bit. So, we could have had that deal!

FOOT   PATROL

JAZZ !   FUNK !   FUSION   DANCERS

SAMSON   ZIPPA   GODFREY   RICKY

DAY:- 061 227 9453   NIGHT:- 061 226 3337

FOOT PATROL

Following right after The Jazz Defektors, when they'd moved on, the Foot Patrol became enormous and feared as dancefloor warriors. Like IDJ in London, even when they became professional and achieved so much, they were still out there battling it out. Foot Patrol also showed the way that you could dance jazz to House music, and some say, they helped break House at The Hacienda.

Godfrey - I'm older than the others in Foot Patrol and so I saw all the dancers like who were in *The Jazz Defektors*, and I'd go to Colin Curtis' clubs like *Smartys, Rafters* and *Rufus* – where all the best dancers went. *Legends* with *Greg Wilson* was great as well, He'd give us an hour of Jazz.

I was in a group called J.A.B – which stood for 'Jazz At It's Best.' There was six of us; Me, John Silcott, Richard and Derek, Steve Richards and Pob, which was the same time as The Jazz Defektors. We trained at the 911 Centre in Moss side on Mondays and Thursdays, to sharpen up our moves. We didn't do any professional work. There was plenty of battling though.

Samson - I came over from Jamaica when I was eight and moved to Birmingham then came to Manchester and that's when the Northern scene was dying off. There was a lot of Funk and Electro. Manchester had a big Breakdance crew called *Broken Glass*, and they were Jazz dancers that got into the breaking. You started getting a few Jazz dancers incorporating a few Breaking moves, and in clubs they were doing Jazz breaks in amongst the Electro.

You went to dancing school didn't you?

Samson - When I left school. The Sheena Simon School Of Dance.

You were Jazz dancing when you were at school.

Samson - I was shuffling my feet yeah, but I just wanted to hone what I was doing. Be more graceful. It was good to know. It made me a bit more polished.

How did The Foot Patrol start?

Samson - It started for us around '86 when we saw I.D.J on the *Working Week – Venceremos* video. It opened our eyes, and from then we wanted to be where they were. It gave us the hunger. The line-up was me, Godfrey, Little Ricky and Zippa and we were all known in the club scene as dancers anyway – everyone knew of us - but you never know who's watching. Michael Jackson was going to play at Aintree in Liverpool and one day we got a call at the place where we trained – Proctors in Moss Side – and they asked us whether we would dance with him. When that came through we were buzzing. You can't get bigger than that. Unfortunately it fell through.

Even though it fell through, it must have created a buzz around you.

Samson - Yes it did.

How did you get established?

Godfrey - From the TV work and clubs. We were definitely known through doing TV shows like 'Opportunity Knocks.'

Samson - That put our names up even further. We tried to take it to the mainstream. Try to branch out. That wasn't the four of us, just two of us – me and Zippa.

Millions watched that series.

Samson - I know. From there we started making waves. Our name was plastered all over the place. We got a lot of TV. work for the I.T.V. channel Granada. Anytime they needed dancers they'd call for Foot Patrol. We did shows with *Carmel, Swing Out Sister*…we did loads of TV. We did big shows like the Jubilee Centre in London. We just did so much.

I've been told that people seeing you dancing at The Hacienda to House was one of the main things that broke that music in the North.

Samson - Yes, but there were others dancing there as well - a good fifteen. But we were there in our suits. We had a Pass. We were dancing to House music there because the Jazz was dying up here.

Godfrey - Everyone knew us in the Jazz scene, but there was money to be made in the dance (House music) scene. We'd 'shuffle foot' and those people had never seen anything like it! That's the way we made money. We got known at The Hacienda.

Other shows like' Hit Man And Her' came through, which not everybody would want to do but we thought "Why not? It's TV work, and if it's going to pay and give us a name then lets do it."

Samson – We did it every week. It was a profile thing for us and it worked because even though it wasn't our music we'd still wear our suits and spats. When people saw us wearing those shoes a lot of people went out and bought them. We got ours from Shelleys in London. We'd take umpteen days off to get a train to go and get them – sometimes they'd have run out! To be in the scene you had to have the shoes! We just went on the show to spread the Jazz moves and get the name around. The presenter [and record producer] Pete Waterman wanted us to make records and all that – like *The Pasadenas*, but some of the guys didn't want to do it.

You did make a record though (1989).

Godfrey - Zippa produced it. He was strong at the music. It was a House tune. Zippa did the lyrics and he'd MC when we did performances. The rest of us performed a routine to the tune. We'd do two clubs a night. There was only so far you can go as dancers, so we thought that could help broaden it all.

Did you get on well with The Jazz Defektors?

Samson - We got on really well. In the end they were doing more singing than dancing. We even danced for them on a gig once. They weren't competition. They'd moved onto the next level, and they left dancing for the 'Foot Patrol' to patrol (laughs).

What tracks did you do dance routines to?

Samson - *Pat Metheny –Third Wind* and *Chick Corea – The Slide*. We were always searching out for tunes. I used to make Mike Chadwick's life a nightmare in *Decoy* records in Manchester. I'd just get him to play through loads of stuff when he should be serving others. I just said, "It's got to be fast." I must have driven him mad.

Were you still going to clubs or all-dayers?

Samson - Yes. We always met up with the London dancers at the Nottingham all-dayers. That's where the battles happened.

Did you battle as a crew or individuals?

Samson - Both. It was like a 'western' in there: everyone waiting for IDJ to make the first move. It was like 'who's going to draw first?' It was really like that. A lot of dancers feared I.D.J but then the battles would start and it'd be heavy. There will be people that say they beat I.D.J but they didn't. It just made you work harder to improve to get on top and it enhanced what you do and got you talked about. People knew about Foot Patrol.

I think the scene was all about London and Manchester.

What about Birmingham?

Samson -Yeah, but they were rough, them. They always wanted to fight on the floor. In those battles, fighting took place. No guns, just fists. Looking back, it was all fun - boys will be boys. There were some fists flying. Some people got humiliated. Everyone wanted to be the best. In the later days everyone respected each other though.

Did you ever go to the *Jive Turkey* in Sheffield?

Samson - A few times. We had some fierce battles there which ended in fighting and we got thrown out. There were great dancers in there too but no organized crews, like us. We thought we were hard nuts, and they did too and we had this reputation for kicking off.

Battling on the floor, not fighting...

Samson - Both (laughs). They thought they were 'the boys' but we were the boys up-North and they took offence and the battles got out of hand. There were bad vibes there. We didn't want to fight any more; we just wanted to dance. We always got on well with the Leeds dancers. The battles never got to the fighting stage.

Godfrey – In the end *Fusion Beat* took care of the battling side of things. We'd been there and done it and wanted to move on. There was money to be made. We went abroad, did tons of work; we did one hell of a lot. We got equity and did extras work.

What happened to The Foot Patrol?

Samson - I went to prison in the early 90's and that was it really. I was doing all the pushing for us and all of a sudden I wasn't there.

Godfrey - It carried on a little bit longer. We used other dancers: Dave Burton (now known as DJ D'Lite) and Derek 'Dinky' Tauk to cover. The scene was dying off too, and also I started DJ'ing. I'd been collecting since 1979.

FUSION BEAT

Snapping right at the heels of Foot Patrol time-wise, this crew often gets mixed up with them, as they traveled together a lot of the time – and there was also a Samson brother in each troupe. Again, they were heavily rated and achieved such a lot. They also remained battling until the end.

Dave, your Brother formed *Foot Patrol*: Which group came first them or *Fusion Beat*?

Dave Samson - Foot Patrol came after The Jazz Defektors, then us. Foot Patrol were working everywhere. They gave Manchester pride.

What's the difference in styles?

Dave - We're more of a mixture between hardcore floor-work and swing. We got ideas and tricks from the Nicholas Brothers and blended it with us. We mixed in the older dancers styles of *IDJ*, *Brothers In Jazz*, and *The Jazz Defektors* too.

Why did you form Fusion Beat?

Dave - I looked at Foot Patrol and thought "They're good but we could be better." There was just two of us originally – me and Vince Dixon - and then we brought in Roger Mitchell and Ian De Pezia to give a different flavour.

Roger, how did you get into *Fusion Beat*?

Roger - Dave came up to us with a dancer called Vinnie who were already Fusion Beat, and said: "You two can dance. I like what you do" and invited us to join. Fusion Beat was already well established so we leapt at the chance.

You and Ian were from a House background weren't you Roger?

Roger - When we were about 13 we danced fast footwork (Fusion) to House records like *Harlequin 4 – Set It Off*. We first saw that style from a dancer called Sinclair Page who brought it up from Birmingham. I thought: "Wow, I want to learn that". He was quick. He learnt it off *Bulldog* and that crowd. I always look at Fusion as broken-down Tap dancing.

Me and Ian De Pezia were later in a House music dance group called *Special FX* and we'd go out dancing to all styles of music. One night we saw *Foot Patrol* dancing to some Jazz and we were blown away and wanted to try it. Everyone wanted to emulate *Samson* from that group - they were *all* known dancers actually.

Dave - We trained hard three nights a week, Monday, Wednesday and Friday at Proctor Youth Centre at Hulme

Roger - We all had nicknames too: I'm known as *Ninja* (or *Sandman*), Ian is *Sweet P*, Dave is

Smoothie D and Vinnie is *Styles*. We went absolutely Jazz mad, crazy on it. We loved the dance group IDJ, but we were really inspired by the *Brothers In Jazz*. I love Jazz. When I dance it I get that inner feeling. It's in my heart, soul and spirit. I move to the direction the instruments go, like the sax or piano. We'd dance Jazz to House music.

Did you have to change your style much to dance to House?
Dave - You can do more tricks; more movements because it's slowed down.

It's said that Foot Patrol established dancing Jazz to House music at The Hacienda.
Roger - Yes. But we'd all go down there and mash it up. There'd be big circles.

As *Fusion Beat*, did you battle much?
We did shows all over the country but we didn't do the challenging as a group, I mean, we went to all- dayers and battled but not as a group. We were just representing Manchester.

Dave - We did battle, but not as much. We started doing school summer shows; street festivals; a show in Cardiff; we were regulars at the national music BBC TV programmes *Behind The Beat* and *Solid Soul*; we were on the video of *Carino* by *T–Coy* and we toured all over promoting the single – that was Mike Pickering's project, who was the main DJ from the Hacienda. He formed the band M-People later. Foot Patrol and us livened up the crowd at The Hacienda. We'd mash it up. Someone said in a magazine review that we were 'The Mafia Of The Dancefloor.'

We used to go battling to places like *MacMillans* in Yarm and take over – leave our mark – we feared no one. I wish we could have battled IDJ from London. The first time I saw them at all-dayers it opened my eyes. Manchester was the only crew that would have had the nerve to go in against them.

There was always a good relationship between both areas.
Dave -There was great dancers from everywhere but we'd just go straight in and battle. Guaranteed.

Why did Fusion Beat stop?
Roger - Commitments. Kids. We never fell out. We're all still friends. It just fizzled out. Clubs changed, with all the drugs, and it just wasn't the same anymore. Too many bad boys.

DEAN JOHNSON

A respected Black music DJ (equally as at home playing Reggae, Funk, Soul or Jazz) and Journalist, Dean has never held back speaking his mind, and so I have included, I feel, some various important observations from him here.

"There were dancers in Birmingham that were doing intricate steps to Funk (before there was Jazz Funk) – and all that. They were doing the *throwing the hanky on the floor and picking it up whilst doing a cart wheel* stuff. To me, that's all that steppers (Fusion) is."

"I think that the dance style didn't evolve up here until you got Colin (Curtis) playing *real* Jazz records."

"For a hetrosexual club, my recollection of Colin's night at Rufus was: going for a piss and seeing huge muscular black men changing their clothes and the overpowering smell of aftershave."

"There was all the 'small room at all-dayers' thing obviously, but the importance of *Berlin* was that it would start off with a bit of harsh Jazz and the second set was always more accessible to the women. In between was amazing Soul music. It wasn't packed every week but one week if there was only sixty there, I'd know them all. There'd be all of *A Certain Ratio*, all of *Kalima*, all of *Chapter and Verse* (Colin and Aniff) assorted DJ's. The club was superb. It was my favourite. If it was packed there'd be no fancy dancing; the dancefloor was tiny."

"*The Hacienda* keyed into the Berlin thing – promoting the *Jazz Defektors* and getting them to dance on stage, with John Tracey or Hewan Clarke playing the tunes. Hewan was the first DJ at The Hacienda.when it was dead. I did '86 to '88 at the Hacienda."

"I've always played Jazz from when I started to DJ in ''83. By 1985, when I was doing every Saturday night at *The Venue* there'd be a Jazz break, and at The Hacienda – which I did for two years on a Saturday (from '86 to '88), I'd play Boogaloo earlier on and harder faster Latin later on – more Mambos and Descargas. There'd be 1,400 in there but you could hold the floor with that. If you couldn't you'd be out on your ear."

"They fired me because I wouldn't play House music all night. Playing a mixture of music was no longer acceptable there."

"Absolute Beginners killed off the scene. It did more damage than good. Also, at the time (85/86) there was the first Chicago Acid House records coming through. The guys who'd like to do the fast footwork would suddenly give it loads of foot to that. It took over from Jazz for these guys, except the more balletic dancers. In certain clubs, where'd there'd been Jazz breaks they'd have breaks of these 'strange records from Chicago!' "

LEEDS AND BRADFORD

Although the initial scene all revolved around Ian Dewhirst and Paul Schofield at The Central and the dancer Oki and his crew, the majority of the future Jazz DJ's seem to come from Bradford (just down the road) – Lubi Jovanovic and Chris 'Chico' Murphy, and 'The Educated Jazzmen'. Other than their clubs, there was only the *Time And Place* discoteque. Although a rated club for what it was, it hasn't ant relevance to this book. Leeds, with it's incredible dancers, became a rock-solid foundation for Jazz Dance through the endeavours of Lubi, Chico and Gip Dammone latterly known as *The Dig Family* - with their many, many sessions (with both live bands and DJ's) and their opposition: the DJ collective *Take Five*. Leeds had a solid Jazz Dance scene that still continues to date.

WAR · LONNIE SMITH · TRAMMPS · FANTASTIC FOUR · L.T.D. · JIMMY McGRIFF · MASTERMIND

"QUITE SIMPLY THE NORTH'S NO 1 SOUL SPOT!"
LEEDS CENTRAL
CELLAR CLUB, 2 CENTRAL RD., CENTRE OF LEEDS, PRECINCT BEHIND WOOLWORTHS!
PAUL SCHOFIELD and IAN DEWHIRST
THE BEST FUNKSMACKINDISCOLICKINMOTHERSHIPPIN CONNECTION!

IT HAPPENED ON A DARK, COLD NIGHT IN NOVEMBER WHEN PAUL 'FOUR EYES FUNK' SCHOFIELD AND IAN 'QUICKDRAW DISCO' DEWHIRST MOWED EACH OTHER DOWN WITH AN UNFORGETTABLE FUSILAGE OF FUNK, DISCO AND JAZZ ON THE HIGHEST CALIBRE!

LICENSED BAR AND FOOD   FRIDAYS 9 – 2 a.m.

GARNET MIMMS   RAMSEY LEWIS

CHIC · MANDRILL · PAMPLEMOUSSE · KING ERRISON · THELMA HOUSTON · E.W & F. · ALL THE NEWIES

IAN DEWHIRST

Known from the Northern Soul scene to just about every other one to do with UK Black Music club culture, on the highest level, it is his club *The Central* that, along with DJ partner Paul Schofield, gave a focal point to Jazz on the dancefloor for the first time in Leeds.

I went to Los Angeles looking for Northern Soul records in 1975 and all I heard on the radio stations like CUTE FM – were tracks by artists like *Ronnie Laws, Marlena Shaw, Bob James* etc... and I started buying all that. When I got back to the UK at the end of '75 I started going to the hipper clubs in Leeds and the main one was *Primos*, where the DJ was my friend Paul Schofield. Primos was very sophisticated – with about a 90% Black crowd. Paul would be playing stuff like *Donald Byrd – Flight Time*; there was nowhere in Leeds that you'd hear anything like that. When it closed it caused a vacuum. I wanted somewhere to hear Funk and Jazz Funk, and I suggested a club called *The Central* - which I knew from DJ-ing Northern Soul there. We got the club on Fridays and the timing was perfect. This was the night everyone was looking for and it was a killer from the word go.
This must have happened before Colin Curtis broke away from The Mecca then?
It must have been, although Colin has always been contemporary; interested in new records as

well as old. We had a very fashionable crowd and people traveled for it. We didn't get many 'townies' - we were after those into the music. If you were into your music, our club was the place to go. We didn't really have any competition.

Did the dancers influence your music?

Yes, Originally we had the nucleus of the Primos crowd who'd been around since day one, and these new young dancers who came from The Precinct - which was a pub that played a lot of Funk. These guys were *Oki, Steve Caesar* and *Glen Campbell*, They integrated well and used to love the extended Jazz tracks like *John Klemmer - Brazilia*. You could see that they worked on their moves from one week to the next, but the problem was that the floor would clear to watch them – so we would tend to save a lot of that till the last hour. We were always rammed almost as soon as the doors opened so when it thinned a little at 1a.m. that was the chance to play the Jazz. It was only a part of the night. Oki had a huge contingent of women following him around. The Central was as much about his crowd as the music. They were seen as the fashion go-getters of Leeds. He's a sophisticated guy. I like to think that The Central was instrumental in him getting into all that music. They created an environment there - the atmosphere - although it was like a stand-off between him and us sometimes, like a 'western' (laughs). He was the leader of the gang and he had his own power-base there. He would stand there with everyone dancing – looking at us, saying, like: "Are you going to play some *Azymuth* or what?" He was an incredible dancer and would want some esoteric stuff that I wouldn't be prepared to play, I just didn't want circles breaking things up. People may leave. You'd build up and build up and there's these two guys having a dance off and the attention comes off the music.

You were at the legendary Chris Hill gig at *Manchester Ritz* weren't you?

Yes I was. There was plenty of Northerners and the powers-that-be that wanted to see him fall flat on his arse that night, but he came straight on with *Ashford and Simpson – Love Don't Cost A Thing* and absolutely rocked it. He made a massive impact. He brought up a level of showmanship that we'd never seen before. My DJ partner Paul Schofield perhaps took the showmanship bit a bit too far dressing up as Dame Edna Everage and all that. I was just there for the music, but we had great fun with the 'human pyramids' and the 'mooning.' We got the entire balcony at the Blackpool Mecca to 'moon,' did you hear about that? 5 or 600 people. We got banned from there. That's where our 'Botties Over Britain' idea started. We did an eight week tour around the clubs. I think there was a bit of novelty introduced to break up the all-dayers a bit because they were so long it gave a bit of variety, although I'd have been happy with it just being music. But all these all-dayers were huge events: I'd come on at eight o'clock to 3000 people and I'd be fucking pissed. It was so exhilarating. You felt you could do anything with the crowd. I stripped off once to my underwear and stood on a speaker conducting the crowd, or you could get them to sit down en masse.

Well, this was what started to kill the scene countrywide wasn't it, when, after all this light-hearted stuff started to attract idiots in that weren't there for the music?

Yes, it had peaked and it was getting too pre-meditated. There was also a level of elitism coming in too, which wanted it more intricate - which I wasn't happy with. I was always more mainstream, and also I'd taken an interest in mixing so I went to *The Warehouse* from ''79 to ''82 which had quite a sophisticated crowd.

OKI

Oki – real name David Okonofua – was considered the first of all the great dancers that came from Leeds. He was equally known for his trend-setting fashion-sense. He and his influential crowd were the intimidators of many a DJ, because of their music knowledge as well as dance skills.

We used to go to the Northern Soul club The Wigan Casino 1974, 75 and 76. The Blackpool Mecca was still the same scene but they'd play more innovative records. You had the Northern (Soul) scene and you had the 'Blackpool Mecca' sound ; it became a lot different - the older DJ's just stuck to the Northern scene and they played records that just weren't relevant.

Primo's - with DJ Paul Schofield - was about the first Jazz Funk club in Leeds wasn't it?

Yes. There was *Liquid* but that was more Modern Soul. Later there was *The Central* and *The Precinct*. At Primos you'd hear tracks like *John Handy – Hard Work, Black Byrds – Rock Creek*

Park and all that kind of stuff. I remember buying *Expansions* by *Lonnie Liston Smith* on a 7" in 1975 and I took it down to The Precinct and got Paul Schofield to play it and he said: "This is crap Oki" and took it off.

It was ahead of its time though. Do you remember when out-and-out Jazz started getting played there?

Well, at The Central, Paul Schofield and Ian Dewhirst were playing Northern Soul and they closed it for a month and when they reopened it was all the new stuff - Jazz Funk, you know, like *Running Away – Roy Ayers*, stuff by *George Duke* etc

Did they do Jazz spots?

No, the Jazz thing came in gradually. I think one of the pinnacles of dance records once it came in was *Opus De Lopus - Spyro Gyra* with the two or three minute long drum solo. Every spin, every jump was in with that solo. *John Klemmer – Brazilia*: that's another one. They were seven or eight minute long tunes, and you needed a lot of stamina to take them out, and another set of clothes!!!

I heard about something called the 'Oki Five.' What was that?

(Laughs) That was a dance that nobody could get right. What happened was, that I went down to a club in Brighton called *The Alhambra*, and the people in there were wearing plastic macs and tapered trousers, pointed shoes, mohair jumpers and I thought they looked really funky so I went out in Brighton next day and bought all the stuff and a feather earring and I got back to Leeds on the Friday and thought: "Right. On Saturday I'm going to hit it big time." I walked into Primos and everybody stopped and looked - including my friends. Anyway, I plaguerised this dance I'd seen at the Alhambra mixed in with a bit of 'Northen Funk' style dancing and danced to *Lalo Schifrin – Jaws* and people just stopped dancing to watch me on all three floors. The lights went up and I felt like a film star or something and Paul Schofield kept playing it about five times. Anyway, next week I went to the club and loads of people were dressed the same way (laughs). There was five of us that did this dance: Glen Campbell, me, Steve Caesar, Roland and Simon Andrews. It wasn't a routine though. People used to recognize us by the way we were dressed up and people would stop and watch us dance. People knew we were from Leeds

when we used to go to Blackpool Mecca and people used to think we were the leaders in dance for about a year and a half until these [Jazz] dancers from Birmingham came along. Fantastic dancers. They took it to the next level. I remember when they came up to Smartys; we thought we were cool but they came in doing all these ballet moves and all that. We picked up a few things off them and everybody was friendly - before all this 'competition' stuff on the dance floor: you know, when people would get in your face when you're just trying to get lost in a track. I came out of the scene in 1981/82 because I got disillusioned. I was still buying records though.

GIP DAMMONE, LUBI JOVANOVIC and CHRIS 'CHICO' MURPHY

Between these three, the bullet-proof scene that they had going in Leeds kept it all going to an exceptional level there when it had all-but faded elsewhere in the North. Their sessions were some of the biggest and most creative in the UK.

Chico - I was into Punk and New wave. A lot of the clubs up in Bradford played this or Reggae.

I went from Punk/ New wave into bands like Rip, Rig and Panic and Pigbag and from there into Blue Note, and I imagine Lubi did as well.

Lubi – Yes, I was a first generation Punk and later, post-punk, you had that Punk Jazz movement as Lubi says, with bands like *Rip, Rig and Panic* and *James White and the Blacks*, and through them you got to Joe Bowie's *Defunkt*. A guy in a record shop recommended 'Rip Rig and Panic' by *Roland Kirk* and I'm like "What?" He was putting me on to all the original influences of what I was listening to, introducing me to *Fela Kuti* and Soul and Funk, and by '80 I'd got into Jazz - but I wasn't aware of the Jazz Dance scene. I went to Bradford Jazz festival in '80 and saw Freddie Hubbard and Gil Evans. There was all these Jazz dancers dancing to Hubbard and I didn't know where to look: the stage or them. They were amazing. I got to know them after that.

Chico - Lubi and I got ourselves involved with that festival for six years. They put on other ambitious gigs like Art Blakey, Johnny Griffin, Art Ensemble Of Chicago – right across the spectrum. We learnt a lot there and it got us really into Jazz. Club-wise, there weren't really any for us, so in '82 Lubi started The Hot Club at The Subway Bar, Bradford Universisty.

Lubi – I was playing Punk, Jazz, Latin and Fusion, and on the last night thirty dancers came down and took over the floor, and one of them asked if he could play some tunes, and so he playing all that hard Fusion. I wasn't even aware of the all-dayer scene before then. That lasted for six months. Also in '82 we Dj'd the Bradford Mecca playing Punk Funk/Punk Jazz and Jazz Fusion too.

Chico – In '84 – for two years - me and him started The Wild Style at *The Checkpoint* – which was at The West Indian Centre. It was the two rooms; one breakdancing and a Jazz room - which was as heavy as you could get.

That's exactly like The Electric Ballroom.

Lubi – Unbeknownst to us. It was hardcore. There certainly wasn't anything like it before.

Chico - We didn't do much live stuff, but we got IDJ up to dance and the Jazz Defektors, and we brought *Hewan Clarke* up a few times to do a few heavy sets too.

Where were you picking up your records from?

Lubi - It was easy to buy records round here, they were all over and cheap plus we used to buy mail-order from Paul Murphy's record shop.

Chico - I was picking up records left, right and centre. Actually, Bradford had an extensive record library and I used to sort through that, finding out what I liked and what I didn't, and go out and buy them.

Were you aware of what was going on elsewhere?

Chico - Yes. I had friends in London and we used to get tapes off of the pirate radios - Gilles' show and all that, and we knew of Paul Murphy and Bob Jones, and we heard what Colin Curtis and Hewan Clare were playing in Manchester.

Lubi - We also learnt from the dancers and the DJ's *The Educated Jazzmen* what was going on elsewhere. We went to Colin Curtis' night at *Berlin* but it wasn't quite our thing: There was a lot of Mambo being played and people in 50's baggy suits, but we wanted it 'nose-bleed.'

Did you check out the charts in Blues and Soul as well?

Chico - I think those charts were the first reference point for us - for me anyway. A good, initial source.

Where did you do after The Checkpoint?

Chico - We started a session called the Jazz Cellar in 1985. It was beneath the Queens Hall, Morley Street in Bradford and, Jazz wise, it was quite diverse. The tempo's were varied and we also did some live bands - local bands mainly. It only lasted a year.

With the scene starting to pop in to the mainstream with Sade, Matt Bianco and previously Blue Rondo A la Turk, it peaked with the hype of the film Absolute Beginners. As we knew, the film was a disappointment and it did damage to the scene down South, what about for you?

Lubi – Me, Chico and our girlfriends, and the Educated Jazzmen all went to see it and sat there stunned at the closing credits. I didn't want to be any part of that commercial side, certainly after that. Forget it. We kept it going underground.

We started hearing about this man opening up a Jazz venue in Leeds.

Gip – It was a restaurant with a live room upstairs called *The Coconut Grove*, Lower Merrion Street (1985). I did a Jazz night every Wednesday and, eventually, we got some decks and I started playing records. It wasn't a Jazz dance session, but I was playing just Jazz.

Chico – He used to put on live bands – our kind of bands. I think Gip only started DJing because he couldn't find the kind of DJ to play the kind of music he wanted to hear, and he had a big collection. He used to play the right tunes.

So wasn't there a night in Leeds like this before?

Chico - No, Ozzie and Chris (The Educated Jazzmen) and me and Lubi used to hang out at there as it was the only place that played what we were after, and we met up with Gip. He got a lot of the major Jazz acts from the States played there, and he used to get jazz dancers in there, as well. We (Lubi and Chico) had taken up instruments by then as well, and played there.

Lubi – On Monday it was student night, but we ran a heavy Jazz room upstairs and on Saturdays we also, again, had a heavy Jazz room. That's what the dancers wanted.

Gip – I was never involved in the Jazz dance scene until it came to me. Fucking Hell!!! The shock of seeing people dance to Be Bop! I didn't even know there was Jazz DJ's until I started putting Jazz on!

Lubi – The Coconut Grove was on three floors: the top was the Jazz venue; the middle was the restaurant and the bottom was the club that was called Ricky's. And in there [in '86, for a year] I started a night called Club Afro Latino. It was 50% Hard 'Fania'-type Salsa and 50% African. Leeds never had a night like that before.

Chico – We'd all started DJ-ing all over the place, and by '87 me and Lubi started doing Latin music promotions at a very famous old Bradford venue called The Royal Standard. Manningham Lane and also The Queens Hall cellar. The nights were called *Mambo show*. It wasn't a Jazz dancer but we were running in parallel with our other Jazz things.

Lubi - It was Bradford's first Latin music night, which ran until '89.

Chico - We had other nights running about then. We had *Dig Dis!* at Rickys on a Wednesday.

Lubi – And in '88, on a Saturday there, we did a night called *The Downbeat*. We all just guested regularly at that one, and so did Andy Bex [also a Jazz dancer and member of 'Bamboozle']. We'd play a lot of hard jazz. Dancers came from everywhere for that session. Our band 'Sonando' were resident there too.

> "I used to play regularly at The Downbeat. The advantage I had there was, as a dancer, I was on their wavelength. I was notorious for playing a tune and getting on the floor and dancing to it and getting back behind the decks and showering my records in sweat!"

> *Andy Bex*

Chico - In '89 we started *Destination Out* there, with all five of us. The venue had just changed it's name to The Gallery.

Lubi - We ran it for a couple of years. Acid Jazz had come in by then so we were playing more groove based stuff; 'Hammond' stuff. By '91, I dropped out for a year.

Gip – In '91 we started *Dig* there with The Educated Jazz Men, Chris Goss and Ez. In the main club we were playing Fusion, Latin and Be Bop and in the back room was Hammond grooves, Acid Jazz, Jazz Rap.

What did you think of Acid Jazz?

Lubi – I didn't like it. I didn't like *Galliano* or any of that. Paul Bradshaw kept on phoning me trying to talk me into booking them but I wasn't into it. Obviously both our nights *Dig* and *The Cooker* really went mad around '91 when Acid Jazz was at it's height. Instead of 100/120, even the opening night was 400, then 500, then 600 people.

Gip - When I started Dig the main room was Jazz and the smaller room was Jazzy - more groove based, and by '91 everyone wanted the groove stuff and wasn't listening to the Jazz, and that's when you realized that scene was moving away from the Jazz.

Lubi – It was a huge change. I could see it.

What did you think of *Dingwalls*?

Lubi – We played there four or five times with our band Conjunto Fuego. The first time was amazing, and we then played four or five months later and something had changed. It was different. It wasn't as good as *The Wag* in '84 - there you had Paul Murphy actually playing Jazz; there was the smart suits; bands like *Tommy Chase*. It was a special club.

THE EDUCATED JAZZ MEN – OZZIE LEBAD and CHRIS THOMAS

From Bradford, Ozzie and Chris went from dancers to respected Jazz DJ's and heavy-weight collectors.

Ozzie - I remember about ''83 when a lot of the slightly older guys dropped out when this other dance style style came in....

Chris -.....Foot Tapping (Fusion)...

Ozzie - I rejected the new style at first. I'd come up on the back end of the 'Ballet-style' and that's what I was practicing, and then, all of a sudden there's these guys from Nottingham and Birmingham....

Chris - They were coming in with this intricate footwork. I thought, "Hey, that's not what it's all about."

Ozzie - Yeah, I mean, they were doing that intricate kind of footwork to Electro in the other room - before Break Dancing came in - to *Planet Rock* and all that.

Chris - I remember not liking it at first.

Ozzie - I first saw it at Nottingham Palais and I thought: "What is going on? Where's the pirouettes?" There was all these intricate moves going on in a tight square and they never glided across the floor. I thought what's this? I didn't understand it. I didn't like it.

Chris - The Ballet dropped away and this was the new style. There were a lot of 'foot-tappers' standing around who wanted it faster. They wanted it fast.

Ozzie - DJ's were catering for it. You could tell. You had both styles of dancing but you couldn't do Ballet-style to *that* speed.

Chris - We were waiting for the fast tunes and the hardest tunes.

Ozzie - The scene fizzled out around '85 didn't it? We stopped dancing and got into listening. Gip, Lubi and Chico [The Dig Family] were a big influence on us. They were turning us onto some unbelievable Jazz.

Chris - We started collecting seriously and decided to start DJ-ing on the back of that commercial Jazz scene. We had a lot of the Jazz records that the other DJ's had, so we thought: "We could do this." Gip gave us a break at *The Coconut Grove* in Leeds. It was our first gig. We knew Lubi from Bradford. He had the tunes, and Chico. They all got us into the serious side of Jazz.

Did you go to The Central?

Ozzie - No we were too young, but it was legendary. There was a club in Bradford called Textile Hall and it was a very 'Black' club. Dovel and Wayne used to go there on a Friday night.

What DJ's did you rate?

Ozzie -Jonathon. He had the tunes – he didn't disappoint. He started a fantastic Friday night at Nottingham – Rock City with Colin Curtis downstairs playing Jazz all night, and it was just like a 'dayer. It was packed, and people were traveling from all over the North. Everyone was checking each others moves and fashions.

What kind of stuff were you DJ-ing? Was it commercial?

Ozzie - No. Mainly straight Jazz. Bop.

Chris - Again, Gip's name comes up. He said: "I've got a club – educate the crowd." It was a lot of Bop,

Where were you buying your tunes from?

Chris - All over, but *Powercuts* in Manchester was great for Jazz. They'd got a lot of records that were used for ballast on ships, all kinds of music, but a lot of Jazz, for, like, 49 pence (laughs). They didn't know what they had. We were serious Blue Note collectors.

Ozzie - We used to play a lot of Blue Note.

Chris - We got disillusioned about 1989 with all that 'Acid Jazz'. We started going to a lot of festivals and Jazz gigs. We didn't want anything to do with the Acid Jazz scene.

Did you have any residencies?

Ozzie - Other than Checkpoint (Bradford) No. We used to put a lot of nights on ourselves, and people just got to know us. We were purist and got known for that.

TAKE 5

As the name suggests: there were five of these DJ's. A collective playing rarest-of-the-rare tunes to an alternative crowd to Gip, Lubi and Chico.

Tony Jacobs - I came out of the Reggae scene in around 1983 when that Ragga rubbish came out, and around '84/85 I got into 'Rare Groove' - a few years later I started getting into Jazz and Latin. I'd been friends with Aff since school and he'd always be playing tapes of all that when I had the reggae sound system. It wasn't my music at the time but I got into it. I used to see Joe in this second hand record shop and I noticed we were buying similar things and got talking. He was friends with Michael and we all got together to try and start a little something with this music

So you missed all the early 80's Jazz thing?

Tony - Apart from Aff, we all came out of the Reggae scene. We all had 'dreads'.

Aff Ahmed - I was into Soul music and around '80/82 I met Irven Lewis (Brothers In Jazz) and Leroy and hung around with them. They were well into the Jazz. We'd travel to clubs like *Berlin* and go to *The Gallery*, all-dayers, weekenders. Colin Curtis just blew my mind. I wasn't a dancer, I just watched envious!

What about *The Central*?

Aff - People would clap the records. It had the vibe. From there it became a passion. That club kick started it up here. A lot of dancers that came from Leeds went there. The top guys. That was it for me, anything with a Jazz groove. I went out looking for the music. I started buying records from there. There was nowhere in Leeds to buy from, you had to go to Manchester - which was an Alladins cave: Afflecks Palace, Expansion records....

We started out on ABC radio - the pirate radio scene. That was the only way to get the music out there. Mike had his own show.

Tony - Our first gigs were for Gip at *The Cooker* but we were doing other places: Harveys (on a Sunday) The Bank wine bar - just playing Jazz, and a live session at Café Max...

Mike Walwyn - .....which was our first foray into promoting.

Everybody loved our music on our radio show. We had a very positive reaction, so when we started doing clubs, we didn't realise how hard it would be. It was difficult to get the numbers. If we played at an established club that had a big crowd they'd go mental.

Aff - We were fighting a battle to put the Jazz groove in Leeds. *Gip, Lubi* and *Chico* cornered that scene. I've played for them quite a few times. For music, no one could compete with us though – we had the groove, we had the vibe.

Mike - There was five of us all bringing our own selection. There was me, Joe Gatewood, Tony Jacobs, Afaq 'Aff' Ahmed, Micheal Richards. We were all collectors. We had the music. We were competing and trying to out do each other. One of us – Joe – would think nothing of spending £200 on a record and we'd go out playing all this exclusive stuff – rare as anything. He was our advantage.

Tony - We weren't paying a lot of money for a lot of it though. You could find loads of rare stuff in Manchester, way cheaper than London.

Mike - We were buying a lot of rare Jazz and Rare Groove.

Aff - Because there was five of us playing different styles, we never overlapped.

Mike - We must have been daunting.

Aff - We don't know why, but we kept getting doors closed in our faces though.

Tony - which was a good thing because it made us go out and do our own nights.

Mike - I don't think that, at the time, we realised how big we'd got and how much influence we had. We were doing two or three gigs a week. We converted a lot of people to Jazz.

Aff - We did a lot of parties. We aimed them at the right people. Charge a fee which included the drink. We had a crowd that followed us.

Did you go to Gip's club *The Coconut Grove* to see the bands?

Mike - Loads of times. It was a good little scene. It was new and fresh and we needed something in Leeds at the time. It led onto their other sessions *Dig* and *The Cooker* so...

So you started, more or less, when the *Acid Jazz* thing was happening

Aff - It was just coming up. It seemed to kick-start the whole Jazz thing again. It was good and exciting.

MILLER THE DRILLER

I'm talking to one of Leeds main dancers from the mid-80's on.

I went dancing at the original 'Fame' school in Leeds - *Middle School* in Hare Hills. I was there with *De-Napoli Clarke* and *Edward Irish*. That's where I learnt contemporary. The teacher was Nadine Senior. It was a regular comprehensive school but dance was on the curriculum, I didn't take it serious at first. I learnt a lot just from watching, thinking, "I could do that."

An inspiration was watching *The Firm* practicing at The Mandela Centre. They were more Funk dancing really but you wouldn't see dancing like that in the clubs. My friend Paul 'Willy' Wilson aka The Doc said: "I can't teach you how to dance but I can show you a few moves, and when you go out you practice. Get in to the circle", and then I met Mad Max, Dovel Morten, Tony Blackman, Huggy and from there it fell into place.

Dovel's name comes up time and time again.

What can you say? He was the man. Seeing is believing. Way ahead of his time. He didn't like to get into battles. He was in his zone. No one would battle him, they'd show him respect. He was articulate, a big fashion man too, dressed immaculate.

You didn't get your nickname for nothing.

I had no fear: get in do your stuff, get out, job done. It'd improve me. I always had Lloyd Olpherts - *Mad Max* and Wilson to back me. The contact could get out of hand: occasionally fists might fly, but that's the problem with contacts.

I've even heard of people kicking with both legs in the chest.

Or headbutt. You may get a dancer who doesn't want contact but the other one does, so I'll say "Step out of the way. I'll take him." It was glorified bullying in a way.

There were other rated dancers that I should mention like *Rudy, Dean, Knocker, Dufus, Michael Harvey, David Sutton, Huggy, Donald Henry, Terry Isaacs, Junior Patterson, Ruan, Pedicook, Nobs, Tony Blackman* and *Boxer.*

IAN HYLTON

Again, one of the most respected of Leeds dancers.

I was a 17 year old rude boy and I met these two Punk girls and they said: "We've seen this funny dancing in this club" and we went to look. I saw *Glenroy Rawlings* and *Frank Millet* dancing full on Jazz, and that was it for me straight away. I watched and practiced.

Everyone used to go to Tiffanys. They had a Jazz room. There was dancers like Pitt, Paul Wilson, Paul Sandeford, Chris Saddler – but they were more funky at that point – and of course Wayne and Irven. Then I heard about Dovel Morton. The first time I saw him, he was wearing an army helmet and goggles, jodhpurs, cravatte and riding boots. Outrageous. I was going to say something but then he got on the floor. Oh my god, leave that one alone! He was way ahead. I learnt a lot.

I started going to *The Warehouse* in Sommer Street – when they'd let me in! – and I met the dancer Mad Max. That was the first time I saw the style of Fusion. I saw the battling, and a headbutt and tripping, and I thought: "Is this what this Fusion is all about? If so I don't like it." I've never got involved in challenges, anyone will tell you that. I used to question Miller (The Driller) why he had to challenge. I didn't get it. It always seemed that it happened to Fusion. The dance floor seemed like a battle-ground and I didn't like it. It got tedious everyone dancing the same and looking the same.

Fusion isn't versatile with tempo either. What do you think about the crew Elite? They were Fusion specialists.

They had so much energy. Very powerful, but totally Fusion – as you say. I thought they were excellent. They actually said "Come down to the West Indian centre and teach us some moves," and I said, "What can I teach you?" They looked great as well.

ELITE

As every major city had their main crew that took it from the floor to performances, Leeds had Elite – a hard working unit that did a lot of shows.

Edward Irish - I first saw Jazz Dancers Marvin, Pete, Derrick and Sean at an all-dayer in Bradford and I thought "I want to do that." I was about 14.

Marvin Ottley – My Uncle was a contemporary dancer and he used to talk about all the old dancers at the clubs *The Precinct* and *The Central*. The stories used to excite me. I was a Breakdancer, but when I saw Fusion….!

Edward - We first got together at the *Tiffanys* all-dayers in '85.

Marvin – We did it just for the fun of it originally and all of a sudden, we were doing all the practice and we thought: "Let's do something." We admired IDJ, we said we'd like to be like that, so that's what we did. We weren't just a dance group though, we were friends. If one of us didn't have money, we'd sub each other and we'd go to clubs together and do routines on the spot. We got work like that too. We went out every night to different places.

What was the line-up of Elite?

Marvin – Other than me and Edward, there was Derrick Savery, Pete Springer and Sean Clark.

Edward – We used to dance for Gip at the Cocoanut Grove; we'd do routines for him, and eventually we did a lot of work everywhere. We did the TV shows Def 2, Inter-View (which we hosted) and Hit Man And Her. We were lucky to get all these because there were so many dancers about. The work kept on coming in, and we didn't know from where because we didn't have management for too long.

Marvin – We formed a girl group as well with Bridgit Houghton, Mirrium Shott and Angela Jeffeson; it was an aggressive one, who did all the moves that the guys did. We were working hard rehearsing our routines and trying to work on theirs too and it got too much. They were called the *Elite Girls*. They did quite a few gigs with us.

Edward – You had a lot of Fusion dancers that were great with footwork but when they got down to floor-work they were limited. If you could be good at both you were 'The Don.' Mad Max could do that, I could, Marvin, Ian Hylton, Dovel. As a group, we adapted our style to do some contemporary in with the Fusion too. We didn't want to just be yet another group that just shuffled foot. A lot of groups couldn't change style.

Don't you call floor-working 'Drilling' up here?

Marvin – Exactly. There were specialists in it.

Edward – You couldn't put a contemporary style up against a *driller*. You'd put the drillers in together.

Marvin – Like, if you were a driller, it'd be 10% footwork 90% drilling. You'd do your drilling and finish with a pose. You'd say "Let me go in and drill him." Drillers always wore trainers and looked a bit sporty.

There was always a massive build up for all-dayers, wondering who was going to be there.

Edward – Yes, it'd all come out at all-dayers. Everyone would be there. You'd acknowledge the other crews, but you wanted to be the victor, at the end of the day. If you ever got beaten, you'd always come back with a fresh new move. You wouldn't know where they'd come from sometimes.

Marvin – MacMillans in Yarm was a great place for battling. They'd come all over for it. There was always someone that wanted 'The Title.'

Edward – There was a place in Halifax…. so many places that I can't remember the names of….. *Josephines* in Sheffield…..

That's a new one on me.

Edward – In interviews we wanted people to realise that we didn't start the Fusion style but we were following a tradition. We always made sure that other crews were name checked in them too, out of respect. Here in Leeds there was *The Meanwood Posse* – The M.P's. They were drillers. Very street.

Marvin – Eventually through commitments, we lost Pete, Sean and Derrick. Me and Edward decided to carry on as Elite.

Edward – We got loads of work even then. The Sunday Times did a piece on us - a photo shoot and everything. It was a six-piece spread.

You know, we never, ever said we were the best, I just think that as a group, we did really well. We were really good at getting work doing jazz dancing. We stopped dancing in about 1992.

DE-NAPOLI CLARKE AND EDWARD LYNCH

Two incredible dancers that went as far as forming dance company's. Edward was one of the founders of the famous Pheonix Dance Company and De-Napoli was later one of the founders of RJC – Reggae Jazz Contemporary – Dance Company; who formed a little after the subject of this book ends.

Edward – I'm one of the founder members of Phoenix Dance company with David Hamilton, Donald Edwards and Vilmore James. They formed on 1981. We formed it to be a Black, athletic, male dance company, as there was nothing like that at all. For 8 years we played theatres, schools, colleges, universities, prisons, garden festivals, galas, community centres, arts centres, wherever; which is why we became house-hold names.

What's your dance background?

Edward – My older brother Donald used to dance Jazz Funk/ Jazz Fusion. He was always trying to get me out, and he dragged me to *The Central*. Oh it was sweet! I got the bug.

You had the dancers Oki - the main man, Steve Caesar, Glen Campbell…

Edward – All those, plus the Jazz Funk dance crew *The Tuxedos* - they were Dovel Morton, Paul Henry, Pete Saddler, Anthony Huggins, Sean Odu, my brother and a couple of white guys. There was *The Firm* too. Leeds Jazz dancers had something special. I don't know what it was, but they got inside the music. We were always getting challenged but I never liked all that "I'm better than you" thing.

I always preferred that old 40's style of dancing. I honestly believe that I'm from there – The Nicholas Brothers and all those. Dovel was my inspiration though. He could move from one style to another, which is what I aspired to.

De-Napoli, how did you get interested in dance?

De-Napoli – When I was 11 years old, I went to Earl Cowper Middle school in Chapel Town which had a youth dance group led by the P.E teacher Pete Huggins. I was into martial arts studying and training occasionally with (the Jazz dancer) Pete Springer, and I got into that dance group after the teacher saw me leaping and kicking about, doing my martial arts. In '86 I got into Northern School Of Contemporary (NSCD) but I also got accepted for Leeds United under 18's as well! I went with the dance, as there was no Black role models in football – actually in '88 they still pursued me and I did the trial again, and, once again got in (for the under 21's) – but I still didn't do it.

I remained with NSCD until '89 and went to the *Kokuma* dance group in Birmingham for a year. Jackie Guy - the artistic director - wanted to merge Contemporary with African and Caribbean dance styles.

Where did you first encounter Jazz dancing?

De-Napoli – In '87, I was about 15 or 16, and saw the dance group *Elite* dancing everywhere, doing their Fusion dancing, and also IDJ came to NSCD to do a collaboration show with other styles of dance. I went home and tried to do Fusion but it just wasn't me. I didn't want people saying "You dance like so and so" so I just did my own thing. I consider myself to be a versatile dancer, not a Jazz dancer. I can dance to all styles and all tempos.

What did you feel about the dancers battling?

De-Napoli – I wasn't into that. I wouldn't like someone laying their hands on me. I've battled a couple of times, but that's it. I'm not interested.

What dancers did you rate?

De-Napoli – Pete Springer was the one who really stuck out. He was Fusion, but he had a clean-style, using his arms. You could see his Martial Arts training in his style, which is also what people say about my dancing.

Did you realize you were a rated dancer?

De-Napoli – People do tell me. I'm complimented, but I just do what I do.

Did anyone try to get you into a crew?

De-Napoli – Elite tried to get me to choreograph for them, but it never happened. I never moved with anyone.

SHEFFIELD

A very important area for Jazz Dance. Although the city hosted the odd all-dayer – as most did – the area is most famous for two ground-breaking club's: *Dollars* and *The Jive Turkey* - which, with the exception of *MacMillans* in Yarm (in the North-east), was the last of the great, regular battling grounds of the Jazz Dancers in the North. It was ran by legendary DJ and promoter *Winston Hazel*, local hero DJ and Record Producer *Parrot* and DJ and Jazz Dancer *Andy Bex*. The success of Dollars in 1980 was astounding. Even though it only lasted a year, the Southern DJ, *Pete Girtley*, commanded a huge and loyal following on his jammed-solid Monday nights. For Jazz in Sheffield it all began there, and it's reputation still reverberates in the city even now.

PETE GIRTLEY

Me and my wife Wendy, used to go The Blackpool Mecca for the Jazz Funk with Colin Curtis, and also the Wigan Casino. We were well into the music.

I started doing a mobile disco, playing as much Black music as I could get away with, and one day in 1980, I went to an all-dayer in Sheffield, and was so disappointed with the local DJ there, that I thought I could do better than him. The next day I went to this club called *Dollars* in Sheffield (formerly *The Penthouse*) and convinced the management into letting me do a night. It was a Monday and the first week there was 150 people – you know, nothing special, and it was like that for six weeks, then I invited *John Grant* to guest - his session with Colin Curtis at *Rafters* in Manchester was the top session in the North. He brought 5 coaches from Manchester with him. Unbelievable. We had about 800 – 1000 people. The next week I thought we would be back to normal, so I casually turned up at 9pm, and people were queuing all the way down the road. That was it! It was monstrous, and it stayed like that. I then got invited to guest at the *Nottingham Palais* and by the time I'd done it a few times, I was taking 8 to 10 coaches with me, approx 4-500 people. We were dominating. I did *Clouds* in Preston, *The Blackpool Mecca*...

At Dollars, I used to do a Jazz-hour in the middle of the night, and that was popular -remember, we opened at 9, but it got busy at 10.30, so considering we closed at 2 a.m that was a fair proportion of the night. It was 85% Black, but I remember one of the best dancers was a White guy called Warren.

The crowd craved the jazz: we played a lot of the Japanese Jazz that was popular at the time; *Chick Corea-Central Park* was huge; *John Klemmer – Brasilia... John Payne- Dreams Zone 9* was about the biggest track – massive.

"DOLLARS"
DIXON LANE, SHEFFIELD
(at the side of Woolco Store)

Jazz Funkin'

EVERY TUESDAY — 9.00pm-2.00am
DJ — PETE GIRTLEY

75p Admission
Licensed Bars — Restaurant
Smart Casual Wear

STOP PRESS

TUESDAY 19th FEBRUARY 1980

For a fist full of dollars we are hiring **John Grant** plus his **Rafters Rangers** from Manchester for a shoot 'em up showdown!! at Sheffields newest Jazz Funk scene —

BE THERE!!

The night only lasted twelve months unfortunately, even though my night remained packed. The other nights didn't do so well so the club closed. We tried another club called *Pennys*, but the atmosphere just wasn't right.

WINSTON HAZEL

One of the original rated dancers, Hazel became an important DJ promoter in the mid-80's. With Parrot he co-promoted *Jive Turkey* at Sheffield City Hall – one of the Norths best all-time club sessions.

After *Dollars* closed, there was a void for a few years in Sheffield. A lot of my friends settled down or stopped going out or dancing. I got involved in DJing. I was the only DJ playing the Electro-Soul like *Shannon – Let the Music Play* and *Dennis Edwards – Don't Look Any Further*, and I'd drop the odd Jazz track like *Art Blakey – Night in Tunisia*.

You were a noted dancer.

Well, there was a posse of us that used to go to a youth club in Low Edges, South Sheffield called Rawlinson and it used to be packed. It was predominantly Black. We used to dance to Electro like Tyrone Brunson – The Smurf, but the majority of us were *floor-workers*. After there, we would go on to a place called *Chats* where this guy – Mr Chatoo – used to kill chickens. He painted it red and put sawdust on the floor and it had one turntable. He held Reggae-Blues in there occasionally. About twelve of us would go there and practice our moves, and this dancer – *Chris Ventnor*, was top of the pile. I was seen as the top floor-worker in Sheffield at the time, but, to me, he was "Whoa." He was the man. He was the dancer.

What were you practicing for?

We were going to the all-dayers. I remember at one all-dayer at the Birmingham Powerhouse, they had this video jukebox and it had *Malcolm McLaren – Buffalo Girls* on it. No one had seen Breakdancing before so it was watched so much that the machine packed in from too much money inserted or something. At the next all-dayer people had started practicing what they'd seen in that video, and were dressing in that way. We started a crew called *Smac19*.

They're a famous Breakdance crew.

Yes, well we were versatile. We had specialists in Body Popping, Flares, Spasms and me and *Andrew Bandoo* would take care of the footwork and take care of the Jazz room. We could cover all the other styles too, as I say: we were versatile. People couldn't replicate my moves because I didn't know what I'd just done. It was 'battle' and it was intense, and you'd have your posse supporting you. We started challenges by throwing a beer towel onto the dance floor.

How did the name 'Smac 19' come about?

A friend was in the Royal Navy and when he left he had access to these bomber jackets. We were going on a six week Scandinavian tour and got kitted out in them. They all had 'Smac19' on them which stood for Ships Maritime Air Control 19, so we named ourselves after that.

Tell me about *Jive Turkey*.

For the North and Yorkshire Jive Turkey was the only super-club that was happening at the time. It held 1500 but we had way more than that and there was always queues. After the all-dayers stopped in the mid-eighties, there was not one place to go and dance, so this was a haven for people into all kinds of Black music. We'd play House next to Electro next to Soul and get the same response to all of them and our Jazz room had an influx of all the people into these styles of music too. People literally traveled from all over the country to go there. We had the monopoly for 7 or 8 years. Originally it started at a club called *Mona Lisa* from 1983 and I'd be doing it with a DJ friend of mine called *Parrot* - who was a fashion guru then. That was weekly and Jive Turkey was monthly at Sheffield City Hall at the same time.

Was there a Jazz room before Andy Bex did it?

No. It was all styles of music- including Jazz, because that wasn't right in the main hall anymore. Andy was the perfect person but I was having a big result in the main room.

PARROT

Influential DJ, recording artist and producer, Parrot (real name Richard Barratt) co-promoted Jive Turkey with Winston Hazel.

Jazz was a minor part of what I did. The 80's was a voyage of discovery with music for a lot of people. Hearing something like *Art Blakey – The Sacrifice* for the first time would really knock you back.

I realized that when the jazz foot-workers said they were into Jazz they meant 'more percussive stuff' like *batucadas* because they wanted to footwork to it. If you played some Bop, they weren't that bothered; they'd go off and dance to some House music. I'd rather play something like *Mas Que Nada* and get the girls dancing rather than get all train-spottery, and play to two people. I did have trouble with jazz for a while because of that.

Because the music became too hard?

Exactly. The scene became too male and narrow. By the late 80's I'd stopped playing Jazz. In the early '80's, when I was learning, Andy Bex helped show me the way with Jazz, plus you had the

Jazz Juice compilations that helped. I found things going through them.

People told me that you were important as a DJ here in Sheffield, and that you had a big following. You'd play all different styles, just doing your own thing.

I did. I really got into all the original House music and it did cross over in the North to the Jazz scene because the foot-workers danced to it. I'm not totally convinced that the foot-workers were *that* into Jazz, I think they were into foot-working - although the House scene up here was very Black.

You were one of the originators of *Jive Turkey*.

Yes at *Mona Lisas*. I brought Winston Hazel in there after seeing him play at another club. I was surprised at the time seeing foot-working to House, which I associated with Jazz. We were in and out of Mona Lisa all the time - the owner thought the crowd was too Black - so we started doing illegal warehouse parties and then we started Jive Turkey at Sheffield City Hall. We had the main room playing all styles and a Jazz room too. And those nights were fantastic. People came from all over the country. The night collapsed because the council restricted attendance and so we couldn't get enough people in there to make an atmosphere.

Sheffield had some amazing dancers.

One thing about the dancers here that I haven't encountered anywhere else except Leeds, is that with the foot-working – or Fusion style, as you call it – here you will get specialists at different elements of the dance. Whereas in the dance, usually, you'll get floor-work and footwork but here you get dancers doing floor-work *or* foot-work.

Yes, like in Break dancing.

I'd say it's like being in a union: 'Industrial working class culture' as realized through the dance-floor – from the shop floor to the dancefloor – "He does that, you do that, I can't do that." Sheffield is very much like that: specialists putting all the parts together to make a whole.

ANDY BEX

One of the countries top Jazz Dancers, Andy is included in both here and the North east section (where he became based). As well as being a member of the North east Jazz Dance troupe *Bamboozle* he's also a DJ, and as a DJ, amongst many other clubs, he DJ'd in the jazz room at Jive Turkey.

The main club there was Dollars with Pete Girtley, and when that closed down in '82 there were various jazz things happening later. I did a club at the City Hall called The Kat Klub, which re-energized Sheffield. It lasted four months and was closed down by the council. Sometime after that there I did Jive Turkey there. It was a lovely old ballroom, and we had two rooms. We emptied all the clubs on Saturdays. In my room I was playing more straight Jazz like John Coltrane – Blue Train, and there'd be Jazz Funk and Northern Soul, but the main event was the Jazz. There was a mass of dancers that'd travel from everywhere but the cream of those wanted to be in the House room and mine, so they'd flit back and forth.

The main interview with Andy Bex is in the North east' section about the Jazz Dance group 'Bamboozle.'

BERNI

Berni is one of Sheffield's most rated dancers, known all over the country.

All the dancers used to go to Rawlinson youth centre. We'd play tunes on a Sunday afternoon to dance to. This was the beginning of Breakdancing. There was a good fifteen of us. There was us and the Shanti Posse too, and others.

I was in Smak 19 with Winston, Spanner, Carlos, Bandoo... I was a dancer that went into Breaking but Winnie and Bandoo would still do *Footwork*. When Breaking died down I got back into the dancing but we were doing it to House music. I was merging my Breaking with the foot-work and when I went down to do floorworking I could stay down for a long time. We would travel and we would battle in the name of Sheffield.

The Jazz room at the Jive Turkey was amazing, it was non-stop challenging. By then there wasn't many Sheffield Jazz dancers left here. There was a crew of Jazz dancers called the XR4's. There was about fifteen of them. They were older guys. They had great dancers but they were more *ballet* style and we came from a battling background, and fought our fights. We could hold our own, Smak 19 was the top crew though. We had everything covered from the Breaking to the Jazz.

TREVOR DARIEN – MISTER T

Everyone said "You must talk to Mister T." This hairdresser was there from the beginning, and he and his friends were some of Sheffield's very original main Jazz Dancers.

Trevor - Originally here, there was *Crazy Daisy*, but they played a mixture there. There'd play 'Alternative' stuff and you had band's like *Human League* and *Cabaret Voltaire* in the crowd, but when they'd play Funk, Soul or Jazz Funk, it was the real stuff - no messing. That stopped in 1980. But it all really started up with *Pete Girtley* with the club *Dollars*. We saw him originally at Earl Marshall youth club on Friday nights, then at the First Park Hotel and everyone went there. Dollars followed and people traveled from everywhere. It was very Jazzy. He'd say "If you don't like it, go and get a drink."

You're a rated dancer, were any of them in your crowd any good?

They all were. We liked to go to both rooms at all-dayers, - for the Funk and the Jazz. I'm a dance floor man through and through. We used to take our changes of clothes, and all that, in a 'camera case' and we'd stick them up in an area of the Jazz room. There'd be loads of them stacked up, and one person would take it in turns to stand guard over them.

The camera cases were a Sheffield trademark without a doubt.

We'd wear neckerchiefs, frayed jeans, patent leather shoes, spats (putties) from Army and Navy shops, and even those long tail dinner jackets with white jeans, white t-shirt and spats. You couldn't be a good dancer and not look good. I was a fast foot worker - big spins; sudden stops. That was my style – very funky, but I could switch to Ballet as well. I never did much floor work - perhaps a knee spin. Winston Hazel was similar to me. He was a rated foot-worker. Some of the older dancers inspired us, like *Phil Campbell*. Sheffield had a lot of dancers – at least thirty heavyweights – *Earl Roper, Eric Reid, Roger Bell, Dave Aitch, Winston Norman, Paul Gordon* - who went professional, *Tony Baraclough*....

Everyone knew each other in the Jazz Funk scene, but it was divided, city-wide, into two posses: you had the Zebras and the Shantis, The Zebras wore stripey tops. I wasn't in either.

Was the rivalry serious like the Convicts and Smethwick Spades in Birmingham?

No. Nothing like that. It was friendly.

Did you get involved in challenges?

Oh yes! I've challenged everywhere but never got into trouble. I've seen confrontation especially over scissors (leg traps) - some people would want to kill you for that. Some of those moves were naughty.

When Dollars closed in '81, where do you think the Jazz went to?

It didn't go anywhere to great strengths. That was the pinnacle in Sheffield. I came out when Electro came in. It had changed totally for me.

NOTTINGHAM

This city was firmly on the map through its club sessions and all-dayers at The Palais and, most importantly, Rock City. Run by DJ Jonathon', Rock City's jazz room was, without doubt, one of the most legendary and revered battle-grounds in the UK.

JONATHAN

Forever associated with the venue that he managed – Rock City, you could say that serious record collector and DJ Jonathan Woodliffe was one of the Norths higher-echelon of Black music tastemakers. He was a permanent fixture on the all-dayer circuit and would be just as at home playing to 200 in the Jazz room as playing Soul to 2,000 people in the main room.

I was collecting from 1975 and got roped into DJ-ing from 1976. From 1978/79 I was buying new releases – new LP's/ 12's from what I was hearing at The Blackpool Mecca on a Saturday night when Colin Curtis and Ian Levine were changing over from a strict Northern Soul perspective to then playing new releases from the states…

That upset a lot of people.

Yes it did. But a lot of people trusted Ian and Colin's ears for music and accepted new releases. It was then that I was made aware of these records.

What was going on in Nottingham then?

There were a handful of things going on in. There was *The Italian Club* on a Sunday night with the DJ's Mick Fields and Andy Lee, and they were playing all the new Jazz Funk. They were two DJ's that went to The Mecca and started buying the new releases; they got them from Kev and Paul Thomas at *Arcade Records* here - which is where all the new releases came from. Kev had a show on Radio Nottingham at the time and that's really how the scene started here.

In 1980 I started DJing new releases so I sold off all my Northern Soul collection. I bought all new release LP's and 12's. There were other DJ's in Nottingham like Andy Fields and Andy Lee. We couldn't get access to main nights like on Fridays or Saturdays so they had to be Sunday nights etc. It wasn't really until the early 80's that we had a scene. I got a prime night at a club called *Camelot* which I turned round from 'pop' to 'new release' in two years, and then I started at *Rock City*, doing a Funk and Soul night every Friday – starting October '82 - and by the beginning of '83 we'd gone from 300 people to 1500 for no reason. It just clicked. This lasted till '86. I was also doing all the all-dayers all over the midlands and North. There was many at Rock City.

Were you aware of your countrywide reputation?

No. Colin and I just did what we did. There were records that were big in London that weren't up here and vice versa, perhaps that was because Colin and I were from a Northern Soul background, so we were perhaps listening for a slightly different sound. People never pestered us at Rock City either. We could play what we wanted and everything was new - no oldies. Sometimes we could 'break' seven or eight new releases in a night. I could play anything and the crowd would accept it and go berserk, and when it was eventually consistently packed every week, we opened the room downstairs and that's when Colin went down and started the Jazz room.

They tried to get Colin Curtis involved down South.

Colin was keen, and had a lot of respect for Chris Hill as I did as well. Musically, Chris had a slightly different approach but as an entertainer, no one could better him at that time. I've always stood by that: a great entertainer and a great taste in music. Colin was keen to get involved with Chris and the 'Funk Mafia' down South. Colin and I spoke about this; he also wanted to bring a lot of those DJ's up North, but it wasn't to be.

Colin told me he was furious at the way Chris was treated at the Manchester Ritz. He stormed the place apparently.

He ripped the place to bits. I was there.

Were there other DJ's in Nottingham keeping the scene going by now?

Yes. There were three or four doing rooms in back rooms of pub's and all that, that were searching out tunes that Colin and I were playing. The scene was made strong by people like these - not only here but in Manchester and Leeds, and those kind of places.

I heard you DJ'd at the Electric Ballroom.

Yes. In the main hall with Paul 'Trouble' Anderson, not in Paul Murphy's room. Paul had taken it to a very extreme way - faster, faster and faster. It was one big circle with people challenging each other. It was great to see but I felt it diluted things a bit. I mean, people got really excited when Paul Murphy would come up here to the Jazz rooms but that created pockets of people all over the Midlands and the North that just wanted it fast, which excluded a lot of the girls that used to like dancing to the mid-tempo Jazz. It was near on impossible for them. When the really fast stuff started to get played, in the space of a month the style changed from the almost 'Ballet thing' to the 'footwork style'(Fusion). Everybody was doing it. The hardened Jazz dancers were, like:"We're taking it this way now." The music was there to back up the moves. The dancers practiced a lot. They took it very seriously. Unlike Paul, I played heavy tracks in my set, but I was more interested in playing across the board tempo-wise. I wanted to involve everyone in the room - anyway, I couldn't stand there and listen to two hours of furious paced Fusion. I went upstairs at The Ballroom a few times and watched, and there was no doubt that it worked to devastating effect, but it did have a limited shelf life. Paul did turn up some absolutely incredible records as well. Let's not forget that.

I'm sure theres enough stuff that you and Colin have turned up over the years: *Quartette Tres Bien – Boss Tres Bien* **was one of Colin's ...**

We both put a lot of work into finding tunes, Colin more than me. He was always out looking.

PJ – PATRICK JOHNSON

A dancer that has been there from the beginning and seen it all. I wanted his views.

We used to go to *The Rum Runner* in Birmingham from Rugby. We were twenty strong. *Charles Antiobus* and my older brother *Leroy* were the main dancers from our area. We used to call the Birmingham style 'Fly away' - spinning, and all that. The dancers were strong like Rick and Ty [The Twins] – which brought Charles and Leroys game up. The *Footwork* style [Fusion] was just coming in. Then there came a massive switch and the 'fly away' got moved to the side. The tempos went up, and the challenges came in.

I always felt, at the all-dayers that the best dancers were round the edge of the dancefloor. They didn't want to challenge; they didn't want to go in the middle, trouble is, you didn't get recognized until you got in the 'arena' and once you did you had to stay there. *The Foot Patrol* were *bad*. They had the combinations of footwork and drops. They were fast, and dangerous. You wondered what the hell was coming next. The Jazz rooms could be rough though, you would have dancers saying "I don't want to see you dancing tonight. Don't dance".

We always knew that the funk dancers were the heaviest. You put them up against a (Ballet-style) Jazz dancer and they'd win every time. That's all the *Fusion* jazz style is: speeded up Funk to take on the Jazz music.

We took a lot of moves from the Martial Arts movies: jumps and spins. A lot of moves were taken from those films and incorporated. When you watch them films you'll see. It wasn't the kicks or strikes, but the spins and the drops on the knees. Martial Arts films were massive for the Black community. We used to hire the videos just to steal moves. We noticed it in dancers from other areas like Birmingham and Manchester. We never knew what to do with our hands – it was always all about the feet – until we saw the Nicholas Brothers. Then we knew. Fred Astaire was too slick for us to take anything from, but they had the 'hands.' We didn't know before, we just had our arms by our sides (*Penguin*-style).

We went to a *Caister Soul Weekender* once because Jonathon was going to be doing a DJ set in the Jazz room. A coach load of us went – about fifty two. We were so used to the hostility of our Black crowd from the all-dayer scene that dancing in a room that was predominantly White dancers was different for us – we'd never encountered that – no hostility. We were now mingling with the Essex crowd. They knew their music, and even all the matrix numbers (laughs).

JEFF CAMPBELL, PJ, GILLY, FLOYD SCOTT, PABLO, ERIC MILLER and ERROL DAVIS

I got a group together to reminisce. A top dancer anyway, Jeff's brother Owen is also considered as one of the originals. PJ is there again, with Gilly, Floyd and Eric – who were part of the crew *The Groove Merchants***. Eric, Pablo and Errol were also the Jazz DJ's keeping the scene alive there on a week-to-week basis.**

Jeff - For dancers in Nottingham, there was Colin Carruthers, Gary Maxwell, Rico, Louis Costello, Burton Davis and Chris Foster .

Floyd - The main dancers for me in Nottingham then, that influenced me was Owen Campbell, Randy Francis and a guy we just knew as Greg. They were fantastic. Even when the Fusion style came through I still preferred their way. That was my style.

Pablo - *Chris Foster* was the main man here. When we were all doing the twirling *Ballet* thing, he freestyled in an entirely different way that we'd never seen before. His style would be just as suitable to the Electro room as to the Jazz at all-dayers, I think that it was his style that influenced what we call *Tap-Style* or *Step-Style* (Fusion). A lot of his moves were copied. I saw him mash up dancers at The Ballroom, You may correct me, but we'd never seen that style before.

Floyd - He could take anyone at any style. I introduced him to the scene and was aggrieved when he changed his style from Ballet to Fusion (laughs). I saw it as the enemy, seeing all these young puppies coming in and taking over. We were getting forced out.

P.J. - It was a progression.

Floyd - What saved it for us was when the Mambos and Bossa Novas started getting played by Colin Curtis and Baz Fe Jazz. It equalled things out again.

Eric - You always knew, as a dancer, that the better you got you were going to get challenged at some point though. That was all part of the fun. When Paul Murphy came up was when I first saw the full London crew come up; which was a different scene. That was when I first saw signs of the intense challenging. I thought: "These guys are out to kill us." The dress styles and dance styles were different. The styles clashed, which, to me, was great.

Did you see much trouble up-North?

P.J. - I remember Birmingham dancer Bulldog battling someone and sticking a learner-driver *L Plate* sign on the other guys back. It's that kind of humiliation that causes fights.

Floyd - At *The Powerhouse* in Birmingham, the IDJ dancers from London challenged locals *Lizard* and *Stretch;* IDJ did this thing where one would leap out of his shoes and the next man would jump in and carry on dancing, then the next one and the next one ....then Birmingham went in: First Lizard, then Stretch and then another guy - but his style was portraying violence. He was giving IDJ *the finger* and all that and.....whooompf .... a fight went off. I remember that night because after the club closed and me and my troops were going to the train station, both crowds rushed past throwing bottles at each other .

Errol - Those days were wild.

P.J. -With the *fusion* dancing, you'd get people jumping on each others backs . That used to start violence. You'd get dancers doing those kind of things to stop other dancers doing their killer moves.

You'd see dancers trapping other dancers legs with a *scissors* move with their legs. P.J. - That would cause trouble. That always happened.

That was the new-wave of dancers.

P.J. - They went out to battle on the floor and they'd do anything to win. If there was trouble, it was usually 'Birmingham versus this town or that town'.

Floyd - They were a very aggressive dancefloor force. Let's face it: Birmingham had a force; they had quantity; they had guys that could dance Funk *and* Jazz, and they looked after each other.

Gilly – It got silly though. It got too aggressive.

There must have been area rivalry.

Floyd – There was. I got on a coach coming home from an all-dayer there and it got stoned. All the windows got smashed.

P.J. - There was fierce competition between Birmingham and Wolverhampton. When this all-dayer had finished, I was walking toward the train station and I could hear windows being smashed there. These guys came flying past me running for their lives from some Birmingham guys.

Floyd – Was this when the town centre got wrecked?

P.J. – Yes. What happened was: Wolverhampton went in the jazz room and they were dancing well and Birmingham didn't like it and the animosity spread to the main room and escalated into a near–riot. When we heard the windows smashing behind us, we jumped into a bush. The rivalry was bad. All this because a guy pulled a move.

It was the good moves that happened before trouble was what you took home; what you remembered; what you wanted to practice. It was all about who could pull off the best move, at the end of the day.

You know, you had people starting to say that they weren't going to any more all-dayers because of the violence.

Pablo, Errol and Eric used to back up all the big DJ's at Northern all-dayers but their names never appeared on any flyers, and yet they were local heroes:

P.J. – When I moved here from Derby, Pablo was already doing his stuff. He was the main man. I knew that him Errol and Eric were the Jazz DJ's. They weren't names but they were *our* guys, and they ruled. It was always "Pablo's playing here, Errol is playing there…" Jonathon was friends with all those guys. Eric was the fast Latin percussion man and he used to go to London and bring, what was big there - he was raw; Pablo was real deep and Errol was your 'Airto' style.

Eric Miller – I was originally part of a reggae sound system but got turned onto Jazz by Pablo. You didn't hear much Jazz up here like you did in London. There'd be a few tracks played in other types of nights which is why we started putting our own nights on. We weren't getting catered for elsewhere.

Pablo – We kept the scene alive so that the big-boys could come back and see it's still happening. No matter what level you were at, it was important to keep pushing at it. Colin's cool, Jonathan's cool, but we made more things happen than we were given credit for. We used to find tunes for them; turn them on to certain artists and even lend them records . I'm not saying that we were unsung heroes, all I'm saying is that we did our best.

Are you saying that Colin Curtis got more credit than he deserved?

Pablo - No. He deserves every bit of it. All I'm saying is: that between the all-dayers that they were playing a, we were still doing things and circulating records. We were the *field workers*. Look, it went like this: we'd go to the all-dayers and have records with us. If one of the DJ's was late or didn't turn up we'd jump on. We were just supporting the scene. We didn't ask for recognition. We'd get in to the gig free. We had a chance to play the music and were happy to be around the people that were doing it. We were probably stupid giving away tracks we discovered to some of the big guys on the scene but for people to walk in to a club and see you behind the decks was a pretty big deal. We just wanted to be part of it. Sometimes we got paid, sometimes we didn't. We knew we were playing better records than most.

Errol - We also used to phone up promoters and get on all-dayers and play our stuff before Colin would come on at 10 o'clock and we'd probably do the last three hours as well. Our names were never on the bill. We kept it all alive between all-dayers, perpetuating the scene.

Gilly - Later on in the 80's Pablo did *The Hippo* on Tuesdays which was 80% Jazz - all the dancers went there. It was the main first weekly that we had for years.

THE GROOVE MERCHANTS
Possibly Nottingham's first Jazz Dance troupe.

Floyd – It was me, Gilly and Eric Miller.

Gilly - We started early 90's.

Floyd - It was swing style. We got our cue from *Brothers In Jazz*.

Gilly - We were influenced by them but then we tracked back to their influences - Berry Brothers, Nicholas Brothers… It suited our style.

Floyd – We did quite a few performances.

Gilly – We then became a collective. There were other dancers coming in and out, plus we had a couple of DJ's. We were a package. There were so many people dancing Fusion in the scene by then that we weren't sure whether to switch styles. It wasn't so artistic though.

Floyd – No, Fusion was just raw and fast.

Gilly – Everyone was doing it, whether you were a good dancer or not. Anyone could do it. There are people that are absolutely fantastic at it though.

Floyd – It became a craze. It could become violent.

Gilly – There was no contact with the contemporary style though. It was more about intimidation - doing a move that someone had to follow. There's more etiquette with that style.

KILLER JIM
Jim Bernadini has been there through it all, sticking to his no-messing, hard-core selection.

I went through Northern Soul to Jazz Funk and quickly into Jazz Dance. At Rock City the dancing blew me away. I could never understand though why some dancers took it too far, when there could be trouble. Just fucking dance! Leave it at that! Whats's the point, all that aggro? There's no need for that.

When did you become a DJ?

I was building up a good collection – mainly late 50's and 60's *Blue Note* Be Bop – and I'd pick out the odd track that I thought would be good for the dancers in case I ever DJ'd. I kept the titles to myself. Toward the late 80's I had an idea for a Jazz dance session but to have a live band to bring another crowd in, so I had *Tommy Chase, The Jazz Renegades, James Taylor Quartet, Incognito* and others. I did these events at three different venues *Eden* in Greyhound Street, *Venus* in Stanford Street, and *The Old Angel* in Stanley Street. All the dancers came and I'd DJ with *Chris Reid* and I had *Jonathon* too.

So you'd never DJ'd before these events?

Not really. Bits and bobs. A few places. There was one place – *The Heart Of Goodfellow*, about '83/84. I was very blinkered musically, Jazz, Latin, Bop, Hard Bop....

Who did you rate as a DJ?

Rhythm Doc. He was electric. He played stuff I'd never heard of, same as Chris Reid. I built my collection up quickly. At one point I had 4000 Jazz albums. I owned a clothes shop and I had more money than sense. I stopped in the early 90's because I was concentrating on getting money together to buy a house.

What did you think of *Dingwalls*?

What, The Acid Jazz thing? I fucking hated it. You could say it made Jazz more popular but I thought it was detrimental. I couldn't even stand saxophonist *Courtney Pine. Dick Morrissey* was the man but Courtney had all the hype. No, I disliked that scene. It moved it into a totally different direction. Where are all those bands now?

BIRMINGHAM

With such a vast scene – like London's – there was no way I was going to physically talk with everybody. Again, like in London, Birmingham also had (and has) what they now term a 'World Music' scene – with very important Tropical DJ's such as Brian Parsons and Babatunde (as London had Tomek; Sue Steward; Dave Hucker and John Armstrong) who would occasionally (and often) put a foot into the Jazz Dance world too, but with a strong Jazz Dance line to follow from Chaplins; Rumrunner; the all-dayers and the eventual demise of the midlands and Northern all-dayer scene because of constant violence and disruption from the Birmingham football-hooligans - The Zulus, I couldn't afford to deviate from the story too much. There were so many troupes as well, that I had to talk to many, many people to get to the bottom of it all. Of the many that I didn't get to (this time) I would like to especially acknowledge the important contribution of the Jazz DJ Chris Reid.

GRAHAM WARR

In Birmingham, the roots of their Jazz Dance scene began with the barrier-breaking DJ Graham Warr and his club Chaplins.

My residency at *Chaplins* in Fiveways was borne out of frustration. Firstly because I was frustrated at selling records to normal punters and collectors, and secondly, the so called big DJ's would listen to fifty new releases and virtually pass on all of them, and thirdly: there was nowhere that you could dance to these records.

I went to Chaplins and told the manager that I wanted to start a night. I said: 'This is how I want the club to run, this is the door policy, this is the music policy, this is the dress policy, and I control the lot. You provide the club I'll provide the punters."

Which was unusual then.

Especially in Birmingham. Clubs here had racist door policies – just a few token Blacks in. Our music was unique and you couldn't play to normal punters. The first night we did it – Saturday 10th August 1977, we gave out 500 free tickets. The place filled up. We moved to every Friday after that. There was no conflict of interest with our night, we weren't really competing with anyone. Colin Curtis came down virtually every Friday night, and he'd come to my house too and buy almost everything new. He was a class act you know. My favourite DJ.

Because I had a shop, I was turning over such a lot of music. I'd play a different set every week, unless it was the same Jazz like *Eddie Russ – Zaius* or *Jeff Lorber – The Samba*. There was so much stuff coming through you couldn't physically play it all. I was fortunate because I heard everything that was coming through and had the time to track through albums. I had a receptive crowd.

Colin Curtis said that the first time he encountered Jazz dancers was at Chaplins.

Yes, that's true. We had The Twins – Rick and Ty Hassell, Carl and Lance Lowe, Errol T, Shaun and Pete Williams, the Baptist brothers. They were amazing and far ahead with fashion. They were always starting things. I was very lucky to have them. They reacted to everything I played.

How much of the night was Jazz?

I'd experiment at the beginning of the evening and the last 30 minutes to an hour would always be Jazz, so musically, about 30% of the night. It was funny, really, because Chaplins was a small club. You couldn't really sit down. It would be packed with people dancing all around you and you had nowhere to go, if you did want to leave the floor you had to dance! We'd have coaches come up from all over the country but unless they called us in advance we physically couldn't fit them in!

How long did Chaplins last?

Until January '79. I turned up one week and there was a new owner, and the old head doorman was given the managers job. He said: "This is the way its going to be now," so I left and never came back. It folded after two more weeks. I went from there to a club called the *Elbow Rooms* - doing Thursday nights, but they didn't like the Black people coming in so I went searching for another club. I approached *The Rum Runner* – which was owned by *Duran Duran's* managers Paul and Mike Berrow, so I started in March 79 for three months.

SHAUN WILLIAMS

A rated dancer and a peoples-champion as one of the early pioneers of the Jazz dance movement.

> "Shaun was someone that I respected more than anyone I knew from the all-dayer circuit. He had a phenomenal taste in music and helped make Birmingham what it was. The Rumrunner had incredible dancers and a lot of people were jealous of them. There were six or eight that were even exceptional, like The Twins (Rick and Ty). When I DJ'd in Birmingham I had to take serious Jazz there."

DJ Neil Neale

You were known as a dancer before being a DJ. Did you go to *Chaplins*?

Yes, it was a meeting place. The dancing was incredibl: Rick and Ty, the Baptist Brothers, Carl Jones... My brother Peter was an amazing dancer, he was an aggressive dancer. I was more smooth. I was known for my spins.

I was spending £100 a week on records on imports mainly from Graham Warrs' shop at that time. That was also a meeting place too.

What did you think of Graham Warr as a DJ?

He played Jazz and Disco Funk. He was an influence. He played some good stuff. Colin Curtis and Greg Wilson were also influential.

How did you meet your DJ partner Dave Till?

In Graham's shop. We got on well and started our Monday night at *The Rum Runner.* The owners – the Berrow brothers – liked my style and wanted me to do a Sunday night but it wasn't really my music. I won't bend. The music was too controlled. Our Monday nights started with twenty five people and really took off after a few months. It held two hundred and fifty people but occasionally we'd get Colin Curtis and Jonathon bring a coach down and we'd have four hundred in there! I had a following. People would travel from Manchester, Nottingham, London…. It was predominantly a Black crowd but there were some great white dancers too. Musically I'd play Jazz Funk like *Wilbert Longmire – Black Is The Colour, Alphonse Mouzon – By All Means, Chick Corea – Fickle Funk* and *Central Park,* tracks by *Poncho Sanchez*… It would vary. I wasn't so into playing the fast-step stuff that *Bulldog* and that lot were into; having said that, I'd play stuff like *Slick - Ramsey Lewis.* If you played too much heavy stuff the ladies would complain, so I'd keep them happy with some Soul or mellow Jazz and then up the tempo. There was real talent there. It was probably the busiest night they ever had.

Was it an equal partnership with Dave Till?

Yes. We had a record shop too, called D&SCO. Sadly, it only lasted six months. I could sell a lot of records on recommendation though because people knew me. We were DJ partners for about two years. He was different than me. He was more mellow, I was aggressive. I can't knock him though, he was a great DJ. He had a fantastic selection.

Me and him used to take coaches up to Manchester to see Colin Curtis. I remember going to *Rufus* - which was excellent, but Birmingham ended up fighting in there. It was putting me off a bit because some of the guys were carrying weapons. I DJ'd at lots of all-dayers too, with Colin.

Did you change your style to adapt to the tastes of people traveling from all over the country?

No. I just did what I did. They seemed to like it. I got turned on to a lot of records by Colin, and I like to think I turned him onto a few. I remember recommending *Mardi Gras – Lonnie Liston Smith.*

Dave Till left The Rumrunner.

I don't know why Dave stopped, but I know that he didn't like the change when the fast Jazz was in demand. He'd say enough is enough. When he left The Rumrunner I would give guest spots to DJ's like *Eric X* and (the dancer) *Smiler,* to give them opportunities.

> "I used to do warm up at Rum Runner from 9 – 11. It got popular. I'd play experimental tracks. I never saw being a DJ as something that I wanted to do though, even though Sean was trying to give me an opportunity."
>
> *Smiler*

How did you feel when the Jazz started to get more manic on the dance floor?

What I called the fast-steppers….It was interesting. It was a new generation. I started playing a bit more Electro Boogie. Jazz was my first love, but to survive I had to go that way.

What happened to The Rumrunner?

I don't know. I was there when it closed down, when it was raided, but I don't know why.

RICK AND TY HASSELL – THE TWINS
with COLIN JONES, SARANJIT 'SAM' BIRDI,
MANISH and BULLDOG

Some of the original dancers gathered to reminisce.

So, Chaplins: Who were the main dancers there?

Rick: Well, we'd dance with Errol T, there was Shaun Williams and his brother Pete, Colin (Jones), Carl and Lance Lowe, there was Smiler….

Bulldog - All legends.

I heard about the Baptist brothers.

Rick - Yeah, well there were five of them. Some could dance but they were more *the faces* really.

They went to the best places; dressed well.

Bulldog - Some of you guys, I didn't know your names. I just knew you, (Rick and Ty) as 'the twins'.

Colin - Some people may not have known my name but they knew my moves. I've seen people dancing my moves.

Ty - Someone challenged me once – with *my* moves (laughs)! In Birmingham as well!

Rick - We used to travel everywhere in those days. People did. As many as we could get in a car. But we didn't go around saying, 'We're from Birmingham', like people did in the 80's with all the coaches going to the all-dayers.

Ty - We wouldn't tell people if we found somewhere we liked as it was just a small crowd of us. If word got around, there would be a coach going or something.

Rick - We used to go up to Manchester every couple of weeks. We were always dressed up, looking good. There was some animosity but we got on with some of the *Jazz Defektors*. When we'd go back we'd see that some people had found the clothes we were wearing and that they'd been copying our moves, but they'd taken it their way. It was always evolving.

Ty - We didn't practice really, except they had big mirrors at *Chaplins* so we'd get there early to work on ideas. The DJ Graham Warr might drop a few fresh tunes for us early that we didn't know to try them out. We'd start as soon as we walked in, because it was non- confrontational. We danced with like-minded people really.

Sam - It was very sophisticated. Everyone was dressed up well. It wasn't intimidating The dance style was a mixture of ballet and funk, and the dance floor was small.

Colin - I can do whatever I need to in a small space, probably because I trained myself because of the lack of space. That was my education.

Sam - It was an education. You learned every time.

Rick - I think it was welcoming in Chaplins. I think people would always come back – but they'd want to come back better (laughs).

Colin - We'd always get there early and I'd walk around the floor and put the talc on the floor and wonder if I could get five or six spins out of it. I went to Woolworths and bought these slippers and the next week at the club there were others wearing them, sales of slippers must have rocketed at Woolworths!

Manish - I bought a pair of trainers that weren't good enough for Chaplins so I sprayed them gold!

Colin - Slippers or Ballet shoes - you'd take them everywhere…to the all-dayers…

Ty - Well, the ballet shoes…we'd check out *Ballet Rombert* and *London Contemporary* for moves. They were an influence. It was a style that we never saw when we traveled down to Crackers in London or The Lacy Lady. It was all about the body and the hands.

Colin - It was about being individual. Individual style – look different.

Rick - Also, we'd mix classic fashion with street fashion. You'd have, say, stretch jeans with riding boots. All of us into fashion would buy our shoes and boots from Shoe Scoop in in Wolverhampton, they were slight seconds of classic brands like Grensons.

Now, Graham Warr. Do you think he had a different selection of records to other DJ's because he had an import shop?

Rick - Well, yes, but it was a two-way thing in my opinion: We'd learn from him and we'd tell him about tunes we'd heard from traveling to other clubs too.

Ty - He played Jazzy stuff but it was at *The Rumrunner* when it *really* got jazzy, with the DJ's Shaun Williams and Dave Till.

Rick - The Monday was all about the Jazz and the Jazz Funk.

Colin: We turned up at Chaplins one week and it was closed, down so we went down the road and came across The Rumrunner – which was empty. After a short while we got it busy which is why I feel passionate about it.

Ty - They'd play stuff like *Bobby McFerrin – Dance With Me*, *Al Jarreau – Spain*, anything *Jeff Lorber*, that kind of thing. Sean was a noted dancer so he knew what we wanted.

Rick - It wasn't all frenetic. It was stuff for everyone. There was mellower stuff by people like Grover Washington – stuff for the women as well.

Sam - All the dancers would get there early at 9.30 and have an hour and a half before everyone turned up.

How did you feel about this new dance style – *Fusion* – coming through?

Rick - Well, we were ten years older than these guys. We'd had our time. You get married and have kids and that sort of thing. It wasn't important anymore. It was: 'Hey, it's moved on.'

Ty - When we wanted to do something with dancing, that was way before, when we started our dance group *Expansions* in '76/77,which was like 'Hot Gossip' - there was hardly anyone. We did some shows, but there was job commitments so *that* was just play.

This was in the disco period. Did you go into competitions?

Ty - Well, what we'd do took a couple of hours on a dance floor not all crammed into five minutes. Most of the best dancing was on the dancefloor not competitions. I remember seeing the World Disco Champion, Grant Santino, dancing at the Lacy Lady. He was terrible.

RICK HASSELL of THE TWINS – RICK AND TY

The Twins were talked of by dancers all over the country – as much for their dress-style as their influential dancing. Colin Curtis brought them and their dance group Expansions to Manchester to introduce jazz-dancing there.

West Side Story was very influential to us. We liked the coolness of it – the skinny jeans and sneakers. We always used to check out London Contemporary and Ballet Rambert. We'd be in the first five rows hoping for some inspiration. I suppose, for a short while you always had, at the back of your mind, 'I wish that was me..' You always identified with the Black dancers, even though there was hardly any in the company.

You used to go to *The 100 Club* and *Crackers* in London.

Oh yes, and we were at *Global Village* in London once and we saw *Trevor Shakes* on his own. As a dancer, he was just on another level. There was a few guys: *Paul Anderson, Kelvin* and *Mohammed Yermack* – who were our favourites. We mixed in a bit of their style with ours. In terms of our education, Crackers was it. We went every couple of weeks. We've been to Upstairs At Ronnie Scotts and Lacy Lady.

You used to have guys come up to Chaplins from Bristol.

Yes. When we went to their clubs they'd jump in your face. That's the first time I really encountered that battling mentality. Their dance style was entirely different to ours.

What do you think of Colin Curtis?

Oh God. The main man! He totally understood the dancers. From a Jazz point of view, he got it right.

What was your favourite club of Colin's?

Rufus. We'd get there when the doors opened and just dance to Jazz before the people really started coming in.

Colin tells me of getting dancers coming up from Chaplins to introduce Jazz dancing, and they came on the floor with stockings over the faces, shocking everyone.

That was us. It was at a Blackpool Mecca all-dayer. I've never been so nervous in my life, we hated every second. We'd never choreographed anything before, the stockings weren't meant to be a military statement, we wore them so that if anything went wrong no one would recognize us (laughs). We almost didn't go on. We did it in three parts: a choreographed piece, a mass 'Bump' and then the freestyle – which is the only bit we wanted to do. We called ourselves *Expansions*. It was a 'Hot Gossip' type group.

SPATS

I mixed the James Brown dancing with Tap and elements of Break Dancing, and gymnastics. That's where I come in. Basically, I was watching Errol. T championing all those movements and I wanted to do that, but do my own thing. I was too young for *Chaplins* and it took a while to get into The Rumrunner but that's where I was hearing the Jazz. I used to stand on the side of the dancefloor thinking,"When am I going to get a chance to dance?" You had to gradually get on the floor and gain respect. I felt the aggressiveness of the dance. It had to be dark, so I'd go away and practice. A lot of them were copying the London dancers and coming back, at the time, but I was trying to work on different moves. I met a lot of the dancers at The Locarno. That was where the real battling took place. That was where the hand over was happening from Errol T to the new generation.

ERROL T – THE GODFATHER

As dancers go, every major area had their main-main and original influence; Errol T was Birmingham's.

Around '76, London was two years ahead of anywhere else. It had close links with America. The only club here that was 'doing it' was Chaplins with Graham Warr. He had a record shop, and that's where we all started from. My crew were *the* dancers at Chaplins, plus you had the other crew: 'the twins' and all of them, but we were rough. A crew of trained American dancers based in London came to the club once and white-washed us, and on that day I swore it would never happen again, and I started practicing and focusing on my dancing. They came back a year later and we took them. They'll remember me! I carried on doing my own thing working on my own style. I've influenced many people, and if young dancers couldn't get in I'd always make sure they did. I'd bring crowds to the clubs too.

> "Errol T was a 'people-person'. He was everywhere, and an incredible networker. He's great at putting the word around and bringing people into your club. He had a bag of records three inches thick that he'd take around to clubs and sometimes get DJ's to play them."
>
> *Bruce Q*

I used to spend all week buying records and I would travel all over the North going to clubs with a small bag of records and try to turn the DJ's onto these sounds; try to influence them. We knew all the dancers from visiting London and the other areas and they'd come up and stay too. Other than the music it was all about three things: the socializing, the dancing and the fashion, and we dressed well.

In the early 80's the next generation came in: Bulldog, Lizard, Brezhnev, Stretch.... all those, and I was mentoring them. I was still there going out though, and if I was in the room I'd give everyone something to think about. People think I play an instrument because I'm finely tuned to the music. I was never going to take the dancing further though, because to me, it was all about pure enjoyment.

Midlands meets the Metropolis at a JAZZ-LATIN All-NIGHTER *latin bossa nova batacuda mambo samba salsa bop* only £3.50 for 8 hours of music & film PA by IRE KERE!

DANCE to DJs from the Midlands CHRIS REID & RHYTHM DOC and from London BAZ fe JAZ & EL DORADO

WATCH rare archive film featuring, from Cuba BENNY MORÉ, RITA MONTANER and from America BIRD, GILLESPIE & many more

SCALA Cinema, Kings X 11.30> SATURDAY 21st SEPTEMBER

RHYTHM DOCTOR

One of the new-wave of important heavy-weight Jazz DJ's that came through in the early 80's.

I became a DJ in 1976 playing Punk and Reggae at Coventry polytechnic. I was mixed up with the 'Two Tone' scene in a big way (British new-wave Ska music of the late 70's). All the bars and clubs I did were frequented by members of *The Specials*. I was in a Two Tone group called *The Swinging Cats* and we made a record for the Two Tone label. After that, I got into Rhythm and Blues, and then Jazz. I used to go to the old Locarno all-dayers which had Shaun Williams and Graham Warr in the small room – The Bali Hai. That room was absolutely packed. It was absolutely undescribable, and from there you had The Rum Rummer. There wasn't many people there that weren't great dancers. Earlier on in the session serious dancing was going on – that was in that kind of Ballet-style.

I would travel everywhere with the DJ Baz Fe Jazz. He was an old friend from Coventry. I got on to doing the all-dayers through him. He used to push me, and suggest to other promoters to book me. We were brothers in collecting. I used to work in record shops in Coventry that he'd buy from: first at Virgin, and then I had my own department selling imports and pre-release Reggae above Jill Hansons records, and *Inferno* records. Believe it or not, I used to get a lot of Samba records from HMV. They had a great big section. I used to buy all the Batucada albums blind there! I was also buying from a Birmingham shop called the Jazz And Swing and *Sonet* - my own shop (around '83). I used to also buy a lot of my records from Chris Reid - he worked at *The Diskery* in Corporation Street and Baz - who worked at Paul Murphys shop, and we'd swap and trade. I wouldn't want to play what everyone else was playing, great as it was. I had to find my own stuff too.

I did all *The Rock City* all-dayers - with Colin Curtis, Jonathon and Baz. I was the one there that was more extreme in tempo, in retrospect. I was honoured that a man as legendary as Colin thought that Baz and I were the men pushing the whole scene on. I just thought I was a young upstart! I loved the all-dayers because you had about fifteen different cities all represented there, like tribes. Of course there was always the bad element. It was a shame that the whole all-dayer scene imploded.

Did you DJ in London?
I did Gilles Peterson's pirate radio station KJAZZ once with Baz, in a shed in his back garden, and a big event at the Scala cinema, but that was it.

You were doing Greens, Clarets, Roma's - which was billed as 100% Jazz. Did Coventry have a lot of great dancers?
Not really. Baz and all his friends. There were great dancers coming from Rugby and Nuneaton but it was just a microcosm of what was happening in Birmingham really.

Were you strictly a Jazz DJ?
No. I mixed it up. At the all-dayers I just played Jazz, but I'm passionate about many styles. I couldn't go to a specialist night and listen to one style all night. I'd last a couple of hours. It was my livelihood, so I would play other stuff.

Was it a situation that when the all-dayers stopped you stopped playing Jazz?
A bit like that, yeah.

LINFORD 'FANNY' TAYLOR
As both a dancer and spectator, Linford has seen it all happen in the Jazz Dance scene. He traveled everywhere and still does.

My crowd from Smethwick went out and got these baseball jackets and we called ourselves *The Smethwick Spades*. We used to go to the Crown And Cushion in Derry Bar (near Handsworth) on a Thursday night. It was like that film 'The Wanderers' - we used to walk through Smethwick through Handsworth to the venue in our jackets and the word got out about us, and we'd be dancing against the 'elite' of Birmingham.

We'd travel anywhere. Hardly any of us had any work so all we worried about was getting to where we wanted to go, like Manchester or Scotland. We didn't worry about getting back, we had nothing to get back for. We used to go to Greg Wilson's night at Wigan Pier near Manchester, and our first objective, when we got there, was to siphon off petrol from other cars. We'd just go round to the car park, sometimes we would just roll into the car park where we'd have just enough petrol to get there. We'd go to Rum Runner in Birmingham Mondays, Wigan Pier Tuesday, Legends, Manchester Wednesday, Cassinellis, Standish on Friday. Cassinellis was my favourite club of all time. If we didn't get to any other club we had to get there. There was something about Colin that was electric. He inspired me. A few of the lads, like Stretch and Lizard started going to The Electric Ballroom and told us all about it and saying: "You've got to go," and from that moment on, London were the Gods. The first time we went was an eye opener: The lads went there to do the business and all they ended up doing was watching (laughs). One of us went in, Clive – but the rest of us were more 'contemporary' style. Their scene was intimidating. Years later, they didn't understand why we'd put them on a pedestal. It was intimidating going to The Rumrunner in Birmingham for the first time too: all the older dancers that we looked up to were there, like Rick and Ty - The Twins, Smiler and a guy called Lance Lowe. The twins had their moves, and anybody would have been silly to take them on, and they all did such fast moves that we couldn't work them out. They were friendly to us and gave us encouragement. The DJ Shaun Williams there was a legend. It was an amazing session. It was an experience. The dance style was more contemporary there until the boys starting going up to the Electric Ballroom bringing the *fusion* in.

Did you see many battles?

Thousands. The best battle I ever saw was between Dovel Morten from Leeds and the Birmingham dancers. He was doing moves we'd never seen before. He took us on single handedly and beat everyone. There was an arrogance of like: "Yeah, I know I've beaten you," and if you tried to shake his hand he wouldn't, but I have to admit on that night we were beaten hands down. There was a bit of animosity between Leeds and Birmingham for a while after.

ERIC X

Just like the Rhythm Doc, again: here is another one of the new influential young heavy Jazz DJ's of the early 80's.

Around 1980, I started DJ-ing at the *Crown and Cushion* battle-ground on Sunday afternoons. I was still at school then. It was originally a mobile disco with two DJ's and was promoted by John Tully – who went on to run the all-dayers in Birmingham. I used to bring my records because I knew I had the tunes that people wanted to hear, so eventually they let me DJ.

I was going to London clubs like *Spats* and *Crackers* and all those clubs, and go to buy records there too. I'd go with Paul Murphy and others. London was more upfront than Birmingham. That was evident. There were bigger pockets of the scene there. I was playing all the music I heard in London which was new to the Birmingham crowd, like *Barry Miles- Magic Theater.*

Through John Tully I got booked straight into the Jazz room at the first Powerhouse all-dayer along with Chris Reid, Baz Fe Jazz and Colin Curtis.

What were you doing outside of the all-dayers?

Well, all-dayers were spread all over the North, and I was doing all of them, so that kept me busy. They started off monthly and then went every two weeks. I did a few all-dayers in London at *The Electric Ballroom* too. The Powerhouse in Birmingham, and the *Rock City* in Nottingham were the pinnacles in the North.

I heard Murphy once got a round of applause as he walked across the floor to the decks at the Powerhouse.

(laughs) He did. He got a great reception here.

What was your impression of The Ballroom?

Dark, dingy and it was a battleground!

What happened when the all-dayers finally stopped?

Well, by then I was buying a lot of House music and playing that. To me that music is a continuation of Disco, which I was always into.

Did you stop playing Jazz?
No. I guested at *The Wag* a few times and did *Dingwalls* quite a few times and a *Jazz 90*.
So were you playing Acid Jazz?
No, I never bought into that. It was refreshing but I didn't go into overkill. Not at all.

THE FUSION FEW

This troupe were one of the first to take the Fusion dance steps and put them into a performance. Fusion Few was comprised of the elite of Birminghams new young Fusion dancers. Stretch and Lizard talk here, and these were the dancers responsible for initially spreading the London Fusion style all over the country.

Stretch – The first time I went to an all-dayer at *The Locarno*, the music was amazing, and there'd be amazing dancers like Rick and Ty, Shaun Williams and Errol T – The Godfather. I was surprised when I heard Jazz, I thought, "What's this?" and there'd be these guys dancing like contemporary dancers. Someone said I should check out *The Rumrunner*. It was an intimate club and the best I've ever been to. The music was unbelievable. I saw the dancers and I wanted to be like them. Everybody knew them and they had the best women.

I got opportunities to travel with other people: people traveled all over the country to clubs then. The first time I went to London was to *The Horseshoe*. I went in and sat down listening to the maddest Jazz Funk and someone said, 'Hey, have you been in the other room?' I went in and heard stuff by *Airto Moreira* and *Flora Purim*, but it was the dancing that got me. It was rough but smooth. We were thrown. The footwork was unbelievable. After that night, it changed the dance style of Birmingham forever: We went straight from there to The Locarno and explained what we'd seen, and from there it caused a bit of resentment. The older dancers said that us young wild youth had brought in this style of Jazz from London and ruined the scene. There was animosity. They didn't like the *Fusion* style. We readily admit that we 'teefed' the moves, 'teefed' the style, did it our way and took it round the country.

Lizard – Yeah, our group would go down to London – we were young, we were stealing moves, we didn't give a damn - watching all these guys and going back and practicing. We would travel all over the country and after a while you started seeing small crews doing the Fusion style. It was like a virus that was spreading (laughs). Wherever we were going people were trying to challenge us. We were the new wave and we were moving on. At first, at the all-dayers in the Jazz room, you would get dancers from all over the country but dancing in the contemporary style. They hated what we were doing. They would say: "That's not right" and went on and on…..."That's not Jazz," they would say. They would get in our way to make it hard to dance. We never saw 'Contemporary' – like they danced at The Rumrunner - as a street dance. When we brought the *Fusion* from London there was a lot of resentment. People couldn't understand it.

One night we went to The Horseshoe early and we saw this black guy wearing a vest and beat-up basketball trainers and he set a square - five feet by five feet – he was dancing to *Herbie Hancock – Actual Proof* – and we watched him dancing and realized that if you were dancing Fusion, you had to make it precise and everyone should see what you were doing - rough but neat. His name was Chalky. He had his head up proud, as if to say: "Beat this." We learnt that day.

Stretch – We found out that the dancer's from The Horseshoe didn't travel for some reason, but we started traveling to other parts of the country, and, to me, that is how the Fusion style spread all over the country. We went to Nottingham, Leeds, Preston – mashing it up. We were taking it. We started running out of ides and then we heard that the Electric Ballroom had started with Paul Murphy. I didn't make the first trip but I waited up until 3a.m. till the guys got back to hear about it, and they all just shook their heads. They said that Jerry Barry was still on top and raved about this 'battle' tune *Barry Miles – Magic Theater*, and they were talking about this new dancer - Milton. They said that now all the dancers were 'busting a cut' and I said: "What is that?" It was pulling a competitive move on another dancer in a challenge – "A man is holding his foot while jumping through with the other and all that." I went next week and shook my head. It was raw. I was seeing 'patent shoes' and 'crown slippers,' I saw people with short-cropped hair - all dyed multi-coloured, and I was watching people challenging - dropping cuts hammer-and-tong. I realized it'd moved on to another level.

We asked why don't they travel and they said that they had it all there. The only reason they did start to travel was because someone from here went to London boasting: 'Us Brummies can tear up the Londoners.' The Londoners came up to one all-dayer and brought a crew up called *The Murder Squad*, because they only came up to burn Brummies. It started a bit of rivalry. We tried telling them that we just come to London to learn the moves etc but they weren't having any of it. They were cold-hearted. Nothing major developed. When London decided to start traveling they wanted to go to all the main areas and then come for Brum. We knew that the cockneys were our 'World cup.' We'd take on anyone.We used to test our mettle when we traveled up North, but London? It was a different game man. Godfrey would say: 'The Cockneys invented it but we're taking it to another sphere' but what we didn't realize was, they were doing it too - they were riding the riddim same as us, but they were lucky: they had the music 24/7 on tap! That was the only difference between us and them: we had to beg to get the tunes. We were hopeless.

Lizard – I became good friends with Milton. I never saw him before their first trip up here, but he must have destroyed London. They'd sent him up here to do damage! I met him in a challenge. There was shouting like you hear in a riot in this packed room: people were shouting: "Bulldog's losing to Milton!!!" and I was pulled onto the floor. We went head to head for three tunes. He'd be dropping lots of cuts – so did I. We rowed afterwards but, then, as I say, we became close friends. We danced at The Electric Ballroom as well. We danced solid through six tunes, cut after cut. Everyone was there. The weight of Birmingham was on my shoulders. For that challenge we weren't friends. On the coach I went out like a light straight away.

Stretch - We probably killed the scene in Birmingham because we spent so much time traveling. We should have been at home nurturing. We just got on with it.

***The Fusion Few* has been acknowledged as being the first Jazz dance troupe in the Midlands.. When did it start?**

Stretch - Early '80s and lasted for about ten years. Our weakness was our organization. We were very disorganized. We had no business card, no idea, we had no ambition. It was all a bit penny-ante. We could have gone a lot further. We needed guidance. We were originally called *Wild Youth*: that was Bulldog, Brezhnev, Lizard and Pablo. They were raw. Out of them came *The Convicts*. There were thirty or forty of us, and to be a member you had to have a criminal record!

Lizard - There was a lot of rivalry between the Smethwick Spades and The Convicts at the Crown And Cushion. They used to come in with the same Baseball jackets with a 'spade' on the back – about twenty of them – and we'd be there waiting to bury them. We were mob handed. We all became *one* in the end.

Stretch - Out of the Convicts came The Fusion Few – round '85. Lizard came up with the name (after seeing an advert for Paul Murphys record shop).The original line-up was Lizard, Brezhnev, Bulldog – in the beginning, then Godfrey and Stretch. There was a dancer called *Little Ronnie*, who was an amazing dancer. He had some intricate moves. He joined *Fusion Few*. He brought a character to the group: the funniness. We were deadly serious and he lightened it up. If you asked who the best dancer is in Birmingham though, you're talking about *Bulldog*. He's number one. He can dance anything. He can drop the cuts.

Lizard - We used to practice at the Summerfield centre and we put loads of hours in there. We started because we were practicing down there individually. When we did our first gig at the Hummingbird, Milton said to me "Right, we're going to have to go away and do something."

Stretch - We tore the place up. Bruce Q said that he turned round to look at the reaction's of Marshall and Jerry - future members of IDJ - and they realized that they had to step up their game. We were looking to be where they were. We'd go to all the all-dayers and our arses would be on the line every time. If one of us had an off day and a man burned you, you had to get on with your training and work on your stamina and work on your cuts. We actually wrote a book of all the moves: combinations of cuts, footwork, spins. We gave each move a nickname and we'd call them out.

Like American football tactics.

Lizard - We knew them off by heart. After a while you could shout out "Dead man," "Surfboard" and all that. It wasn't really dancing in the end. It was just about getting one back. It'd be nice just to dance sometimes! People never remembered the dancing though, it was all about who dropped the baddest cut?

Stretch - We played in many places that never knew about Jazz dancing and we'd get standing ovations. We did one long set at the Mac in Cannonhill park and one of the routines we performed using chairs that we took from the film 'Singing In The Rain' with Gene Kelly and Donald O'Connor - where they danced on chairs, and we took that out.

I've seen a few dancers dance on and over chairs in challenges. I never knew it came from you.

Stretch - We were developing. We took stuff from the Nicholas Brothers, everywhere... it got heavy. Lizard took to dancing Fusion as easy as drinking a glass of water. Brezhnev was left-handed so he came out with harder moves. Me, I was a footwork man - I'd stand up straight like Marshall (IDJ). He was one of my idols. That guy could 'bust some foot.' His spins were tight and his cuts were clean. Afro (IDJ) had some vicious footwork again - really clean. He'd dress like a sticksman (a pimp), and Milton (IDJ) was the hooligan wideboy – fast feet, murderous cuts; cuts to die for. He took Fusion to a standard that has never been passed.

Lizard - If you went up against him you had to give as good as you got or you'd get buried.

He'd think about moves all day.

Stretch - So did Lizard. All day. His mum used to complain about him ruining the carpet from practicing all day. He was always working on his cuts.

What was your impression of The Electric Ballroom?

Lizard - Well, at The Horseshoe, everybody was different, and after the short gap when that closed and The Ballroom started it had all changed. It was mainly footwork.

Because it was so small you were in the middle of it and you felt that at any time you could be pushed into a challenge. You could literally turn round and you could be in a challenge (laughs).

The dress then was different. People wore Crown slippers, stretch jeans - I saw leopard skin trousers, short dyed hair or shaved heads, but at The Ballroom you had a lot more boots, riding boots, these red Indian type boots, leather jackets, spats, those patent shoes with the bows -we all had those - green gazelle trainers. Because you had delicate shoes on it felt like you had nothing on your feet – the steps got more intricate.

Did you see the changeover there between Paul Murphy and Gilles Peterson?

Lizard – Yes. Well it was hard to follow someone like Murphy. I wasn't enjoying it for a while. I think that we all wanted it hard and he *would* play that, but he'd take his time getting there.

Stretch - When The Electric Ballroom had finished, we didn't know anything was happening and people told us about *Dingwalls*. It was like time stood still. We noticed that there were a lot of fucking amazing White dancers in there too, and women. Not so many Black dancers.

Like Michael Knott. He was in IDJ.

Strtetch – He was *bad!* We had this thing that none of us were going to go up against him and lose. None of us went toe-to-toe with him because if you went toe-to-toe with him you'd have to be tooled-up: come with the cuts, come with the foot, come with the stamina; hammer and tong. If you said: 'Let's go for three tunes straight' you'd have to murder him because if you didn't, every body'd know you got burned. You know the old dancers expression: 'You get burned to learn.'

In challenges, I panic. There's too much pressure. You've go to go in and drop as much cuts as you can. You haven't got time to move about. You're facing your opponent, he's not going to give you space to do what you want to do - one minute the circle is big then it tightens in. You can't do anything. I like to take some time over some songs like *Airto – The Road Is Hard*. That's my tune. Other songs, I'm in quick fffffffff! – cram all the moves in.

Birmingham had a terrible reputation for being violent.

Stretch – Yes, people say we're rough but it was the people that rode with us. That story in Manchester when it kicked off (violently) in *Legends*: they had to handcuff one dancer to the bar. Manchester, Leeds and Huddersfield all joined together and bricked our coach and run us out of Manchester. One of the dancers got cracked ribs. We were being attacked with hammers and all that. My boys weren't at that one. It got to the stage where the police knew our nicknames and knew where we'd travel to. This was when I had the misfortune of being arrested and put in a police cell. A policeman would say: 'I know you Stretch. I know you go to The Electric Ballroom in London blah blah.... we know about you lot and your all-dayers. We've been watching.' I was open mouthed. They knew everything.

There must have been plain clothed police at the all-dayers.

Stretch – Yeah. They just wanted to know who-was-who and what was going on.

Lizard – There was a lot of robbing - stealing purses at the all-dayers. The hooligans were following us because it looked good. They came on the coaches and there was always incidents.

Stretch – The problem was that the (multi-racial) Birmingham City Football Hooligans – *The Zulus* – starting coming to the all-dayers. You see, in the mid-eighties, with the Burberry, Tacchini, La Coste, Farrah fashions – the 'Casual' look - *that* style seeped into the dancers. We saw some of the London dancers, like Milton, wearing it so we took it to Birmingham. The problem was that the Birmingham football hooligans were wearing all that too. This was the problem at all-dayers: you couldn't tell who was who. We had a mutual respect. We knew them – they knew us – and they always heard when and where the next event was, so they'd always be there. We had our fair share of dance challenges, but nine times out of ten there'd be a massive fight at the end of the night. It got to the stage where you'd hear on the microphone, 'Mind your handbags, the Brummies are here.' People thought we were all hooligans.

BULLDOG
A dance-institution in Birmingham. The greatest ever from that area?

Rick and Ty, Baptist Brothers and Errol T were my inspiration but I became the main dancer up here, If you mention Birmingham my name will be mentioned first nine out of ten times. There are a lot of people who have grown up knowing about me. Often I would turn up to clubs, and before I can put my bag down or take my coat off there's almost a queue of people going: "Are you Bulldog?" wanting to challenge me. I'll take them all on. It's like I'm going 'Ok, next…next..' It kept me on my toes. I've taken them all on and come out on top.

I heard about Milton McAlpine from IDJ challenging you and he span off the floor leaving an egg there.
Yes, I did that move first, but leaving behind an 'L' plate. I've stuck those on peoples backs too. That's my way of saying "Come back when you're ready!" Everybody started to do novelty stuff like that. People came out with some outrageous stuff. You don't need novelties though, If you're a good enough dancer, that'll do the damage for you. I'm an all-rounder.

Was there ever trouble on the floor?
Yes, there was a stage when there was body contact. You could get kicked in the chest, people would try and trap your legs in a scissor movement to stop you doing your move - that'll start fights.

What was your feeling about The Electric Ballroom?
I was determined to make a mark there. We gave as good as we got. We held our ground. We'd back each other up.

It sounds like 'tag wrestling.'
It was. We'd watch each other's back

Birmingham used to travel everywhere.
Yes. It caused a lot of problems when we went to other areas to dance because we went there to beat them on the floor and to take their girls. It caused resentment everywhere we went. You would do the challenging and at the end of the night there'd be gang fights. It was too crazy. There'd be two or three hundred of us at all-dayers. The Zulus destroyed the scene. I didn't want to come out of a club dodging bricks and have trouble trying to get to my car or coach. They killed the all-dayers. I remember once coming home from Manchester we had to go back in a coach with every window smashed in. We got surrounded and bricked.

Birmingham did it to others though.
Fair enough, that's true.

I heard of a coach from London had trouble at the Blue Note in Derby. As it arrived Birmingham went over to the coach as the people were getting off.
Yes that's right. I remember. The dancers weren't up for that. We weren't interested in all that.

What was 'Spectrum'?
That was me and Robert Johnson. We did gigs here and there and we just got known around in the clubs as *Spectrum*. We just got out of the big crowd before we got injured. Me and Fire also had a troupe called *Two Of A Kind* and did a few shows wearing the suits and spats.

RONNIE HENRY aka FIRE and ROBERT JOHNSON
Dancers from various troupes and important faces in the scene.

Fire – I was a 'Smethwick Spade.' There was about eight or nine of us, and we were all friends. We were rivals with The Convicts, and would battle them at the Crown and Cushion and The Rumrunner.

Tell me about The Crown And Cushion?

Fire - I can't remember who the main guy's were (see interview with Eric X) but I remember Eric X playing there; although he wasn't the main DJ. The session was in the function room, and they played Funk and Jazz Fusion.

Robert – I hated Jazz at the all-dayers originally, I think it was the dancing to it that got me into it.

Fire – Same as me. I got all my spins from the Northern Soul dancers. I was fascinated by it.

Robert – I used to organize all the coaches to go on the trips all over the country.

Birmingham had a terrible reputation. The football hooligans 'The Zulus' got on the coaches didn't they?

Robert – Yes, well, some of those guys just went for the women and the fighting. If they didn't come on the coaches they would have got there somehow. But the violence was at a lot of the all-dayers. It ruined the scene.

Fire – They were idiots for spoiling it all. It would still be going now if it wasn't for them.

Robert – I got more in to the contemporary. I never wanted to be a Fusion dancer.

Fire – I really got into Breaking and would dance in both rooms at all-dayers. I formed a Break dance crew called *Ace Squad* and later joined a well-organized Break Crew called *The Rough Squad* – ran by Martin Jones. I stopped traveling all over jazz dancing because I was now earning money at Break dancing. The Rough Squad organized a big major event at Cannon Hill Park which was televised for Central TV called 'Thriller In The Park.' The idea was to bring all styles of dancing together. The Fusion Few danced at that.

Robert – There were lots of Jazz crews around. I was in one with Bulldog called *Spectrum*. There's a dancer called Rico who had a crew called *Mahogany* with Micheal 'Big John' Hall, Steve Seymour and Gary Edwards. They got a few gigs too.

Fire – I was also in one with Bulldog – I think, at the same time – called *Two Of A Kind*. We did routines in podiums in the clubs dancing a mixed style of Funk and Jazz. Other than that we just did three or four shows.

I actually auditioned for the Northern Contemporary in Leeds in '90 or '91 – the same time Chris Hibbert, Derek Tauk and Rob Hylton were there. I got in, but I never pursued it, through personal reasons.

FRIDAY 21 & SATURDAY 22 MARCH 7.30pm

ART BLAKEY & THE JAZZ MESSENGERS

with

IDJ/THE JAZZ DEFEKTORS/JAZZ FIVE

"Art Blakey! What's left to be said about the ageless master of the traps that hasn't already been spoken? After thirty-two years bossing the toughest, most consistently exciting jazz group in the world, Blakey seems as fired as he ever was – a keeper of the flame without parallel" RICHARD COOK THE WIRE OCTOBER 1985

For these special concerts, Blakey & Co are joined by the best of Britain's Black jazz dancers – Manchester's Jazz Defektors, Birmingham's Jazz Five and London's IDJ. The Big Three will sweep the stage with their innovative styles of Jazz dance (first spotted in clubs such as the Wag, Camden's Electric Ballroom, Birmingham's Powerhouse and Manchester's Hacienda), their fast and furious footwork interacting with the hard be-bop of the Jazz Messengers

£7 (£5)

MAHOGANY / THE JAZZ 5

Dancers Rico and Michael 'Big John' Hall give us the brief history of yet another of the rated Birmingham Jazz Dance troupes.

L to R - Rico, Gary, Big John and Steve

How did the Jazz 5 start?

Rico - Marshall from IDJ liked what we did at an all-dayer at Rock City in Nottingham and he came up to me and asked if we'd form a troupe of five dancers to perform with them and the Jazz Defektors with Art Blakey at the Shaw Theatre in London. He asked what we were called and I blurted out "The Jazz Five" because there wasn't time to think about it.

Big John - There was only a short time to the show but we got together quickly. We rehearsed twice a week. We didn't dance Fusion, we danced contemporary, but we were unique because we were physical and very powerful; which was unusual for those contemporary-style Jazz dancers. Jazz Defektors had more finesse, and wore suits and all that and we were all short and muscley - if we'd stood around wearing suits we'd have looked like doormen (laughs). We changed our name to Mahogany because the name suited us – I came up with that - the Jazz 5 just wasn't right, and also one of us, Wayne, dropped out, so we'd only had four in the troupe anyway.

Who was in Mahogany?

Rico - There was me - Rico (Michael Hamilton Bowen), Michael 'Big John' Hall, Gary Edwards and Steven Seymour.

Those two nights with Blakey were filmed for the documentary 'Art Blakey – Father Time'. I've seen it and you're not in it, what happened?

Big John - On the Friday, Jazz Defektors had to perform on the Channel Four program 'The Tube', so we danced with IDJ then, and they did it with IDJ Saturday. It was Saturdays show that was filmed for the Art Blakey documentary unfortunately. When we rehearsed with Blakey you could see how pleased he was that we could interpret his music. We'd danced to *A Night In Tunisia* and on stage towards the end of the routine IDJ battled with us.

Did they mean it?

Big John - Well, it was playful but edgy!

Rico – I thought they meant it. I gave them as good as I got, I know that!

What else did you do?

Big John - We did a lot of shows. A lot were local, like at The Dome, Powerhouse and The Irish Centre; we danced at a lot of colleges and we danced twice with Tania Maria at the Shaw Theatre - that was incredible. They really loved what we did.

How long did you last for?

Rico - About 11/2 to 2 years. It was quite high profile, to be honest. By '87 the Jazz Dance scene here was dying, and we all went our own ways. There was nothing acrimonious.

SMILER

Never affiliating with any crews or troupes, Smiler just danced and influenced so many all over the country.

I got into Jazz Funk when I went to a club called *Romulus* in Birmingham in '76. The dancing was amazing and I was hooked. I then started going to the all-dayers at The Locarno hearing this amazing music and it was the first time I saw dancers like Rick and Ty – the twins, and Carl and Lance Lowe, and I knew that this was where I belonged. I could always dance but I just used to watch at the first few all–dayers and I said to my sister Sharon (another rated dancer): "I've got to take Ballet", and I did. I went through all the grades with my sister and I still teach now. That was just because of the all-dayers.

We were different than the others. We had our own style, we went to many all-dayers and its been lovely to hear dancers say to me: "Oh you're Smiler. If it wasn't for you…." It's lovely to know that I've left some kind of mark. The DJ Colin Curtis came up to me once and said: "I brought this track because I know you can dance to it" and that was awesome to me.

What did you think of the Fusion style when that came in?
We got a bit envious, but things move on. Their time had come.

Were you in any crews or troupes?
No, I never really noticed all that that was going on. Me, Sharon and my brother Brian liked to be individual. We went to enjoy it not to get involved in challenges.

BRUCE QURESHI aka BRUCE Q

In some ways, Bruce was the alternative to whatever else was going on jazz-wise in the City. Without following fads or fashions, he did it his way.

Jazz was always around his house as a pre-teen, and it was checking out the *Miles Davis – On The Corner* album at Birmingham City Library at 10 years old that sent Bruce on a discovery. Taking in Funk and Soul and Dub Reggae along the way, he started DJ-ing in 1976.

It was at the Midlands Arts Centre at Cannon Hill. We had one Garrard deck and a tape deck. There was about thirty of us and wed play 75% Jazz records like Herbie Hancock – Wiggle Waggle just to shock people, and trip them out a bit. We moved to the African Centre in '77 on a Sunday night, on the Moseley road. A friend said that if I liked that music I should go to Chaplins, which I did. I carried on with my nights too. There were a lot of guys into martial arts - Kung Fu - that were into dancing and some were going to the Birmingham School Of Dance and they'd come down to the Midland Art Centre and congregate there, which enticed me into the more Jazz Dance side of things.

I started then going to The Rum Runner - to me, the greatest club that there ever was. It was full of like-minded people and I have never heard a sound system like it in my life – the sound would embrace you. Shaun Williams started something culturally within our music scene and is a big part of what the Birmingham music scene is.

I started a night called the Kitten Club which started in '83 till '86. It wasn't just for the dancers, it was about a bigger picture. I didn't want it to be anal and incestuous like the hardcore scene. It wasn't about 'me and my friends.' When The Rumrunner died everybody moved on to the Kitten Club.

What kind of Jazz was played there?
A lot of Fusion, stuff likes *Miles Davis – Bitches Brew*; more accessible Jazz Funk. There was a void when The Rumrunner closed. Musically, '85/86 it all started to change with music production, and artists like Roy Ayers and Herbie Hancock just weren't there anymore. It wasn't right. The breath of fresh air was when the Acid Jazz thing came in, so we were trying to get that in, as it was a shift away from the Jazz we were playing. I wanted to promote it.

THE MIDLANDS

Even though the city is in the midlands, I've given Birmingham a section of it's own due to the enormity of the Jazz Dance scene there. Not so enormous, but equally as important for their contribution are Derby, Stoke-On-Trent and Leicester. In each of these areas, there has been the one very important club and DJ that needed documenting for their achievements. In the case of *Neil Neale* and The Blue Note in Derby and *Trevor M* (real name – Trevor Molloy) and The Place in Stoke-On-Trent, both venues became classics on the all-dayer circuit, as did the DJ's – who both had enormous followings. As with these two DJ's and *Tony Minvielle* and his many promotions in Leicester, when it comes to their respective areas, it was a 'one horse race.'

NEIL NEALE

I was into the Northern Soul scene and crossed over to Jazz Funk late '76. I got a break almost immediately at a club called *Tiffanys* in Newcastle-Under-Lyme. The DJ there – Neil Allen – was giving up, and he'd been borrowing some of my records anyway so he offered me the spot. That was early '77, and before then I was doing Jazz Funk nights at college three nights a week, and that's where my buying habit started. I was taking all the door money! It was an instant bug. I went crazy.

Were you checking other people's nights out?

Yes. I went to the *Blackpool Mecca* to see Colin Curtis and Ian Levene, but I was going to loads of underground nights as well, that you never heard of. The Mecca was the key venue.

From '77 to 81/2 I was going to the US – particularly the West Coast – on buying trips three to four times a year. I wasn't buying to sell, this was for my own collection. I'd go to warehouses, charity shops, markets….

Did you go to any clubs out there?

Yes. You heard some of the bigger Jazz Funk tracks in more commercial nights, but it was way different than ours. I'm sure there were more underground clubs. The clubs were mainly Black as opposed to over here. In the early days it was mainly White. I mean, at The Mecca you could count the amount of Black people on two hands.

Was Tiffanys the only place you were working at?

No. I was doing all-dayers, all-nighters… the same circuit as all the others. If it was a bank holiday, I'd do a club on Friday, club on Saturday, all-dayer on Sunday and an all-nighter Monday night. I went all over the place. I was regular at Pete Girtleys Monday night at *Dollars* in Sheffield. That club was so good I would go and stay at Petes house to go to the night, even if I wasn't working. It was fantastic.

I heard it was about a third Jazz, musically.

Yes it was. He had a fantastic taste in music. I guested at Colin Curtis night at Rafters in Manchester too, all over…. I would always take two or three coaches - sometimes four – to these places. I put a lot of hard work into publicizing myself and got a hell of a following, and I played as up-front as humanly possible. That gained me respect.

When did you get involved in *The Blue Note* in Derby?

From '78 to '82. The sound system was the best I'd ever heard and it held 500. We had all-dayers there but it was remembered for the Sunday nights. People traveled from all over the country. It's talked about today.

Which is why I'm here (laughs)! You were known for your Jazz bias.

The only reason I know that was because *Baz Fe Jazz* gave me a mention on the sleeve of one of his Jazz compilations. He'd come to stay at my house and we'd just play Jazz in to the early morning.

I'd never play Jazz, or anything, on it's own, I liked to mix it all up. I played one hell of a lot of Jazz, but I saw at other clubs that did Jazz 'breaks' that the floor would clear and a circle would form for two or three records, which could be detrimental to the club - and it was a male thing too. There was too much of a Jazz element in some clubs by the early 80's which was a mistake. It started to intimidate people and they stopped going. You had to get the balance right, which we did. Some of the jazz was starting to be obscure. It was different if I was playing in a dedicated jazz room; it was a pleasure to be there playing to those incredible dancers. Again, things started to change when Electro came in. People got into it in the South quicker than the North and that caused a few problems because people didn't want it up here, which put us in a precarious position.

But for the amount of DJ's that stopped playing Jazz, there was a new amount playing really hard. The all-dayer circuit had Jazz rooms.

Yes, Jonathon and Colin Curtis got involved in all that and I played some, but by '83 I started to pull away - even though I've never stopped buying. I think a lot of the Jazz was going up it's own arse; people playing obscure stuff – only five made–type of stuff - although Paul Murphy made a massive impact on the scene. He certainly did up here anyway.

TREVOR M.

I'd already had a taste of Jazz Funk from this woman who DJ'd at this school disco, but going to *The Locarno* in Birmingham and hearing Dave Till inspired me further – he had a real Jazzy edge. It made me investigate from there. The buying addiction started. That was it. Nothing else mattered.

There was a guy that had a mobile disco at The George Hotel (in Stoke-On-Trent) that held 400 that wasn't having much luck, and a few friends of mine were pushing him to let me have a go. He did, and because of all my dancer friends telling others, the night took off quickly, and they heard about it at *The Place* (Bryan Street). I went there and they gave me a chance, and within three weeks I got Saturday nights and so I've done it from '79 to a couple of years ago!

Were the all-dayers at The Place your idea?

Yes. They were reluctant. It's a big venue, it held 2500. We did six or so, but they were big successes. It was the success of the residency though that got me noticed to play regular on the all-dayer circuit – word of mouth. I played with Colin (Curtis) and Jonathon a lot.

I was told your Jazz sets were unique.

To me, it was just part of the Black music spectrum. I was playing jazz breaks on a Saturday night, but obviously at the all-dayers I would just totally play Jazz, plus I'd always be doing the main halls. There was a circuit but I mainly played the midlands [Derby] but I also did them at Manchester, Birmingham, Stafford, here and Nottingham - I was so nervous the first time I played there I had trouble putting the needle on the record!

Were there many great dancers in Stoke or did they travel in?

It was the crowd I grew up with: Lee Scott, Carl Henry, Eugene Brown, Raymond Notice, Linton Salmon. We were good dancers. There were challenges, but nothing aggressive. We made lots of friends traveling around.

Was there anything else going on in Stoke-on-Trent?

Well, apart from me, Colin Curtis is from here and Neal Neale. People talk about the big cities but people used to travel from all over to come to The Place. It was strange though that, on occasions, I would DJ at an all-dayer in a different part of the country with Colin and Neal on the same bill - three DJ's from Stoke-on-Trent!

Were you on 'a mission' buying the Jazz?

No. I was buying what was available really, I wasn't a connoisseur, but I loved my Jazz. I just loved seeing people dancing to it. There were certain records that made my hair stand on end.

I heard you were quite ruthless

I took it as an everyday thing. I just did my best. I played what was big and other stuff that would work with that. I didn't realize at the time, but I've since been told what affect my music has had on people. I had no idea what it meant to people.

TONY MINVIELLE

Tony moved to Leicester when he was 19 but was born in South London and had a club diet of *Cheeky Petes*, *Lacy Lady*, *Barracudas* and *The Royalty*.

I went to *The Electric Ballroom* to see George Power but when I went upstairs to the Jazz room for the first time to see Paul Murphy I was completely blown away. I'd never seen anything like it. That was it for me. I was a dancer anyway and me and my friends Salv and Derek used to dance in the corner.

Did you find it intimidating in there?

No, I was dancing, doing my thing. It felt exclusive in there. You felt part of something. I went to The Wag a few times and Sol Y Sombre too, and then I went off to college.

Were you buying then?

Oh God, yes. It was a fever. I worked in a record shop in Kennington Oval in London called *Page 43*. I got paid my wages in vinyl. They got all the American Soul and Jazz imports – which I creamed off, and I used to buy at the jazz shop *Honest Jons*. When I moved up to Leicester in '82 to go to the Polytechnic, I was shopping at *The Diskery* in Birmingham and *Rob's Rare Records* in Nottingham – which was an absolute goldmine. I started DJ-ing then, when I was at the Poly, but I was playing everything. They said I could also do a Soul & Jazz Funk night, which I did, but I was still looking for *that* extra buzz. In '84, a venue in Leicester let me do a night called *The Jazz Basement* which was a Jazz room at *Viceroys*. It was a small basement where I could play jazz to like-minded people. I was playing a lot of mid-tempo 'Blue Note' Jazz and stuff like *Jimmy Smith – The Cat, Art Blakey – Moanin'* and a little bit of Jazz Funk. I did *Greenwich Village* in a bar called 'Helsinki' playing the same stuff; just keeping it all going. I moved The Jazz Basement to a bigger venue called *Jazz Company* (St Nicholas Circle, which later became the famous venue *Mosquito Coast*) because it was in tune with what I wanted to do. It was opposite the Hotel 'Holiday Inn' and all the bands used to stay there when they were playing in the city, so we had a lot of them coming in to my night. One night Larry Blackmon from *Cameo* was going through my (Jazz) records !!!. The Jazz Basement lasted until 1987. Around that time, with friends O.J, Alps and Manj, I started a crew called *The Foundation*. We played a mixture of Soul and Jazz and we did one-off's and parties – we were an oasis amongst a sea of homogenous House music. So many thing's started in '87. I started at a club called *The Bear Cage* in the High Street, and did a night called *Calling All Cats*, and then a long running session called *Bag Of Rhythms*. Again, it was just jazz, and it seemed to attract a wider audience.

Jazz was pretty fashionable then wasn't it?

It was different. A lot of Jazz Dancers started to come down. I'm proud to say that almost all of them went on to be trained dancers – some have got dance companies now. They saw it as an art-form.

What kind of Jazz were you playing though. It was a Saturday night, right?

Yes. I got away with unbelievable stuff actually, because I had a full floor with the Jazz Dancers, which encouraged others. I played a lot of Fusion, like *Lenguas* by *Raices* etc and stuff like *Manfredo Fest – Jungle Kitten, Willis Jackson – Nuthin' Like Thutherin'*......We carried on long enough to embrace the 'Acid Jazz' scene too.

What about The Giant Step? They were huge and important events.

Yes. I did those at The Spectrum Arts Centre and Leicester Poly Students Union. Again, I started those in '87, with Rob Childs. We had funding. *All* the bands played there, and it lasted for about three years. I stopped it for three reasons: promoting bands just wore me out, continuous *lack* of funding (in the end) and I started a family – so I had family commitments.

THE WEST COUNTRY

BRISTOL

If you speak to anyone in Bristol about the early days, they talk about the dancer *Clive Smith* – an institution in the Bristol club scene, and one of the originals. The next generation of dancers were the powerful Jazz Dance crew - *The Floor Technicians*. Through various members, I give detailed background of the Bristol scene and document their unusual background too. Also interviewed is another institution of the Bristol Jazz Dance scene - the DJ *Tin Tin*.

CLIVE SMITH

I used to tape Robbie Vincent's radio show and he used to play Jazz, and that's what I used to dance to. Now, I never named it Jazz, but going to all the clubs in the scene and dancing, that's what it was: we were dancing Jazz. There was the Funk element in it and the Jazz. I met *Dennis Richards* at this dance competition. I'd heard about him and we were rivals. It was at a club called *Granarys* with the DJ Superfly (Mike Barnard) – and his brother Seymour was a DJ too and another brother Junior 'Bernie' was a well known dancer. I was dropping moves that Dennis had never seen before; I'd been away in Luton for a couple of years so the crowd knew Dennis more so they were shouting for him, but Dennis said, 'No, he was better than me.' We became close friends after that, traveling all over the place. We'd go up to London to the *100 club* on a Saturday afternoon or the *Wheatsheaf* here in Bristol or *Charlottes, Tiffanys* or the Granary. You'd always get a Jazz break and people would crowd around. We'd go all over the country. *Princess Court* was a big club for us here. Dennis Richards and Seymour DJ'd then and Dennis would play the Jazz. A dancer from London – *Wayne Fairclough* moved down here and some of his family were Jazz dancers and they'd come and visit, or the Pinky brothers from The 100 Club would visit. Everybody knew each other in the scene then. It was a scene where blacks and whites were together. There was no racism at that time. Everybody was moving as one and traveling.

We created a dance group, that wasn't rehearsed, called *The Mirror Squad*: talented dancers. We could just read each others mind's. I'd do something then he would, and he would, and he'd do a somersault…people thought we were doing routines but we were making it up on the spot. The DJ Martin Starr created 10-4 – we were *both* of those crews, and that's when the World Disco Dancing Championships were around. I won that one year, and that's where I met *Clive Clark* – the rubber man. He challenged me at the 100 Club. What I had over him was that I had more moves, but he was amazing. *Trevor Shakes* - another big dancer – used to come and stay at my house in Bristol and there was *Paul Anderson, Phil Tann*…we were the originals.

We had a dance group called Mahogany; that was around before Hot Gossip. We went on tour with the British Jazz Funk band *Light Of The World* and the Reggae band *Third World*, and we went to The Goldmine - Chris Hill's place, then 'Hot Gossip' came out and got on TV, on Top Of The Pops. They stole our thunder, because we were down here and didn't have the connections.

Were there any clubs in Bristol that just played Jazz?

The only club that was Jazz in Bristol was at *Smiths* on a Saturday afternoon. That was Dennis Richards and Martin Starr. *Cinderellas* - with Dennis again – didn't have Jazz breaks, it was part of the whole night. No other club was like that.

With challenges it'd be, 'I'm going to teach you a lesson on the dancefloor.' I used to do some moves 'cause I also had the martial arts training – so did Dennis Richards – we'd mix the two. I'd go Bam! – Bam! Drop down, spin around, pull their legs away, embarass them. That was the move – or I'd do certain moves and just leave my shoes there and *that's* the move, and you'd won – finished! I would never dance all night though, unless it was with a woman! We might go and dance in the corner and work on moves but if people gathered, we'd stop. We would only dance on a Jazz break or if it was a dedicated Jazz room, nothing else. The Jazz-era for us was from day one. There were only a few guys. You'd challenge and then be friends after – swap numbers or stay at each others houses, up to this day, we're still all friends.

The dancing that the *Floor Technicians* do now isn't the same Jazz that we used to do. It isn't flowing enough, but became a style that's around now, but I remember when that style started, from who we called 'The Gossip guys' – *Junior 'Aggis' Mcphee, Steven Thompson, Carl Fagan*. Those were the guys that started doing it. We used to take them up to London on a Saturday afternoon and then they'd go up on their own and then *Gossips* started, and because they couldn't do the Jazz the way we used to do it, they created their own style within it – simple. They came back to Bristol with this style - a mixture of what we do and what they'd learnt in Gossips. There was a step in there called 'The freaky deaky.' You know it? We'd done it all; mind you, there's nothing new that we did back then. If you go back to the old dancers in America – not that I was at all influenced by it – and see old footage of tap and dance and you'd think "Hang on. These are moves that we do"- moves that I thought I'd invented.

Did you go to The Electric Ballroom?

I've been there but not when it was Jazz. That was Oscar's era (Oscar from The Floor

Top- Oscar. L to R - Hameed, Saeed and Nathan

146

Technicians). I'd come out of it by then: I was artistic director of the Arts Opportunity Theatre - which was teaching the youngsters the skills I had - dance, music and drama, and many have gone on to do things you know? *Smith and Mighty* – heard of them? *Ronnie Size* (the massive Drum & Bass DJ), *Gavin 'Cleo' Cornwall* – who has choreographed in London and US, and other people who have gone on to do TV. I now direct documentaries and films to do with my culture.

THE FLOOR TECHNICIANS
NATHAN LEWIS

Around mid to late 70's in the funk days of *Clive Smith*, he had presence. He was intimidating. When he walked in everbody trembled. In *Cinderellas* you had *Delston Brown*; that guy had some of the sharpest moves as a *Funkateer* and you had *Ranky* as well, but every now and again there'd be a battle and Clive would come in and you'd think "Oh God, here we go" and he'd chop down a move and you'd think "Damn". That club was the home of the Funkateers and the Jazz boys because it was owned by Dennis Richards mum – and Dennis was one of the main dancers. If you were an underground dancer and had the moves, that's where you'd go. Every now and then there may be a local dance competition like at *Reeves* with Raymondo DJing, and of course the dancers from Cinderellas would turn up in droves – dancers like *Louis Barratt* and *Cliff Brown* - who had the fastest footwork. The floor would be rammed with just pure dancers. If Raymondo put on something like *Cameo – Knights Of The Sound Table*, you didn't know where to look. The moves were coming thick and fast and then you'd get a burn up – no forget that – it'd be a *rip-up*! Me dance? You'd have to be joking. I'd stay in the corner and practice. In that era, Clive Smith ruled. I'd be proud to have his legacy. He took on all corners. He'd take anyone, any style.

We have to talk about the DJ Martin Starr. He was the Don Daddy of the record box and where he went you knew you were going to hear the tunes. Especially in *Sinatra's*. You had other DJ's like *Seymour, Doodlebug*, of course Dennis Richards - who was a brilliant DJ as well as a legendary dancer. He was bad. You had *Princess Court*, Cinderellas and then, *Romeo and Juliet*s - which was the place for competitions. This was the venue that Clive Smith and Dennis Richards went head to head. The crowd went wild. It was legendary. It was the living burn-up, I saw moves that I'd never seen before. Clive won, but you couldn't say really.

Clive and all the top dancers had a crew called 10-4 and you had *Minor League* and *The Sweat Hogs* and from there 10-4 and Minor League became *The Mirror Squad*. After the Mirror Squad you had *The Renegades*. This was around the period of *The Electric Ballroom* and *The Hummingbird* in Birmingham. I remember going to the Birmingham Powerhouse and watching Bulldog and all those other dancers plus The Renegades. I was still breakdancing but watching them dancing, I thought I'd better start practicing or I'll get left behind. By then, the whole 'Funkateer' thing had disappeared, but to me the Jazz style was just speeded up Funk steps anyway.

Exactly. That's exactly what it is. Countless people have said that. Tell me about the club Reeves.
(Laughs) That place....either you have it or you don't. That's where you'd practice. It was on Sunday nights, and anyone but anyone danced there. It was outright battle. People used to save up their best moves for it. It was vicious. Dancers would travel from all over - like Birmingham. It carried on until 1984.

Tell me about Oscar.
Oscar was the next generation coming through. He opened our eyes to knowing that you can make it if you practice. People knew him from all over the clubs in Bristol. He wanted to be mainstream; out there being seen. I remember seeing him in a disco dancing competition on TV in his yellow jumpsuit. That man could do robotics, then disco, the Jazz, and that takes some doing.

The Renegades - which was *Dave Brown, Vernon Walker, Andrew Samuel* and *Cecil Walker* were the new wave of Jazz Dancers (Fusion) and Oscar would just take them on; battle them. He could switch styles. He was versatile. Clive Smith is the legend of his generation and will always be the daddy of us but for our generation Oscar rules. I've rarely seen him defeated. I latched onto him and learned. You see, I came out of the scene to get into Breakdancing and got back in again around '87.

I remember Hameed and Saeed Esmaeli having one hell of a battle against the *Foot Patrol* at the Hacienda in Manchester – two against twenty! They would beat some but got annihilated because of the numbers, and they'd come back here and tell Oscar and Darren Thorne to go back to battle. They'd travel to London to Dingwalls and The Wag and slowly got known.

I'd been practicing my jazz moves and one day Saeed said, "How come you keep practicing but never dance with us? You should join us." but I stayed on my own until one night in this club called *Papillon* I saw the best battle ever: It was the Floor Techs versus dancers from Reading – and these were great dancers. The Floor Techs were out numbered, so I stepped in – we were doing these moves and the crowd were going crazy – it looked like we'd rehearsed but we hadn't – and I was running up the wall and all that. Reading stopped! Oscar said that they were going up to London and asked me along, so that's when I started following along. I went to Dingwalls with them (but Oscar didn't come along the first time) and I walked in and saw Irven and Trevor from *Brothers In Jazz* and Marshall from *IDJ*. Hameed said to me, "If you think you can dance, then here's where you prove it!" but I got my butt kicked. I didn't have the tools to do it yet. I didn't know this scene existed so the occasion got to me. Hameed and Saeed did really well though, they'd been going for a while. Anyway, I practiced with the Floor Techs and did a show with them in Hereford town hall. I ran up the wall in my dirty spats and you could see my footprints (laughs). I felt great that I was a part of it, and I did a few small shows with them, but then we went up to London to do a Jazz dance competition at *The Underworld* and all the crews were there. Darren couldn't make it for family commitments so it was me, Oscar, Hameed and Saeed. We had to go first, but to this day, it was the best we'd ever danced, and we won. There hasn't been a group competition since Darren stopped dancing, but I want it on record to say that: he'll always be a member of the Floor Techs. He was a founder member. Anyway, this was my journey to being a dancer.

Also, I've got to give respect to Tin Tin at the Thekla. He would encourage us and name-check us. He would play hard jazz for the first hour and a half and we would dance. We'd be practicing and honing our moves. He'd book us for other events too.

OSCAR (PAUL ANDERSON)

Oscar, you were a rated disco dancer originally.
In 1978 I was 6th in the U.K disco championships out of 4000 entrants, I got a lot of publicity around that.

Did you go out much locally?
In Bristol,we had *Cinderellas* – all the dancers went there: *Scamps, Tiffanys The Blue Lagoon, Top Cat* and we had dj's like Martin Starr. We traveled a lot out of the area- two coaches went to *The Goldmine* in 1979. It took 4 hours. Those days there were loads of dance competitions to get people into the club. I remember battles in those days in the late 70's: dancers like *Pinky, Dennis Richards, Clive Smith*.....

Was it Jazzy?
We had the Jazz-Funk but we had to go to London for the real stuff.

What was your impression of The Electric Ballroom?
Well, it was a dark room and everyone used to stand along the wall watching the dancers. The music was so fast. Even though I was a Disco champion and getting into the Jazz, I thought:, 'This is speedwork. I've really got to work on this', so I went away and practiced. People noticed that my style had changed. I started going to the all-dayers where the Birmingham dancers went and all those.

Did you get involved in the battles?
Yes, yes. There was all this pushing and kicking - I remember getting kicked in the chest. Those days were lethal. You had to have a head on your shoulders: they would try and block your moves and trap your legs but I was always too quick for them. They were just trying to prevent you from

doing your moves - I had a move where I did a 'scissor' movement and wrap my legs around their waist.

A big place for the dancers in this part of the country was The Brunel Rooms in Swindon.
Yes, in the mid Eighties. There was a room there called *The Ampitheatre* and I used to get 'butterflies' walking in there. There were excellent dancers in there - *Clive King* and all those. All the Bristol dancers used to go there. The DJ there- *Paul Lewis* – used to give a time countdown until the Jazz sets: "Only 20 minutes to go" etc...People would be waiting in anticipation. He always started with the same one, a slow one, for us to warm up to: *Dave Valentin – Crotona Park* (from *Flute Juice*), then he went into the heavier stuff. These were jazz-breaks for 20-30 minutes, because the majority of the music was Soul. It was a very special place. People would travel from everywhere, so the standard was very high.

I think Bristol was starting to get active by then. You had the Wheatsheaf, and Vadims with the DJ Paul Morrissey, and events by DJ's Paul Dudbridge and Tim Williams. They used to play a lot of fast latin at Moles in Bath (near to Bristol) and other places. They ran events called Birdland at Rummers in Bristol.
Yes but The Thekla!! WHAM!! BAM!! Every one was up dancing. The DJ there - Tin Tin - played some fast Jazz. We were all dancing there and in the end they would book us to dance on stage and the place went mental. We danced for 20 minutes but we had the energy. We felt fresh.

So, how did The Floor Technicians start?
A dancer called Hameed came down to live from Blackburn and he approached me one day because he'd heard about me. We'd dance against each other and one day he suggested that we go up to a club in Blackburn called the Peppermint Place. We went up there – just me and him – and we had crowds around us. We found out that they had jazz- dancers up there called Foot Patrol (from Manchester) and they came to the club late and someone told them that these dancers were in – us. They took us on and we gave them a battle and a half. Two of us against four. They were friendly afterwards. The next time we went there we were three- a guy called Darren. It was there that we thought of the name The Floor Technicians because there was I.D.J and The Foot Patrol. We got back to Bristol and started practicing, watching the old films and routines, and it all took off for us – Holland, Japan...

How did the Japan thing happen?
Well we already knew that Brothers In Jazz had been there and we were watching this TV show about how the Japanese enjoyed themselves, and they showed dancing. One of the hosts of the show joined them and started doing jazz dancing. We recognized the style- it was 'Brothers In Jazz' style that they were doing. We thought that'd be great if we could get out there, so anyway, when I was on holiday I phoned one of the lads for a talk and he said that a guy was coming to check us out for Japan. Within 10 days we were off. We met the dancers from that show and we took them on. They were great, but we just edged it.

This must have been around the time of Acid Jazz.
We heard about 'Acid Jazz' coming in, and thought it sounded promising. It was a slower type of music and we still needed to move to the hardcore. We started going to Dingwalls. It was the top place. I.D.J were there, Brothers In Jazz... I remember Hameed and Saeed having a run-in with them there over dance floor space. It could have turned nasty. There was a lot of respect there though.

HAMEED ESMAELI

How did you and your brother Saeed get involved?
Saeed and I came over from Iran over 20 years ago; coming out of the revolution. I came from a background of Break dancing – which came over from the west; not to the standard of the guys over here. There was a scene, and then when the revolution happened, everything shut down. Breaking didn't stop but it went underground. I first came to London and started seeing the Breaking and got more into it and dancing, and that summer I went to Bristol and that's where I first met Oscar. I saw him in a shopping centre doing 'robotics' behind a shop window with a crowd of a hundred people watching him and thought it was good but I didn't think much more about it. I moved up North to Blackburn to see a friend after going to college for eight months and he and his friends were into the Jazz, Breaking and dancing so I hung around with these guys and went to all these clubs. I'd never seen Jazz dancing before. A friend was into Jazz and I

started watching (the British version of) *Soul Train* on TV and was taking notice of the dancing for the first time and started to work on some moves. I went to this club in Blackburn called *Peppermint Place* and it had two rooms: one was playing Jazz, Latin, Soul Funk etc…heavy, and this was the 'mecca' of the scene in the North west on a Saturday. All the dancers used to go there from Manchester, Leeds, Preston… I remember watching Bulldog and Robert Johnson from Birmingham, but it was so different than what I did, but I still went on the floor. I'd go away and practice and practice. I came back to Bristol and went to a club called *The Papillon* and I recognized Oscar from the shop window. He's like a local celebrity. Everyone knows him. I'd seen him in a few adverts by then. Anyway, he was dancing and had a crowd around him and I was just dancing in a corner and people started noticing me and so did Oscar, we got talking and I told him about this club in Blackburn - there wasn't a club like that in Bristol, and that's how we started dancing together. There was another guy called *Darren Thorne* who was a great dancer, strong but like breaker/disco, and we all went to clubs together. I started practicing with Oscar and we'd go around challenging and all that. We used to go up to Swindon, to *The Brunel Rooms* and actually seeing what the Jazz rooms were like. We'd travel up to Blackburn and take on the *Foot Patrol* (from Manchester) – two of us, and four of them. It always felt more like a conflict than dancing, because me and Oscar never backed down. We got to know them, and they respected us.

There were all these crews that had names but we didn't. Darren came up with the name *Floor Technicians*. We got the DJ to mention our name so that people knew we were there. We always asked the DJ's to name-check us to help get our name around. I had another friend called Spencer Ellis who went to Ballet Rombert and he'd been part of the scene since 'day one,' going to all-dayers and all that. He'd travel all over the country going to clubs like up to *MacMillans* in Yarm (near Newcastle) or wherever, and I'd go with him. This is where my brother Saeed started coming in (late '87). He was too young to go to clubs but he'd watch us all practicing and he'd go off and practice. I never took any notice. We all went out one night and he started doing the footwork out of the blue and we were shocked. He's an athlete anyway and had the speed and fitness of a sportsman.

We'd already heard about this club called *Dingwalls* from a previous visit here from Gilles Peterson at The Papillon but he came to play at The Thekla where we danced and Jerry IDJ, Perry Louis and someone else came with him, and us, Saeed and Spencer were battling them. They said that we needed to go to Dingwalls on a Sunday lunchtime and we started to go. We couldn't afford it but we had to get there. It was amazing and we went every week. Dancers wanted to know us – they thought we were Puerto Rican! – but we had a run in with the *Brothers In Jazz*: They had their own 'circle' and we kept bumping into each other and the next thing we were taking them on and the whole of Dingwalls were thinking "Hang on there's newcomers taking on the heavyweights." We didn't know them. It went on for ages and got tense, but we stood our ground. Gilles gave us a name check and we were so proud. We did have our problems with the Brothers for a while – pushing and shoving – but me and Saeed are fiery. I'd say: 'You don't know who you're messing with. We paid to come here and that's it.' But they said that we should respect them, that they'd been around since the beginning - 'You're new to Jazz so you shouldn't come in trying to take over,' but anyway we shook hands after that. Back in Bristol, there was a Jazz guy who got into breaking who was dancing again called Nathan Lewis, and we never saw eye-to-eye and we'd always be battling each other, but I saw him and told him about Dingwalls so he started driving down there. Nathan sat there and watched and we said "This is the place to prove yourself." Nathan did a lot more gymnastics in those days, and he jumped in and people thought 'wow!' Nathan had joined the Floor Technicians by now and we'd go and do routines on the floor. We took Oscar down there at last and people couldn't believe what they were seeing with him. They'd never seen anything like it. We started to get noticed and getting lots of work – like going to Japan, and we won the National Jazz Dance competition in 1991 at the Underworld in Camden (run by Marshall of I.D.J). Every group was there.

Oscar has been a local celebrity for the last 30 years in Bristol being an extra in films, TV shows, adverts, on the front of a record, he was in the media, disco dancing champion, whatever style of music is in the clubs everyone knows him. He's an excellent showman. I remember once he phoned me to go and watch a video He said that I must watch it as there's these guys in grey suits and spats, and it was I.D.J dancing at Wembley stadium on the Nelson Mandela concert. That was a major turning point for all of us. We started shifting straight away. In the early days of the Floor

Technicians the Jazz was mellower. Oscar was choosing the music but that was more his background, with this line-up now of Nathan and Saeed – who was full of energy, and fast too, things were changing. We wanted it to. It all speeded up.

The first time we started going to the Southport weekenders I was on my own. I walked into the Jazz room and I recognized the dancers from London but there were so many from all over the country that I'd never seen before. They were all coming up for a challenge and there were all these different styles, and you had to survive. If you couldn't dance you had to walk off or they'd laugh at you, make you look silly. Because of the dedication of the dancers, you had to practice hard or they'd wipe you out. You could never come back. The scene was too hard. You were going against the best. And they *were* the best. People would call you names, there'd be fights sometimes: Like at MacMillans at Yarm on a Sunday there'd never be fist fights but they'd kick, and some push and shove and it would go *that* far. We didn't think they were good enough and they didn't think we were. We said they we too slow - doing ballet moves, and they weren't ballet trained. We had the speed and the stamina. They would say that we weren't dancing to the music. It was a good thing. It made us improve.

You were ridiculously busy weren't you?

At first it was competition with I.D.J, Foot Patrol, and Brothers In Jazz. If one of them got a TV appearance we'd get one, and it went on like that. Things went mad: we were getting three gigs a week and doing all kinds of stuff. We had a manager for ten years called Andrew Baldie who got us tons of high profile stuff. We're lucky, we're still busy even today.

TIN TIN – STEVE SYMONS

My first residency was at the *Moon Club* – which went on to become *The Lakota*. I persuaded the manager to let me do a Jazz night and I got (British Jazz legend) Andy Shepherd to play live. On the night before he went on stage there was hardly anyone in there and the manager threatened to set his dog on me if I didn't play some conventional music. Luckily people suddenly turned up and it was a good ol' gig, but the manager was serious. After that I put the Jazz Defektors on at the Bierkeller in November '87. I sold it so hard and we got 900 in for them and that's when I thought that I needed to do this in a permanent venue.

What got you interested in all this then?

I was on a catch-up love affair with black music. It wasn't just Jazz. I was an old Punk and moved to Bristol because of bands like *Pig Bag* and *Rip, Rig and Panic* – the 'Punk Jazz' thing. I got here at the tail end of all that, but what it unlocked in me was the experience of black music and, like a lot of other people too, it was a matter of going back – right back – and checking out anything from Blue Note to Studio One Reggae to 'Kent' Northern Soul. I had that fast track 'educate yourself' drive, and Jazz was one of the major flavours for me. I was driven more from the funky side of it.

By getting the J.D's live, were you aware of the Jazz dance scene?

Yes, I was aware of people like Gilles Peterson and Baz Fe Jazz. We were loving the fast, rhythmical thing and wanted to put it more central to what we were doing.

I was getting involved with the charity 'Bristol link with Nicuragua' at the Sandinista time, and we did some benefits. We got Baz Fe Jazz down to DJ and the venue flooded at the last minute so we tried to move it to this West Indian club called the *Western Star Domino Club*. The guy let me talk for a while and said "What denomination are you boy?" and it wasn't till I convinced him that I was a good Christian boy that he let me have it! We did a few more gigs around town and then that's when I started at *The Thekla* with another DJ called John Stapleton. This was probably in 1988. We called the night *The Cooker*.

Was The Thekla an immediate success?

Yes. But I don't want to give you the wrong impression. We were just as excited about the instrumental b-side of a Hip-Hop tune as an old Jazz track. We mixed up the styles, but there was a part at the beginning of the night when it was pure Jazz – 100mph – just for the dancers, for years. It was a real draw for people to come in early. We had a very upfront crowd that would dance to stuff that they perhaps wouldn't normally dance to.

We played stuff like *Michel LeGrand – La Passionara* and stuff by *Art Blakey* and *Tubby Hayes*. The Floor Technicians were always there and another twenty or thirty great dancers too. There was an amazing dancer called Spencer. A black guy in Somerset was strange enough, but to be a dancer too….!!! He was probably the best there.

By the time you started, the 'Acid Jazz' thing would have been coming through.

Musically, yes, gradually, but it didn't have that name yet. When we first heard that name, it actually fitted what we were doing playing Jazz next to Acid House!!!

Did you have any competition?

None.

Why did it finish at The Thekla?

We were turning away so many people each time that we decided to move to a much, much larger venue, the Lakota. It only lasted a couple of years though, with big numbers you have to water things down a bit and then you start to lose heart with it. It's a spiral. It wasn't making sense really.

You had another big session happening didn't you?

After The Cooker had been going for a while, I said to John that I'd like to do a session just focused on the Jazz dancers, so there was this enormous club called *Busbys* that held fifteen hundred people that had a small room in it, but we had to have the whole venue. John suggested putting on a Wednesday night House night - which was rammed solid each week, and I was happy-as-Larry playing Jazz upstairs to four people!! The night was called *Vision* and it started around 1989. It lasted a couple of years. It was the first House night here. Bristol was probably the last place in the country that House music took off.

Was the Jazz room successful?

No, not really. In the end we thought that we should do something else in keeping with the main room, otherwise it would have been self-indulgence gone mad!!

SWINDON

There was no competition for The Ampitheatre at The Brunel Rooms in Havelock Square, Swindon. Generally, there is only room for one place like this in any one area, and, given that the city is only 30 miles from Bristol, it wasn't surprising that it attracted so many dancers from there, and eventually – once the word spread – all over the country.

PAUL LEWIS

I was on in the Ampitheatre which was part of the Brunel Rooms and I started there in 1980 until '86.

I got the job there when I was about 18, from doing a half hour spot at a wedding for one of the part time DJ's from the Brunel Rooms. All the directors were there and offered me a job at the club. The music policy was non-commercial: I'd start with laid back soul, then move into up front imports and I'd do an hour Jazz set. I started the Jazz mellow and built up to the frantic stuff, because I had the time to do it. Dancers would come from all over the country to have burn-ups there. I was fortunate, because if people didn't like what I was playing, they could just go in to the main ballroom which was commercial. It was ideal. I could literally play what I liked, with no limitations. The last half hour of the set would be full on for the dancers, and it made a bit of a show for the others, that's why I could get away with it. The management were fantastic there. They actively encouraged the dancers. The dress code was open – which was unusual then. People bought in whistles and air horns too, so it got very noisy in there sometimes!

The problem with dancers is that when they battle it causes a circle and that breaks up the floor.

We never had that problem, because of the layout of the room. As it was layered like an ampitheatre people could dance on different layers and still see what's going on.

The session was so popular it was always packed. There'd be two or three coach loads traveling in every week.

I know people that traveled from Leeds and Birmingham.

Chris Dinnis from Exeter came up often and he just couldn't believe what he could play. He could play some of the hardest stuff he ever bought and the floor would be packed. He loved it. I was fortunate to have worked with him.

Did you have any local competition?
No, not really. The other clubs were mainstream
When you left, did the music principle continue?
No, the DJ wasn't into Jazz, so the dancers stopped going and it lost its direction

DEVON

Some have been surprised to hear that there was a very strong scene – not only for Soul and Jazz Funk but for Jazz - in the beautiful county of Devon. It only being unusual because of it having the tiniest of a Black population there. However, considering the close proximity to Bristol, Swindon and, less so, Bournemouth, it isn't so surprising. You would have read interviews elsewhere in this book, from DJ's or key punters who have been inluenced from visits to Devon in the 70's and 80's. From a Jazz-bias perspective, *Chris Dinnis, Nic Wakefield* and *Duncan Uren* were the DJ's greatly influencing the area. I have included an important reminiscence from *Groove Weekly* magazine owner, journalist and DJ – *Ralph Tee*.

CHRIS DINNIS

Down here in Devon, how did you get into the scene? Was there much Jazz Funk being played?
From the mid to the late 70's it was like a religion down here. There were a lot of people passionate about it. The first place I heard Jazz Funk being played here in Exeter was a club called The Timepiece and there was a club in Torquay called Sindys. I actually started d.j.ing in Sidmouth in 1978 with another guy called Andrew Pinney. It was more Funk and Jazz influenced.

There wasn't really any Soul being played by us at that point. We had guest DJ's like Sean French, Chris Brown and Robbie Vincent. There was a club called The Yacht as well, DJ'd by a very influential guy called Duncan Uren, who was deeply into Jazz and at the time was completely obsessed by Jap Jazz. He was very important. I went from Sidmouth to Boxes in Exeter.....

And the rest is history!!!

Yeah (Laughs). The whole club was dedicated to that music. I was there for 6 or 7 years. The club was half local and half traveling. People would come down regularly from as far as South East England. After the club had closed people would just sleep in their cars in the car park.

At a lot of the best Jazz Funk clubs they would play a couple of Jazz spots. Most people would dance to everything, but you had some that were just waiting for the Jazz.

Absolutely. We had that at Boxes. You'd have some guys - I can still picture them now - that would stand by the wall and bug you all night until you played a full on nose-bleed Jazz set. It was more of a male thing. They would only dance to that. They'd come for the Samba Fusion. There's never been an out-and-out Jazz dance session here though. I remember playing tracks like *Kathryn Moses – Music In My Heart, David Benoit – Life Is Like A Samba, Naobi Yagi – Mimi Africa, Billy Taylor Trio- Mambo Inn, Sadao Watanabe – Samba De Marco* - this was huge, *Chick Corea – Central Park, Mikio Masuda - My Delight, Clare Fischer - Descarga Yemaya, Barbara Carrol - From The Beginning*; I remember those in isolation as being big tracks when the scene was at its height.

You did some legendary sessions called The Hummdinger

This was a special night I did that was a traveling session, and perhaps once a month, but no more. It was for the purists that were really into the music you know; no compromise - real Soul nights, real Jazz dance nights.

I went from Boxes to Monroes in Torquay – well actually they overlapped – but those two were probably the two most important clubs in Devon, even Cornwall and Somerset, for this scene. Monroes was owned by a Jazz enthusiast and Managed by someone who was into the scene.

In Swindon, I was booked regularly at this club called *The Brunel Rooms*. It was a huge club and it had this side room called The Ampitheatere and the crowd was very Black. A lot of times I was just booked there to do a Jazz set. It was one of the most upfront clubs anywhere, full-stop! They had some superb jazz dancers which meant it gave you license to play some fierce stuff!! This was the mid 80's. It didn't get much national coverage but people traveled from everywhere to go there. There was another great club that I guested at a lot in Yeovil, called The Electric Studios. Jon Coomer used to be the resident there. Our crowd would go to his and his to ours. Jazz sets were a big part of it.

"My DJ partner – Chris Rennie – had moved to Exeter (in Devon) to go to university there. He did a soul show on the campus radio station and his show became so popular that he put on an event there, which was completely rammed solid. I was doing *Groove Weekly* by then and I met *Chris Dinnis* there and he invited me to DJ at his club called *Boxes*. To this day, I will say that it is the best club that I've ever worked at. I said to Chris that, even though I live in London, if he wanted to take a night off at any point, I'd like to cover for him. So, for a couple of years I was his stand-in and I built up a bit of a rapport with the locals.

There was a rival scene down there in Sidmouth, at a club called *Carina*s, with a DJ called *Nic Wakefield*. Nick was well into the latin jazz. He used to play a lot of that. Even though Chris and Nick didn't see eye-to-eye, I organized a west-country weekender where I took a load of people down from London and we went to both clubs.

I remember DJing at boxes once when the whole video-promo thing was brand new. Boxes was one of the first clubs in the UK to have a video screen, so the day before, I'd been at the Motown office in London and they gave me a video with the full length version of *Stevie Wonder-Do I Do* with the *Dizzy Gillespie* trumpet solo. At the club, I was playing the audio of it with the screen off and when it got to the solo I said on the microphone: " Ladies and Gentlemen - Mister Dizzy Gillespie," and I turned on the screen. The crowd went absolutely wild. It still gives me goose-bumps to this day thinking about it.

What was it that made that club so special?

It dripped with atmosphere, even when it was empty. Also, it was unusual to have a club manager that would allow Chris to play such music. A lot of the Exeter University students went there as it was *the-place-to-be*, so it was a combination of those three things. Chris did a column in my magazine too, which gave more profile to him and the club, plus he had a radio show at the time.

Chris told me that he never used to hold back with the jazz.

His club was the first place that I ever heard *Eddie Russ-Zaius*, and I daresay that there were many other Jazz-Fusion tracks that you heard there that you wouldn't hear anywhere else."

Ralph Tee

NIC WAKEFIELD

I started off as a mobile DJ in 1975 and got an agent. I'd DJed at *Carinas* in Sidmouth, Devon, four times before, through the agent, and fell in love with the place. I'd travel down in my Luton Van packed with equipment. I could get away with records there that I got away with in London. My van broke down there one day and I boldly walked in and proposed a deal that they accepted – the beginning of a love affair. I started early summer 1978. The front of Carinas was a pub and the back was a club. The customers were very special: I had a crowd called the *Sid Valley Jazzers* who really knew their music. There were about twenty five of them and they were great dancers, really great. They lived, breathed and eat it. They were known for it. Rhymically they were phenomenal. Not one of them couldn't dance. The only time I saw dancing like that was when I would do a Jazz set at the *National Soul Festival* at the Lyceum in London – all these Black guys coming out with their spats on and baggy trousers, probably a hundred of them.

How did you nurture a local crowd?

Before Carinas, the Sid Valley Jazzers used to travel up to see *Chris Dinnis* at *Boxes* in Exeter, who was very well known – and my archrival – (laughs). I had to do all I could to keep them at Carinas. His nights were well known and he got the real heavyweight's guesting so I really had to be on the ball musically. I'll admit that I was jealous sometimes when I saw that he'd booked Chris Hill or Robbie Vincent. It was good for the scene that he did bring them down.

You had a reputation for your Jazz.

Yes, I used to do a half hour guest spot on on Tim Arnold's show every Saturday on Radio Devonair – which turned into 45 minutes. That was predominantly Jazz. This was in '79. We used to do phone-in competitions, which were quite difficult. If no one could get the answers I would get my flat mate Frank to phone in under the name Denzel! In the club though, Jazz-wise they'd like anything from *Sadao Watanabe* to *John Coltrane*. Some of these tracks were breakneck speed.

I moved on to a great club in Torquay in '82. called *Monroes* - a four hundred capacity. Our Saturday nights were very upfront. People came for the music like they did in Sidmouth, but by '85 the Jazz had become too specialist - for the minority - by now, and unless you had a tiny small club it was no longer going to work. Times had changed.

DUNCAN UREN

Starting DJing in 1971 and having many residences and working abroad for agencies, Duncan settled in Torquay around 1976/77.

I secured a residency at Sindys, which was a small club on the waterside, where I could keep the music underground. I did a couple of years at a club called Monroes, but the local crowd at the time didn't understand the scene and probably would've preferred it more commercial. It was great when I moved on to The 400 Club. I was selling imports from an area which used to be the cloakroom. This was great because at the end of the night I could see which tracks had the most response. Tony Monson used to supply me with the records. The 400 Club really took off when we formed (the tribe) *The West Coast Jazz Freezers* - I used to take coaches up to Exeter to see Robin Pele at Boxes; he was a Black guy with an amazing taste. He was very influential. I got jazzier because of him. He was the original in Devon

Was there many in the WCJF?

There were about three coach loads. They'd buy me drinks all night. It made me feel good to have that support.

I was told by many people around the country as far up as Newcastle, what an influence Torquay was.

Really? The locals hated me for playing so much Jazz. I was the only one playing it in Torquay. I feel that if anyone had heard it there then it was through me. The 400 changed owners and the new owner didn't like me playing so much Jazz Funk so I told him to fuck off and I went next door to a club called *The Yacht*, but I lasted just 9 months to a year there.

You were noted as being militant with the Japanese Jazz.

I was. I was searching for something new. Again, I heard it first from Robin Pele. There was a group of Scottish guys there that if they heard someone complaining about me playing that kind of stuff they'd follow them into the toilets and beat them up. It was horrendous, but they were so passionate about the music. I was bitten by that stuff. I would say that the night consisted of a third Jap Jazz, but it went out of fashion here in a year. I loved it, but it was a short-lived thing. I couldn't maintain it.

When did you move away from the Jazzy side?

Early 80's. I was a Record Company rep and you got brainwashed. It was drummed into you and I moved away from that scene. It affected my opinion of the music industry. It ruined it for me.

"**Michael** - All the fashionable clubbers from all over the country used to go to Torquay: from London, from the Mecca, you know, wearing the mohair jumpers and the jellybean sandals. Everyone used to go to The Yacht.
Peter- The more I think about it, the more I think The Yacht was like the Lacy Lady - very Black and great dancers.
Duncan specialized in Jap Jazz. Alex (Lowes) told me that he got turned on to a lot of that there.
Michael - You had Sindys, which was more upmarket."

Michael Powney and Peter Duncan from the North east. Friends of Alex Lowes

KENT

Tony Matthews – known as Maggot - and his crowd were the top Kent dancers and inspiration to a young DJ: *Pete Tong* – Kent's most famous Black music export from that county. Pete, of course, has now risen to become one of the World's most important and influential DJ's. There were many great club's and DJ's in Kent, but of a jazz-bias 'Tongy' stood head and shoulders above the others in the county's important Jazz Funk scene. Along with his brother Terry - also, confusingly known as Maggot! - Tony was there every step of the way, as well as traveling around London, Essex and the home-counties battling other dancers. Michael McDonach is also considered as someone who lived and breathed the Kent scene that revolved around Pete Tong.

TONY & TERRY MATTHEWS AND MICHAEL McDONACH

Tony, you were singled out as one of the main dancers.

Tony - Well there was also Pepe, Timmy Misson, Colin Pellan, Johnny Skates, Tommy Mac, Keith from Sidcup, Stan from Ilford, Stan from Margate...Margate was an enclave for Soul and Jazz, at *The Atlantis* and *Hades* nightclubs. Every bank holiday was the time. People would come from everywhere; everyone had their turn on the dancefloor, you had serious face-offs. The standard and competition of dancing was as good as you'd get anywhere including *Crackers, 100 Club* etc...It was the best I've ever seen. The club was influential. People wanted the music the hardest and newest. It had a commited crowd.

Terry – You could only equate it with *The Goldmine*.

Michael – Other big dancers I remember were Tony Maxwell from Margate, Clive Francis,

Frenchie, Budgie, Mole and Akim.

Tony - What inspired me was when I first saw Tommy Mac at Global Village. He was an icon. He blew all the Black guys away there. The Jazz dancers weren't necessarily Black; most we saw were white then ('76). It was a pre-sub culture of 'Soul boy' that was there before Punk, and kept going on for a long time. We started moving out to Pete Tong's clubs *The Kings Lodge* and *Hilltop* and *The Hunting Lodge* in Larkfield.

Terry – That's where you had the tribe *The Larkfield Loonies*, who knew their stuff. We were *The Gravesend Groovers*.

Tony – We went to *Kempton Manor, Wings* in Gravesend - with the DJ Colin Hudd. Kent was buzzing. But wherever Pete Tong was playing that was the epicenter of the Kent scene, but the dancers knew their music as well as the DJ's.

Michael - There was a huge scene in Gravesend – some would say that they were the focal point in Kent, and there was a huge scene in Maidstone, a big crowd in Margate, Ashford, Rochester and Gillingham too.

Pete Tong was the 'hard man' of Jazz at one point.

Tony – He was, and it was our influence that pushed him on, he'd admit that. He sussed it all out very quickly

Michael - Pete was very Jazz focused. For me, him and Paul Murphy were the forerunners of the Jazz dance scene. Paul Murphy actually used to come down to the Kings Lodge and The Hilltop with the Lacy Lady crowd. He used to bring records to sell.

For a six month period, there was no better playlist in the country than at The Hilltop, and people traveled for it - aggressive musically but beautiful. There was an individuality to the club and people knew it. Typical tracks I remember Pete playing were *Sweet & Sour - Crusaders, There Are Many Stops Along The Way - Joe Sample, The Thang - Charles Earland, Hades - Kenny Barron, Do It To It - Jimmy Owens, Far Out - Crown Heights Affair, Music Is My Sanctuary - Gary Bartz.*

Tony -We loved any thing on Blue Note, and records like *Mass Production - Cosmic Lust, Brass Construction - Sambo / Ha Cha Cha, Hudson People - Trip To Your Mind, Crown Heights Affair - Far Out* were OUR tunes, but, of course, the ultimate was *Lonnie Liston Smith – Expansions*. We went into a club and we'd clear the floor. We had a network. All the dancers knew where all the others were going. There was a crew from Lewisham (South east London) – about eight of them, and all dancers – would always be there.

Terry – They were the forerunners of that area.

Tony – London was much more into the hard Funk, but the Jazz thing was outside in the home counties then. It moved in later. For some reason it was a very White scene. Then from London out to us there was probably thirty main dancers who you knew you'd be up against. It was very competitive. Each club had their few resident dancers. It was their territory. You would always go in and shake their hand and have a quick chat and then you were off competing with them. You'd always travel with a duffel bag full of spare clothes, another pair of shoes in case of different dancefloor surfaces and a beret, and legwarmers, handkerchief round the neck, you knew you were going to be competing against someone each time.

Terry – It ran parallel with that really hard Jazz scene in London.

Tony – It was the forerunner. I saw it all. Starting in the South East in *The Goldmine* and *The Lacy Lady* in Essex and in Kent, and we took it into London and spread it out from there.

PETE TONG

I wanted to be a drummer, a guitarist, a pianist - very much a drummer - and at school we had a bad Rock band playing Black Sabbath and Deep Purple covers At a school disco I saw a DJ and it seemed fun and exciting so I wanted to do that instead.

My first gig was with this guy Nigel Burns and we had two belt driven Garrard turntables stuck together through a domestic amp and some speakers borrowed from my dad, and we probably hired some too. Although I was available for weddings and all that, I was hiring village halls doing gigs riding around on my bike putting up hand drawn posters. We'd get 150-200 people to some of these and we'd make loads of money. My dad supplied the security because he was a Bookmaker and he used to have a couple of useful guys around – there was a huge black guy called Eric who was our main man. I was a promoter as well as a DJ but also ruining peoples weddings, inflicting my music on them too!

Was it all kinds of music?

Yes, but I was into James Brown and Funkadelic, listening to radio shows by Emperor Rosko and liking the odd track there; this is before listening to specialist shows. I liked the Jazz influenced groups out of California like Steely Dan and all those. Later, Robbie Vincent's show on Radio London and Greg Edwards one on Capitol were a big influence.

In 1978 you were doing *Kings Lodge* on Mondays at West Kingsdown, Tuesdays in *Hades* in Margate, Thursdays and Saturdays at *The Nelson* in Gravesend and Fridays at *The Elizabethan Barns* in Tunbridge Wells...

They were full on Black music by then. I was still doing the odd wedding but they were falling away. By the time I left school in 1978 I was running around in a Transit Van 'available to hire' but also doing my own gigs.

You were underage when you were doing your residencies

I certainly was when I was doing the Nelson.

How did you get involved with the Funk Mafia?

I was working with this guy called Tony Littley who was promoting, who would've booked these guys to guest at The Kings Lodge. I also went into the scene head first throwing myself into pirate radio on stations in London like LWR and JFM. I started working for Blues And Soul magazine in 1979, In 78 I was actually in a DJ competition in Leicester Square (London) sponsored by the National Tea Council and there was Goff Abbey and John Hassinger who ran that magazine. I came second but these guys said, 'We really like you, come and work for us.' I was actually multi tasking, I was there selling advert space for Black Music but offered to write for Blues and Soul and established myself there. Contacts were building through there.

You obviously played a varied selection of styles of black music but The Hilltop had the reputation of being very Jazz biased.

I don't know whether that was conscious. It was the music I found myself drawn towards. The first

Elizabethan Barn
LONSDALE GARDENS, TUNBRIDGE WELLS, KENT

Friday, 17th November

FANCY DRESS
FUNK PARTY

WITH

Chris Brown

TOM HOLLAND

SEAN FRENCH

PETE TONG

8.30 p.m. to 12.30 a.m.
Licensed Bars

Admission
£1.50

NB. THIS IS THE VERY LAST FUNK NIGHT
AT THE BARN TILL 9th FEBRUARY, 1979

records I was infatuated with were things that Chris Hill was playing. Chris you had to see to experience him but Robbie Vincent you could listen to on the radio. Robbie was a little stronger influence whereas Chris became a mentor and a great friend. Although Chris is very passionate about Jazz, Robbie could stretch out more because of the radio show. We were all heavily influenced by Chris but I found my niche. I had a great relationship with City Sounds records and was known as the 'Jazz Boy' there and they'd give me a pile of Jazz album's on 'Muse' and say: 'Tongy, go and find the track on those', and I started tracking back older records. They were still new tracks, if you like, because they were only just discovered. So often it was all the cut-outs (deletions) that were around. I always found it disappointing sometimes, interviewing people like

Donald Byrd who couldn't quite get his head around the fact that our scene loved his albums that were ridiculed in the States. We were completely freaking out about all his Mizell Brothers production stuff and yet he wasn't popular at home. I met a few musicians like that.

> "The Hilltop was amazing. It was on a Monday night and it was actually inside Brands Hatch race-track and so there were no neighbours, therefore the noise didn't matter. Some Mondays it would run over the closing time by hours! Pete would play a lot of Blue Note jazz and infact, he could go quite esoteric with the Jazz he played - the harder the better. He found the crowd pushing him on and he went that way."

DJ Chris Brown

The Hilltop was noted for it's dancers. You had people travel from South London, Essex…
Timmy Misson, Chris Pollard, Tony Matthews, John Wooland and Clive Francis were the senior dancers. These were the older crowd that got me into the scene. Where I really became aware of that style of dancing – the spinning and all that, and the fashion - was at the Margate all-dayers at The Atlantis. It was the obsession. You had the Mods and Rockers outside and inside it was dancing to very fast Jazz records and hard Jazz Funk stuff like Crown Heights Affair - Far Out and Lonnie Liston Smith - Expansions. That crowd was very much the core of the Kings Lodge, and The Hilltop continued on as the meeting place for dancers. There was one dancer called Tony - who went on to dance for The Bluebells in Paris – who was the best dancer in the South East definitely. All the dancers knew the Essex dancers and The 100 Club dancers and they'd meet up at Margate.

Previous to Paul Murphy coming along, you were seen as the 'Hard Man Of Jazz'
A trait of mine which has followed me through my whole career is; I'll latch onto something. I don't want to seem not committed to what I'm currently in to but I'm also fascinated by change and new things. Paul was a great friend for a while - I used to play with him at The Horseshoe, but it all got a bit too serious and laddish, and all about catalogue numbers and people leaning over the booth. It got a bit po-faced. As much as it was a major part of my life and continued to be on the radio, some switch went off in my head at that point.

I read that you were annoyed at Murphy for advertising that there was to be a residency at The Horseshoe with you both when you never said you'd do it (10/1980)
Yes, well there was some friction there. I think we wanted different things. We were close; there was probably a bit of ego involved (laughs). I was very much on the coat tails of Chris Hill and Robbie alongside Jeff Young then – them being the dominant force. Maybe we had other plans. My residency at Barracudas was starting to loom and that was also on Fridays and that was my own night.

When did you decide to stop playing Jazz?
I never turned the tap off. There was less good stuff coming out. I mean *Quartette Tres Bien – Boss Tres Bien* was huge for me for six months to a year, and that was a little later so I was still playing it. I guess I didn't want to align myself with the 'Jazz Fundamentalists' (laughs). I was trying to avoid that. Gilles Peterson was part of that but he was nowhere near as hardcore as Murphy - *he* was the Jazz Fundamentalist. I was still a big buyer of it at City Sounds, Honest Jons and Rays, and go shopping with Gilles, but there was other music coming through and I think the obsession with looking for Jazz records that were old was starting to move into Funk.

For more about Kent, go to Mark Webster's interview.

> "Pete Tong had a lot to do with the jazz getting played. At The Kings Lodge there was originally just forty of us and he would be playing Blue Note stuff like *Donald Byrd – Think Twice, Wind Parade*… He got me more into jazz with all that stuff. He was going out hunting that stuff down. The club built and built and it went bang – 250 people! It was so special. We'd be discovering all kinds of music. This is where I discovered that I liked Jazz."

Gary Dennis

BRIGHTON

Really, this city should have been included in the Sussex section, but it really needed to be highlighted on it's own. One of the 'Funk Mafia' DJ's, Paul Clark's many achievements in the vast Southern Jazz Funk movement are not covered here, but, although Jazz was just a part of what he played, he was still the first to feel committed to push Jazz on the dancefloors here. You had Paul Murphy and Ed Stokes' Jazz Room sessions at Churchill Palace Hotel and The Escape – running in tandem with Murphy's session at The Electric Ballroom – in the early 80's, and DJ and promoter Russ Dewbury's absolutely massive event's called The Brighton Jazz Bop – initially aided by DJ Baz Fe Jazz. All of these promotions made immense impact on the Jazz Dance movement.

PAUL CLARK

Paul - I was resident at a club called *The Papillon*, doing various nights. The DJ Mick Clark and me tried a specialist Jazz night in 1979 on a Thursday (18/8/79) but it only lasted two weeks. I did have attempts to do straight Jazz nights. On my regular nights, I always tried to throw half an hour of jazz in if I could. I was always looking for something different but I like my jazz with a good melody like *Neil Larson-Demonette* or *Sudden Samba*.

I did a jazz night on Tuesdays at a club called *Deacons* (13/6/81), which was great. The night was called *Jazzin' It Up*. It was a small crowd but knowledgable. There were a lot of people for jazz in Brighton.

What kind of jazz were you playing?

A lot of Jap Jazz by artists like *Sadao Watanabe* and *Terumasa Hino*. The night lasted four months.

Was there anyone else playing jazz in Brighton?

No. Not at the time.

I notice that you had a Jazz All-Dayer at *Busbys* (25/8/81)?

The Long Good Jazz Sunday, yes, we had about three hundred people to that. It was all jazz.

You DJ'd with Paul Murphy and Ed Stokes at The Jazz Rooms.

Well, I knew Murphy from coming to my clubs, but that night he just came in with a few guys and played a short set and cleared off!

Did you ever attend their night in Brighton?

No. I never went to his night. People in Brighton loved him. I actually DJ'd at the same club, but on Saturdays. I wouldn't have got away with jazz there.

Did you ever go to any of Russ Dewburys nights?

Once or twice. I love my jazz, but I wouldn't want a whole evening of it; although, to be fair, I did really enjoy doing Deacons.

RUSS DEWBURY

Russ - I got into Jazz Dance through the Mod scene. I'd been a Mod since 1979 and later got into the ultra-Mod scene: made to measure suits, living the Mod ideal etc...

I used to go to this club in Bedford, where I'm from, called The Modern Club and there was this fantastic DJ there called Glenn who had this incredible collection and used to play such brilliant Soul and R&B and all that – in fact it was him that got me into appreciating the excitement of rare records. One day he told us that there was this club happening in London with this DJ called Paul Murphy, playing all this Jazz and Latin music. It was The Electric Ballroom and the night was called *The Purple Pit*. This was the beginning of 1986. He was playing records by Grant Green, Hank Mobley, John Patton, Mongo Santamaria, Art Blakey and this was the first time I'd heard this music. It was life changing. All the Soul and R&B that I'd previously been listening to was a prelude… it set me up to hear and understand Latin and Jazz music.

The minute I heard that music, I seriously got into buying Jazz records and within six months I started wanting to DJ, basically. There was this little club in Bedford where I started out, but there wasn't many people there. I was playing Jimmy Smith and Art Blakey and all that for the first time and I was also going into London all the time checking out Gilles and Baz Fe Jazz but

I seriously wanted people to hear this music I was into, so at the end of 1986 I moved to Brighton. By the February 1987 I'd started *The Jazz Room* which continues today.....

It was a different venue thought wasn't it?

Well, yes, but what happened was, when I moved down to Brighton, Sunday night in the top bar of *The Escape Club* with a DJ called Justin Robbins was the only thing going on. He used to be Paul Murphys back up DJ when he was in Brighton in the basement of the Churchill Palace hotel

Bazz Fe Jazz and Russ

- which had been christened as The Jazz Room - plus other places, That venue hadn't been used for a year and a half. I liked the look of it, and started every Saturday night and called it 'I Like It Like That' and it took off straight away. The thing was, that everybody remembered it as The Jazz Room and referred to the night as that rather than the name I'd given it, so it progressed to The Jazz Room after six months.

Where did you move to from there?

We got thrown out in July 1988 and we went to *Nash's Basement* for a year, and another venue for six months. I was getting fed up with keeping on moving but I found this venue in Ship Street that hadn't been used for a few years. It used to be called The Cavern. We started there and that's where we are today. It took about six months to get it going though. That was in July 1991.

I started initially on my own, but I truly felt that, even though I was living in Brighton, it was London where it was at and I was desperate to do something in London too, but I didn't have the name so I needed to do it with someone who did. Baz Fe Jazz was an obvious choice. I'd known Andy McConnell for quite a while – he was Baz's partner then as well. I got Baz to do a night with me at a club called *The Gazebo* in Argyle Street on Fridays. It was a disaster but we had bands on and guest DJ's. I cut my teeth there as a promoter but I lost an absolute fortune. The good thing was that I formed a relationship with Baz who'd 'fallen out' with Gilles and there was a bit of acrimony in London. He was looking for something new, and loved DJ.ing in Brighton as a guest at my club there - that's how we forged our partnership; although only on the big events called *The Jazz Bop*, not at The Jazz Rooms. He just guested there. After 6 months at the Jazz Rooms, I tried some other residencies in London as well, that didn't work out, like *The Dip* at The Whippet and *The Connection,* and other gigs in London, but The Jazz Rooms remained solid throughout.

Andy McConnell was mentioned earlier. How did you meet him?

I was going to The Wag weekly and always talked to Andy about records. One week he said, 'Are you a DJ?' and I told him I was sort of one in Bedford. He mentioned that Baz was away the following week in Japan and did I want to come down and do half an hour? So I was about four records into my set and this Italian guy came up to me and told me how much he liked my music and that he wanted to book me in Italy. The following Monday this guy phoned me and booked Andy and I to DJ in Milan and Bologna. Unitl then, all my DJ experience had been half an hour at The Wag! (laughs) I only had fifty records! When I got back, I used all that in my press: "I've just been to Italy..." It all helped.

Did you work with Andy much after that?

No, he actually gave up soon after. I never found out the reason why.

How come you went with Baz rather than Gilles or Chris Bangs? They all had different sounds.

Well firstly, there was Baz's image. I come from a Mod background where you HAD to wear a suit, so I related to Baz - who always wore suits, and also his music style of more 50's and 60's jazz suited my taste more. I couldn't see anything past 1969 being that important at that time. Baz, for me, was *that* sound. He was the logical choice!!

How did your famous Brighton Jazz Bop concerts start?

It was difficult in Brighton for people to take me seriously. There was a straight live jazz club at the Concorde and I'd try and convince them into letting me DJ for £25 if they had Mark Murphy there, or I'd try and get them to book Tommy Chase etc... Baz and I managed to talk them into funding a concert with Art Blakey at the Top Rank, which held 1800 people, and that was the turning point. They didn't like the idea of DJ's and we insisted on the IDJ dancers performing. They fought us every step of the way until the night came when it was packed solid. It was one of the most exciting moments of my life. One minute I'm playing Jazz to eighty or ninety people and all of a sudden I'm playing the same records to 1800 people! The highlight was when IDJ came on with Art Blakey. People had never seen anything like it. The Jazz Bops led on from there directly. Our first one was an all-British line up: Tommy Chase, The James Taylor Quartet, and The Jazz Defektors, and – bang – 1800 again!!

I was on a buying trip in the US and I walked past this little bar lounge in New York with this sign advertising 'John Pattern', and I couldn't believe it was actually the famous Organist on Blue Note records – John Patton!. He was playing to twenty or so dis-interested people. Well I met him and took his number and when I got back to the UK I suggested to Baz that we bring him over for a Jazz Bop in February 1989. After that we decided that each Jazz Bop would be one US act, one UK act and dancers...

Weren't the original Jazz Bops Radio London events in London with Gilles and Chris Bangs?

Baz did the second London one and suggested to me that we did a 'Brighton' Jazz Bop. The term seemed to sum it all up.

What did you think about the Acid Jazz thing down here in Brighton? I remember Baz wasn't overly happy about it....

Acid Jazz never meant anything to me in terms of a 'logo' or a 'tag'. We never used it on any posters. Actually, on Baz's advice we tried to stay away from it as it seemed just a 'fad', basically. Again, I was more into the 50's and 60's side of it. I was more into Tommy Chase than James Taylor Quartet.

Did you ever go to Dingwalls?

Every opportunity. It's easily the best club I've ever been to. Inspirational. As far as Acid Jazz though, we bypassed it in Brighton.

But you booked these bands at The Jazz Bops.

Yes, that's true. It would have been suicide not to. My plan was to, say, put on The Brand New Heavies but also put on Johnny Lytle on the same bill so people could see the REAL music.

Did Art Blakey get what was going on?

Well he'd only just done the TV documentary with the IDJ dancers six months before...

Yes, but I'm sure some of those bands just thought The Jazz Bop was a festival or something. They probably turn up 15 minutes before they're due to perform and leave straight afterwards..

I think that they understood after they'd done it - when you get twenty people backstage with their records of the artist that the artist doesn't have! I don't think John Patton got it, or Jon Lucien and Terry Callier; I don't think Johnny

Lytle got it either. Charles Earland did at the time, so did Bernard Purdie and Pucho and many more that we've had since.

Read the interviews of Paul Murphy, Ed Stokes, Sheldon Willox and Baz Fe Jazz for more information on Brighton.

SUSSEX AND SURREY

There was so much going on in these home-counties that it would be impossible to document it all – particularly Surrey. In many other interviews, club's and DJ's from this area are spoken about all the time. Remember, Gilles Peterson and Chris Bangs resided in that area, and they are two of the most important DJ's in this History Book - not forgetting Kevin Beadle and The Mambo Cartel – Andy Dyer and Mark Higgins.

CHRIS BROWN

Always an individual, Chris has always been known for his taste and musicality. Certainly, he is one the original Southern DJ's to influence Jazz on the dance floor. He's also one of the original members of The Funk Mafia team.

Chris - I started going to *The Twisted Wheel* in the mid-60's, before the term *Northern Soul* was used. It was a great club; wasn't licensed and open all night. The club had a dedicated following for all types of Black music.

I moved South in 1967 and it took me a while to find the kind of clubs of the calibre I was used to, which led to trips to London.

Me and some music enthusiast friends started a Monday night session in the basement of a pub – nothing serious, and then I went away for a season to Spain. When I returned, I got talking music at a local club called *Pantilles* in Bagshot, and they suggested that I do a Sunday night there [1973] - which was successful – and in 1977, I got offered a night down the road at a club called *Frenchies* in Camberley. It was a much more of a specialist club and a big break for me. It lasted until about 1980. It must have been successful because people were traveling from Bristol [120 miles], Manchester [240 miles] and all over.

What were you playing?

Lesser known Black music. Of course there was soul, funk and disco, and there was stuff coming through with jazzy riffs in it. I played quite uptempo through demand of the dancers who wanted to show off their skills - which is why a lot of people travelled. We were specialist, with all that CTI sound and other jazzy funk tracks. It was a learning curve: you'd see a musician on one album and check out other albums with them on, and so it went on. The more we got to know the more the crowd got to know, and it opened up doors to make people more experimental in what they listened and danced to, so you could be a little more avant-garde as time went on . We weren't inventing anything – there were others playing similar, but I played what I wanted. If I liked it and thought I could get away with it, I would.

In 1978 we hi-jacked a Northern Soul all-dayer in *Reading*, where we had a small room for jazz-funk and the main room was Northern. I was doing the jazz-funk room and booked Chris Hill as a guest and he brought two coach loads with him (100 people). There was so many people jammed in our room and the main hall was not too busy so we took it over. One of the Northern DJ's took off one of Chris Hills records while it was playing and tried to break it in protest, so the crowd surged forward to get him. Hill himself had to help him out before they killed him.

After that was the *Purley* all-dayers (approx 5000 people), and the logical conclusion to the success of the all-dayers was to do a weekender. *Caister* was the first one [which still continues today], and featured a lot of Jazz in the smaller second room. The Northerners invented the concept of the all-dayer but the Southerners invented the weekender.

What other residencies shall I mention around then, as there were quite a few ?

At the same time as Frenchies, there was *Americas* in Southall. That was on a Thursday and had a midnight finish; although it was packed by 9 o'clock. Myself and *Sean French* did alternate weeks with a guy called Fergie as the resident. It was, and still is, a very big Asian area and so it was a very mixed crowd, and Jazz was featured very heavily there. I used to do a Jazz-Fusion night called *Jazzin' It* at Jacksons in Staines (Middlesex) on a Tuesday night (21/10/80) with Mike Sefton. It lasted for about three or four years. I could go heavier and more experimental there -

I gave it the full hammer! Mainly, all the people were jazz-heads and loyal so we went 'hard at the feet.' A lot of other DJ's would come and check it out.

Were you buying from Murphys record shop?

Yes. From Exmouth Market and Berwick Street. It was the real stuff. We could get away with all that at Jacksons. Around 1980 I started a Sunday lunchtime out in Ascot at a place called *The Belvedere*. It had a live jazz group called *I.C.Q. – The Ivan Chandler Quintet* - there every week and had a great following. They brought me in to play a bit of background music, as dancing was not allowed there, but it ended up as a meeting place and full all-year round. We used to get between 600 to 1,000 people every week and we were only open from midday until 3pm!

I.C.Q. released an incredible record – *The Final Approach*. Were you involved ?

Yes. I helped out at the mix and helped promote it. I suggested that they release that particular song as a 12" single.

That must have made The Belvedere even busier.

I used to advertise 'Don't bother coming down to The Belvedere on Sundays as it's sold out!' which made people come even earlier. There were cars parked everywhere and it became a problem.

***Gilles Peterson* was also running another venue called The Belvedere at the same time.**

Gilles used to come down to us. Actually, it was quite abstract because I would look out into the crowd and see Gilles, Bob Jones, Paul Oakenfold, Chris Bangs, Nicky Holloway – the lot! All the faces. It was an excellent community. It lasted about six years.

IVAN CHANDLER of I.C.Q.
(The Ivan Chandler Quintet)

ICQ were the resident band at the Belvedere in Ascot along with DJ Chris Brown, and this Sunday afternoon became one of the most important places to go in the South of England. The band's record 'Final Approach' absolutely exploded onto our scene – just on promo 'green' label. This important record is rightly regarded as an all-time classic and will be fondly remembered by most of you readers.

Ivan - We started off by playing in 1980 on Sunday afternoons in the bar of *The Belvedere* in Ascot. The line up was me on keys, Andy Hamilton on Sax, Paul Carmichael on Bass and Miguel Acciaioli on drums. For ease we called ourselves The Ivan Chandler Quartet but then switched it to ICQ. Miguel went on to percussion and Theo joined us on drums but it didn't matter being a quintet with a name like ICQ we became more popular and they moved us to a bigger area and brought in the DJ's Chris Brown and Mike Sefton. At first we did it every other week because I'd been divorced and that was the day I saw my kids. Eventually we did it every week and we brought in a trombone / guitarist called Spike Edney.

Chris Brown suggested that we make a record, so a friend of Spikes was training to be an engineer at Tony Visconti's Good Earth studios and he managed to get us some free time and we went in there. For the recording a new drummer joined us called Larry Tollfree and a new bass player called Roger Sutton. He said that he had a track called *Final Approach*. We'd been playing it out and decided to record it live in the studio. Chris suggested that we press up 1000 12inch singles and give it a green label. I saw it in the *Record Mirror* club charts at 33 and thought "Ooh there's a bit of fame there!"

Did it get a formal release?
No. We formed a label called 'Unsquare Records.' We followed Final Approach up with *Soak It Up*, which didn't do quite as well, and then *Flight Of The Vendo Hair*. I was working for Motown's publishers 'Jobete' and by 1989 I just ran out of time trying to work there and run a six piece band.

What happened to The Belvedere residency?
It ran for four years. It had to end because it was so successful. There were too many cars everywhere. The neighbours were complaining and then they found out that The Belvedere was not allowed more than two musicians to play there!

SEAN FRENCH

Whether he liked it or not, Sean was known for his ruthlessness with the Jazz and with the dancers. He gave them both-barrels of the gun. He would massage the egos of the eagerly-awaiting punters by gesturing to his record case and say, "I've brought along the 'A' box tonight, because we've got the right people in." As another member of the important 'Funk Mafia', he made a massive impact.

Sean: I got into Black music through Pirate Radio: Radio England, Britain Radio, North Sea International Radio... I used to record the shows. My brother used to listen to Motown, so that was an influence.

There was a guy called Tony Hall who taught me to DJ, and by 15 years old I was DJing regularly. My DJ partner would tell me off for playing too much Soul.

My first big club was called *Dantes* in Bognor Regis. By 74/75 this club became progressively Black music orientated. We started a Soul night and regularly got 3 to 400 people - sometimes 500 - in this small little club. They used to queue around the block on a Sunday night to get in. Chris Hill came to have a look and was impressed. The doors opened at 8 and closed by 8.30. In its height we were turning 2 to 300 people away. Later, a big break was the first Purley all-dayer....

I was there!!!

I took four and a half coach loads of people from my little club!!! That really put me on the 'circuit.'

Lets talk about your residencies: The Stateline, in Southampton 1978....

That club was owned by Pete Mathhews. He ran a lot of all-dayers and put all the money into that club. I was doing *Americas* in Southall at the same time- Thursdays with *Chris Brown*, and *Fergie* Sunday night. There was a lot of Jazz getting played.

In a review it said that "Americas was one of the most elite Jazz Funk clubs in the country."

I was playing stuff like *Herbie Hancock - Hang Up Your Hang-Up's* and *Expansions – Lonnie Liston Smith*. A bit of Jazzier stuff was going down well too. Not everyone liked it obviously. In 1980 I had a residency at *The Royalty* in Southgate [North London] with Chris Hill. I was basically the warm up. Maybe two out of every ten records I played was Jazz.

I always remember you as particularly evil with the Jazz.

I liked to pace it up a bit.

I always knew I was going to get it when I saw you.

Lets put it this way: I got away with more than a lot of other DJ's tried to. You couldn't always, but there was an element of the crowd that expected it of you. I didn't hold back.

I've seen you break the dancefloor down just to play to the few.

I'd put my head on the chopping block.

Bogarts **in Ealing was one of your classic clubs. What was it about musically?**

Well me and Chris Bangs played imports but of course

with Chris it was always going to be Jazzy. In fact it was almost a Jazz club. He was my back-up DJ and we shared some of the same crowd as 'Americas.' A very knowledgable and friendly crowd.

In 1981 you did a Jazz Fusion night at *Wheelers* (Henley on Thames) on a Saturday night with Andy Gill. How did you get away with that on a Saturday?

It was a limited market, let's face it. It had a terrible sound system and was hard work. We were getting 150 – 200.

That's not a bad attendance.

It had its moments. It wasn`t a local crowd - mainly travellers.

You were probably one of the first to try a dedicated Jazz–Fusion night. Did you get any good dancers there?

We did, but then there was a lot of good dancers about then. The best one was a White guy called Rob Utley from Southend-On-Sea. There was no two ways about it, you could put him against any of the best....His family moved to Bognor Regis. He used to go to The Goldmine, by the way.

In 1982 you were doing a Jazz Fusion night at Jacksons in Staines.

That was Chris Browns baby really. I only did it about ten times. Tuesday nights were quite successful but it was a tiny club though. It was packed with a hundred people.

ESSEX

It makes no sense why this county with such a small Black population has been so influential in so many of the British club-culture cults: the 1950's Rock and Roll scene never died there in the 60's as it did elsewhere in the country (with the exception of Bristol), so became the first focal point in 1971 with the massive national Teddy Boy revival; the mid-70's Rockabilly movement started there; most importantly, the Mod 1960's Mod movement started there, and it was also where the first Acid House Rave happened (but acknowledging the many illegal warehouse-parties around the country playing that music before). Of interest to this Jazz Dance book is the all encompassing influence certain Jazz Funk clubs and DJ's had there from the beginning until the decline of the subject of this book.

CHRIS HILL

What can you say about this maverick, controversial DJ known as 'The Godfather of The Funk Mafia'? He has been acknowledged, historically, as being the UK's first Super Star club DJ. Along with Sean French, Robbie Vincent and Chris Brown, his area was really the whole of the South and South-east, but The Goldmine and Lacy Lady were in Essex - and this interview mainly centre's around those two important clubs. This is not meant to be all about Chris' career and achievements – other than Jazz-related – so the all-dayers and Caister Soul Weekenders etc are not covered here (although, let's not forget the immense importance of the Jazz Room at Caister). Other than London, where George Power ruled, the South of England was Hilly's - as the North was Colin Curtis.' Without doubt, between what Chris and Bob Jones achieved, Jazz-wise, on the dancefloors of Essex, the Jazz-Dance scene of the South undisputedly began with them, as, again, it began with Curtis in the North.

Chris: It wasn't unusual to hear jazz in the early 1960's. It had already crossed over. Dave Brubeck had a hit with Take 5, Stan Getz had been in the charts; infact, jazz was the music of club-land. You'd walk into The Flamingo [Soho, London], and saxophonist *Joe Harriot* would be playing, and in between the bands you'd hear songs by Cannonball Adderley, Nat Adderley-Work Song. Every UK R&B band from Chris Farlowe, Zoot Money to Georgie Fame would play tracks by *Big John Patton-the* Organist more than Jimmy Smith. The whole Organ thing was happening. It was normal to hear this music; It appealed to the hipper crowd. There were 7 inch singles: Sidewinder, Mercy Mercy Mercy, Walk Tall, Country Preacher, Jive Samba. Song For My Father-Horace Silver was a song that everybody knew. People would grow up with these. Thelonius Monk-Blue Monk - you'd hear the bloody Milkman whistle that! John Coltrane - Blue Trane; these were Pop tunes - well they *felt* like Pop tunes. You wouldn't think "Ugh! What the hell is that?" The theme from the film *Alfie* - we grew up with it. You went to see a Tubby Hayes gig and you'd see people dancing up at the back. Jazz was on the juke-boxes, *Johnny Stacatto* was a top-ten hit, and you went to parties and you heard M.J.Q; you'd hear Charlie Mingus - Oh Yeah, Miles Davis - Sketches Of Spain...The west-end was jazz-driven. There was the club in Ham Yard called *The Scene* with the DJ *James Hamilton* - this was around the corner from The Flamingo. Guy Stephens (who owned the Sue label in the UK) started it and then James took over. *Jazz* as a new dance-form in the late 1970's/early 80's? BOLLOCKS! Charlie Parker used to play in a dance band......

Yes, but what happened in the 1970's was different though.

Yes, well I suppose that there were very few DJ's like James and I that actually *lived* that west-end scene, so it was natural to draw on those times. It wasn't a stroke of genius to say, "Let's play a jazz record" though.

In the 1960's Chris worked at Fords, he did Reparatory Theatre and had a record shop:

It was in Westcliff-On-Sea, in Essex. I had it with two other guys. This was in the mid-sixties (when I started DJing) and we had this competition to see who could sell the most outrageous record: whatever a guy came in for, the idea was to sell him something else as well, that they weren't after, so this guy came in for a Beatles album and went out with *Sonny Rollins-East Broadway Rundown* !

Did you always DJ Black music?
My first serious residency was at *The Cock* in Orsett, Essex in the late 60's and I always opened with *Miles Davis - Milestones*, I was playing Soul/Motown music - It was a conscious decision; I've always played what I believe in. Even later, when I'd had my two top-ten hits with *Renta Santa* and *Bionic Santa* and was being offered shows on Radio 1 and Capitol Radio, I still wouldn't do it unless I had total freedom. Why would I want to do it? I couldn't imagine Radio 1, to this day, allowing me to play what I want to.

Tell me about The Goldmine.
The Goldmine owner – Stan Barrett and manager Kenny Faulkner came to The Cock and offered me the residency. They'd heard about me. When I started at *The Goldmine* on Canvey Island (Essex) in January 1973, people there didn't understand a 'Soul' night. I'd get poison-pen letters from people saying things like "Why are you bringing these coons onto the Island?" Why did Canvey work? Why did Wigan work? Well, there were no locals and also, it was special for people to come to the club at the end of the country. Everyone was there for one reason. We had a great door-policy: if the

Doorman didn't think someone was the right kind of person he'd say, 'I don't think it's your music?' and if they went 'Why? What is it?' they were caught out. They weren't coming in.

Monday nights I did an import-only Soul night that was packed out and had coaches coming from everywhere, and eventually I did it on Thursdays too, and Friday and Saturdays I played records by bands like Roxy Music, Gary Glitter, Rod Stewart, Little Feat etc mixed in with Soul and Funk and we had a resident band – like almost all the discos had then. By early '74 it was totally black music and no band. Initially Johnny Stainse (the owner of the famous *Moondogs* record shop) was my back-up DJ on the weekends and he and I used to go over to DJ in Belgium (note: at what are now known now as 'Popcorn' nights) .We were invited over by the guys who used to come over here and go all over the country to the clubs up North -to *The Twisted Wheel* and down to The Goldmine. In this club in Belgium the biggest record was *Song For My Father* – not the original but a different version, and they'd play all these Soul/Jazz standards as well. It was all at a similar tempo and feel, and they'd do this 'Ceroc' type Jive to them. I couldn't believe it. I thought: "I've got all these records," and although there were hundreds of DJ's in the South, I was one of the few that had this background. I always saw Funk and Jazz together.

What about the huge Swing revival that happened at the Goldmine in '76? I'm sure it was a bit of a laugh, but was there a Jazz element leading up to it?
Of course, or I wouldn't have done it otherwise.

What kind of things were you playing?
Funk instrumentals that crossed over, nothing retro, no *Blue Note* or no Be- Bop at that time. The CTI label – that worked. I was playing Swing as a party idea: Louis Bellson, Basie, Ellington, 'Jump' stuff - tracks that people knew. Also, of course, at the same time, Bette Midler and Manhattan Transfer were doing jazzy stuff too. We played these plus the Jazzy Disco and with my previous knowledge, it didn't take long to get a set together. Remember that 'The Hustle' dance was a big thing and was a *couples* dance, so it was easy to get people Jiving in couples. I mentioned over the mic that, "Next week I'm playing glamorous music, and I want you to dress glamorous," so, the next week a few girls did, and some started wearing army fatigues and within a month the whole club was wearing these 1940's war clothes! Again, a similar thing happened a few years later when I was at the Lacy Lady: we had a very fashion-student crowd and all the Bromley crowd used to come down – *Siouxsie, Billy Idol, Steve Severin*, members of *The Subway*

Sect, Bernie Rhodes -the manager of *The Clash*, and various members of that group. We were open on Boxing Day for the first time and I did a fancy-dress party. I said I wanted people to wear their X-mas wrapping, so people were turning up in black bin liners made into dresses and all that, some held together with safety-pins, and some of the Punk wear ended up getting mixed into it and it all fell together. That was the first time that look appeared.

This became a Soul boy look countrywide quite soon after.

The Swing thing was short lived – Jimmy Lutchford and a few things on *Specialty*, Blues, Jimmy Rushing etc. The thing that hooked everybody was *Glenn Miller-In The Mood*. You must remember that I'd just had a big hit with Renta Santa and the newspapers were trying to get an angle on me: "Who is this Chris Hill? He's a DJ". A guy called Colin Irwin got sent from Melody Maker – he was a Folk and Jazz writer – and I was only playing, like, a half hour of Swing and he walked into The Goldmine and thought "Fuck me!!! I've just seen the most amazing thing. Everyones dressed up in 40's style and Jiving." We were in The Sun, The Mirror (a double page spread), The Evening Standard - all in one week! Vogue did a big article on it as well; it was everywhere. TV crews from Australia, Canada, 6 o'clock news. Bizarre! Glenn Miller was a hit again in the charts and dancers came up from The Goldmine to do *Top Of The Pops*. More importantly, it was the first time a DJ was famous for being a DJ starting a scene. That's why I left The Goldmine the first time, because it got so huge. I had to walk away from it, so The Goldmine manager, Kenny, went to the Lacy Lady, Ilford and one week I was at The Mine and the next, The Lacy. Stan Barrett, was mortified, but he understood. The club was full of people nobody knew because of the popularity. I thought: "I'm going now...." I wasn't sure where to go next and James Hamilton gave me the idea, because he said: "Go back to your roots and start again – the 50's/60's Blue Note Soul Jazz etc." When I went to the Lacy Lady it was a very Black crowd and had an edge to it. At first, everybody expected me to play Swing but I didn't; that Black crowd wouldn't stand any of my novelty stuff. The crowd wanted it all new, and with so many fantastic new releases why play anything old, so I didn't play much of that at The Lacy - but it was always at the back of my mind.

Between '76-'78 we played records like *Lonnie Liston - Smith-Expansions, Roy Ayers - Evolution, Bobby Lyle - The Genie, Lalo Schiffrin - Jaws, Dexter Wansal - Life On Mars*... now *that* was the sound of The Lacy, and the whole thing became more selective. Good quality Black music - *Liston-Smith, Roy Ayers, Gary Bartz - Music Is Sanctuary*....these were big records at the time on 7" single before the albums came out.

Expansions wasn't made as a dance record.

No, but it fitted into what we were playing in '75 and '76; *The Bottle - Gil Scott Heron*, his *Lady Day and John Coltrane* – I used to play the 7" of that. It got a UK release for gods sake. These were new records at the time.

I went to New York on business and found copies of *Sonny Stitt - Slick Eddie, Jack McDuff - Sophisticated Funk, Ingram - That's All* etc as failed new releases. I bought them home in a big box and, bang - overnight they were huge.

Ingram. Was that in 1979?

No. This was the first time around. Ingram and all that were huge at The Lacy.

What started it up North was the album *Mister Magic - Grover Washington Jr*. They got it through *Supership - George Benson* too. It sounded like a Northern record. Mr Magic was particularly significant as it was funky *and* jazzy – you could do a whole night around that sound: Steve Khan's version of *Darlin',Darlin' Baby*.....I wasn't the only one playing Jazz-Funk then - everybody else was- but we popularized it. In the North, they kept records to themselves - "I've got this record and I'm going to cover it up so nobody else knows what it is," but our attitude was "I've found this record by Lonnie Liston-Smith (for example) and you should buy it, and I'm going to keep on playing it until you *do* buy it and make it a hit - make the music bigger, make the scene bigger!" I've no sense of shame to keep on plugging the music rather than cover it up. Roy Ayers understood what we were doing. Donald Byrd thanked me - he was absolutely amazed. The payback was seeing these artists in the charts and knowing that our scene did it. Ian Levine has the same attitude. He's a popularist

When I went back to The Mine in 1978, the environment had been created for real Jazz: 60's jazz that works 'with *this* that inspired *that*.' I thought, "Now we're going to start playing *real jazz.*" There was none of that at The Lacy: a sense of 'This is real Jazz', it was just great US contemporary Black music. No sense of retro. All new.

By this time, it wasn't a lone quest, as by then Jonesy (Bob Jones) had also established a situation where that could also be done. Bob came through very un-pressurised – with a loyal, loyal following, and, musically, he was always left of centre. There was now an audience to play a whole night of Jazz to if you wanted to. That didn't exist before. I mean, (Paul) Murphy was a punter at The Lacy, and there were other DJ's doing similar things, and it escalated fast after that. The scene would never have been the same without James Hamilton (his DJ page in Record Mirror was the DJ's bible) or Robbie Vincent because of his radio show on Radio London.

I remember in my area: as soon as his show finished on Saturday afternoons, all the DJ's would go down to Colin and Trisha Snow's *Record Man* in Rayleigh, Essex, trying to buy what he'd just been playing on his show. The shop would be empty until then.

His show was absolutely crucial. It was the connection of the people: If he mentioned a gig, it was packed. It had a huge impact for years. The thing is, it went from being a show with a few listeners to becoming this huge show that was a point of contact for all these listeners. The pirate station *Radio Invicta* was important for the same reason.

How did the Jazz-Fusion music get introduced?

A style of dancing emerged that needed feeding, which is one thing the House music scene has never had, which is why it has stood still for all these years. Every year a dance style would come out – The Bump, Hustle, Rock – suddenly a dance style emerged - not the complex one that people danced at (Paul) Murphys clubs - but like, a fast, double-time frantic dance which you thought, "Fuck me, I've got to find stuff to fit this." I found more stuff, and it went around in circles, finding stuff to make the dancefloor erupt.

I heard that you would never tolerate circles on the dancefloor. They are to be avoided, from my experience.

Well, they are all about exclusion, not inclusion. They are intimidating. We rarely had them at The Goldmine or The Lacy, although, occasionally, we'd get them at The Royalty because it was such a vast room. I'd let them dance the track out and then immediately change the music, because it's me that controls the dancefloor not them. Never let the punters control the room, even if it's a hen party or a crowd of blokes.

How about Paul Murphy?

With Murphy it wasn't a suburban thing anymore – Essex and outskirts of East London. He took it into London. Whether people like it or not, Essex was the heartland and it wasn't an accident. It goes back to the Mod thing that started in Ilford, you know, and North London, out to say, Basildon in Essex It was the same with the Jazz-Funk thing - East London Black fused with White Essex-boy.

I was playing in some clubs to thousands of people and it was getting increasingly hard to play the uncompromising jazz. You could play the odd one but Murphy took it back to a small room crystalising down to Hard Bop, like Art Blakey, and it revolved around the jazz dancers. The punters ended up as spectators. This goes back to the West Indian culture of dancing-off against each other. I use to hate all that because, everybody in the room was supposed to be dancing and enjoying themselves, not standing round watching a mock...like...er...two cockerels fighting. Whilst Jazz Dancing was great to look at, I didn't want a whole night built around it. Murphy found rooms and found ways of making it work. Jazz-dancers became the focus. It was intimidating for a first time punter who would walk in. Where as I would try and get everybody to dance, *there* you had to be good enough to get on the floor. That wasn't my thing at all.

But I remember you playing very heavy jazz like McCoy Tyner - Love Samba as well as the softer stuff, and that, to me, was laying the foundations for people wanting to hear more of the stuff.

Well there was the Japanese Jazz as well. We were looking for new stuff to dance to because the US Fusion had turned into elevator music by the early '80's. The Japanese were making some frantic dance music, although, looking back, there were only perhaps two-dozen great ones.

I'll agree there. A lot of it sounds terrible now. Did you shop at *Fusions* (Paul Murphys record shop)? I heard you had one of everything that came into the shop.

No (laughs). Paul's partner, Dean, would phone me and say: "I've got a couple of copies of this. You and Paul would have the only copies" and I'd say that I'm not into all that, but he'd find me pieces and say: "Don't tell Paul I sold you that. He thinks he's got the only one!" (laughs). I'd say to him "Don't sell it to me if you don't want to. I'm not interested in being the only one." I'm sure a lot of those records sold more on import than as a domestic release.

Chris summarized - My thing was to make Jazz normal, like it was normal for me in the early 60's to walk into a party and hear Cannonball Adderley or Charlie Mingus played alongside the Beatles. I wasn't brought up in a jazz ghetto, but I heard as much Jazz as I did Rock and Roll. Marvin Gaye, Miles Davis, James Brown, John Coltrane: to me they all were linked and you wanted a whole room to experience the same feeling that you did when you heard it all for the first time.

That's the main reason you become a specialist DJ.

The same reason kids go around in cars with the window down with their music playing loud: they wanted people to hear it. Luckliy, I was never labeled 'a Jazz Jock' - I'd rather play a good Soul record to a bad Jazz record. If there were no new Jazz records out I would do a night without playing any and yet some weeks it would be the majority.

I went to Brasil in the late 80's and the people were dancing to the wildest stuff at their local dances and just dancing as a matter of course, and it all started to make sense - "This is why we did it!!"

BOB JONES

The people's champion and one of the originators of this scene. Where as Chris Hill did everything in an extravagant, extrovert and forceful manner, just fifteen miles down the road, in Chelmsford, Bob was sharing and helping shape the tastes of the knowledgeable punters of Essex in his unassuming but authoritative manner in the smaller clubs. Bob has been at the forefront of so many different styles of Black music – sometimes years ahead – but it is Jazz we are talking about here.

Bob - I got into Jazz through my R&B roots as a young mod. At 13 or 14 years old (in the early 60's) I was taken to a recording of popular music television programme *Ready Steady Go* and seeing James Brown and Otis Redding and the like, by one of my two sisters, Linda. I used to go to the Chelmsford Corn Exchange on Saturdays seeing bands playing, like Georgie Fame and go to the Rainsford Youth Centre up until the age of 18 or 19 where I

would see bands covering R&B classics. Another influential club for me was a Blues club at Havering college (where I was an apprentice electrician) where I saw artists like Howling Wolf.

I would initially shop at Daceys where I first bought the Sue Story Vol's 1 and 2 (British Sue) with tracks like *James Brown - Night Train* and *Jimmy McGriff - All About My Girl* (and records like *Jimmy Smith - The Cat*. There used to be a list in the shop with what was out the following week, so I would order anything that sounded Black. There was a shop called Pop Inn in Chelmsford that was owned by Martin Havelin who later opened another record shop called 'Extacy' which was opposite DJ'S. I worked there on Saturday mornings selling tunes that I'd played the night before at DJ'S.

Was Dee Jays strictly a Black music club or was there any chart music played?

Initially, in '73, it was chart music, as I was filling in for a guy called Paul Owens who was a DJ on Radio London. He didn't turn up one week so the management asked me. I wanted to play Soul and whatever was going on. My whole collection was Black music, but I had to integrate the pop hits of the day. By 1974 people were there just for the Black music. They would come to me on Fridays and go to *The Goldmine* and see Chris Hill on Saturdays, plus his Monday night which was all imports. He had his record shop DISCO 2+2 in Rainham.

A birthday present from my dad in 1970 was *Jimmy Smith - Back At The Chicken Shack*, and this was typical of the type of R&B that was getting a lot of play at Dee Jays. Despite this and the jazz-influenced Disco and Funk that was being played there, at this point, there was no intention of playing jazz as such. By 1976 of course, you had the Jazz Funk stuff like *Jack McDuff - Sophisticated Funk* and the *Eddie Russ* albums on Monument and then I started to introduce Fusion. I'd virtually stopped playing Soul, but not quite.

How did you introduce Fusion though? It seems to me that you were into the R&B thing. That's a totally different sound.

What nudged me was that there was a dancer called *Mac* at Dee Jays. I think he came from Colchester (his brother Andrew later, was the lead singer with *Animal Nightlife*). He came down early one night and asked whether I could play a track off of an album that he'd bought with him - *Chick Corea - Return To Forever* called *You're Everything*. I could draw comparisons to the sound that I was playing but it was in a direction that I didn't know much about, and that was the turnaround. I went searching for that style after that.

Did Mac see it as a dance record?

Oh he saw it as a dance record alright, but these tracks didn't work overnight. You had to persevere.

Did you feel that you were on a mission to promote this music?

I felt it had a place in what I was doing, yeah, but I didn't 'fly the flag', and say that 'this is the future," I just felt that this was an alterior side of dance music to James Brown, Cameo or Kool And The Gang, you know. When I get behind something I'll plug it to the year dot.

At Dee Jays, we opened from 8 until 2 am and by '76 people were queuing right down the road at a quarter to 8! It was a big night.

By that point it was predominantly a Jazz night.

It was Jazz AND Funk. The only Soul tracks that were played were in the two ballad sessions a night.

That was quite common until the early 80's wasn't it. Ballad sessions.

Yeah. The music at the club was generally Jazzier earlier until about 10pm. It would've cleared the floor later than that. But seeing people dancing to Jazz, I thought, "Yeah I'm onto something here" - all the preconceptions of dance music went right out of the window. This was the turning point: me playing it in the suburbs and other people following suit. I can only talk from a Southern perspective, obviously.

In 1979 I left Dee Jays and started up at *The Countryman* in Chelmsford: Mondays – Soul and Funk and Wednesdays – Pure Jazz. Paul Murphy was a regular there and he used to push records to me, as he worked as a buyer for Our Price records in Leicester Square, London. He even used to give a few free records to me that were too slow for his taste such as *Ryo Kawasaki – Trinkets And Things* and *Ivan Boogaloo Joe Jones – Black Whip* - which became Soul boy Jazz classics, as you know. Paul was more into Funk but would be enquiring "What's this? Whats that?" What is so important is that eventually it was Paul that took the Jazz scene from the suburbs to the City.

One of your secret weapons as a record dealer at that time was Tony Ashby of *Tonys Imports*. Clacton. In fact, it was years later in 1982 that I was working in Clacton as a Red Coat at Butlins that I came across him at Clacton Market and I said: "Oh, so you're Bob's secret supplier!!" I remember him selling me *Clark Terry – Flintstones* (Vanguard) as a 'big Bob Jones' track and the *Pharoah Sanders* album – Journey To The One (Theresa) with *You Got To Have Freedom* on - which I back-heeled at the time as I couldn't see, in our scene, how people could dance to Be Bop. This was a good five years before it was a classic.

I was introduced to Tony through Paul Gratue from Witham, who DJ'd at Crackers in London. It was Tony that put me onto *Mr PC* by *John Coltrane* (Atlantic) and I played it at the Caister Soul Weekender in the alternative room in 1980. At that time, a lot of Fusion was getting played so I played Coltrane as a rebel gesture; Be Bop. I distinctly remember that (Radio Capitol's) Martin Collins was on before me and I said: "Before my first record, open your ears to something different....." It threw the crowd. They were all stunned and it cleared the floor, but by the solo it all went mad. After that, people were on the search for similar stuff. I just wanted to show that there was different Jazz you could dance to. It didn't occur to anyone to play that style, I mean in a discoteque for goodness sakes!!

Anyway, Tony used to come over on Wednesdays to sell records. He had some great stuff. He made it easy for me because he came to my house to sell to me. There was a crowd that came to The Countryman all the way from Royston and they started booking me every other week at *The Bull* on a Saturday, and moved it to Thursdays. It was absolutely packed and we had a hell of a lot of jazz dancers in there. It drew people from Cambridge, Peterborough, Hartfordshire, Essex... That lasted until 1983. We also did a club in the late 70's (Oct 78) called *The Exodus*, ran by Paul Murphy. It was on a Tuesday night at a club above Hornchurch bus station and I did it with Paul Gratue. It was on the same night as Tom Holland's at The Lacy Lady in Ilford, just down the road. He wasn't that happy about it. Tony Monson used to come and guest. Tony had *Flyover Records* in Hammersmith and was responsible for the Japanese Jazz Fusion boom in the scene. He used to supply City Sounds records in London and Robbie Vincent's Radio London show [note: all over the country actually]. We were playing Jazz as well as the order of the day. It was very eclectic. It lasted for about six months. It went from a few people to being rammed solid. It closed because there was a murder there - on a different night I may add! Paul Murphy also made his DJ debut there.

> "I never ever missed a week. Tuesday nights, for about three weeks it was just me and my friends, and the fourth week it took off. It was mobbed. There were people queuing from 9 o'clock."

DJ Gary Dennis

I did another club once with Murphy in the early 80's at *Devils* in Earls Court Road. Paul would be playing more Wayne Handerson / Roy Ayers-ish Jazz Funk and I played the Jazz. The cloak-room, was actally behind the DJ system! There was no evidence of that fast footwork jazz dancing yet. That wasn't until The Electric Ballroom and the Caister Jazz Rooms.

Did you ever go or DJ at The Horseshoe or The Electric Ballroom?
No. I went to see the Jay Hoggard and Heath Brothers gigs there, but never went socially or DJ'd other than that.

What did you think about where Murphy took the scene?
It was his own world. I could see the attraction of it.

What did you think about his record shop?
It echoed his taste. You couldn't go to City Sounds and buy that stuff. It was very limited in music styles but it was an 'Alladins cave.' You had to shop there or miss out.

Pete Tong was getting a reputation in Kent for his Jazz at the time too.
Tongy was responsible for that whole Kent thing. He flew the flag and played top tunes. It was him that broke *Last Poets – It's A Trip*. No one else was playing that. Don't forget that there were loads of back rooms in pubs and wine bars with DJ's playing Jazz (and other music) too. These

were the backbone. It was purely underground and all over the country. I would speak to Colin Curtis up North weekly and we'd be exchanging tunes.

What else were you up to?

I guested all over as a freelance, but before *The Royal Oak*, Tooley Street, Nicky Holloway got me on regularly at his previous venue *The Swan And Sugarloaf* (1983) in Jamaica Street on Mondays and I'd have guests like Sean French. Gilles Peterson made a point of coming to see me. He came down with three or four others and he'd ask me to play the most obscure jazz tracks that he knew I had.

After Baz Fe Jazz left The Wag, You started doing it with Gilles and Chris Bangs.

Yes, with *Sylvester* and *Phil Levene* upstairs playing hard jazz. I would be playing tracks like *Lou Donaldson– Reverand Moses, The Delegates – Pygmy* and my big discovery – *Johnny Lytle – Selim*. These tracks were all road-tested at the all-dayers and weekenders. I searched hard for tunes. Without realising it, some of these type of records changed the face of the scene. At this time, myself, Bangsy and Kev Beadle would go round to Gilles place and we'd suggest tracks that were big for us for those *Jazz Juice* compilations on the Street Sounds label. It was a real family affair. Those albums became legendary.

Weren't you writing for *Blues and Soul* magazine as well, at the time?

Well, Murphy was approached originally but didn't have the time, so I got offered it. I called it 'Dr.Jazz.' I loved doing the page and I did it for quite a while but I handed it over to Mark Webster in the end. It helped the scene, talking about the clubs and reviewing the new releases. I also had a radio show on the pirate station K.JAZZ. It was freedom of expression. No play list.

You, Phil Levene and I did The Hi - Hat at the Moonraker in Southend-On-Sea in '87 didn't we. That was all Jazz but with a 'No Funk' policy, because we felt that there was too much getting played at Dingwalls.

Great sessions and really busy. You know, I did the original sessions at Dingwalls, with Gilles and Kevin Beadle. The first two were promoted by Radio London and were very busy. On the strength of that they offered us regular Sundays – this is before Patrick Forge was doing it. I didn't like the way the scene was going. To be honest, I got out of it, I didn't like the musical direction or the politics.

STEWART and LAURENCE DUNN

These brothers were always there with their influential crowd at all the right places – musically and fashion wise. Their crowd was where the dancers were and the dressers of cutting-edge fashion. Most importantly, they really knew their music and searched it out.

You and your friends were the faces in the Essex scene. It was as much about the dress as the music.

Stewart – Absolutely. We were border-line punk. We were into that. The only safe place a Punk could go was the Soul clubs. The mohair jumpers, peg trouser and plastic sandal look came from Essex.

From the Lacy Lady. Where would you buy all that?

Stewart – From *Seditionaries* and before that *Sex,* in the Kings Road, London.

You were regulars at Bob Jones legendary club Dee Jays in Chelmsford.

Stewart - Yes, Dee Jays was like a pre-fabricated kind of building – the kind that got put up after the second world war.

Laurence – It was all on one level, with a semi-circular dance floor, with the DJ booth on the far side of the dance floor also at ground level. The mixture of people was locals, students and a lot of people traveling. When we went there, there was about fifteen of us.

Stewart – Bob was very special and his selection was different than anyone else's – more Jazz orientated. Every track was heavy and blinding. Edgier. He was in it for the music – like the DJ George Power.

Stewart – You had to get to Dee Jays early and Bob Jones would be warming up with some great mid-tempo Jazzy stuff. It set the mood. It was worth getting there early just for that. Bob was very open to showing you what he was playing.

How was it different from any other club?

Laurence – Only in that the Jazzy warm up set the tone. There were a lot of people that considered them selves to be good dancers there, like Mac, that came early for it.

What kind of stuff was Bob playing?

Stewart – I remember him playing *Walter Bishop Jr. - Soul Village, Hubert Eaves - Esoteric Funk*, all that stuff on labels like C.T.I. and Flying Dutchman; *Wayne* Henderson - *Big Daddys Place*; stuff by *Hubert Laws, Roy Ayers, Lonnie Liston Smith, Chick Corea*; records on the Groove Merchant label by artists like *Jimmy McGriff* and *Joe Thomas; Al Di Meola - Elegant Gypsy*.....

Laurence – I never would have thought about buying a Chick Corea album before then.

Stewart - We travelled around to all the London clubs too. We were regulars at Billys, Crackers, The100 Club with Ronnie L…. The Lyceum and Global Village were too commercial.

You disliked the (Funk) Mafia DJ's like Chris Hill and yet you were faithful to The Goldmine.

Stewart - Oh yes, totally. It was our safe haven. You couldn't go to many places and dress the way we did at The Mine. The dress was totally outrageous.

Yes, there was a massive link with St Martins Art and Fashion college in London and Southend Art and Fashion college and they all went there didn't they.

Stewart - We all wore American 50's clothes for a while – College jackets and the haircuts and all that. The Clash were dressing like that at the time. It was that kind of vibe. It was definitely an Essex Soul boy look.

Around Essex, who were the rated dancers?

Stewart- Elvis Da Costa, Tony Shaw, Rob Uttley, Mark Benjamin, Steve Giocardi, Ozzie, and of course Mark White - a brilliant dancer. Him, Elvis and Tony were the big time boys though.

Mac of course….

Stewart - Oh yes, Mac again. You can't forget him.

TONY ASHBY - TONYS IMPORTS

Of course there were loads of fantastic record shops selling great Jazz - like the cut-out kings Bluebird, in London, and A1 Records in Glasgow, Rays Jazz, Mole Jazz, Blue Monk, Diskery in Birmingham etc - but, in the early-80's, if you were deadly serious about DJ-ing Jazz Fusion, you had to be buying the unique selections from both Paul Murphy's shop *Fusions* and from his nearest rival – Tony Ashby.

I had a record shop originally in 1978 called *First Flight* in Clacton, Essex. I was into Progressive Rock, then Jazz Rock, and got into labels like Impulse – artists like *Pharoah Sanders*, and then into *Roy Ayers* and *George Benson*. I was selling imported Independent Punk records and started to sell Jazz and Jazz Funk too. I started to get to know *Bob Jones* through there – I'd sell him stuff like *Gene Ammons – Brother Jug* and *Rusty Bryant – Friday Night For Saturday Night Brothers*. I started to get fed up with the shop but got a lot of specialist interest and I started to get contacts for deleted records and opportunites to buy interesting albums, so I evolved into 'Tony's Import Records.'

I closed the shop down and began selling at some interesting clubs and a couple of markets in this area. There were great collectors around here plus some half decent DJ's. I was selling at *The Embassy* night club in Colchester - which had a good congregation of knowledgable punters from all over the area like Mark and Paul – *The Harwich Boys* – who were serious collectors…

I remember. They worked on the ferries to Holland and were picking up endless amounts of rare Jazz and pissing the DJ's off with them.

I did Clacton, Ipswich, Southend and Dartford markets, and then *The Countryman* for Bob Jones…

Which was all Jazz.

…Then *The Bull* in Royston for Bob Jones again. That was an important venue, and your *Whispers* in Leigh-On-Sea. As well as the UK, I had a contact in the US who would just hoover up records for me out there. I was taking gambles on deletions by association of musicians playing on the albums. I discovered loads of stuff like that. I worked hard. I had a source of seriously heavy Fusion, plus labels like Prestige, MPS, Milestone… I was lucky, because all the clubs I was selling at, the DJ's were playing to knowledgable punters and those people liked to buy.

Certainly down South, you would have been the only dealer to have competed with Paul Murphy's record shop.

Yes. I'd meet Paul occasionally actually at places like The Countryman in Chelmsford where he'd bring records down for Bob Jones, but he wouldn't sell there. We were rivals you could say, but he was picking up different stuff to me so we co-existed.

What did you think of The Bull in Royston - Bobs other main residency?

It was my favourite. It was in the middle of nowhere. Close enough to attract people from Chelmsford and Colchester, plus it was also far enough up country to attract some of the Northern Soul crowd. It was healthy there and had an edge. To me that's where Bob established *Ivan Boogaloo Joe Jones – Black Whip*. It was an important place.

GARY DENNIS

Gary has lived and breathed the Jazz Funk scene since the mid-70's. His almost photographic memory and passion for the music is what has made his record shop Crazy Beat one of the greatest in the world currently.

In 1984, Gary came back in to the scene after a divorce. Quite soon he was back in the clubs, collecting records, and he also now started to DJ Although not relevant here, Gary quickly became a force to be reckoned with – domineering the Essex scene, and was one of the main players in the 'Rare Groove' movement of the mid-80's - although his very important contribution is still undocumented.

Gary: The first time I concentrated on just purely Jazz was in '85. I did a Jazz room at The Goldmine on Saturdays every week with *Phil Levene*, which was fantastic. We did it for maybe two years. We played Latin, Fusion and Bop. Phil had never DJ'd before and didn't take too kindly to soiling his collection, but he played all manner of tunes that I'd never heard of before or since. He felt very personal about his records and felt that they were becoming a tool - which he never wanted them to be - so he wasn't overly bothered when The Goldmine finished. He did start playing at other Jazz sessions after that though.

You had your famous Rare Groove sessions running at the same time.

Well then it was *The Hadleigh Suite* (London Road, Leigh-On-Sea). The Jazz that Chris Bangs and Gilles Peterson played was popular there, mixed in with the other stuff, but we were on the phone to each other all the time anyway, and went record shopping together. I was finding stuff too. *Maynard Ferguson – Mambo Le Mans* was massive there.

Your following legendary club - Chesters – which changed it's name to Waves (Southend High Street) – had a similar music policy to Dingwalls, which started later.

Well, I'd play Rare Groove, Soul and Hip Hop, and Jazz was just a part of the night, but fitted perfectly. Gilles was the most popular guest we had there with queues all the way down the road.

PHIL LEVENE

Phil was a reluctant DJ initially – he was always a collector first and foremost, but he has been involved in some way with virtually all the most important clubs in London and Essex covered in this book. Considered the DJ's DJ.

My brother was into Jazz. I was exposed to it from an early age. I was into Blues originally, then Funk and by 14years old I started getting into Jazz. I would go through my brothers collection pulling out Coltrane, Donald Byrd, Cecil Taylor, Miles Davis… just listening out of curiosity. You see, my brother was a Jazz-reviewer and got sent lots of it- Lonnie Liston-Smith, Dom Um Romao ; all the Jazz-Rock Fusion stuff like Weather Report. I had a lot to draw on.

When I first started going to clubs in Essex like Zero 6 (and later on, The Goldmine), I was into the Jazz-Funk stuff by artists like Eddie Henderson but I was still listening to the jazz at home. I hadn't put them together at this point until I went to Lacy Lady and heard Herbie Hancock being played next to James Brown and it all made sense all of a sudden. The same at The Goldmine with Chris Hill playing *Miles Davis -Milestones* etc…It never

occurred to me to hear *that* in a clubbing context, that's when I started looking at my own record collection. I was checking out the DJ Bob Jones wherever he was playing too.

Later, when I went to The Electric Ballroom in '82, the room was madness. I thought:, "I've got these records!" and I understood immediately what the dancers were into and I felt it would be easy to play to them. I had done a bit of DJ-ing since 1979 but it was in the Goldmine jazz room that I started to take it seriously. Gary Dennis did it first there and got me to come down and do it with him. I was playing heavyweight stuff-probably too heavy - and I'd play an entirely different set each week. I was DJing a varied set of music at Gary's other club - The Hadleigh Suite as well, but one day I decided that all I wanted to play was Jazz.

So how did you get involved with *The Wag* in '87?

Through Gilles. I knew him through *Solar Radio*. They had a closing down party (1985). We had a chat and afterwards I kept bumping into him. We'd always chat about Jazz. I was going to The Wag anyway, and on 3 different occasions they got me to guest with Sylvester upstairs, and then they stopped doing guests and I ended up doing it every week.

Did any opportunities come out of doing The Wag?

No none! I don't think I hung out at the right places!!!

The *Hi-Hat* at the Moonraker in Southend-On-Sea must have been around the time of The Wag?

Yes, February '87, and I think Dingwalls overlapped.

Yes it did. If you remember, at The Hi - Hat we had a policy of not playing any of the Prestige and Blue Note style organ-funk that was getting played at Dingwalls at that time.

More purist. We thought it was a bad month if we had less than 200 in the club, which for a heavy duty session was superb. We had record stalls, guest DJ's…so I was DJ-ing in Southend *and* London. I felt like I was making my mark.

What did you think of Dingwalls?

Brilliant. Amazing. Actually, I guested there on three occasions. Even though it wasn't all jazz it was a great place to go socially, and all the DJ's would ask one another about what they picked up that week. I was glad to see Patrick Forge doing well there. I knew him from him working at Reckless Records in Soho (London). I worked in Soho too, so I used to go in there three times a day to check out the new arrivals, from the day it opened. My wants list soon went down! Eventually, when Patrick started working there I would often put him onto jazz albums in the record racks that he might not know. I hunted all over London for records. I was (and am) dedicated.

Gilles Peterson, Snowboy and Phil

MAD MARX/ SNOWBOY

I'm sure you'll forgive me including myself in this, but I was (and am) very active for the cause of Jazz Dance.

It says in the preface how I discovered the music and scene of which this book covers, so I won't repeat that. As the resident DJ at school at the age of 15, I already had some experience when, in 1978, I decided to hire out The Goldmine monthly to put on my own nights as Mad Marx' Roadshow. I'd only been collecting records for a few months, but I just wanted people to listen and dance to the music I loved, so as a 17 year old I had the idea of booking two other popular local DJ's with me each month on a Wednesday, hoping that their following would like me, and support me in the future too. I called these events *Jazz Funktions* (a terrible name I know!) and, right away, from the first one, in late 78, they were successful. The idea was to use two different DJ's every time, but on the second one in early '79 I used two by the names of Russ Burcham and Graham 'Grumpy' Brown – who had their own disco system *The Fighting Machine Roadshow* (which was just as well because Chris Hill wouldn't let us use the expensive in-house Mat Amp system), and they ended up doing the next twenty four of my events in the end (in fact Russ took over the running of them). We all dabbled in Jazz, but of the three, I became known as the Jazz specialist. We'd all guest regularly strictly playing Jazz at The Blue Note Jazz Club at Crocs in Rayleigh High Street, Essex every Wednesday in 1980, which was an important event for us locally. Bob Jones was the resident.

I got approached by an old school friend, David Davies, who was now a local music promoter. He put on various events headlined by myself with varying degrees of success; although I do remember having to play 'Celebration Suite' by Airto three times in a row for the Jazz hungry Tribe I was involved with - *The Black Kidney*, and I was very grateful to the support of the Chelmsford Tribe *The Pre-Clones* – who were Jazz specialists, and *The Souldiers* from Southminster, Essex. Around the country, I've since found out, that Tribes were looked down on as some kind of numbskulls, but believe me, the higher echelon ones such as *The Brixton Front Line* and the *Funk Master Generals* (along with the aforementioned) had far more knowledge than 95% of the DJ's.

I lived the Jazz Funk life of an Essex Soul boy: going to many clubs, all-dayers and events (although, I swore I'd never go to Caister again after the second one!), listened to Robbie Vincents Radio London show every Saturday lunch-time and read Blues And Soul magazine, and then it happened: Paul Murphy started The Horseshoe and opened his record shop 'Fusions'. I was on the dole after leaving college but I spent what I could there, every two weeks. The amount of music he was uncovering was quickly changing the scene with so many incredible records, and all of a sudden there was way too much to buy. The Jazz Funk scene was floundering and we could always see that a dedicated Jazz Dance night was going to happen – it was obvious; there was too many of us just waiting for the Jazz to be played in the Discos. There was discontentment. We wanted the music hard and lots of it.

The Jazz Funktions continued on in the early 80's but I took a detour briefly when I became a *Red Coat* entertainer for Butlins Holiday centres for a summer season in Clacton in Essex in 1982. One of the Redcoat girls there, Lesley – ironically a 'Goldmine regular'- tipped me off about a Jazz record stall at Clacton market run by Tony Ashby, who had been supplying the revered DJ Bob Jones. My entire wages went on records every week from him and my poor parents had to drag back the one hundred and fifty or so Jazz albums that I'd built up by train for me. While I was away, my friend and fellow Jazz-head Darren Gale wrote to tell me that Paul Murphy had started his Jazz room at The Electric Ballroom, so I knew things were changing and moving on.

At the end of the season at Butlins I was given a bonus which brought me my first set of Congas the same day I returned. I had already bought a bit of hand-percussion (like the Brasilian friction drum *Cuica*), because I was inspired by seeing Chris Hill play some over the records at The Goldmine. Now I wanted to be a percussionist. I was a failed Comic Artist, but my parents encouraged me to play my Congas. I used to spend seven hours a day practicing, eventually being taught by the esteemed Robin Jones. Meanwhile, I continued on from where I left off with the Jazz Funktions. By now Chris Hill was also letting us cover for him at The Goldmine on Saturday nights when there was a Caister Weekender happening or something, which was an honour, believe me, As the Jazz Dance scene got heavier, I got more and more inspired, although I found time to go berserk about the new release independent 7" Soul releases- of which there was quite a cult–scene developing. I was also one of the original 'Rappers' (as they called them them) at the U.K's first Rap night *The Language Lab* at Gossips, Meard Street, London on Monday nights too.

In august1984, in the local fishing village of Leigh On Sea, I got a weekly Sunday residency at a wine bar called Whispers in Leigh Road. I subtly called it 'The Hard Tackle Club', and played predominantly Jazz; but also Funk and Soul. The place only held 70 or 80 people to be honest, but there was nothing like it locally. Tony Ashby sold records there and Bob Jones guested when the budget allowed. It lasted for two years, and my abiding memory of it is, at a rammed Christmas special playing *George Shearing – Mambo With Me* with an explosion of riotous dancing and people dancing on the tables too – such was the anthem it had become.

Things changed in Southend for the good in early1986 with a huge wine bar called *Scruples* in Milton Road, Westcliff On Sea, under the superb management by Will Hutton and Deb Neild-Wildsmith. These two open minded music lovers put DJ's on every night like Gary Dennis, Cosmic, Grumpy Brown, Russ Burcham and later, Bob Jones and Ed Stokes. I myself, had two Jazz nights and a Soul one, and it was packed most nights. This place did so much for the local Black music scene, it had to be seen to be believed. It was a golden-era, just previous to Gary Dennis giving us the Rare Groove explosion at his nearby club Chesters in March 1987 (also later managed by Will and Deb. They organized the original Essex House music 'rave' too, by the way!).

On the 9th of April, my friend and Scruples regular - Simon Abel, offered to promote a night for me in Southend, so we did 'Southends First Latin Night' with Chris Bangs, Gilles Peterson and myself DJ-ing with Robin Jones' *King Salsa* playing live (of which I was, by now, the Bongo player). It was one of those nights where everyone was there and the drinks were flowing well (especially in my direction). I got so drunk that I fell off stage when Robin introduced me and I was later sick in the lid of Gilles' record box (all of this was reported in Blues And Soul, to my shame!), and I was eventually carried out. All-in-all a good night!

Most importantly: in June 1987 Bob Jones, Phil Levene and I started a Jazz Dance-only night at the Southend United FC Supporters club 'Shrimpers,' – again, promoted by Simon Abel - and the night was called *The Hi - Hat Jazz Club*. We moved from there after one to it's new home - the nearby 'Moonrakers' in Westcliff On Sea. It was a big dingy basement function room and we had guests such as Gilles, Chris Bangs and Baz Fe Jazz and a different record dealer each time. Considering the nature of the night, we were disappointed if we had less than 200 people in (which would have been packed). There was an overkill at Dingwalls of the Prestige/ Blue Note label Funky Organ Jazz at the time, so there was a ban on that at The Hi - Hat; it was just Fusion, Be Bop and Afro Latin Jazz.

I started to do a Jazz room at the newly-owned Goldmine in February1988, but there was a new hooligan/gangster element which I didn't like. It was horrible watching Jazz dancer friends of mine being taunted on the floor by these idiots at the bar. I tried a short-lived Wednesday Jazz night above the club in The Waters Edge pub too but it never worked. To be honest, the golden days of The Goldmine were over by 1984.

Musically, by then I'd become a professional Percussionist under the name *Snowboy* and had released three 12" singles – one called *Bring On The Beat* back in '85 on Arc records; *Mambo Teresa* and *Wild Spirit* in '86 on a local Folk music label called Waterfront, and another called *A Night In Tunisia* and *Ritmo Snowbo* on Gilles Peterson and Baz Fe Jazz's BGP record label in '87; I'd started touring with the singer *Basia* - who'd previously been the lead singer with the Jazz Pop group Matt Bianco, and, as I said, I was playing for my teachers Salsa band. I'm not giving the blow-by-blow account of my music career here for obvious reasons but if you're interested, go to www.snowboy.info.

By 1988 Phil Levene and I inherited a monthly Saturday night at a basement club below Saks wine bar in Station Road, Southend. It was originally called *Floorworkers* and was promoted by Gary Lucas and Dave Elmer. Gary continued the night and Phil and I renamed it *Back To The Tracks*. With just a few Funk tracks thrown in it, was 95% totally Jazz. We were lucky to get support from the heavyweight Jazz dancers from a 100 mile radius. Phil knew them from being resident at The Wag. But, to me, this was a whole new crowd, and they were dedicated. It was hard core all the way. This night continued until 1995 and, with the exception of the Jazz room at Alex Lowes' Southport weekender, became the only club for years just for the Jazz dancers. There was less and less Jazz being played at Dingwalls and when that closed London – briefly – became Jazz Dance free.

During all these periods, I continued to support all the other sessions: traveling up to The Special Branch events at The Royal Oak and The Wag with Bob Jones and was a regular – both as a punter and performer – at Dingwalls too. As a musician I'd become the percussonist with Lisa Stansfield in 1990; I'd become the Conga player back in 1989 with The James Taylor Quartet; featured on the Acid Jazz compilation on Polydor – *The Freedom Principle*, and my first album *Ritmo Snowbo* was one of the first released on 'Acid Jazz' records, so I lived through, and was a part of, all that was happening then, from a Southern perspective.

TONY POOLE

The size of this piece doesn't, at first, do justice to a DJ and Broadcaster who made such a great contribution to our scene on the radio and in the clubs, but all the info is here. Tony worked hard to give us our regular and well-presented jazz-fix and he more than deserves his place in this book.

Tony, who was a mobile DJ, got into the Jazz Funk scene through reading about it in James Hamiltons influential DJ column in Record Mirror in the late 1970's and got turned into the Jazz Dance by going to see Paul Murphy DJing at The Wag playing Art Blakey and such like. It blew him away and got him hooked.

Tony was station manager on a hospital radio station which gave him great experience when, he eventually (after helping out for four years) presented the respected *Jazz First* on BBC Essex for two years. In March 1985 Tony started sessions at The Square in Harlow on Sundays, weekly. This was a live night with DJing and lasted for at least two years. Once a month it would be a big Jazz Dance one with bands like Plan B, Annie Whitehead, Tommy Chase.....

Any guest DJ's?
We had Gilles down there.

A great reaction locally?
Oh yes, but we had people from London, like Eddie Piller, traveling - loads of people. Musically it wasn't ultra-heavy Jazz though. After The Square we did Bop City at *Cheeks*. I was the promoter there. We had guest DJ's like Martin Collins, Grumpy Brown, Baz Fe Jazz, Sylvester, Gilles – his nights were always the best, and Bob Jones as well. It was a one-man crusade to a degree and it was hard.

For more Essex see Andy Ward and Andy McConnell – The A2 Connection and Paul Murphy.

LONDON

ROBBIE VINCENT

He needs no introduction surely? The immense importance of his taste-making Saturday afternoon radio show on Radio London above all other Black music radio shows can not be over-emphasized. He had the power to fill a record shop within half an hour of his show ending and was listened to [and taped!] by everyone in the scene in the South. Everyone relied on the show for essential information of 'what was happening and where,' and you heard the music first there. No one could deny that he is one of the most important people in this book.

I was a journalist at the Evening Standard and left to join the newsroom on BBC Radio 4 and then to BBC Radio London in 1973. I started doing phone-in shows and a music show.

I learnt my trade there. It was an FM station and most people then couldn't get FM. I doubt if there were fifteen hundred people listening, so I could get away with being a terrible DJ - which you couldn't now.

I played all kinds of music – actually Emperor Rosko had all these great US import pop exclusives and I'd record them off air and be playing them two minutes later on my show! I didn't make a big deal, but just play them.

I started off playing Rod Stewart and Slade and all that, and had a half hour at the end where the music was Blacker. It slowly evolved into a policy of Soul, Funk and lighter Jazz. I think I was right to have changed the policy. No one was playing it. We take it for granted now, but I was the first person to play Luther Vandross on radio! I would play from Donald Byrd to Grant Green to Vandross to the Commodires. Originally, the show was Saturdays 11.30 – 1pm, and then 12 till 2p.m which was the perfect time, as clubbers would be getting up around then.

Yes, in my local import shop it would be empty on a Saturday till 2pm and then when your show finished it would be packed with people wanting to buy what they just heard you play!

On a monthly basis I started doing a section called the Fusion 40 – which was forty minutes of Jazz Fusion. It was a bit risky, but I felt justified that there was a market for it.

We needed it. It was essential.

I stuck with it. I didn't see it as a public service per se, but I felt that as it was a publicly funded station it should provide to a minority – tens of thousand – or, in my case it was hundreds of thousands. Of course, the show exploded beyond my wildest imagination. I had no idea that the scene would become as big as it was. The Caister weekenders were my idea, and I never had an idea that *that* would still be going twenty seven years later or that 8,9 or 10,000 people would want to go to one.

If I made ten people go out and buy a *Donald Byrd* album from listening to my show, I'm happy. I've always felt – from a radio point of view - that I'm a privileged position and I *should* be abusing that position to persuade people to go out there and buy those records, and I meant it. I was very serious about it. If I didn't give this music exposure over here, nobody would. I was crusading.

Did the Fusion 40 start with just a few tracks?

Yes. It ended up as forty minutes because I felt that was what I could get away with. Because it had to be accessible I played less accessible in amongst it but got away with them without people noticing too much. There was stuff played that was right for the radio but wrong for the

dancefloor. I would play through hours and hours and hours of Jazz records – some of them bored me to tears – and then a track would leap off of an album and I'd think: "Wow, I wish someone would play this for me so I could dance to it."

Everybody listened to your show in the South and I know loads of people in the North that used to have tapes of your show sent up.

I was told when my show finally finished, that it was the most taped in the history of radio. My tapes have been heard all over Europe, even Australia and the US.

As a radio DJ you must have been getting records far ahead. What day did the imports arrive?

I used to go to an importer – a friend of Chris Hill's – in Blackheath, and get the records before they got in the shops. My relationship with the shops was that they would call me. Tony Monson (owner of Disc Empire distribution and the pirate station Solar Radio) used to stop off at my home with his van delivery. He was good to me. His music taste is exemplary. I got all the acetates, and any promotions people worth their salt would be waiting at the station for me Saturday mornings. That was lovely.

As you were further ahead than the shops, I guess all the big DJ's had to check out your show to hear the new stuff.

Even Chris Hill did, although he'd never admit it (laughs). A lot of the main DJ's guested on my show, and they'd be searching and searching for tunes and play stuff I'd never heard. I think all the DJ's had to work hard to find new stuff; I know I did. There was great competition. It was all very exciting.

In the early 80's a lot of the DJ's started to drop Jazz from their sets because the tempos were getting faster, and a lot of them saw it as antisocial: Did you follow through with this?

No. It separated the dancefloors. You could have a 'Paul Murphy' element, but not all night. I'd always mixed all the elements. I couldn't play some of those very fast Jazz Fusion records or some of the more esoteric jazzy records that the Jazz dancers were brilliant with. Most people couldn't dance to them, so what would be the point of wrecking my dancefloor? Because there was a market for that somewhere else, the jazzier side of our scene developed its own underground scene as rap did.

At the height in the early 80's you were the voice of the scene on the radio. Everyone listened. Did you realize what power and influence you had?

No. Not until it finished, unfortunately. Then it dawned on me.

GEORGE POWER

Of all the great DJ's there would have been in our capital in the 70's, there was none more important or influential in London than George (alongside Greg Edwards, to be fair). He also almost, single-handedly, made it possible for Blacks to (finally) get in to the Disco's in town by refusing to work where there was a racist door policy (and there were many in the 70's). George had a large, loyal following of *the* very finest dancers at his many residencies and promotions.

In the early 70's I had a mobile disco doing all the weddings, pubs and all that. I went under the name of 'Cosmic Power Discoteques,' I owned twelve systems in the end and employed other DJ's. I was in charge of the London Union Youth Clubs and I'd do roadshows with Jimmy Saville and Alan Freeman, and be on his show on Radio 1 on Friday afternoon with the 'Youth Club call!' I was going to be a solicitor but I had to give it up because I had so many bookings coming in. I decided that I wanted a residency playing Soul. I got into that through Motown and Stax/Atlantic and so forth – so, in 1972 I hired the hall in *The Nightingale*, Wood Green (North London) on Sundays. I packed it out with 3 to 500 people. Then I was approached by *The Royal* in Tottenham who used to get 1,000 people in on Sundays. I DJ'd with a guy called The Baron and he'd play a half hour of Reggae and I'd play a half hour of Soul in rotation but my crowd didn't get on with the reggae and there would be fights. In 72-73 I moved onto *The Royalty* in Southgate but they got rid of me because I attracted too many black people. So this was the best thing that happened to me because I went from there to *Crackers* in Wardour Street, and occasionally *Mash* in Greek Street. I was brought into Crackers by a DJ called Nicky Price who was a DJ on the Wheatleys Tavern organization circuit and Crackers was a Wheatleys. He didn't have the records or the interest to do Soul nights so I covered for him at first and then I was also given my own Sunday night and trebled the attendance of his Friday afternoon session, and I just played commercial music on Saturdays. From Monday to Thursday I was at *Studio Valbonne* off Regent Street, plus I was still doing mobile discos.

With Crackers, I started off earning £3 and ended up running the place! It was the best place - the best dancers, the best fashions. If I wanted to break a new record I would get my dancers to dance to it. They knew they had to do it. Wheatleys also gave me a Wednesday at *Bumbles*, Wood Green. I used to get 600 people there but they would be mainly from South East rather than North London. This was more of a reggae area and I didn't want them in. The crowd was 70-30 white to black and Crackers was the opposite. Bumbles lasted until around '80.

I was doing a lot of gigs around that time. *Gossips, Bouncing Ball* in Peckham, *Charlie Browns, Americas* - I was getting approached all the time because people knew I could attract a lot of people. I was everywhere. I used to like working hard because it kept the kids off the streets causing problems. Give them what they want to hear.

It must be your youth club background.

Yes. They had no outlet to hear this music so somebody had to lead the way. I've opened the doors for a lot of black people to get into the clubs.

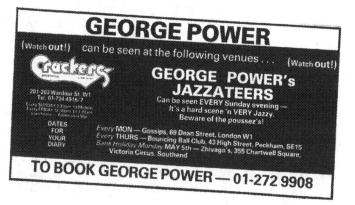

You ruled London didn't you? Your only competition would have been Greg Edwards.

He's a close friend of mine. We get on very well. He's a fantastic radio DJ but more commercial in the clubs. I'm hardcore.

His session at the Dun Cow in Old Kent Road was real hardcore Funk. You shared a lot of the same dancers.

Well yes. There was no competition there whatsoever though, as I say, we're friends.

I've met dancers from all over the country – particularly Birmingham and Bristol – that were regulars at Crackers.

Yes. The best dancers were born in Crackers.

Your reputation was very Jazzy.

I would please everyone. Funk: Philly Soul: Latin Jazz: Fusion. I had to play more Jazz because it was in demand and the best dancers wanted it. I used to cover-up all the record labels because people wanted to know what the records were.

You were holding regular Jazz Dance competitions at Crackers and at a night called Funks at Lazers

Yes, we had competitions for the ladies as well. It was a different Jazz than at *The Horseshoe*, It was more Jazz Funk.

Why did Crackers close?

It was sold, and when Crackers closed I went to Gossips in Dean Street for a while. I did Saturday lunchtimes and Sunday night. From there I went to Spats, which I did every Thursday and Sunday.

So, after a while when you started 'Jazzifunk' at The Horseshoe, it was two rooms; you and Paul Anderson and a Jazz room with Colin Parnell and Boo.

Correct. Like Paul, they used to follow me about and they loved the Jazz so I let them do the room. Because they're Londoners they knew what would be required. They did well but they got tired of it, as far as I can remember. When Paul Murphy came in he had his record shop and a following and we all worked well, He was the original Jazzman.

Why did The Horseshoe close?

Again, it got sold. From there we did The Electric Ballroom. We had Paul Murphy doing the Jazz room and eventually Gilles Peterson took over from him, but there we couldn't get it right up there for quite a while. It was sad to see Paul go, but it did end up a good session.

Your night was one of the first clubs in the country to embrace Electro and the Breakdance phenomenon.

Its true. Personally it wasn't my kind of thing – I like to hear a song. Where did all the songs go? By the time I moved The Ballroom session to *Ambassadors* I was more interested in Radio.

How did you get involved with Pirate radio?

Radio Invicta approached me to do a show which I did. I was encouraged by Paul Anderson and others. I was against it at first because I was worried people would copy my style, but I did it and it worked well. I started to attract a lot of listeners. I did another pirate station called *City Sound* – which I financed – which didn't last too long – and then did LGR (London Greek Radio). Then, with Gordon Mac, I started Kiss FM but being a Cypriot Greek and knowing the community station stood more chance I went with that station. If I'd stayed with a pirate it could have damaged the chances of me getting a license. So I sold Kiss FM to Gordon Mac.

TONY HICKMOTT – OBJ'S

Although, perhaps not a house-hold name in the Jazz Dance scene, Tony, a DJ, was there when others weren't, believing in what he was playing against all—odds. Most importantly: all the *right* people knew him and supported him!

I always played to a majority; very good, hardcore of people – mainly from East and North London: Hackney, Wood Green, and some of West London - but it was mellower there.

It seemed, by the adverts from your clubs that you were really pushing the Jazz.

I always was. I was always working out how I could slip Jazz tracks in through the night.
Like Jazz-breaks?
No. I wanted the Jazz to be a part of the night generally. There was a demand because of dancers like Paul Anderson etc. The Jazz I played wasn't like was played in the '80's – Be Bop and all that, it was more Jazz Fusion like *Jeff Lorber - Samba, Chick Corea – Central Park*...
You were very early playing Jazz, before most others.
I wasn't influenced by others. I did what I wanted. I was never a follower of fashion or check out what other DJ's were playing. It was a long furrow but there was enough enthusiastic followers – key people – that encouraged you. I never took the easy route, but I never looked at it as a career.

I used to have a record stall in '75 in Brick Lane, East London and then Kingsland Road, and through that I started DJ'ing. I did *The Prince Of Wales* in Hammersmith, but the management didn't like the crowd (too many Blacks). From there I went to *Charlie Browns* in Tottenham for a year. It was hard - it wasn't a barnstormer, say, like a 'Chris Hill' gig,, but the crowd were faithful. I was too soon with what I was playing but I was flying the flag.
What does OBJ's stand for?
I'm from Blackburn in the North and there was a beer you could buy called OBJ – O Be Joyful, so I thought that'd make a good catchy name.
How long were you selling records off a stall?
I started working for City Sounds records on Fridays in the late 70's and was still selling then. Then I started delivering import records to other shops for them so I had to go to the airport to pick the records up, which meant that I had immediate access to all the records everyday before they went into the shops. As a DJ I was as upfront as you could be. That gave me a big help and a reputation. In '81 City Sounds and Tony Monson formed a company wholesaling import records called Greyhound and I became a minor share holder with a guy called Paul Callaghan and a year later we bought Tony out - even so, I was still doing my market stall until '83, just selling new release Black music. I could shift more units of individual records than the record shops!
As a DJ, when did you stop playing Jazz?
Early '80's. I still played the odd one, but by that time Paul Murphy had come along and it'd all turned into something else.

TONY MONSON

Tony started his radio broadcasting career on Radio Bermuda ZBM1 in the 60's and eventually became the 'King Of The Pirate Stations', some may say, and as a record distributor he was second to none. It was Tony who single-handedly started the entire Jap Jazz craze country-wide:
Well what happened was, I had a shop in Kings Road, Chelsea, called *Disc Empire* and got friendly with the owner of *Flyover Records* in nearby Hammersmith. He specialized in Japanese Imports across the board – picture discs, Status Quo, Elvis etc.. and Jazz was a small part of it. We merged with him and took over the importing. We started experimenting more by bringing more Jazz in, and so all this happened almost by accident. There were big sellers like *Dave Grusin – Mountain Dance* and stuff by *Sadao Watanabe* and we were hearing records by other artists such as *Shigeburu Mukai* and *Termasa Hino* and names that no one had heard of, and this caused a massive underground interest. People would come from miles around because you couldn't get them from anywhere but us. This was about 1981.
But records like *Hiroshi Fukamara – Hunt Up Wind* are earlier than that.
It was an older record but wasn't known until we brought it in, because we started going through the back catalogues. Because all the Mafia DJ's like Chris Hill, Chris Brown and Sean French were buying them, I would get an immediate response and Robbie Vincent would play them on the radio. There was a good backlog of Jazz in there when we took over, so we also had the advantage of listening to those too. It was more of a Rock shop previously, so people from our scene wouldn't have gone in there before. Another track I'm quite proud of was *Ned Doheney – To Prove My Love*. Its not from a Jazz album, its more soft rock, and I heard it quite by accident in the shop when one of the guys who worked for us was a Folk and Rock expert and was just checking the album. It was already an old record when it was huge in the UK, but it was new, because it was a new discovery. I almost went mad when I heard it!

There was a scene for Jap Jazz all over the country. There was a fever.
Yes there was, but it went national later. We'd wholesale to key shops around the country after a while.
How long did that scene last?
Well, the shop went bankrupt in '82 so we wouldn't have been importing Japanese stuff after that.
Was there anyone else bringing those records?
Originally, it was just us. The process of bringing records in was very complicated and most wholesalers in Japan weren't selling that stuff anyway. Remember, there was no fax or E-Mail then, it was just Telex and was a long process. Kumu Harada from The Breakfast Band did some correspondence for us which helped enormously. People were falling over themselves for a long time trying to find out who we were using and by the time they did the whole thing was fading anyway.

TERRY JONES
Although known as one of the UK's finest Soul DJ's, Terry had a brief flirtation with Jazz at his legendary pub The Norfolk Village. His session - although nothing really to do with the build up, or running in tandem with, the Jazz dance scene as we know it - was so unique and added a different dimension, it is well worth documenting.

I started *Jazz In The Afternoon* at The Norfolk Village (Shoreditch High street, East London) in the summer '81 because Neil and Taffy from the tribe *The Funkmaster Generals* liked it and requested it, so I played a bit on Fridays with the Soul, like *Rinder And Lewis - Blue Steel* and *Dave Benoit - Life Is Like A Samba*, but there was somewhere they were going for Jazz on Sundays that had stopped for a break - The Belvedere - so they asked if I could do something at The Village. I took over as the manager of the pub so had carte blanche to do what I liked, so once the traders from nearby Petticoat Lane market left at 2pm I'd play Jazz from 2 – 5. I'd play stuff like *Janet Lawson - So High* and *Pat Lundy - I Believe In Love*. Being a Soul man, I'd be searching for Jazz tracks on Soul albums like *Aretha Franklin - April Fools, Quincy Jones - Moodys Mood For Love, Carmen Mc Crea - More Today Than Yesterday* and *Elusive Butterfly, The Spinners - Don't Let The Green Grass Fool You*, and even stuff that you wouldn't expect: like Motown artists doing Jazz standards, and *Bobby Darin*, I'd play *Ella Fitzgerald, Dinah Washington* and *Esther Phillips* plus there was the Jap Jazz albums. I'd play some other different records like *Doobie Brothers – South Bay Strut*. It was that popular, we tried contacting the record label to try and get it issued as a single, so there were loads of left-field tracks that I played there. It was a learning curve.

It was more driven by that *Goldmine* crowd that used to come down. They'd bring records for me to play too. I wasn't adverse to that. It was a different session for the Jazz heads who knew their Fusion, because of my Soul background - rather than Jazz - so it was great playing them a different set than they were used to.

It was intended to be a summer–only event but it lasted most of the year, each year until '84. Because there was starting to be popular Jazz events on, on Sunday afternoons elsewhere, it was about time to stop it.

RALPH TEE
DJ and journalist, Ralph's much-loved magazine Groove Weekly was absolutely essential country-wide, and was the first to truly document the Jazz Dance scene properly.

Even though I'd been DJ-ing before, I really got established from doing my magazine *Groove Weekly*. People would want me to come and review their club so I would say: "If I'm coming to your club, how about letting me do a DJ spot?" I got to see a lot of clubs.
How long did Groove Weekly last for?
Two and a half years: May 1980 to the end of November 1982.
It was important documentation. It was out at the height of the Jazz Funk scene - going into the Jazz.
Earlier, the Jazz Funk was truly integral to the scene that I was on: you could play *Roy Ayers - Running Away* next to *Phyllis Hyman - You Know How To Love Me* at that particular time, and the Caister Soul Weekender had a Jazz room. When the Jazz Dance really kicked off in 1981, it was

slightly separate from the Caister Jazz Room' type thing.

I felt that I was on top of all of the new release music in soul, funk and jazz, but when I went to see Gilles Peterson at The Electric Ballroom, I was hearing loads of stuff that I didn't know; stuff that I must have missed. It was a fresh new scene but playing records that were, perhaps, a lot older.

Funk Mafia DJ's went to Paul Murphy's record shop, so some of those records would have been played at Caister.

Yes, well when Paul came along, it was the first time that I was buying *old* records. It had never occurred to me that you would go out and buy an old record. There was old records breaking through for the first time; previously it was all about being up-front with all the new releases. He'd find a batch of records that got missed from a few years earlier and make them available. He'd identify tracks on missed albums and import them in just for the shop and create an awareness. He had stuff that no one had. I remember him playing me *You've Got To Have Freedom - Pharoah Sanders*. He busted that.

I used to go to the Horseshoe to see the bands that Paul Murphy used put on there and I'd be at the decks continuously – 'What's this? What's that?' It used to drive me crazy, and then I'd go down to his shop and buy *whatever* and say: "What else have you got like this?" That's what it was like for me.

Why did Groove Weekly close?

It nearly killed me. It was a victim of it's own success. I got lots of interest and lots of advertising, but advertisers weren't paying their bills, so I got to a point where I was owed so much money that I couldn't afford to print the magazine. Towards the end, it wasn't weekly; I'd have to spend time debt collecting. I was doing it all on my own.

PAUL MURPHY

It is almost pointless giving an explanation about Paul. In some ways, this book is all about the lead up to when he exploded on to the scene [and it's surroundings] and the aftermath of when he left it. There was no one like him on the scene before and hasn't been since. His musical influence blanketed the whole of the UK, as did the dance style that came from his clubs.

I first DJ'd at *The Kingswood Club* in Ilford (Essex). It was above a Funeral Parlour and was a villains club. The good thing about the club was that it was by a bus garage, so all the buses stopped there. In 1978, I used to book Bob Jones and Paul Gratue to DJ for me, and one night it snowed so heavily that neither of them could get there. I had to DJ myself - with my little box of records! I got hooked. It was a buzz. The club only lasted for six months but was really packed; especially the last night. The owner couldn't handle the amount of people in the end.

I had a good job working for ATV Music Publishing at the time, as an office boy. I was earning £12 a week and spending most of it on soul music in Contempo Records in Hanway Street, London [owned by Blues And Soul magazine owner – John Abbey]. I used to go to the night club above Ronnie Scotts Jazz club on Thursday nights and The Goldmine soul night on Mondays and then to The Lacy Lady in Ilford with Chris Hill. People came from all over the South of England for this club. The music was spot on. He would play anything from *Nina Simone – My Baby Just Cares For Me* to *Grover Washington Jr*; some oldies; hard Jazz Funk. Through that club I got into Jazz, and then I started The Kingswood with Bob Jones, because he was jazzier than any other DJ around .

JAFFAS present

LIVE

THE HEATH BROS

(Percy Heath, Jimmy Heath, Stanley Cowell,
Tony Purrone. Akira Tana)

at "THE HORSE SHOE"
Tottenham Court Road, London W.1.

£3.50   SUNDAY 12TH   JULY 1981

TWO SETS PER NIGHT

From 7.30 p.m. - 12.00 a.m.

JAFFAS present

Live

The Jay Hoggard Quartet

at "THE HORSE SHOE"
Tottenham Court Road, London, W.1.

SATURDAY, 15th AUGUST, 1981

£3.50   From 8.30 p.m. - 2.00 a.m.

open 8.30   Band on at 10.30 p.m.

FUSIONS *Records*

present

ONLY U.K. APPEARANCE LIVE

Tania Maria

at THE Y.M.C.A.
Great Russell Street, London, W.C.1.

Monday, 14th June, 1982

Starts 8 p.m.
(Tottenham Court Road Underground)

Tickets £4.00

190

You were also running the Exodus club. What was that?

We were all young and most of us couldn't drive, so we built up subs to pay for coach-trips to other clubs like *Frenchies* in Camberley with Chris Brown and clubs every where. We went to Margate once and I took two double-decker buses there with 150 people. There was a lot of all-dayers and great clubs at that time, but I think that it was the big jazz festival at Alexandra Palace in 1978 that helped the interest in jazz in our scene. *Willie Bobo* was on the bill and his track *Always There* was a monster in the clubs at the time, so we would be like: " Wow! There's Willie Bobo!" There were loads of people from the Jazz Funk scene there, along with the regular jazz crowd. It was the next one though, that did it for me. Alexandra Palace had burned down the following year, so they moved it to Knebworth. There was *Ella Fitzgerald, McCoy Tyner,* well.....a huge gig. Every artist was big, and I was laying there in the sun thinking: "Yes, this is it for me," and I was hooked. I am a voracious reader and I just read tons of books on jazz after that. Tons.

I guess *The Horseshoe* was your first main session.

Yes. This guy I knew called *Ray Reeves* offered me a Friday night there. It was an old Victorian Music Hall on Tottenham Court Road. It took off straight away.

"Ray Reeves was a bloke (with a beard) with a mobile disco who used to do various London pubs, and got Paul to do The Horseshoe with him. I never saw him play a record!"

DJ Chris Bangs

How did people hear about it so quickly?

It was a community. We'd been through the Jazz Funk scene and there were people that wanted the music harder. People soon heard about it that were interested.

I started wondering whether I could get any live acts there, so I tracked down drummer *Alphonse Mouzon*. He cost a fortune, but we broke-even even on that one. After that I got Vibraponist *Jay Hoggard* ...

How on earth did you get these artists?

They'd be over doing festivals. There was a lot of jazz festivals over here then. The Hoggard gig nearly didn't happen: We'd hired the only set of Vibes in London and they were broke. What were we going to do? All of a sudden, this hippy-type bloke comes in and asked about what time the gig starts so I told him the story, and that the gig may not happen and he said: "I've got some Vibes in the car" – It was *Roger Beaujolais*! We also booked UK acts like *Morrisey and Mullen, The Breakfast Band* and *Paz*, and then I booked *The Heath Brothers*. I put them on for three nights and it was jammed. Percy Heath said that he'd never seen people dance to jazz. The last night was the night of the Brixton race riots. In the Spring of '82 I was offered *Tania Maria* but by then The Horseshoe was closed so I put her on at the YMCA down the road. The gig was a nightmare. There was work-permit problems and I had to get a TV in the dressing room because Brazil were playing Russia in the World Cup at Football. They wouldn't go on until the game was finished and the audience were giving them the slow handclap! Anyway, the gig was absolutely unbelievable. Incredible.

So, *Devils* followed The Horseshoe.

It only lasted for a few weeks.

But it was legendary....

Sorry to disillusion you (laughs). It was the only thing going on like it at the time, so .... They used to shout: "Murder" after every tune!

You had your own Jazz record shop.

I used to work for *Our Price Records* from 1979 to '82 in Leicester Square, so I thought I would open my own one: *Fusions* in Exmouth Market. I was a terrible business man. I couldn't do the accounts; I was totally uninterested. I was great at selling though. I got a lot of my contacts from *Billboard* and *Cashbox* where I'd send off for these lists from the adverts and, in one of them there was all these amazing albums at 99c. I was going: 'Yes.I'll have 100 Ingram - That's All, 100 James Mason, 100 Charlie Rouse - Cinnamon Flower, 50 Janet Lawson, 100 of each Tarika Blue albums ...' It was $2.40 to the Pound at the time, so you could get a lot for One Pound! To show that I was a bad businessman, I sold the records way too cheap.

Yes. They were ridiculously cheap!

£2.99 and £1.99 and the odd expensive import for £6.99, but, yes, it was bad business. I got burgled there and had to close down and, also, I owed some money. While all this is going on, George Power offered me this residency at The Electric Ballroom for £50 a week. That kept me afloat for a long time.

Did George buy a lot of Jazz from you?

A bit, but all the DJ's were playing a bit of jazz then. I was DJ-ing in Manchester, Birmingham, Nottingham ....It was a Black circuit. What happened was: because of The Ballroom, a Black jazz-dance scene started very slowly moving along. Before, there was no 'gelled' scene, although there were people dancing to it. There were pockets dotted around....

Wasn't the music Jazz at The Horseshoe?

I was playing hard Jazz Funk and Jazz as well, like *Janet Lawson - So High* and various tracks by *Airto* but, at The Ballroom there was competitive dancing – "If you can't cut-it, go and practice it in the corner."

Was it a continuous *circle* all night long?

What used to happen was that I DJ'd the whole night from 10 til 2am and I'd play an hour and a half of the hardest and fastest jazz until I wore the dancers out, then I'd change the tempo. There was other jazz DJ's around the country as well, like Colin Curtis, Jonathon and Baz Fe Jazz, that had a scene, but the further North you got, the more different the dancing got. In London it was more footwork, whereas in the North it was more *balletic*. It's funny actually, but I went out with a Ballet dancer once, and she came along and said: " They're so un-disciplined [laughs]. They're great though." Curtis had been doing the same thing as me for years.

Did The Electric Ballroom take off immediately?

Immediately. Downstairs you had Paul Anderson playing Electro, and upstairs I was playing mainly new jazz. It was very contemporary. That's why it had a Black crowd: they're into what's new not retro. It was packed solid.

I remember that there was this group of white guys in there that were dressed different from the regulars. One of these came up to me: it was *Simon Booth* [later of *Working Week*] and said: 'I live here in Camden, but I never knew this existed. I did hear that people were dancing to jazz ...' By that time, it was full-on fast and heavy all night and I was having to keep up the interest by finding tracks with big breaks and I was pulling out tracks by Art Blakey and stuff like that. Not old Blue Note, but new. It was full-on, the way they wanted it.

I did a club called The Titanic in Berkley Square after The Ballroom, but it really did sink without a trace (laughs). We used to go to Sol Y Sombre on Thursdays to see Dave Hucker and I ended up doing Fridays there for about two years.

Was it heavy jazz?

No. It was salsa and latin-jazz. Within a few weeks we were getting five hundred people in there. It ran in tandem with The Wag really. Musically it was the same.

How did *The Wag* come about (9/1/84)?

Simon brought this journalist down to The Ballroom called Robert Elms from the magazine *The*

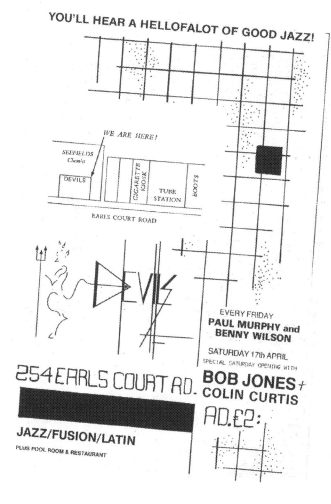

YOU'LL HEAR A HELLOFALOT OF GOOD JAZZ!

WE ARE HERE!

SEEFIELDS *Chemist*

DEVILS

CIGARETTE KIOSK

TUBE STATION

BOOTS

EARLS COURT ROAD

DEVILS

254 EARLS COURT RD.

JAZZ/FUSION/LATIN
PLUS POOL ROOM & RESTAURANT

EVERY FRIDAY
**PAUL MURPHY and
BENNY WILSON**

SATURDAY 17th APRIL
SPECIAL SATURDAY OPENING WITH
**BOB JONES +
COLIN CURTIS**
AD. £2:

Face and then the phone starts ringing: Chris Sullivan offers me *The Wag* on Monday – which is where I met *Dean Hulme* - who liked what I was doing and wanted to put some money into a business with me, so we started another shop. I knew Chris Sullivan from The Lacy Lady. He was a regular there. I thought: "Out with the old and in with the new" and I started playing old Blue Note records. People were coming away going: " I've been to this club and I've heard *Miles Davis- So What* on the dancefloor", and that's how I did it. It was great. It was like being in the film *Absolute Beginners* although, it's a shame they made that film because the scene would have had more longevity and taken a life of its own. That film killed it. It was a ludicrous film. I couldn't even watch it.

Weren't you doing a residency in Brighton at this time?
Yes, the same time. I did it with Ed Stokes. I knew Ed from my record shop and he'd guested at The Ballroom with me a few times. He used to drive me down there. The gig was organized by Andy Hale and Stuart Matthewman from *Sade's* band. They lived in Brighton. We did a place called The Jazz Room, and it lasted for six months. We never made a penny!

I know that you did a legendary all-dayer there with you, Ed Stokes, Baz Fe Jazz and Bob Jones. Mark Webster and Robert Elms went to it …
Yeah, and Sade came down. I don't remember it though (laughs).

You started a record label around this time.
Yes. We'd moved the record shop to beneath Record Shack in Berwick Street in Soho and decided to start a label - *Paladin*. We got an album by Paz, which they couldn't get released.

Did you have any input?
We suggested stuff. We never made a penny out of it, or any of our records in fact. Anyway, then I approached Dave Bitelli of *Onward International* to do something. By then, the press was going mad because of The Face article that Robert Elms had done and doors started to open. I became friends with Robert and he was going out with Sade at the time. She was doing an album and let us use the studio when they weren't in there – as they'd booked it out for 24 hours a day [a lock-out]. All we had to do was pay for the engineer, so we got Onward International in there to do three tracks. Me and my business partner Dean Hulme blew whistles on that!

Things went from a slow pace to out-of-control. The music that I was playing was on the edge and my lifestyle was on the edge. I was walking this tight-rope for three years. I've always been someone that lets things happen. I don't take control. I just went wild. All of a sudden I've got Simon Booth telling me that he's got an idea for a band (Working Week). He wanted to do a cover version of a record that I'd been playing: this was a test pressing for Hi-Fi's and they all were all going mental to it. It was called *The Bottom End* and was used to demonstrate the 'bottom end' on your Hi-Fi speakers. It was all happening. In the end, I got sick of it and I sold all those big Ballroom records. They were doing my head in. I sold them on the last day that my record shop opened.

They were queuing down the road at 9am.
And I didn't even get there until 11 am! Gilles had some of them, and whoever. I said: 'I've got to get out of this.'

Was this before The Wag started?

No. I was about three weeks in to it.

We did a deal for our label with *Virgin*, but they screwed us. We were so naïve. Simon Booth had done a brilliant record for us called *Venceremos* – a brilliant record. It will stand up forever. We got Julian Temple [director of Absolute Beginners] to do the video . It all went very wrong very quickly though, trying to get gigs and we had money problems and all wanting to go in different directions. It fell apart immediately. We ended up hating each other's guts and I had a punch-up with Simon in front of everyone at The Wag.

Who won? (laughs)

Richard Branson! None of us were winners. It was all over a mis-quote by Robert Elms in The Face. He made this cutting remark and it looked like I'd been quoted, so Simon was going: "What's this all about?" and off it went!

Why did you leave The Wag?

Purely money. They kept on buggering me about with it. I wasn't being paid much and I wanted a raise. I decided to leave, so I went to The Comedy Store in Leicester Square. I booked Mose Allison, Georgie Fame, Tommy Chase, Robin Jones ..... It only lasted for three months.

Baz Fe Jazz and Andy McConnell did The Wag after me and then it died, and then Gilles and Bob Jones, but I'd lost interest by the time I got back from Japan. It wasn't going anywhere and it was too retro. I got out for a few years.

You went to Japan?

I went twice. The first time I went there was with Gaz Mayall (DJ at Gaz' Rockin' Blues) and The Jazz Defektors. I'm a pop-star there! I remember that we were in this taxi trying to find this venue and it turned out to be the bloody Playboy Club. I thought: 'This can't be right?' so I went in to see if there had been a mistake. We walked down these stairs and everybody started clapping! I said to my interpreter that I wasn't happy. "I wouldn't have come over if I'd known we were going to play here", and he said:"This is the number one venue in Japan" and I said: "It might be here, but in England it is considered tacky." They gave me a crate of sixteen bottles of Absolut Vodka to quieten me down. Anyway, I had to play background music for the Playboy crowd and then they let the young crowd in. I was so pissed off by then that I started sharing the vodka with the crowd and they got absolutely plastered. They loved it. They asked me back but I didn't want to go. The second time I went wasn't to DJ; I did modeling and a couple of TV adverts. It did my head in. I went mad for a while.

You disappeared didn't you?

Yeah. I was just washing dishes in a restaurant in Camden. I went totally off the rails. Robert Elms walked in one day and he said: "You can't be doing this!" but I'd had enough. I'd been living this crazy life style for so many years.

Eventually, I started back at The Electric Ballroom, but in the main hall, not where I used to be – upstairs in the small room. I called the night *The Purple Pit*. It was too big there really. It was huge. We got a lot of Mods in there – there was all these scooters outside. I also did this club called the 325 on the Euston Road every Saturday. It was unbelievable. It was one of the best clubs that I ever did. It was an illegal Black shabeen, and I was playing jazz, ska and rhythm & blues. It was really exiting. It was a heavy Black crowd and the owner – Johnny Shaft – had half of his fingers missing from a machete attack. Then I moved to a club in Finchley called The Purple Pussycat; which we re-named *The Cat Club*. We were there for a year, and that's when I moved to The 100 Club. Tommy Chase recommended me and I was playing jazz and r&b.

It was playing to a much more Rock and Roll crowd though, wasn't it? You were playing stuff like *Hit The Road Jack* and *Fever*; a completely different sound than we were used to.

It wasn't until the end of 1988 – when Acid Jazz happened, that I came back. My session at H.Q's was happening at the same time as Dingwalls and was opposite. On the Sunday nights after Dingwalls we'd get all these musicians in from there. It was a brilliant time.

Why did you come out of the scene then?

I'd been doing it for a long time and, you must remember that I was always the first to do everything and I'd got really tired and bored and sick of dealing with Club owners.

ED STOKES

For the London section, I could have just used Ed's original interview. Ed's knowledge and clarity was a revelation. He straddled both the home-counties Soul boy Jazz Dance scene and the Black scene revolving around Paul Murphy's clubs, and was experienced in both, so he speaks with authority. Unfortunately for Ed, I had to drastically cut his interview in order for others to have their say too!

I was living in Brixton and I always loved the sound of Reggae and Ska. I remember walking through Brixton market as a young kid with my mum past the record shops and hearing the rhythm just coming out. It gets inside you, so I started buying bits and pieces then, and my record collection started to build up, and all my mates began to acknowledge it. I had no desires to become a DJ I was playing for a football team that was run by a pub in '74 –75 maybe. They used to have DJ's every night of the week except Sunday when they'd play tapes, so I turned around to the guvnor of the pub and I said to him "How about letting me fill the spot? I could bring my own mates and play a bit of music - my own kind of music," and he agreed with it. I went along, armed with a couple of bags full of records, and filled in for a couple of years! I then got a spot in a pub in Brixton on Tuesday nights, and I'd play a few records then introduce a topless dancer!

A major influence on me was Robbie Vincent radio show, especially when he started doing the Fusion 40 - 40 minutes of pure undiluted jazz influenced instrumentals with the occasional vocal or chant in there. That was an eye opener for a lot of people because it was class. He presented it very, very classily. Like everyone else, you sent your requests to Robbie Vincent, and, to be identified as the area you came from you'd ask for a request and then put a little tag in there like " Play it for *The Magnum Force* tribe" or whoever. I said to my friend, Junior: "Think up some names for our crowd" and he came up with *Frontline*. I said: "That's the one," because there's a road in Brixton that's known as the 'frontline' and it was like a no-go area for the police. I was comfortable that it sounded a bit hard because it would give you a little bit of protection; a barrier to people. Chris Hill didn't know us, we didn't know anyone and how we were going to be taken by people, and we didn't know whether we would be accepted or not. Most people we knew that were going to most of the do's were suburban types, and you'd maybe get a little group of Black and White guys from places like Tottenham - not many from South London. You had your little pockets of Rotherhithe gangsters who would just revolve around their own little areas but we threw that away, we didn't want to see any more of the violence and the drug abuse. Personally, I just wanted to get out there. I liked what I saw in the music scene that I got into from the early 70's. I was going out six or seven nights a week as a clubber travelling everywhere. We'd all go down to Torquay, in Devon - which had a big scene - with the whole of The Frontline and I'd been to Manchester a couple of times. They were as up front as London. I went to an all-dayer in 1979, and it was very similar to ours. Colin Curtis was playing. He made a massive noise in the North. He looked above and beyond into the horizon. I realized though, that while it was far and wide across Great Britain, the Essex scene was at the forefront, definitely.

So, I'd had about a two year gap from DJ-ing and I didn't pick up again until '81. It was then that I started getting serious about it. I started doing a wine bar restaurant on Baker St. My cousin used to manage it, and I used to be there on a Friday night with my own mobile disco playing Roy Ayers and Jazz Funk. I was shopping at Paul Murphy's record shop *Fusions* now and the sce-newas beginning to cross over the hill into some very obscure artists; Latin, and also into the Blue Note and Riverside labels. The time was right for someone like Bob Jones or the likes of Paul Murphy, and eventually Baz Fe Jazz. Gilles Peterson was busy, yourself, and myself to a cer-

Flippers Discotheque

presents

The THURSDAY CLUB JAZZ & SOUL

with ED STOKES

8.30pm — 12.30 am. ● Bars n' Food
● FREE admission for First Four weeks ●

Temple Mills Lane, Hackney Marshes, Stratford, E.15

tain extent. We had a lot of influences, a lot of knowledge, we had our record collections, and we knew what a lot of people liked. Jonesy really began to make a mark for himself. It was '81-82 when he became the man everyone wanted. DJ's especially began to take note, because they'd had it safe before then. I mean Sean French would always play a wild set, and Murphy was always looking to dip albums; find one track and take a chance.

The Jazz Room at the Caister weekenders progressed. The likes of Jonesy got to the stage where they could get away with anything. You thought:"This is the business." You accepted it because you trusted him. He had such impeccable taste. Chris Brown could do it without a doubt. He was more laid back, but he could have that effect on a crowd where he would say "Listen, let me have your attention," and Robbie Vincent had that on the radio too.

In '83 I probably had my biggest break. A lot of people already knew me and my collection - even guys from Scotland - and by then I was friendly with Jonesy, and Murphy was quite close then too. When I started to do a club called *Flappers* in Hackney on a Thursday night, Murphy came along to spy on me. It was more out of encouragement than anything, not in opposition but to back me up. I must admit I was aiming at The Goldmine crowd to be totally honest, but because it was an east end nightclub, it was only ever going to go so far. But in that club I was able to play *Fela Kuti - Roforofo Fight* and a lot of the Murphy tackle, mixed in with James Brown, Maceo, Detroit Spinners, Sister Sledge if I wanted to. I was certainly playing very similar to what *Pete Tong* was doing. Murphy said: " Come down, we're doing an all-nighter in The Ballroom," and he said: "Be warned. Not many DJ's can come here and survive. This is the ultimate test. If you can playing Jazz to this particular kind of crowd, not like your Goldmine crowd; you couldn't get away with playing a mid-tempo or a swinger, or light weight Bossa." It really was the ultimate test, because to play that sort of music, breakneck music, and keep them interested is an art. And I went down there and, like you do, you catch the feel of the place, and you go through your box over and over again, working out which order and form you're going to play things. Knowing what his big tunes are, I knew what he hadn't played to the crowd yet. I went on and killed 'em stone dead. Slaughtered them. They loved me, and they came and asked Murphy: "This guy – who is he?" Murphy keep me very much informed as to what used to go down there, so I've always been a good listener, and I knew what kinds of sounds were going down, but because this was an all-nighter, it was rammed as well, and he had his most critical people there: all the main dancers, and a lot of them were collectors as well. Murphy's partner Dean was there as well, and he just gave me the thumbs up.

What did you think about the dancing at The Ballroom?
Well, personally, those fast movements of the Jazz Dancers, I can trace back to Ska. The original shuffle we used to do in the 60's was a lot of the very fast foot movements, the knee trembling effects. If you went to a Blue Beat party, they used to play *Prince Buster* and the foot movements came through, and it passed from one generation to the next. I don't know if anyone's ever addressed it that way before. I used to love that sound, and I used to remember those steps, because we used to mess about doing it, and the handkerchief was definitely in there, you know: going down on one foot and coming back up.

You did other work with Murphy.
Yes, well, from there with him, we began to develop a strong link. We did some funny gigs together, because he began to grow big: he got invited down to Brighton by Dave - who was the keyboard player with *Sade,* and he was there with his college crowd and the people who were trendy in Brighton, to get a Jazz night off the ground, and they knew *Murphy - Robert* Elms and Sade, and the crowd who were floating around at the time, making jazzy noises - and they were beginning to film the 'Absolute Beginners' film. There was a bit of a buzz that Jazz could be a 'direction' again. We played at this hotel down there. The reason he wanted me to come down was because he knew I'd come down and play things like *Breakwater* and the lighter end of it, bringing a different angle, and he knew he couldn't go in there and play 100 mile an hour breakneck-speed Samba Fusion. He thought it was time to move on and to make a break from it. This was New Years Eve '83 and he wanted to play Jazz - not Jazz Fusion. He got into his Salsa period at the same time.

He really upset the dancers I remember at The Wag. He was determined to start playing Salsa, and of course it wasn't the tempo that Jazz dancers could dance to.
He loved the Salsa. He was 100% the influence of Salsa that came into my musical direction. I gave him full acclaim to that. I didn't recognize it as being valid, I didn't ever think "Hang on, I've

been collecting for 15 years, and I need this string to my bow now." It was never an avenue I thought I'd want to go down, but I did and I loved it. Although I didn't go as deep into it as say, Dave Hucker though.

Going down to Brighton, I brought a coachload from Brixton, and he had his college people, and the great thing was, he'd just got hold of a copy of *Sivuca – Ain't No Sunshine* - which was purpose made for a night like this, bearing in mind there was going to be a crowd coming in local who weren't really sure what to expect; Goldminers, who I'd brought down with me, plus some other people, like the Boreham Wood crew came down - and they were Goldmine Jazzers; hard edge. See, there were little pockets of them about, all around the perimeter of the home counties, and when we played Ain't No Sunshine for the first time it was going to be played in England, it then gave the club the right start. So I got a copy off him, and the three or four other copies he had and made sure Chris Hill had one. He really busted it at The Goldmine, so that's how I was quickly elevated. My name suddenly shot out. At this club we literally played from *Fela Kuti* right through to *Ella Fitzgerald -Take The A Train* – 10 minutes long - to the hardest *Blakey*; who was massively featured. Sometimes Murphy would come on and just pay an hour of it Salsa, whereas before him, I'd just done an hour of Blue Note, with congas in there - very experimental. This wasn't a Black crowd, these didn't know, they just followed the music and flew into it, but because it was so small, there would be 130 people in there. We'd have people in the corner, lighting up joints and some people wearing some strange clothes, and normal 'duffle coaters' from the university. It was a real mixture of people.

Sheldon Willox (The Cutting Edge) was a regular there wasn't he?
Yeah, well he used to go round with the Boreham Wood crowd. Sheldon and his mate Tim (Morris) were our two most regular goers that travelled down. We used to call them 'Chas 'n Dave' (laughs). They really, really knew their music.

The next year, after 7 months, Murphy left. I went on holiday in July and he stopped doing it, and so when I came back a few people asked me if we could start it up again, and so I went back there about August or September - so it was about a months break from it. I carried on up until winter time. I don't think I made it a whole year. I spent a lot of time down there and I think by then the jazz scene from '83 to '84 was just going to have an umbrella effect on it: you had the first London Jazz Bop start up; Baz Fe Jazz was massive; you had record labels bringing out stuff; compilations started to emerge and Gilles had his regular radio show coming through.

Really though, although I loved playing the Jazz, I suppose I was frustrated that I might be too bogged down by playing one thing. One thing I always loved about The Goldmine was that you could hear the whole spectrum. Gilles wanted to create the jazz thing and he did it. It became very jazzy, and it had to be because it was in the heyday of the Jazz rooms in Caister, and the likes of DJ's Pete Tong and Bob Jones. It was an exciting period in music, because you broke down a lot of the barriers and opened up a lot of new avenues. You certainly wouldn't have got the jazz scene that eventually came about if it wasn't for those days back then.

SIMON BOOTH

Simon was there from the beginning with his band Working Week. Their debut single Venceremos, was tailor made for the Jazz dancers at The Electric Ballroom, and the video featured the very first performance of IDJ on film. Simon continued through the Acid Jazz scene, and was heavily involved at the beginning.

I was working at Mole Jazz in Kings Cross packing records at the back of the shop. I was an indie-punk, in a few bands – *The Methodiscatune* and *Stepping Talk*. Through osmosis I suppose, I started getting into the stuff I was hearing at the front of the shop – particularly Astrud Gilberto – which was totally at odds with the scratchy 'Gang Of Four' type stuff I was into – and then I heard this band called *The Young Marble Giants* who were doing Brian Eno-type minimalist stuff and they had this great singer called Alison Statton who reminded me of Astrud Gilberto. I started trying to copy that kind of early sixties Brazilian Bossa Nova and sent some stuff to Alison Statton. She liked it and came down to London with her guitarist Spike. We did this song called *View From Her Room*, which was a slow 'soundtracky' sounding Bossa and then kicked into a fast Samba. Robert Wyatt recommended the legendary trumpet player Harry Beckett and we got the percussionist Dawson Miller. The drummer was an incredible sixteen year old boy who

worked at Mole Jazz called Mark Taylor. The band name - *Weekend* was named after the famous Jean Luc Goddard film of the same name. I didn't think much about it but then I found out it was number one in the 'Rough Trade Indie charts'!

After a few months, people like Chris Sullivan started coming into the shop (in his zoot suit) and journalist Robert Elms – he really knew his Jazz, and one day Paul Murphy came in and told me that my record was massive at his club *The Electric Ballroom*. I went down there and I was amazed. There was this whole culture I didn't know about.

This is about the time you formed your band *Working Week*, with (saxophonist) Larry Stabbins.

That's right, and I wrote the first single – *Venceremos*, from the inspiration of seeing the dancers at The Electric Ballroom. It was a song for them. Paul Murphy was very inspiring. We featured the IDJ dancers for the first gigs we did – in fact *Camden Jazz Festival* was the first one they did with us. They came to the studio too, when we recorded the single so we could check the groove was right, and that they could dance to it. I felt privileged to play to the Jazz dancers.

I remember taking a white label of Venceremos to an all-dayer at one of those hell-hole suburban nightclubs with Paul Murphy and Dean Hume in Luton and there was a Jazz room there. I walked in and Bob Jones was on playing *Chekere Son* by *Irakere* and I thought: "That sounds like us." He followed it with *John Coltrane – Impressions*. That guy is a maverick, honestly. Truly. I gave him the 12" and at first he went with the b-side *The Bottom End*, and he talked it up on the microphone and the floor filled. It was unbelievable. An amazing guy.

Other than Venceremos, *Afuche* is the only other Jazz dance track you made, which I was surprised about.

I never wanted to be a dance band. With me it's all about songs and lyrics. Jazz dance was very much tempo-fascism. It was very specific what you could do tempo wise.

One great thing about the Jazz Dance scene though, was that it was so far removed from the rock scene: Keith Richards was originally meant to be playing a part in the film 'Absolute Beginners' and he came to The Wag one Monday and I took him over to see IDJ dancing and he really got into it. I introduced him to one of the dancers and said: "This is Keith Richards" and he said: "What, Cliff's brother?" Keith loved it. He said: "He doesn't know who I am – Brilliant! He thinks I'm Cliff's brother," and laughed.

Unlike other parts of the country, the scene became very political in London didn't it?

It wasn't politically motivated with a capital 'P', but the first 'Acid Jazz' album – *Acid Jazz And Other Illicit Grooves* on Polydor [a title that Bob Jones came up with] was a profit-share. All the bands did it for nothing and it was very fair. All the royalties got split equally. It was a musician run project. It always really depressed me that when the DJ culture thing took over, it all became about peoples solo careers, stitching each other up, and I do find that too competitive. It was a mini example of 'Thatcherism'. It all became about peoples careers and the music was secondary. I found that appalling really. Then it turned into bands just cloning into whatever the latest groove was and it all became very uncreative and that wasn't what *Acid Jazz* was meant to be about. To me, the first 'Acid Jazz' record was our track *Stellamarina* - you've got Jalal from the Last Poets doing this mad Sufi - Mystical poem over a basic electro groove. It was the kind of experimentalism and cutting edge radicalism that I was looking for in the Acid Jazz scene. It wasn't about sitting there playing lame 70's funk grooves.

That's one side of the politics but the scene got political when Jalal from *The Last Poets* moved to London in the late 80's.

Well I bought him over first in '83/84 to do 'Stellamarina'. I think he moved over later because there was a scene, which is when Gilles and everyone got to know him. He was a hustler and good at it, but I never got involved. I got pushed out of the scene. It became about who could be the hippest and trendiest on the block, and I couldn't compete with all that. It got sad. I got forced out. At Dingwalls, when people saw me, I felt it was "Oh there's Simon from Working Week. They're a bit 'yesteryear' now. We've moved on." I ducked out. You have to let the next generation through, but there was a lot of nastiness. It was probably my worst time as a musician.

You always said that: "Acid Jazz should be dangerous and experimental" which was reflected in that big sold-out concert that you put on at the I.C.A. on the Mall (the main road leading to Buckinhgam Palace). You formed a backing band (of which I was in) which backed artists as diverse as a Black poet, a Japanese Opera singer, the street painter - *Wigan* painting on the stage….

The head of the ICA was really into street culture and loved my Acid Jazz projects and he wanted me to do a concert that reflected the multi-media aspect of the scene. I put it together but a lot of people in the scene didn't really want to do it. They wanted to do it their way and on their terms so *that* was the very last thing I did. Really, they were a lot of young white middle class hustlers trying to be cool and black and they weren't. They were being little Tory arse-holes at the end of the day. It ended up with lots of trendy rats from the rat-race running around in their different Duffer Of St George clothes stitching each other up.

To me the ICA concert was an individual expression of what you felt was 'Acid Jazz.'

It was about bringing together generations, bringing together Keith Tippet and

Steve Williamson that'd never played together, breaking down boundaries between musicians and styles of music - Music and Art. That was the spirit of Punk. All the boundaries that were pulled down, two months later after that gig, were re-erected.

You mentioned Dingwalls earlier. What did you think of it?

That was when the next generation got involved. It was unique, but it didn't inspire me. Musically, it was all very retro and my interpretation of it was far more experimental. I saw collaborations with different styles of music and artists, mixing electronic with acoustic – the 'Freedom Principle' album on Polydor (which followed 'Acid Jazz And Other Illicit Grooves') was the best example of the beginnings of that idea.

CHRIS SULLIVAN

Original Punk and Soul boy, fashion (and other) journalist, DJ, promoter and Jazz lover, Chris has seen and lived it all every step of the way. From being a founding member of the band Blue Rondo A La Turk he went on to own The Wag Club in Wardour Street, Soho.

To me, the fundamental dance probably started up North with the Northern Soul dancing. A friend of mine, Tony Gordon, would put in boxing moves, splits and spins, and he was very influenced by Cab Calloway, Nicholas Brothers and Jackie Wilson. Amongst all that really predictable standard dancing there were a few pioneers like him, but then you've got the mid-seventies Funk thing which was predominantly Essex-led. In '75 when I first started going to *Crackers* (with the DJ Mark Roman) in London with dancers like *Tommy Mac* and *Trevor Shakes*, the fast footwork I learnt from the Northern scene stood me in good stead. The dancers, were predominantly white then, later it became a very Black club. I always preferred the Lacy Lady. People dressed well. There was a lot of people into the fifties look. The Soul Boy dress became embarrassing in the end with blokes with their permed hair and painters jeans with a hanky at the back pocket and all that other terrible clothing. That was the death of the scene. Same as the Punk scene when they started spitting and all that. It was about clothes and dressing and all that really. I got out of the Punk scene and got into the Rockabilly. A lot of the Rockabillies I knew came from the Funk scene, dressing in Pink Peg trousers and plastic sandals.

That was a classic Soul boy look.

It was a purely London look. I had lime green pegs, a yellow mohair jumper, green plastic sandals with a green striped 'acme' shirt with a wedge hair cut.- a classic. It spread all over the country. I was coming to London all the time. I'm from Merthyr Tydfil (in Wales), it was so violent there you couldn't go out. I was a shop-lifter at the time and stole all these clothes. Me and my mates would come to London almost every weekend.

Did you go to the Margate all-dayers?

Yeah, yeah, yeah. *The Atlantis*. The dancing was fantastic. We looked forward to it like no other. We'd travel from Wales, and there'd be people from Bristol, everywhere, we had our best moves ready and our best clothes.

That Jazz Funk scene was outrageously stylish. I remember at The Goldmine a lot of the crowd were from Southend Art College or Southend Fashion college and people like (the famous fashion designer) Stephen Linard and his crowd and that crowd called the Corner Gang; The Dunn Brothers and Mick (Ralph) Ricks – who all dressed American 50's style, Haddock, The Davey Sisters and that St Martins Art and Fashion crowd.

I went to college with all that lot. I was in the halls of residency with them late '78 at St Martins. They all came from Southend. Steve Strange started the club *Billys* and brought along all my mates from the halls of residency. History. The New Romantic thing - if you want to call it that – was as much a creation of Steve Linard and that crowd from Southend as it was Steve Strange, very much so. The fashion crowd could make their own clothes. Essex had that great tradition of dressing up. We got a coach to The Goldmine from Wales in '75 for Chris Hill's Swing night. We were all into Roxy Music and were dressed in these '40's clothes.

I've documented that and that Chris had to leave through its popularity and went to The Lacy. That's where you started to get the original Bromley Punk's Siouxsie Sioux, Steve Severin, Billy Idol...

You could wear anything there. That's when you'd start to see the dancers like Tommy Mac dancing in clothes from (Vivienne Westwood and Malcolm MacLaren's shop) Sex – like, red plastic trousers with plastic pockets and see through t shirts, because that wasn't 'Punk' then, it was just fashion. The more outrageous the fashion, the more you 'pulled.' That was the roots of Punk. It was just about outrage. It was fashion to be outrageous. But there at The Lacy was roots of Jazz Dance. You had a Black and White crowd, and face-offs between dancers. People took it deadly serious. I was at a dance competition down the road and got chased out. It was pretty heavy.

There was a lot of great Funk being played in the Gay clubs like *Rods* in Fulham and *Sombrero* in Kensington where you would see people like Bowie. There was *Clouds* in Balham, but that was very Black and a very different scene.

How did you start promoting?

A couple of warehouse parties at Mayhem studios, Battersea, with Robert Elms, St Moritz (because The Blitz started getting silly with badly dressed people) Hell, (with Steve Strange) Le Kilt, in 1980 and Le Beat Route. Then my band Blue Rondo A La Turk took off and I had to stop that.

How did you take over The Wag?
One of the doormen at Le Beat Route said The Wag was doing bad and had heard what we do and would we do a Saturday? I got a lot of the dancers down from years before and it was a big success. Paul Murphy came to see me and I checked out The Horseshoe and liked all that Jazz music myself so invited him to do Monday nights. It had to be tailored somewhat, it had to be more Jazz. I wanted *Young Holt Trio, Horace Silver,* I wanted the *Cu Bop* and *Be Bop, Tito Puente* - that sort of thing, We reached an agreement. I didn't want the Fusion being played. It was a retro session and I booked the bands. I was booking *Mark Murphy, Tommy Chase, Slim Gaillard…* . Because it was purer Jazz we got a different style of dancer. We initially got IDJ but I wasn't keen on that style, I preferred The Jazz Defektors and Brothers In Jazz, who dressed in more 50's style. We attracted that type of dresser. We almost created a new scene, really, because of that Monday night.

They offered me the whole club all week and we got it refurbished. I designed it all.

What happened to Murphy at The Wag?
Can't remember. We fell out badly though. We had Andy McConnell and Baz Fe Jazz next but they didn't last too long, Then I got Gilles Peterson in, but he wasn't quite what I wanted musically either: too Jazz Funky.

For some reason people speak of there being a racist door policy at The Wag.
Yes there was. We were racist about badly dressed people! It wasn't a club for passers-by people – also, there was a bit of handbag stealing and 'steaming' going on so we had to tighten it up on the door. We'd turn away Black, White, Chinese Triads, Football Hooligans, casual sports-wear……..

You didn't like Murphy's Electric Ballroom session did you?
I didn't mind it. It was quite refreshing for the time, but the clothes were awful: tight jeans, leg warmers and ballet slippers, and the dancing wasn't attractive. I didn't think it was very inventive. I was always going there though.

What did you think of the Absolute Beginners film? They were trying to get the essence of The Wag weren't they?
I supplied all the 'extras' for the film. He (Julien Temple) started it off alright, then the money fell out and an American company came in that wanted it to be more poppy. There were hundereds from the Wag in it. I was at all the meetings, and it changed direction virtually everyday.

A lot of people feel that the disappointment of Absolute Beginners helped kill the scene.
Rubbish. How can people blame a scene dying off on one film. It still continued after in different forms - although I never understood what the Acid Jazz scene was all about. Anyway, nothing lasts forever, It only takes the main people to start getting older and settling down for a scene to fall apart. At the end of the day, the Jazz night on Mondays lasted for six years, which was amazing.

ROBERT ELMS

Like Chris, Rob was an original Punk and Soul boy, and also seen it all. His exposure of Jazz Dance in the magazine *The Face*, pushed the scene on to some other level.

The first club I went to was the Bandwagon – just a rural club in Kingsbury. I was the youngest of the group – about 14 – and we went to this club just as the Funk scene had started. Even then you started to hear stuff that was a bit further out, like *Brass Construction – Movin'* and all that. I remember in '75 on Monday nights at the Lyceum Ballroom, among all the funk stuff you'd have heard *Lonnie Liston Smith – Expansions* which sounded different and the term Jazz Funk had just come in. I remember hearing some Latin-y things and a track by Miles Davis and I remember a lot of the kids couldn't dance to it except a couple of Black guys, and I wanted to check this music out.

I started working in a record shop called Sound Recs in Burnt Oak and Paul the owner, who was a Chinese Londoner, said to me: "Right, if you like *The Crusaders* then check this out" and he lent me this *John Coltrane* album and I took it home. I thought: "What on earth is this?" and loved it but was scared of it, and that became my personal journey through Jazz. I was 16 and listening to Coltrane, but also all the C.T.I label stuff like *Airto – Fingers*, but what was weird was, as I was getting into all that, Punk started coming along. So on the one hand I'm out dancing to this and on the other, listening to the Ramones, Patti Smith or Richard Hell and although they're diametrically opposite, it didn't seem it to me.

Well the Lacy Lady was happening then where the original Bromley Punks mixed with the Jazz Funk crowd.

Yes and there were the clothes; what the *Soulboys* were wearing wasn't much different than the Punks. By the end of '76 I was fully into Punk and had to hide my Jazz and Funk records. You weren't allowed to be into that. Musically, I always preferred that, but Punk was so exciting I couldn't not be a part of that, and from there into the New Romantic scene. I would go and dance at Crackers on Friday lunchtime and go from there and buy like, the *Ronnie Laws* album with – *Always There* on for a fortune on Blue Note records. I never stopped buying Jazz like Coltrane or Mingus, it's just that I was going to The Blitz and the New Romantic thing for four years. There was a jazzy element to that scene though like me and Chris Sullivan putting on the first *Defunkt* gig, which was Lester Bowies brother Leslie, and there was James White and the Blacks, and at the same time I was going out with *Sade* who was just starting to form the band, and I was buying Jazz from Simon Booth at Mole Jazz. I'd be watching Spandau Ballet (who Robert named) live and buying *Ornette Coleman* albums. It was two separate things to me.

I went down to The Horseshoe with Simon Booth and it totally blew me away. I hadn't seen dancing like that since Crackers. It was a different style, but essentially the same. I only caught the end of The Horseshoe but that was the first club where I'd just heard Jazz all night and everyone danced the same style. If you couldn't do that, you didn't dance. I found it as exciting and almost as shocking as first seeing the Sex Pistols. It was very aggressive – but not violent. The 'cutting' was very tough. I became evangelical about it, and obsessed. I wanted it hardcore - it was high testosterone and tight trousers! (laughs) With tracks being played like *I See Chano Pozo* by *Jayne Cortez and the Firespitters*, it was never going to be a massive scene.

Did you go out of your way to know Murphy?

Very much so, but it was a two-way thing - I was a writer for *The Face* and Sade my girlfriend and all that kind of thing, so when we turned up people were surprised. We all hung around together, and with Simon Booth, and although Sade was never going to go in that direction, it would've reinforced what she was into. Remember also you had band's like Working Week and even Style Council, so it was penetrating the mainstream, on the other hand you had the indigenous Black British Jazz group *The Jazz Warriors*.

They were the Black '*Loose Tubes*' in a way.

I did a piece in the Face on the great British Jazz revival and one part would be the IDJ dancers and on the other the Jazz Warriors. You had the Manchester scene with the *Jazz Defektors* and *Kalima* too, so for about eighteen months there was a mix of all these things going on. It was at it's most powerful with Paul Murphy. He pushed it and pushed it and went so far out, the sadness was that there were recriminations and back-biting and people splitting up and people accused of selling out.

Other than Mark Webster, you were the only one pushing the scene from a journalistic level.

And I got a lot of grief from it. On one side you had the serious Jazz buffs complaining that we're riding a band wagon and also getting grief from the club kids who just thought it was the latest trend. But no-one knew my background - I was a *soul-boy*. Its funny that that name became a term of abuse for a while and yet it was the basis of everything – Punk; the basis of New Romantic; the Jazz Funk scene; the Jazz scene. I wore the Soul Boy white socks for years, but so would've Johnny Rotten, because that came from there. It's very under-written - the role *that* scene played as a cultural agitator.

You could obviously see the Absolute Beginners film coming.

I was involved in the beginning. I was sort of a music consultant at first. It was intended to be a different film then when it was finished. It had somehow drifted.

What went wrong?

The male casting was dreadful. It should have been a whole celebration of this scene but it wasn't. There was a lot of budgeting problems, but also I don't think they knew what they wanted. They didn't know whether it was a nostalgic film or contemporary. Without the London Jazz scene the film wouldn't have happened, but it wasn't a film about that or of that.

The scene kind of imploded after that didn't it?

It was a big story, and there's a film being made, and I'm writing about it in The Face, so what happens is, people come in for six months and go away. It was a very hard-core thing and very difficult to get into unless you're dedicated to it. A 'bubble' occurred and, like all bubbles, it burst. When it did, it went back smaller than it was before. It never recovered.

What did you think about the Special Branch scene and Acid Jazz, which came out of all that?

It was a watered down version, especially when you've been to a Jazz room when it was really a Jazz room. The Ballroom was its height because it got so tough. I guess with Acid Jazz they just picked up the baton.

Did you realize the power of the printed word?

I didn't do it for that. You were carried along on the energy. What I loved, was that I could get in to clubs for nothing and people knew who I was. That was what mattered to me. It seemed important, but then you were naïve and excited. I don't think there's any magazine now that had the power of The Face. It's a phenomenal magazine, not just in that scene.

MARK WEBSTER

Journalist, Radio and TV broadcaster and DJ, Mark has followed the scene since the beginning. His two Jazz dance pages in Blues And Soul and Black Echoes magazines were one of the first to seriously document the movement. He played a big part as a DJ too.

I didn't know central London existed until the late-70's, because, as far as I was concerned, the whole thing revolved around *The Lacy Lady* and *The Goldmine*. You could then trek around to *Scamps* in Sutton on a Tuesday night, *Frenchies* in Camberley, *The Belvedere....Chris Brown* played very soulful jazz sounds. When you think of the kind of stuff that was played then, they were considered radical, strange records. From 1975 and 76 when club-culture began, the jazz element was in from the start and it provided, almost immediately, an alternate route to go. I thought it was clever to own a *Ramsey Lewis* album. I thought I was clever owning a *Freddie Hubbard* fusion album rather than buy the *Odyssey* album. I wanted something with a bit of edge to it. I wanted what was new; what was different.

I think the dividing line started at the third or fourth *Caister* weekender. That's when I heard my first *jazz* record.

Jazz was being played before then.

I know what you mean, but I'm talking about *John Coltrane - Mr PC*. Straight jazz. Bob Jones played it.

He played it to shake things up.

I would say that the sub-culture of the Jazz Funk culture started around 1980. The parallel lines were never that far apart. It was always the same people wearing the same clothing going to the same clubs, but there were those who stood still when Jazz Funk and Disco came on and those that stood still when the Jazz was on, but everybody bought *Blue Note - Live At The Roxy, Grover Washington Jr - Live At The Bijou, Deodato - Whistle Bump* – that record is corny now, but it was a weird record at the time.

I made more of a conscious effort to buy more Jazz in 1980 because there was a lot of good Jazz and a lot of bad Soul coming out. I wanted to be with the fifty people in the small room at Caister, rather than with the two thousand in the main hall – all those kind of places. That's when I started writing for Black Echoes or Blues and Soul. I'd say bull-shit like "Soul is dead and Jazz is where it's *at*," and other such things really, just to provoke a reaction. I was writing under a pseudonym anyway so I had this provocative page that would upset people – much in the same way that Frank Elson would upset people on his Soul page (in Blues and Soul)...

...fuelling the North / South divide.

I was saying: "If you don't like it, you're sad bastards," to get people involved. I meant it. What I was serious about, over the years, was that people knew that it existed .

You used to check out Pete Tong in Kent at that time.

Big style.*The Hilltop* was the place. Tongys contribution was immense; not least the odd tracks he was sneaking in at Caister and what he was playing at his residencies at The Hilltop and *The Kings Lodge*. These were cutting edge nights. The music he was playing was the alternative Black music scene. You'd get Jazz tracks like *Neil Larsen-Demonette*....

You saw the germination of jazz-dancing there. You'd get these guys utilizing this old-fashioned kind of spinning type of dancing that three or four years earlier they'd have been doing at the Lacy Lady to disco records. It was that kind of Balletical-spinning dancing. There was a dancer from Gravesend (Kent) called *Timmy Misson*, who won through to the national Disco dancing competition, and the dancers that walked on to that stage had leg-warmers, big 'baloony' trousers, glittery head bands doing their ridiculous *Fame*-type dancing :Tim walked on in his jeans and t-shirt and his best slippery shoes and did his club-dancing. He walked off to virtual silence, apart from our crowd shouting. What he was, was a real club dancer and what they all were, was this ridiculous spin-off of Disco that had occurred. This boy was a genius dancer, and you had to learn a fast dancing technique to dance to records like *Crown Heights Affair - Far Out*, *Hudson People - Trip To Your Mind* or *Lonnie Liston-Smith - Expansions*; and that technique definitely crossed over into jazz-dancing . Pete would play these jazz records and those who danced in the Balletic style were getting into that style. I would say, to his credit, that, with the Kent boys and South London boys that would go to his clubs and dance to the Fusion and dance in that style, it's got as much argument to being the start as anywhere else! I'm sure the same thing was going on elsewhere, but he was certainly at it at that very point.

Did you ever check out Jazz Junction?
Yes. It was ran by Darren and Frank Johnson – first, in a basement of a hotel in Bayswater and then at *Spats* in Oxford Street on Saturday lunchtime. The music was as hard-as-nails. Bob Jones had a few tremendous sessions there. The gigs were never packed but, by God, those that were there loved it. Everybody danced.

The Electric Ballroom was more-or-less the same time, what did you think of that session?
It worked because of where it was and it's profile. It wouldn't have been the same in Tunbridge Wells (laughs).

The most memorable moment for me was when someone brought *Will Gaines* there. So, there was this legendary old tap-dancer from *The Cotton Club* standing there watching, and then he jumped in the circle doing his tap – exchanging move-for-move with these young dancers. It all made sense: What is *Cockroach Stomping* if it's not Tap? Cockroach Stomping; Will Gaines dancing – I've never seen anything like it. Unbelievable. You could see in that man's eyes that he'd never seen anything like it – well he had, above 125th Street in New York in 1949, but not since. They were battling to *Art Blakey – A Night In Tunisia*.

When Murphy moved to The Wag, the media jumped on it pretty quick didn't they?
There was one hell of a lot of young people dancing to old jazz, so, of course the Record companies took notice. You can't dismiss the fact that *Sade* and *Matt Bianco* were the commercial face of that scene suddenly. They were aware of what was happening, but they were re-interpreting it. It wasn't an accident. In a way, it was the death-knell of that scene, because it made it a bit corny. At its commercial height it was at its lowest ebb.

That was the time of the film Absolute Beginners (4/4/86).
Even worse.

Everyone had so many hopes for that film.
Simon Booth took director Julien Temple to The Wag and showed him the crowd and he was excited. He said *that* was the atmosphere that he wanted - the vibe -.and what comes out? This piece of fucking crap! Temple might have been inspired, but it wasn't reflected in the film. He fucked it up.

The Jazz Defektors went all over the World promoting that film.
Good luck to them. At least they made a bit of a living out of it. What did anyone in the film or the scene think it would do for it if it had been a success? I've often asked myself this question. I remember so vividly at the time because I was so upset by the film, I thought: "If that film had worked, what would it have meant? You're not going to get better dancers; you're not going to get better clubs or clubbers," so it didn't matter.

Murphy was also doing the Sol Y Sombre (31/7/84).
Yes. I reckon, up until that point you didn't hear him play a lot of Latin music, but you did afterwards.

I remember him playing Salsa at The Wag.
Of course *Hit Man Records* in Soho would have turned people on. They got their Salsa direct from New York and one of the brothers who owned the shop was a jazz musician. I certainly got

a lot, and learnt a lot there.

Murphy played jazz at Sol Y Sombre, but not for jazz-dancers.

Dave Hucker's crowd weren't clubbers as such, if you see what I mean, and Murphy walked in there to a whole new crowd. He knew The Wag crowd like the back of his hand and now he'd found something new. I loved those nights in there. Hucker was a superb DJ and, infact, got used at The Special Branch gigs originally. He came from nowhere with this great collection and knowledge, and it was a pleasure to listen to. He'd play Latin-Jazz, African, Salsa …..it was an education.

He was. People like Hucker, Sue Steward, Tomek, John Armstrong…..they're vaguely related to our scene .

Almost an accident.

They touched us all – musically and educationally.

Definitely. But they'd have done what they did regardless to whether our scene existed or not.

What legacy do you think Sol Y Sombre left us?

It introduced us to areas of music that are with us today. You weren't going to hear sizzling, fast jazz cuts. I'll never forget the atmosphere; it was a back room of a restaurant where it almost felt like a house-party, where you'd push the tables and chairs back. It was too packed and small for showing off heavy moves on the dancefloor.

Murphy had a record label – Paladin (31/7/84).

Yes, Murphy's rise-and-rise through DJ-ing and having the record shop culminated with the record label, co-owned by Dean Hulme (co-owner of the record shop too). It was almost like the *Frankensteins Monster* argument, unfortunately; you're getting the Monster that you created - you're obliged to succeed on a commercial level. The first four or five albums were pretty uncommercial and then he got pressure from upstairs (Virgin records): "We know exactly what you did and why we signed you, now stop doing it so we can sell some units" - type of thing. I think that he fell out of love with the whole thing. It came back and bit him on the arse.

Venceremos by Working Week was on Paladin though.

Working Week is a good example – no two records were the same. *Tommy Chase, Annie Whitehead*….they never did a second album on Paladin. There was even a couple of pop R&B albums towards the end…

Like *Aldeoni*. He was on that label.

Oh yes. We thought at the time: "Great Artist, but why is he on this label?" The label started off as a Jazz label but Paul (Murphy) was trying to convince us that it was just all about talent of any kind.

The label lasted a year, I reckon, and then Murphy disappeared and then the scene fell on its arse. From my perspective, when Murphy wasn't around anymore the big dream had died. It genuinely went underground. People wanted something else to talk about, and they didn't have to wait long before *Acid Jazz* came about!

TOMMY CHASE

The Jazz Dance scene of the 80's was as much about jazz drummer Tommy Chase as anyone. Virtually resident at The Wag Club, the firing, aggressive Be Bop that his quartet played became the favourite of all jazz dancers country-wide.

I already had a thing going before Paul Murphy got in touch with me about *The Wag*. We had a bit of a scene happening at *The 100* club every week with support from the Chevalier Brothers (a Jump Jive act). I didn't know anything about Murphy's one. I went up there late (The Wag) with my manager Honest Jon (as in the record shop owner!) and there wasn't a lot of people up there and I said to Jon: "Forget it" but he reckoned The 100 Club crowd would come over. Stiff records owner David Robinson said I should do it too. It got packed. It even got voted 'Number One Jazz Club' above Ronnie Scott's. It was a great scene, but Paul got discontented there and was going to move it to The Comedy Store and he wanted me to go with him but I told him no. I didn't want to move, I enjoyed it too much. I got Baz Fe Jazz and Andy in.

Did the whole DJ culture thing surprise you?

Well, there was only one DJ as far as I was concerned – Murphy. Before him there was a DJ on

Radio London called David Simmonds – very influential. He brought over the Fania All Stars, he introduced us all to Cajun music, he'd bring over African dance troupes.

Were you influenced by the music Murphy played?

No. I was already playing it.

Did the dancers take to you straight away at The Wag?

When we moved in, it was totally different to what I'd seen before. I got very frustrated with the (other 'mainstream') jazz crowd. They were fucking squares. They couldn't see the benefit of dancing to jazz. It was us and them. I would've thought that they would be delighted that they were getting young people.

I'm surprised that you weren't in the *Absolute Beginners* film.

Absolute Beginners! They wanted me to do this – get this — a Jump Jive number! Can you believe it? Me! I told them to let me do what I do and get a Jump Jive band in. They made a complete fucking mess of that didn't they? It could've been great.

You were in the *Ten Days That Shook Soho* documentary on Channel 4 in '86.

Yes. Half of those bands weren't meant to be on that – a lot of them were crap, but one particular band – *The Jazz Defektors* – they weren't going to put them on – I had an argument with Channel 4 and I said "If they don't go on I don't."

You did so much then. You were playing everywhere.

Actually, you know *Jools Holland* asked me to join his band. I said "I'll do it if you make me musical director." I said "We'll be the best fucking big band in Europe" but he wouldn't do it. He told me he loved my stuff but nothing happened.

You must have had some musicians come through the band that didn't understand what the scene was all about and what you were after at first.

I had some that never got it at all *ever*. The band from the 'Groove Merchant' album period was great (the guitarist – Adrian Utley – went on to form Portishead).

That album came out around the Acid Jazz period. It all started to change.

I didn't like that change. The music started to divorce itself from what Paul Murphy had started with. It was supposed to be Jazz dance not fucking Hip Hop, and it became very cliquey and very commercial. Once a scene disipates you can never rekindle that.

You know, before Gilles did his residency at *Dingwalls* I had one there every Sunday lunchtime, but it changed hands. It was my scene. The DJ was one of the managers. He knew the scene. He used to go to The Wag. We went out one day and bought loads of records and they're what he DJ'd with!

DAVE BITELLI – ONWARD INTERNATIONAL

Although only making one record – a 12 inch e.p, - it made incredible impact. *Samba Doo Bonnay*, in particular,

was an anthem anywhere that had Jazz Dancers. Along with *ICQ-Final Approach* and *Working Week – Venceremos*, we felt that this track belonged to us.

Percussionist Dawson Miller was in Onward International from the beginning. He would be traveling the world and be talking about rhythms from here or there. We didn't know what the hell he was going on about! He's an unsung hero.

I formed the band originally to make Jazz for the dancefloor fusing all different types of music. We did a demo tape and soon found out that Paul Murphy had been playing it out . He told us that *Foot In The Door* was massive and he wanted us to put a record out for him on his Paladin record label. We recorded it at Robin Miller's studio – who was producing *Sade* among others. He just gave us an engineer and left us alone. Paul Murphy and his partner Dean Hulme came down but didn't really get in the way. I was open to advice though.

Did you know the market that you were aiming at then? Had you been to The Horseshoe or The Electric Ballroom?

Never. It was accidental. We just did what we did. Quite soon after the record was released we fell apart. I was encouraged by the sales but that didn't turn into anything. We got gigs here and there but nothing special. We wanted management, publishing and a female singer which we never did get. We went as far as my business acumen went.

It's such a hot record. I hope people talk about my records like that one day.

Well, it sold a few thousand and did well in the club charts which was nice to see.

There's a school of thought that Onward International became Working Week – being the band behind Simon Booth and Larry Stabbins.

Well I see what you mean. The line up is very similar. No. We were all like a university of like minded-musicians, sharing information, moving in the same circle, so it was bound to happen.

ROBIN JONES

Although Jazz drummer and Latin Percussionist Robin, didn't need a career revival – it was already strong – two of his early 70's album's on the small independent label Apollo Sound created havoc in the Jazz Dance club's of the early 80's; thank's to Paul Murphy and his record

shop. The buzz was that big, it convinced Robin to put the band back together for some special gig's. His Salsa band – King Salsa – that he also formed around then has gone down in history as one the country's first salsa bands.

You became popular again to a new generation in the early 80's with the discovery in the Jazz dance scene of your albums *El Maja* and *Denga*.

Paul Murphy was responsible for that. I had an audience that I never knew of. I was in *Blue Rondo A La Turk* and from there Matt Bianco and Chris Sullivan (who was in Blue Rondo) started booking me at The Wag and that's where I found this audience, thanks to Paul resurrecting those albums. I was overjoyed about it.

The legitimate Jazz world always knew of you of course.

But as a drummer. I got forced into playing percussion. I covered for Jack Costanzo with Francis Faye and went from there to *Edmondo Ros*.

Barry Morgan was the main percussionist at the time and decided that all he wanted to play was drums. When he was in Blue Mink, Barry passed me all his percussion sessions. We did the Bee Gees and Elton Johns – Tumbleweed Connection.

Who was Carlos Romanos?

That was the singer Wilf Todd. My sextet was basically the rhythm section in his Latin big band. He managed me too. His band was more ballroom Latin and he made a few albums. My two albums though, were probably the first introduction most people got here to Afro Cuban music. Before us there had only been Kenny Grahams Afro Cubans back in the 50's. I will take credit for being one of the first.

Paul Murphy got you to put that band back together.

Yes he did. I continued to work at The Wag up until it closed, with different line-ups – like my band King Salsa. That bands first gig was there. There was only two Latin bands in London then: us and Roberto Pla.

That first gig at The Wag would have been the first time you saw Jazz dancers.

Yes. It was wonderful to see them relating to my music. There was loads of them. It gave me a whole new incentive. We used to do a lot of double headers all over the country with Tommy Chase, both playing to Jazz dancers, but with different sounds. Tommy liked the combination of our bands.

BAZ FE JAZZ

Real name Barrington Wilmot - Baz, perhaps, should really be in the midlands section, but he established himself in London and lived South of London in Surrey. Other than being totally established country-wide on the all-dayer circuit the vast majority of his work was in London. He was, without doubt, the busiest Jazz DJ ever, and was always in direct competition with Gilles Peterson – despite having a virtually different following.

I'm from Coventry, in the Midlands - the same as the DJ the Rhythm Doc. Back in the late 1970's I used to drive to Birmingham every week with my friends to go to a club called Chaplins to see Graham Warr DJ and also to buy records from his record shop. It wasn't that Graham was an amazing DJ technically, but he always came up with gems that were dynamic. He always had the edge. Perhaps it was from owning a record shop. He broke *Patsy Gallant - Te Caliente* and *Manfredo Fest -Jungle Kitten*; they were his tunes. Chaplins was a predominantly Black crowd and had the best cut of dancers that I've ever seen in a club until coming to London and seeing a different style of dancing. It was very '*balletic*' in Brirmingham, as opposed to the '*Cockroaching*' in London.

As a dancer myself, I used to mix with the elite club dancers, which made me move to London to train as a dancer a few years later. I went to the Arts Educational School at The Barbican for three years studying Stage Dancing but I wasn't cut out for it because I was too into being a club dancer. In 1982, the DJ Colin Curtis, suggested that I become a DJ, as he knew that I'd been collecting records for a while; infact, it was Colin that suggested the name *Baz Fe Jazz* . I DJ'd at all-dayers like The Powerhouse (Birmingham) immediately; obviously low down the bill. Other than Graham Warr, Colin Curtis was my mentor.

What kind of records were you playing when you first started?

Disco-Jazz stuff like *Wilbert Longmire-Black Is The Colour* and Fusion-based stuff by *Airto Moeira*

and that kind of thing. I learnt quickly that to be competitive, you had to be one step ahead of the game so I sought out obscure stuff that people would find hard to obtain. I broke *Herbie Mann - New York Is A Jungle Festival* at one of the all-dayers; that was one of mine. I used to work at Paul Murphy's original record shop *Fusions* in Exmouth Market to subsidise my grant while I was at dancing school. He got the most weird and wonderful records in there. I often ran the shop for him because he was always away sourcing records. It was great for me because I got the records first and told people that certain ones would be coming at the weekend, and Saturday morning they would be queuing up before the shop opened - which was a buzz. I was keen to DJ, and used to go with him to a lot of places, like, up to Scotland.

Obviously, I used to find my own records too. I'd go to Paris with my Wife and get some serious tunes there, and there was an amazing shop in Birmingham called *The Diskery*. They didn't know what they had, and it was cheap. It was an absolute goldmine of a shop. The Jazz DJ Chris Reid used to work there.

This must have been around the time of The Horseshoe.

Yes it was. That was run by George Power and, infact, I used to go to his previous club Crackers. That's when I'd go to *really* dance. He had some tunes. He and his back up DJ – Paul Anderson - liked to play jazz. That club had some of the best ever dancers.

The Horseshoe was the stickiest, smokiest hole. It was a sweat-box, but, my God it was a buzz. I later used to back Paul Murphy at The Electric Ballroom in the early days, although I couldn't get to grips with the dancing - it was all 100 mph. It wasn't for my style of dancing, but I could adapt as a DJ because I knew what was going on (both North and South). It was very intense with tension, and the music was deafening. Musically, I felt that certain records were being played because they were heavy rather than because they were good. I used to take some of my fellow dance students there. Some of them got really good at it. It was quite intimidating with the heat of the competition of the dancers.

When the *cockroach-stomping* started, I thought " What's this all about ?" It was a very ugly dance but it grew on me after a while. There was a great dancer called *Coach* who stood out as having amazing footwork, and my favourite dancer was a guy called Marshall Smith, who went on to dance with IDJ.

I then started to DJ at an event called *The Saturday Night Fish Fry* (4/5/85). It was ran by a guy called Andy McConnell (ex- A2 Connection DJ), and the events were illegal warehouse parties. Musically, it was more 50's R&B and Big Band jazz. The events were absolutely superb. We had dancers from the Jazz scene *and* the Rock and Roll scene so I would play more Cuban and Brazilian stuff to off-set the R&B. I got to know Andy when he had a residency at the Sol Y Sombre, and he asked me to get involved. We formed the partnership *Take 5* when we took over from Paul Murphy at The Wag (15/7/86).

There was some interaction with the World Music DJ's: Dave Hucker, John Armstrong, Tomek and Sue Steward.

Yes, well I got on particularly well with Sue. She specialized in Salsa; Cuban music. We'd exchange notes and we'd compare albums. She was very enthusiastic. She was connected with the arts, and, along with her and *Geoff Wilkinson* (later of US 3), we put on shows for the GLC in London, which was the Labour council who were running London. They put on some big shows; open air ones. Geoff was a big supporter of mine.

I also got very involved with the jazz promotion company – BPK, who had offices above Ronnie Scott's Jazz Club. I used to do my own promotions and help them. They used to pick my brain. They had access to certain acts and I liaised with them to create a framework of gig's around the country because of my DJ connection. I learnt a lot about buisiness through them too.

I'm surprised that you got on well with them, because they represented the older, higher-echelon of the jazz scene and *that* scene hated ours.

Well, Pete King didn't like it but Brian was into making money. I got them to bring Jimmy Smith; Tito Puente and Celia Cruz; El Gran Combo …… I got to DJ at all of the events as well.

You put some huge events on at the Scala Cinema in Kings Cross (21/9/85).

Yes. This is where my new organizational skills came in. I would incorporate DJ's from the North and South of England and we would have a jazz film showing, plus we'd have live acts such as *Mark Murphy*. That was my own creation.

Through my connections with BPK, I got to know Jean Davenport at The Shaw Theatre. I did a lot of things with her. They had the money and they had the sponsorship; it was just *that* fraternity. They had the clout to make things work. We coincided one of my Scala events to be the same night as Art Blakey's show at The Shaw Theatre (which was made in to a documentary – *Father Time*), and be the official after-show party.

It seemed to me that you were running in a parallel to Chris Bangs and Gilles Peterson and all that Special Branch scene. I don't know how many of the clubbers that you shared, but it almost seemed that you were in a different World, but doing the same thing.

Rather than just playing music, I was into productions as well, don't forget that.

You had Gilles doing the upstairs room at The Wag when you were on the main floor. Your partner – Andy McConnell – didn't like what Gilles was doing.

No he didn't. I did. It didn't bother me. Andy got despondant and said that: " If this is the way the scene is going. I'm stopping!" and he did. Gilles took over the main club when we left. Paul Murphy's shoes were very hard to fill when we took over from him at The Wag. The scene was changing and dropping off and only worked at it's best when there was a good band playing. We got ousted and Gilles was in. His crowd was different than ours and they didn't gel. I think that the times we've worked together, we didn't gel actually.

Did you see Gilles as a threat?

We were rivals. We were both high-profile. Gilles had a lot of enthusiasm and obviously loved the music. I didn't have resentment, but he was competition. I got on well with him though, and went to his parents a lot and I was involved with him in the KJAZZ pirate station. We also had a record label called BGP.

Baz and Gilles Peterson.

That's it, although we tried to make out BGP stood for *Beat Goes Public*. BGP was a part of Ace Records and Andy McConnel and I had already done a compilation for them called *Women, Whiskey and Wailing*. Ace had access to loads of labels: Argo, Cadet, Chess…..BGP sprang from there . I later did compilations for Charly Records as well. Of course, Gilles had done the popular Jazz Juice compilations before, so he knew what he was doing. We did quite a few for BGP and the label is still going now. I got Gilles involved originally; he had a lot of the original albums and could see the opportunities.

You had one hell of a lot of residencies: Cocos; Bay 63; Purple Pit; Café Mambo ;Whispers;

Gazebos; Legends; The Comedy Store; The Dip; The Scala; The Wag.....

Yes, we (Take 5) also did the *Bass Clef* jazz club, taking over from Gilles (12/8/86). It was a hard crowd to work, but then it was getting very hard to make it anywhere at that point. I felt that Gilles and Chris Bangs and that crowd were playing more commercial and catchy tunes but we wouldn't break the mold. We tried to keep the authenticity in the music, which could have been the demise of what we were trying to do in the end. although at that point we were equally as successful. Luckily, Russ Dewbury came along and freshened it all up. Although he came from a Mod background, he was into straight jazz and latin, and he took a lot of risks with his club nights. He wouldn't compromise.

Around this time I also did a lot of work in Japan (from 3/3/87), for fashion designer Michiko Koshino initially, and other designers. I spent a period of two months there.

> "Baz was probably better than Gilles in some ways. He was the best of them all in the sense that he'd work his nuts off trying new venues. He was probably busier than all of the Jazz DJ's put together. He kept the momentum going and was much needed."

Mark Webster

You are famous for The Brighton Jazz Bop events. How did the Brighton connection happen?

Well, Russ (Dewbury) was already in Brighton, but for me, our *Soho goes to Brighton* event (10/87) was the first. It featured British bands like *Tommy Chase* and *Team 10*. Tommy was very instrumental in getting that happening. He had a monthly residence at The Concorde in Brighton and was getting tired of that stale, narrow-minded regular jazz crowd and got an opportunity to do something, so he brought us in. We helped each other.

We were informed that *Art Blakey* was coming over, so we got him to do a gig as part of the Brighton Jazz Festival (6/5/88). The idea was frowned upon by the local jazz fraternity and it was predicted for failure. We had 2,200 people there, at the enormous Top Rank night club on Brighton sea-front! We had IDJ dancing as well, which was a nice reunion as they were in the *Father Time* documentary (the Shaw Theatre concert, where they danced on stage with Blakey). He could not believe the concert. And then, of course, came the first *Jazz Bop*:

It was at the Top Rank again. It was hard work, because of Brighton being so staid, but people travelled from all over the country, so it didn't matter. We booked *The James Taylor Quartet; Tommy Chase* and *The Jazz Defektors*. We got 2000 at that gig and so we did a Jazz Bop every six months (to the present day). I think this is where my organizational skills came to the fore that I learnt from BPK. This was the pay-off. Russ was great at the writing side, with the press-releases etc and mine was the organizational side. It was a great partnership. When I think of all the people that we brought over: *Charles Earland, Big John Patton, Johnny Lytle* .....

The Acid Jazz movement had started by your first Jazz Bop. I understood that you were keen to distance yourself from it.

Yes. As far as I was concerned I didn't like the connotation of the word 'acid', and also I felt that it was a fad. The scene was created, so you either rode with it or you can create a completely different niche.

You have booked Brand New Heavies, Jamiroquoi and James Taylor. My band too. We were all on the Acid Jazz record label.

We booked bands from the entire spectrum of our scene. Right across the board. We tried to be fad-free.

Talking about all these British bands, I've been trying to think where *The Jazz Warriors* fitted in. A couple of them were old jazz-dancers.

They didn't fit in to our scene. They were at a tangent to us. They didn't get involved.

Well some of them played at Dingwalls as individual musicians.

Yes, but the Jazz Warriors didn't get involved with us. Tommy Chase *really* got involved.

Did you ever go to Dingwalls?

Yes. It was amazing. It was the coming together of everything that Gilles and his crowd had worked for. It fused together lots of styles and there was great dancing, live music; everything.

Why did you come out of the scene?

The Jazz Bops got so huge that the tax-man started to take an interest and that's when I had to make up my mind whether to help get to the next level or leave, so I left. I left for religious reasons as I was getting more involved with that. It was a conflict of interests with my beliefs.

SYLVESTER

As Gilles Peterson called him: "The Hard Core Champion." Sylvester was totally unique. He was always one step ahead of any one. He just did his bit with no fuss or looking for plaudits, and the other DJ's just listened from a distance in admiration. He really specialized in that heavy Mambo/Afro Latin sound, and had a collection second to none.

I used to go to clubs like The Goldmine .....all those Jazz Funk clubs. I was particularly influenced by George Power at his session at Crackers. He used to play some good Fusion. I followed him to Gossips and The Horseshoe. There was two great DJ's at The Horseshoe that used to do the hardcore room: Colin Parnell and Boo. They played great jazz, although I was just getting in to it. I started collecting bits and pieces. I got heavier into it through the influence of Paul Murphy. I was buying from his shop at Exmouth Market and Dobells; Groove Records and Bluebird. My collecting took over and I was spending all my money! When Murphy did The Electric Ballroom, he had a box of records for sale by the record decks and you could buy some of the tunes that he was playing, and that made me even worse. I just had to have those records!

I met you through Tonys Imports from Clacton, then. How did you meet him?

Oh, just from an ad in *Blues And Soul*.

The first time I met you was when you and I were buying Jazz Fusion records from him from the boot (trunk) of his car in the multi-story car park next to Southend-On-Sea train station. He drove 70 miles just to sell them to you and me that day.

Yes. I got a train there from London (40 miles), and quickly met him and had to be on the next train back to London to get back to work (laughs).

He had amazing records.

He had different stuff than Murphy.

When did you start DJ-ing?

I bumped in to Baz Fe Jazz at The Record And Tape Exchange at Shepherds Bush (west London). I got talking to him because I knew he was a DJ and he pointed out records for me to buy. We got on really well. He got me to DJ at Club Mankind in Hackney [east London] – which was the first time I'd ever done it, and then invited me to play at The Saturday Night Fish Fry at Rotherhithe with him and Andy McConnell. Gilles was doing The Belvedere Arms in Richmond on Sunday night's and once he realized I had a good collection he let me do a few sets and I DJ'd with him at The Electric Ballroom often, as well. When Baz and Andy took over from Murphy at The Wag, they got me to do the upstairs room with Gilles and that ended up busier than the main floor.

When Gilles took over from them, with Chris Bangs, Bob Jones and Kevin Beadle, I stayed upstairs and I got Phil Levene involved. Bob used to play sets up there too. It was strictly hardcore. That's where the dancers were. It was great to have Bob play some sets because when I was younger I would always try and see him DJ if I could, because I always knew that he would play some jazz. Around that time, I got the reputation as a hard-core Jazz DJ, which I didn't mind; that's what I wanted to play. What I liked about playing upstairs was, you had the Fusion dancers like IDJ and all the others, but you also had the Brothers In Jazz, who introduced a different style.

Was there ever any trouble?

Yes there was, but there was a lot of competition.

What else was happening for you around then?

I was doing another event around the time of The Wag called Jazz 90. I found this venue in Hammersmith; just a council hall – I work for the town council, you see – and I suggested it to Gilles. We got Janine involved to organize it, and Swifty did the artwork. The license was til 1 a.m. but we played til 3 or 4. It was strictly hardcore though. That's what it was for. They were once a month while we were at Hammersmith and did a few others in different venues.

Me and Baz used to do the Scala all-nighters. We played in the foyer and put jazz films on in the cinema. They went on until 6a.m. and we'd be playing Latin, Fusion and Be-Bop. They were great events. Also, I started doing the Notting Hill Carnival [the second biggest Black music celebration in the World]. I used to live in Ladbroke Grove [the carnivals main road] and I thought that, as they played Reggae and Calypso, they must like Afro Cuban and Latin Jazz, so I put a couple of speakers outside my window and the guys below and it went down a storm; every body was dancing outside our house. So after that, I said to Baz that we've got to do a Latin Sound System at the next one, so me, Baz and Sheldon Willox (from *The Cutting Edge*) set up at Portobello Road and it all went mad - all the Jazz Dancers came down .The following year Baz came out of the scene (1990) so I got the female Salsa DJ Dominique Roome involved. I wanted to keep it Latin. We got – and still get – thousands. You just can't move.

Lastly: No one knew where the hell you got your special records from. You were playing records that I'm still searching for now.

My Dad was a diplomat for the Ghanaian embassy and he had a friend that had built a collection of old Latin stuff by Machito, Tito Puente and loads of obscure stuff. He emigrated to Australia and gave me most of them. Also, there was an old guy that Baz Fe Jazz introduced me to from Harlow in Essex, called Gordon Braham, and he used to play Timbales in his younger days. Baz used to get all his old Afro-Cuban albums from him. When I went to his house, he had a wall-to-wall collection of Cuban, Salsa and Latin Jazz. It was amazing stuff and ridiculously cheap: like £1.50 for rare collectors pieces! He liked the fact that we were playing the music. He was a goldmine.

THE A2 CONNECTION - ANDY Mc CONNELL and ANDY WARD

The A2 Connection are from Essex but got established in London. Important individually or together, they DJ'd at The Electric Ballroom, Sol Y Sombre, The Wag, The Saturday Night Fish Fry....

How long did the A2 Connection last?

Ward - A couple of years. '81 to '84 maybe '85. When we first started we were doing the 'Chris Hill' kind of thing; Disco, Funk and drop a few Jazz tunes in. Jazz got more and more dominant. I was going to The Electric ballroom as a punter as well. A lot of the people that I knew that used to go and see the DJ Froggy at the Green Gate (Ilford) went there. That's how I heard about it: I used to hear all the hard Jazz/Funk at the under 18's night at Ilford town hall with Froggy and then later at the Green Gate. That gave me a taste for it.

McConnell - The reason I started DJ-ing was watching Chris Hill at the Goldmine. I thought: "I wouldn't mind doing that," but not that kind of music. You'd never get a record collection like his; he'd been at it for too long, I just went for the Jazz element of what he was doing.

What residencies did you have?

Ward - There was *The Regency* in Chadwell Heath, Essex.

McConnell - There were loads of short lived ones. Our first was *The Coopers Arms* (13/ /3/84) playing just Jazz and that's when we first had the idea of putting on an alldayer at The Maze club (above Ronnie Scotts Jazz Club).

Ward: We did it to get ourselves known, no one had done a Jazz all-dayer in London, so we did it.

McConnell - Also, in Essex you had the 'Funk Mafia', and Gilles had another crowd.... There were lots of things happening but we were trying to bring the DJ's together hoping to form a collective for our kind of music.

The line up was Paul Murphy, us, Gilles Peterson, Ed Stokes and Neil A. Musically it was hard Fusion and Be Bop and everyone was dancing in there.

Ward - It was nothing like 'The Ballroom' - there were too many people from Essex (laughs). Too much beer being drunk! It was all Jazz but not all heavy. We got great reviews from it but we didn't get much work from it as hoped. We still continued our local events, and actually we did two all-dayers at The Maze club. The second (23/9/84) had a dance off between IDJ and A Fuego Vivo (a short lived Jazz dance crew) – first, as groups and then individual battles. It was pretty special.

What did you think of The Electric Ballroom?

McConnell - We used to go down there to see (Paul) Murphy, and buy some records from him.

Ward - The atmosphere was intimidating to say the least. I just stood against the wall for three weeks before I could even think about getting on the dancefloor, It was heavy and dark.

McConnell - What didn't help was that the music was so intense. You didn't know where to look. The dancing, though, was out of this world.

Ward - Nasty. It got ugly in there. You just saw people getting humiliated on the dancefloor. Some times you'd see fights after challenges. It was good, but scary. I would come home from there and not be able to sleep because I was buzzing. I was privileged to have gone there.

You both DJ'd there though (23/10/84).

McConnell - Murphy left to start at the Sol Y Sombre and The Wag. Gilles comes in to The Ballroom and we go there to see him and he seemed pretty good. He asked us to open up for him, so we said yeah.

Ward - We panicked. I only just had enough tunes, but between us we could do the whole night.

McConnell - Murphy was playing stuff like Salsa and Big Band Jazz at the Sol Y Sombre ; a million miles away from the kind of stuff he was playing at The Ballroom. It attracted more women there. It wasn't that Essex'y kind of 'Chris Hill' scene, it was more 'London trendy' - more 'Face' readers than 'Blues and Soul'. The music was the kind of music I'd always wanted to hear: Ella Fitzgerald, Duke Ellington, Dizzy Gillespie....

You did the Sol Y Sombre Eventually didn't you Andy (McConnell)?

McConnell - On Tuesdays (22/1/85). It was pretty busy. I was playing the music I love: 50's and 60's Jazz and Big Band. I'd play a bit of Salsa too. I called the night The Cotton Club. From there I started doing illegal warehouse parties. I took a risk. I went to one that Murphy was doing with Jonathon Moore in the Rotherhithe area so I started doing them. On the first Saturday night I was shitting myself and I went round the local pubs near the gig and they were packed out. They were all full of the right kind of people and I was trying to give them leaflets but the people were refusing saying "I don't need that, I'm already going." They were queuing down Rotherhithe Street and it was mobbed. We called it The Saturday Night Fish Fry (4/5/85). I did that once a month. Then I heard that Paul Murphy was leaving The Wag (85) to start a night at The Comedy Store so I saw Chris Sullivan and took over the Mondays residency. It did it on my own initially. I then started to work with Baz Fe Jazz as a joint name of 'Take 5'. He guested at a Fish Fry and started to do Sol Y Sombre with me (26/11/85). We were organizing lots of things like the dance side of the Soho Jazz festival. I put Gilles on upstairs at The Wag and he was playing 'Rare Groove' kind of stuff and he started to attract more and more people up there than on our main floor. When the music started to change I'd had enough of it all by then. I got disillusioned. I did it all for the love of music and I thought that when I stopped enjoying it I should stop. And I was DJ-ing five nights a week. I couldn't relax or enjoy myself- plus, I got engaged as well, so I thought it was time to stop.

What about the monstrous 'Absolute Beginners' film?

McConnell - I quite liked it actually. Everybody thought that would be the thing that would make the music the 'thing to be into'. That music would never be mainstream. The film was for 'Face' readers, fashionable people. It was style over content. Everyone who was trendy was falling over each other trying to get in it as an extra, It didn't have any impact al all. They were the trendy West end kind of people who didn't have passion for anything, as opposed to the 'Essex' scene, which was totally about the music, which I suppose I came from but I liked that 50's Jazz sound that you'd never get there except the odd track from Chris Hill.

You DJ'd at The Electric Ballroom again (2/5/86).

McConnell: It was Murphys night (The Purple Pit])but I did DJ there upstairs with Baz. Murphy had a long argument with the owner of Sol Y Sombre and left and took his crowd with him. It was a big venue for that style of music and it wasn't totally working there. You got a lot of Mods - proper Mods. I got a lot of them at another venue I DJ'd at called *The Soul System*, down the Charing Cross road above the Goodfellas Pizza house.

Along with big band Jazz 50's and 60's and all that, I'd play Wynonie Harris, Joe Turner….My wife was into all that rhythm and blues stuff from going to the Rock and Roll clubs. She'd play it to me and I thought it was excellent. I thought it would work with what I was already playing. It was only being played in the rock and roll scene.

Yes, DJ's Kav and Nino, and Rohan The Man…

McConnell - That's it. Anyway, it had that beat that anyone could dance to and it worked with Jazz instrumentrals. We'd even book Jump Jive acts at The Wag like Rent Party.

Andy (Ward), why did you stop DJ-ing?

I had 2000 albums stolen. They were being stored at my brothers house and he got evicted so they were put in the street overnight! Shortly after the second all-dayer, Andy said he was giving up, so we split the A2 Connection. After a short while he started up again. I stopped and got into sport. A little while after, my parents got divorced so I wasn't DJ-ing then.

THE MAMBO CARTEL - MARK HIGGINS and ANDY DYER

The Mambo Cartel are from Surrey, but included here because of their important contribution working with Gilles Peterson at The Electric Ballroom. Some feel that they were of equal importance to Gilles.

Andy - Mark and I were doing our thing at the West End Centre in Aldershot supporting the band *ICQ*. That was our format for the next two or three years, monthly. We'd never DJ'd before. *Paz* played there, *Tommy Chase, Cayenne*….

But how did you get into it all?

Andy - I used to follow Chris Brown at Frenchies and Jacksons, Froggy, Sean French. I knew Mark from school and when we went to college we started getting into buying the records. We got the bug. My brother took us to The Electric Ballroom. There was two car loads of us, but the White guys couldn't handle it – except Mark. The heat and the smell blew them away. We went almost every week. *Paul Murphy* was the Godfather.

Mark - For us it all revolved around him. We didn't go out for the rest of the week so we could hear what Murphy would play on the Friday, and go and try to buy them on Saturday.

Andy - We were sad when Murphy left. We didn't know who Gilles Peterson was - who was taking over (21/4/84). He did well though, but it was a different selection than Murphys. It was different but good.

The A2 Connection came before you as backing up Gilles at The Ballroom (23/10/84).

Andy - Yes. I saw them at an all-dayer there with Murphy, Baz Fe Jazz and Ed Stokes. They had an excellent collection. I thought they did well. They had the music. We had good stuff but they had a much bigger volume of tunes. There was respect there from us.

How did you get the position of supporting Gilles (19/2/85)?

Andy - We simply got the job by asking Gilles for the gig and he accepted. No big story there. He knew us as regulars and plugged our gigs on his pirate radio show he was doing at the time. I couldn't believe it.

Mark - Gilles had acquired a lot of Murphy's big tunes from The Ballroom - the crowd expected them - which was great, because when Gilles was doing it less and less we'd go to his house to pick up the box of Ballroom tunes – which was great because sometimes I'd have it for a week! We had our own tunes of course too. Andy and I were hardcore all the way, I specialized more in Latin Jazz and he played more Fusion.

Andy - I could see that after a while of taking over from Murphy, that it seemed that Gilles was getting bored or something. His interests were elsewhere, he was doing the *Special Branch* at The Royal Oak on a Friday too, so he would turn up pretty late sometimes. Sometime later before he stopped he was just doing every other week at The Ballroom and we did the others. The DJ Sylvester used to come down regularly and turn us onto loads of tunes .He was a great help. He'd bring stuff down for us.

Mark - Gilles gave us the break, but we were playing Murphys big records. By the end of The Ballroom we were probably playing exactly what Murphy used to play. I could personally say that my box was Murphys box because that's where I heard the records.

How long did you last?

Andy - We had a good three years at it. We didn't want a career out of it. Gilles did obviously. When The Ballroom closed, George Power (who was running the night) said he was moving to another venue and asked us if we wanted to come along; perhaps give ourselves a name like 'Jazzy Sensation' and play music more like Gilles - the Acid Jazz was coming in then - but we declined. That Acid Jazz thing wasn't for me. I was schooled in the hardcore, I wasn't happy about it.

Mark - I went to *Dingwalls* a few times but I just didn't get the vibe.

DISTINC–SHUN - ONKAR BANCIL and NILISH GOSHI

In some ways, this sound-system was west London's secret weapon. Not really known outside of the area, but had a massive pull in their own, to a predominantly Asian crowd and some Black. For those in the know, Distinc-Shun's sessions were very influential and of the utmost importance.

We started around 1978 when we were 12 to 13 years old, going to the local record shop and buying seven-inch singles. We did our own parties at home for thirteen, fourteen people and one day we thought "Why don't we do this for money so we could buy some more records?" Our friend's dad had a van and we begged, stole or borrowed the equipment. We got successful really quickly. We had to just make ten phone calls and the gigs would be packed. People would love it. All it was was a rugged sound system, we used to go and look at *Jah Shaka*, and his sound-system was what we wanted. By the time I was sixteen the money was being ploughed into it.

We went to Hounslow Borough College and got on the committee and was putting gigs on in the canteen or the after-studies and found ourselves very popular. We networked well there. We hired out halls like at *The Osterley Hotel* in Isleworth and other places. It got to the stage where we just turned up and people were there. We played out every Friday and Saturday, We could fill a club with four or five hundred people at 72 hours notice.

We had this great gig we did at *The Milford Arms*. We played Jazz, Soul, Jazz/Funk and Reggae. We thought our crowd would be more from the college and the West London area, and it was a predominantly Asian crowd, but we started picking up dancers from *The Electric Ballroom* jazz room. For the first couple of times they came they didn't dance. They were just checking us out. They wanted to know whenever and wherever we played. These were heavy weight. I knew Seymour and Gary Nurse and Milton McAlpine from school. My brother was 'Mr Cool' for having a brother in Distinc-shun at school with that crowd!

We started getting other sound systems wanting to battle us and we'd take 'em all. We out-Bassed them. Our sound was crystal clear. We'd get cabinets from Froggy, bass speakers from Cliff Richards studio in Isleworth and we had modified amps. We were recognized as a sound system and by the crowd that followed us but we weren't known on the club circuit.

That's right. I didn't know you. There must have been so much going on outside of that circuit. What makes me laugh is that you were underage.

We couldn't buy a drink! It was right place right time. '79 to '85 was an amazing time.

How long did Milford Arms last?

Four years. Sometimes every week, mostly every other week, Saturdays. Sometimes we'd start at midday and go on till midnight. Musically, it was 20% Jazz and 80% Jazz Funk.

How did you play the Jazz? In breaks?

No. It would be when you'd start to see it building. You might get the Southall boys wanting to take on the Hounslow ones for instance and they'd let us know, and that'd be it! You'd whip out the well-hard Jazz tunes. The guy that always took it; the best in West London, was Milton.

Probably the best in the Country.

We went up The Ballroom a few times and everyone worshipped him in there.

Didn't you get trouble with Asian gangs?

We had the Tooti Nung (Punjabi Sikh) and The Holy Smokes – they were almost like mafia - but these were the young ones that just had fights. They never started trouble inside because we had a lot of women there.

Did you feel that you were trying to push the Jazz part of your sound?

Even to this day I listen to a lot of Jazz. I played Jazz when I could, out of my special box. We were jazz-freaks. Deep down it's always been about Jazz.

HUGH ALBERT

Of course, there were many famous Jazz record shops around then – too many to have interviewed or to mention, but there were hardly any dealers who would move from DJ to DJ, collector to collector with a small shoulder-bag full of dynamic Jazz records for the dance floor. These were, of course, very much influencing the dance floor [even though the DJ's would take credit for *discovering* the record's – despite having just paid a three figure sum for certain ones!]. It would be pointless interviewing them all either,

but Hugh was not only doing that, he was a DJ and [is still] a passionate Jazz collector himself. His session - The Cutting Edge was the alternative to all that was happening elsewhere in London. One for those serious about their Jazz!

Originally, when I was at school, I was into James Brown and from there discovering the CTI label – artists like Bob James, Earl Klugh, Ronnie Laws, and then Herbie Hancock – that 'Headhunters' period. – and that was my introduction to Fusion, and I went on from there.

Were you going to the Jazz Funk clubs?

I was going to Lacy Lady, with Chris Hill, occasionally Crackers, Barracudas....

Were these clubs fulfilling your jazzy-needs as it were?

Actually, it didn't matter to me whether I heard it or not, because I was collecting such a lot of Jazz independently that I was fulfilled there anyway. I had a musical mentor called Brian Watson, who was a serious Jazz collector. He was very diverse in taste and introduced me to so much - like the 'Blue Note' sound. At one point I felt like I was in a vacuum because I wasn't hearing any of this music on the radio or in the clubs, I wondered if I way off track. It wasn't until meeting a DJ called *Tim Morris* doing a club called *Bentleys* in Swallow Street (London) playing that kind of stuff that I realised there was something there. Tim introduced me to the Latin sound as well, like *Kenny Dorham* and *Herbie Mann*. I had a fair collection by then (around 84) and he invited me to play a few records. He moved to *Clowns* in Frith Street in '85 and we started *The Cutting Edge*. It was like a speakeasy. The club was flourishing and there was loads of other great places to go too, but at the Cutting Edge you really had a chance to experiment. We were so lucky being in the same street as Ronnie Scotts Jazz Club because there must have been people in our place from there. It didn't take too long to establish the night.

Did you get support from the scene from the other DJ's?

They came along once or twice, but we felt that we were being pressed out of the scene by the powers that be. With the clientele we had and the music we had, we were potential upstarts. I'd started dealing records to most of those guys by then anyway, but we weren't given any other opportunities. I think what caused a major disturbance was that we could get away with stuff there that they couldn't elsewhere.

Did the fall out of Jazz interest after the flop of the Absolute Beginners film or the emerging Acid Jazz scene affect you?

No. We continued regardless. We were aware of what was happening around us, but we just did what we did.

So, what about the whole organ combo thing like *Clarence Wheeler – Right On*, or the 'Baptist-Beat' gospel Blue Note sound?

Ok, I have to say, on record, that I was the originator of that. Gilles and Chris Bangs were playing all that stuff and calling themselves 'the Baptist Brothers' so I said to them, I was surprised that *Hank Mobley – The Baptist Beat* wasn't their theme tune, but they didn't know it, so I sold them both copies, which I think is where the compilation came from. At the Cutting Edge we were offering something different: my DJ partner Tim was into the Eastern influenced jazz like *Yusef Lateef*, which was a welcome addition. I like to think that every week was different.

What did you think of Dingwalls?

I liked what Patrick and Gilles were doing there. Myself and a couple of other guys were servicing them with records and our influence was quite apparent. Dingwalls was a laboratory, a fertile ground - you got an immediate reaction from records that you sold. There were so many records surfacing then you didn't have time to catch breath. It was coming thick and fast. Some of the packages that I would send to Dingwalls wouldn't necessarily be right for Clowns. There was a definite line. I felt that towards the end of Dingwalls it got a bit distasteful, but it was communal and unpretentious.

With Dingwalls, of course, you had Alan Riding selling amazing Jazz in the cloakroom and upstairs you had Soul Jazz records knocking out the funky *Prestige* label stuff.

They were major influences in that.

The dealers never get the accolades for turning this stuff up, it's always the DJ that gets the reputation.

To me, it's a straight forward transaction, There are some dealers that want their name in lights, that was their agenda: looking in sleeve-notes of compilations to see if they've been mentioned.

What happened to The Cutting Edge?

The owner started intruding in our business - which was causing bad feeling - but he sold out to a restaurant anyway. We tried other places, including putting live bands on – which was something I'd done for years anyway – but we didn't want to use our own money and lose our shirts.

SHELDON WILLOX

As well as being one of the 'faces' around the Jazz Dance scene - being close with Paul Murphy, and watching the whole scene unfold – he also DJ'd with Tim Morris at Bentleys and towards the latter part of the barrier-breaking *Cutting Edge* club.

I got into it all through *The Royalty* with Froggy and Pete Tong, the early Caister's, Goldmine, the Pirate station *Invicta* and Robbie Vincent's essential radio show. I started collecting Jazz Funk and then went back collecting earlier stuff buying 'Blue Note' records and seriously shopping. I was buying from Paul Murphy and went to The Electric Ballroom. When he left, it was never the same, That was the essence of what it [the scene] was all about. It was concentrated. I only went once whrn Gilles took over, I didn't see any point. Paul was actually going to give it to me and my friend Tim Morris, but then he said he'd give it to Gilles.

You were DJ-ing by then, obviously.

Yes, a bit. I DJ'd at Bentleys with Tim a bit; Murphy knew us well. We'd travel down to Brighton with him for the Jazz Room with *Ed Stokes*. The music was great there, and there was a good cross section of people. Ed Stokes had a big following in London so a lot would come and support him as well as Murphy.

Was Murphy playing the same stuff as at The Electric Ballroom?

He was starting to change. He played a specific sound at The Ballroom, just aimed at the dancers, everywhere else it was more diverse. I liked going there 'crushing cock roaches' (laughs). I feel that people get a bit intense about it. Really, it was a period of time that was a laugh and a lot of people took it too serious. It wasn't just about dancing. It was about collecting and seeing live gigs. You go and watch Elvin Jones and you know you've experienced something.

Did you follow Murphy to The Wag?

I went to support him but it was a different sound; a different crowd. It was alright.

What DJ's did you rate outside of Murphy?

None really, except Chris Bangs. He's an innovator. Gilles had his day at Dingwalls too. He shone there. Bob Jones – another innovator. The others followed really and watered it down.

You DJ'd at *The Cutting Edge* with Tim Morris and Hugh Albert.

Not at first. That was later, but I went every week.

What was the music principle?

Play fucking great Jazz (laughs).

Did the main players from the scene check it out?

All of them, or they'd send someone to find out what we were playing. To us, it was just about good music, nothing trendy, that's why we were maverick I suppose. It was way further ahead than anywhere else That place was something else.

Didn't you try The Cutting Edge in Brighton?

Yes, in '86 we hired out the same hotel that Murphy did his session at – The Churchill Hotel. It was an all-nighter. It went spectacularly well. It was packed. We would have continued with it but none of us lived there. Not long after, Russ Dewbury started his events down there anyway so....

JEZ NELSON

Of course, by the mid-80's there had been many Black music pirate stations but along with Tony Monson and Gilles Peterson, there had been no one as dedicated to putting Jazz on the airwaves than Jez Nelson or Chris Phillips.

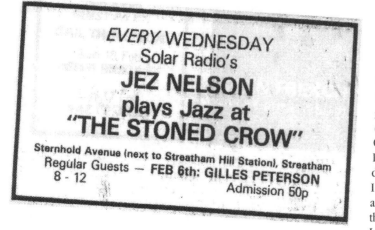

From the age of 13 or 14 (1981), I was obsessed with music and radio. I was living just outside Bromley (Kent) and was spoilt for music. There was two under 18's disco's – one was with Robbie Vincent and the other was Greg Edwards. Fucking amazing! When I was 15, I was going to Robbie Vincent's nights at Flicks (Dartford, Kent), and started going to The Goldmine, The Rio in Didcot, Stage 3 in Leysdown, Isle Of Sheppey (Kent), the all-dayers, The Caister Weekenders – of which I started gravitating towards the Jazz room, and listening to the radio a lot. I got into the Black music pirate radio station *Radio Invicta* on Sundays and I taped everything. I got obsessed by it; it was a life saver. There was an amazing Jazz show on there by Andy 'Jazzman' Jackson, he was buying from Paul Murphy's record shop, so what you were hearing was straight off the racks of his shop. He was the first Jazz dance radio DJ.

When I was at University, I was spending all my time going out, but did a demo tape for the pirate station *Horizon*. I was listening to Gilles Peterson on there a lot, (as I did on Invicta) and

219

I managed to get in there too. We bonded there. We were the weirdos playing the strange music. As a station, it did really well and was making money. I was doing my shows and would cover for Gilles occasionally.

During that period I started to DJ out. I did a Thursday at *Dr. Crippens* in Bromley, Kent, which was full of men. There was always a big fight there, but I had a small contingent of followers that also followed Gilles too. I did *The Stoned Crow* in Streatham on Wednesdays too. It had a dodgy vibe, but I had guest DJ's every week like Gilles and Bob Jones. I was also a regular at Gilles' residency at The Belvedere. I had three or four gigs a week but it was the radio I was interested in. I don't think I've ever been a particularly good DJ I became a DJ because I was on the pirate radio. I had the passion for the music and wanted it to be broadcast. I wasn't into it because it was illegal - after all we were always campaigning for it to be legal.

There was a split at Horizon and Tony Monson started *Solar Radio*, which we did, and after that, Gilles, me and Chris Phillips decided to start a Jazz Pirate station called *KJAZZ*. Eventually we got a great place to put a transmitter: above a hairdressers (where my dad went) in Crystal Palace – a prime location. Our signal was incredible for a while. As well as us, Kevin Beadle was on it, Salsa DJ Tomek, Sue Steward, Baz Fe Jazz and Pamela Estherson. It was around that time that Gilles went off to do 'Mad on Jazz' on BBC Radio London, but he'd do anonymous shows on KJAZZ at the same time. We used to put on a few gigs and Gilles was doing the *Jazz Bop's* at the Town And Country Club, Kentish Town (now the Forum).

When did you start your *Something Else* events?

After KJAZZ I went to Starpoint Radio and did a few shows, I think I then wanted to learn more of the craft and went to college to do a post grad in Radio Journalism. A couple of years later in '89 me and Chris Phillips were recommended to do the new legal Jazz station called JAZZ FM by Gilles, who was on the board. He got us involved, and we'd gone from doing pirate stations in heavy areas to helping set up this brand new Jazz station. I did the nightshift every night, for six months, playing anything from *Archie Shepp* to *Public Enemy* – it was well 'out there' – and then they put me and Chris together to do every evening, and that show was called Something Else! We did that till '91, until they started sacking loads of people, then we set up a production company called ''Something Else'', and ran a weekly Monday night at the Jazz Café in London called that as well, which ran for a long time, and it all built from there. I was basically playing what I was hearing every week plus obscure twenty five minute long tracks off of obscure 'Impulse' albums – I was going deeper and deeper. Gilles' show was mid-day till 4pm on Saturday afternoons and he'd be breaking tracks by the new bands like *Young Disciples* or Jamiroquoi and all that, and from there we'd play them through the week.

What did you think about 'Acid Jazz' and the whole 'Freedom Principle'?

I remember Gilles phoning me and saying "The scenes really blowing up, and it needs a name. Bangsy and I thought of *Acid Jazz*" and I said, "That's absolute bollocks! That's a terrible name." I thought it was a shit name. I thought it's intentions were good. Gilles has got incredible taste and puts music together brilliantly, also, he's fantastic at communicating and marketing. 'Acid Jazz' is the headline example of 'Gilles - The Marketing Person.' I was there, even when Gilles and Eddie Piller talked about forming the label. Acid Jazz got made up and had no meaning. It then meant something for a while and pulled people together and then became meaningless again.

CHRIS PHILLIPS

I bought the *Earth, Wind and Fire* album 'All in all' when I was 13 and with tracks like Brazilian Rhyme and Runnin', it set off my taste for acoustic Latin based music and Jazz, and a little later I'd be going to clubs like the 100 Club with Ronnie L on a Saturday afternoon where he'd play an extraordinary mix of heavy disco funk and Jazz, and Crackers with George Power playing Disco, Jazz Funk and a lot of Jazz. The energy was so potent.

In '81, I picked up the *Paquito D'Riviera - Blowin* album, which was straight ahead Jazz, and through that I started picking up Miles Davis and all that.

By the mid-eighties there was a second generation of DJ's and there was loads of pirate stations – Solar; Horizon; JFM; LWR, so there was a lot of really interesting music getting discovered and played. The most interesting DJ for me was Gilles Peterson. I've always regarded him as a pied piper. A friend of mine was sharing a flat with Jez Nelson who was running a pirate with Gilles called KJAZZ – a Jazz station named after a San Francisco jazz station called KJAZ – and he got me to meet him. The station was being run from a house in Cheam (South London) but was suffering from engineering problems. I was running a little pirate out of Crystal Palace called Radioactivity and got them to move there, where they used my talented engineer and me. We hauled a 40 foot aerial above a hairdressers and they charged us £25 a weekend and we recorded all the shows on cassette and had to keep on opening up the shop on Sundays to change tapes. We played them through an auto reverse car stereo connected to the transmitter. We couldn't go on like that forever so I hooked up with a work mate called Carl who had a flat in nearby Gypsy Hill, Upper Norwood, and we went live from there. Saturdays was Carl's station *Starpoint* and Sunday was KJAZZ. I was a DJ on both.

We lost our engineer, and this genius called Keith Penton – who until two years ago was still with KISS FM – made our broadcast untraceable through microwave and we'd broadcast in a bedroom flat in South Croydon of one of Gilles ex-girlfriends! Kevin Beadle did the Sunday breakfast show and then I would follow. And at first he whispered to me to keep the noise down because the girl was actually in bed sleeping!! Occassionally a male head would pop up from under the covers saying: "Who are all these men?!"

The pirates coincided with gigs that were going on like Gilles' Belvedere. His movement was in full swing. Altogether the station lasted from '86 to '89.

Was there any way of telling how many were listening?

No, but I can tell you who was listening: the guy from the radio investigations department, who once said to me, "Why did you stop KJAZZ? We used to really like it." That would explain to me why regularly on a Sunday twelve stations would get raided and taken off the air but we'd get left on! The other stations used to ask us why we never got busted but *then* we knew at last.

The main man prosecuted me a few years later and complimented me for one station while busting me for another. It was really 'cold war' time then, I'd literally be walking down the road and a car would screech up and a guy in sunglasses and a fawn coat would leap out and take my photo and drive off.

I did all the late night donkey-work - ratcheting of aerials and that type thing, and the DJ's just got on with broadcasting. We all had a part to play. The pirate scene was very key to promoting music.

Gilles went from there to 'Radio London' – legal radio – which was so important. *Roy Ayers* was there being interviewed one night and Gilles played X-CLAN – *Red, Black and Green* sampling one of Roy's tracks from the 1970s and he was flabberghasted. And that, to me was the power of that scene that they loosely called *Acid Jazz*. It was a new energy, defining the music.

The energy of the scene was petering out though where the original crowd was being replaced by a younger student crowd and lads drinking lager. It replaced the music lover with fodder at the gig's, and that's where it started losing it for me. It was a halcyon era and things have to move on but there was a mysticism to it.

Were you a DJ outside of the station?

No, not really. I was much more a radio entrepreneur. I was very much a consumer and punter.

CHRIS BANGS

Bangsy – as he is known to friends – was one the main players in both the home counties Jazz dance scene and the hard-core London Paul Murphy one. He co-ran the famous Bournemouth Soul Weekenders and led all the way through the 80's with his partner Gilles Peterson – he even coined the phrase 'Acid Jazz.' He didn't like where the scene was going eventually and so got out. His achievements are documented here.

Although individual DJ's in their own right, Bob Cosby and Kevin Beadle were very inte-

geral to the whole Jazz circle surrounding Gilles, Bangsy and the whole 'Special Branch' movement (if you will). Their interviews follow Bangsy's.

I started clubbing in 1975, going to clubs like The Lacy Lady; Cheeky Petes in Richmond ; The Toby Jug in Tolworth; The Goldmine a few times and Frenchies in Camberley with DJ's Chris Brown and Robin Nash. It went from Chris Hill to Chris Brown as arbiter of my taste in music. Although playing a lot of soul music, Chris did play a lot of jazz; although, not as heavy as I would go on to play.

By 1980 I'd been DJ-ing a bit with my mobile system, and I'd guested at a few clubs, but the first ones of note were *Bogarts* in Harrow (13/4/80) and *The Exeter Bowl* in Bouremouth on the South coast (5/5/81). It was the only different disco in Bournemouth, and also, there was the novelty of this *London* DJ coming down every week. It started off very funk and soul and I gradually got away with a lot of jazz; nothing clever, but good Fusion and good Bossas. It ended up totally jazz. It had a good, strong loyal following, and a lot of people traveled, as well.. Bogarts was similar. I started on my own and eventually brought in Sean French, who ended up head-lining there. We played quite a lot of jazz-funk there like *Jimmy Smith – Sit On It* and a good bit of jazz.

By now, I'd seen Paul Murphy DJ-ing at The Horseshoe, and that had a big impact on me. By 1981/82, I'd became much more of a Jazz DJ.

Paul Murphy was at The Horseshoe twice, and in between times he moved what he was doing to *The Green Man* (near Portland Street). I guested there a couple of times and I told Paul that I knew a place called the St Louis Club in Earls Court that had a basement (5/5/81). We did it on a Thursday for three or four months. Musically, it was very hard funk and jazz. The funk was very fast and hard. It led me to believe that there could be some Jazz Dance DJ-ing scene going on. The session finished when the football team -Tottenham Hotspur, were in a replay of the F.A. cup, which fell on that day. At the club, it was just me and the bar-man. I never worked with Murphy again after that.

I started a residency at *Jesters* in Kingston with Tarun Sen Gupta (12/3/82). He backed Paul there, and when Paul left we started our T&C session.

Why was Tarun so rated?

He was such a collector. He discovered loads of records that other DJ's would have taken credit for. I don't know where he got his fucking records. I don't think he had any desire to be a DJ, but people would ask him because he had such a great collection. I used to pick up stuff for him when I was DJ-ing at Exeter Bowl in Bournemouth: they used to have loads and loads of people selling records at Matchams Market, where I'd pick up a lot of records from, and I'd go to Record And Tape Exchange on the way back too!

I had a lot of things going on around then, but none had a big enough local crowd to sustain the nights and to build them. There were places like The Crown in Marlow; Osbourne Arms; East Arms in Hurley.....loads of places, all miles out of town. I decided to stop messing around with other styles of music and just play jazz.

How did the Bournemouth weekenders come about?

I was playing it pretty Jazzy at The Exeter Bowl, and I got to know the DJ Bob Masters who playing above a pub in Badgers wine bar. For the two bank holiday weekends in '81 we did a weekender where he moved downstairs to the pub and I went up to the wine bar. I did Saturday and Sunday lunchtimes there and the Exeter Bowl on Saturday night, and from there we moved to East of Eden which is where it all solidified. He knew more of the Reading/ Oxford kind of crowd and mine was more South London, Kent, South of London – Camberely and all that. It was bigger, and really started taking off. It was absolutely packed with hundreds and hundreds of people outside. We moved down the road to Boscombe, to the Show Bar on the pier. It was a huge venue, but we used to ram 1200 in there. It was a slightly older, musical crowd who knew their stuff. We lasted there till 1987.

TG'S ☆ latin
+jazz fusion

8 til 12
EVERY WEDNESDAY
CHRIS BANGS
& TARUN
£1.00 before 10
with this ticket

JESTER'S
CROWN PASSAGE
KINGSTON

Upstairs At Erics would have been a big club for Jazz in Bournemouth at the same time.
Yes, the DJ Graham did the weekenders with us originally - he had a big local following, - then we brought in Gilles; Bob Jones did some and Chris Brown.

How did you meet Gilles?
I met Gilles trough Tarun and we went to see him at Crystals Wine Bar in Cheam village, where he had a great crowd. He used to come to some of my gigs. We got on very well. I did a few shows for him on his KJAZZ radio station. I started using him to warm up for me at *The Rio* in Didcot, but what really started it for us was when we discovered this pub in East Sheen called *The Bull* which had this massive function room. That's where we started the *Mambo Madness* sessions. We used to get about 350 people to those and that's what started giving us a base. Gilles and I were very keen to build something rather than just guest-spotting for other people. We did those

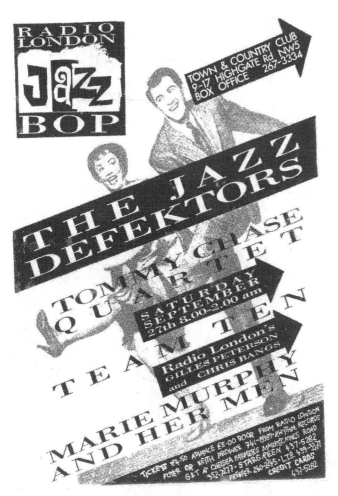

once a month and built it slowly. I got Gilles on my Bournemouth weekenders and we got Nicky Holloway on it as well, so when he started The Royal Oak, he started using Gilles weekly, and I'd do it once a month with him. It all grew from there really.

What about The London Jazz Bops (27/9/86)? That was the same period.
Well they were sponsored by Radio London, which Gilles had a show on and I did the posters. We just put bands on from the scene, like Team 10 and The Jazz Defektors and we would both DJ. These bands would never normally be able to headline at such a huge venue like The Town And Country Club (now *The Forum*) – it held over two thousand people – but the events were big and we got everyone involved. There was a lot going on at that time and this helped to solidify things.

Gilles told me that you were a big influence on him.
I'm not a purist, as you know: as Gilles had come from The Electric Ballroom - with all that fast Samba Fusion, I may have shown him that you could bring the pace down and play something a lot lighter, but still with it's own merits – *Andy Williams - House Of Bamboo* or whatever. We used to play to the girls.

You were known for playing odd-ball records and dressing up too.
Well, yes. I remember when me, Gilles and Bob Jones were doing The Wag on a Monday and the jazz drummer, Tommy Chase said: " What are you playing all the *Baptist Beat* for? All that *Don Wilkerson – Dem Tambourines*, and all that?" So we went and rented some *cassocks* and did a Baptist Beat special and gave out tambourines. We got into the habit of doing things like that. I just felt that, if people are having a good time you can get away with anything. I wasn't too serious and I quite liked the idea of making Gilles less serious. He had a lot of serious jazz; everyone knew what he could play, but at the same time, he wasn't scared to throw in some old Funk with it or whatever.

He's always done that.
We used to go record shopping together and get records from mail-order places together, like *Soul Bowl*. Basically, we'd both be playing certain records at our own residencies and by the time we played together once a month, both of our crowds knew those songs. There was a lot of collusion in trying to get a play-list going.

Could you see where you were trying to get to? What you were aiming for?

We were deliberately trying to cross over a bit. It was when the Acid House club started – *Schoom* – that it all changed. A lot of our hard-core crowd suddenly disappeared . We were very conscious that we needed to change, musically.

How did 'Acid Jazz' come about?

One night Gilles and I were DJ-ing at one of Nicky Holloways *Special Branch* gigs at *The Watermans Arts Centre* and we were the last on. By then, the Acid-House thing had taken hold, and,, being projected on the wall was all this day-glo stuff and the word *Acid* was flashing. I remember Gilles was playing a track by *Art Blakey and Sabu*, and he saw all these projected images and the flashing 'Acid', and said: "What is this all about?" and I said: "*Acid Jazz*, isn't it !". Gilles just picked up the microphone and said: " Acid Jazz!" and that was it - the term was born!

What we'd been playing had less relationship with The Electric Ballroom. We were playing a lot of *rare groove* and jazz and all kinds of stuff, so you couldn't call it a jazz night, as such, anymore. 'Acid Jazz' was just one in a line of stupid names that we came up with, and it stuck.

The Cock Happy events were the original Acid Jazz events, weren't they [26/3/88]?

The Cock Tavern was down a side road in Smithfield Market and was tiny, infact a lot of people missed the first one because they couldn't find it! (note: See Janine Neye's interview for details). At that one we had all the crossed-eyed smiley face 'Acid Jazz' badges and all that. We did Cock Happy's in loads of other venues after, but what really started Acid Jazz was, soon after we came up with the name, a spoof article on Acid Jazz appeared in I.D. magazine. He had contributions from Simon Booth, Eddie Piller, me and Gilles. That got everybody talking.

I slowly lost interest after the second *Special Branch* Ibiza trip in 1988. Amongst the crowd, it seemed that people weren't interested in what others were playing. You had Nicky Holloway playing House, and me and Gilles playing our thing and at the other end, you had Bob Jones and Simon Dunmore playing straight-down-the-line Modern Soul. Musically, the whole thing had just pulled too far apart. It was never the same after that. I made a few records for Acid Jazz records and I got so into being in recording studios and making music that by 1989 I'd stopped being a DJ altogether.

BOB COSBY

From 16 years old, a friend used to drive me up to Blackpool Mecca regularly, which I loved, but I was open minded and used to listen to Robbie Vincent's radio show, go to the Caister Soul Weekenders and read Blues and Soul and Groove Weekly magazines. I loved the Jazz scene and the Fusion sound and used to look forward to the Fusion 40 minutes on Robbie's show and try to track them down. I went to Paul Murphy's shop and other dealers, but I liked the obscurer stuff that Paul sold. There was a Bluebird record shop in Luton [THE cut-out deletions specialists] which I worked at from '82 to '86, which was open on Saturdays and Sunday, so I did that as well as my regular weekly job. So I go tons of cut-outs from there and a discount too! I had access to all the DJ's coming in and flying all my gigs too.

The first gig I did playing Jazz was back in 1980 on a Sunday night at *The Sun* in Leighton Buzzard. We started playing Jazz Funk and got harder into the 'Blue Note' sound and Fusion. We outgrew it and quickly moved down the road in '81, to The Black Horse on Tuesdays. Because it used to get plugged on Martin Collins show on BBC Chiltern Radio, I got people traveling from Hertfordshire, Bedfordshire, North London.... We got guest DJ's like Bob Jones and Chris Bangs, and it was packed. That lasted for about 8 years. I was also doing *The Cross Keys* - also in Leighton Buzzard - on Friday nights – which ran for a year.

Around '85, I got asked to do the *Mambo Madness* sessions in London with Chris Bangs and Gilles Peterson at The Bull in East Sheen. I was just getting great tuition in Jazz. Anthems for me were *Joe Torres -Get Out Of My Way, Tenoria Jr - Nebulosa, Sonny Bravo -Tighten Up, Ray Baretto - Love Beads*, and started developing into the funkier stuff like *Funk Inc -Sister Sadie* and *Let's Make Peace*.

How did you get involved with Chris Bangs and Gilles?

Nicky Holloway used to come to The Black Horse and liked what I was playing, so I got booked to play at The Royal Oak. I guess Bangsy was impressed with my selection from there. I got quite friendly with him and would go record shopping with him. We'd go to a record shop in Chertsey called *Mister Waxie's* which was an alladins cave of records. The owner turned us onto loads of odd tracks that became big for us like *Boots Randolph – Cerveza* and *Perry Como – House Of Bamboo*. I did Mambo Madness from day one. It used to get packed and I'd bring a coach up too, and it then moved to Fulham Football ground. It used to remind me of the Caister Soul Weekender Jazz room. I remember all the phases it went through, like the Blue Note 'Baptist Beat' thing with tracks like *Reverend Moses – Lou Donaldson*, and the Boogaloo phase, and the

Funkier one with Funk Inc, and *Ceaser Frazier – Another Life*, and all that 'wah-wah' roots of Acid Jazz stuff. I liked it and went along with it, but I was beginning to wonder where it was all going.

It couldn't have done you any harm being involved with that.

It was the biggest thing happening in that scene at that time, plus working at The Royal Oak. I was guesting at loads of pubs and wine bars too.

Which is where the scene existed really. The staple diet of it.

There was tons of those places. That;s where it all fermented. The grass roots.I was a Soul Boy at heart, that got into Jazz, and I would say that most of those Jazz DJ's were the same. To me though, by '88, the Jazz dance scene was starting to peter out and I started getting really interested in Soul music. Myself and a DJ friend *Gavin Page* decided to resurrect the sessions at *The Bull* in Royston - that was originally a famous one for Bob Jones - which we did on a Friday night once a month playing Soul and Jazz. That ran until '90.

NICKY HOLLOWAY

At one point in London during the mid-to-late Eighties, so much of the scene was revolving around Nicky Holloway's Special Branch events based at The Royal Oak in Bermondsey. One could argue, too, that it was his original events in Ibiza that started the whole club-culture associated with that Balearic island.

I was DJ-ing in rough Old Kent Road pubs getting £15 a night. There was a big pub scene in Bermondsey, with a lot of Disco pubs.

I went out with a girl who worked at The Swan And Sugarloaf in Tooley Street so I started DJ-ing there (November '83) - I asked the manager, Greg Powell, if he'd let me do a Monday night. My ambition was to be a Funk Mafia DJ and I felt that the only way to get in with them was to book those DJ's and hope that they'd book me, which worked. I booked Jeff Young, Sean French and Pete Tong. I started off with one hundred and twenty in there, which went up to two hundred by the end of the month. It went so well I started doing Fridays there and living there too – rent free – as long as I'd keep the bottle shelves filled and DJ support to the strippers on Friday lunchtimes. I was also DJ-ing down the road at The Royal Oak too. It was the only pub in the area with a two o'clock license, so when the other pubs shut they'd come down to The Royal Oak and it was packed. I did that every Saturday. I played what I wanted

at The Swan and Sugarloaf but played commercial at The Royal Oak. But my way of being commercial was playing old Soul hits like the Motown classics, rather than play the chart-hits of the day.

All of a sudden all the pubs around there got a 2 am license and the pub went dead. Well The Swan And Sugarloaf was closing down for redecoration so in June '84 I suggested moving the idea of my successful Fridays from there to The Royal Oak. I called the night *The Special Branch* and I initially tried it on Thursdays and then Mondays but it really took off in February '85 when I finally started it on Fridays. I did downstairs in the main room with guests and Mark Webster and Dave Hucker played upstairs with the Jazz and Tropical, also with guests. It was Mark that came up with the name 'The Special Branch' actually. Later, Gilles Peterson took over the Fridays, after a couple of months. I was into that whole London warehouse parties/ Dirt Box scene - with clubs like Raw, but also that home–counties Soul scene too so I wanted a mixture of that.

Was it a success from the word go?

Yes. We had the odd bad night through snow, bomb scares or tube strikes but other than that it was all amazing.

So the Special Branch was on Fridays, what else was on there?

It was just a pub. The other nights were nothing to do with me. I was doing special events every two months like the 'Doos At The Zoo' at Regents Park Zoo. We'd have 2000 at those and 300 at the Royal Oak. DJ's like Chris Brown – who did all of them, Sean French, Gilles Peterson, Pete Tong, Jeff Young, Bangsy, Bob Jones, Danny Rampling, Paul Oakenfold, Trevor Nelson...... I did sixteen of those events, and I did weekenders too - the only ones other than Caister.

You really started that whole *Ibiza clubbing culture*; that was a Special Branch event.

That was in '86. It could have been anywhere really, I'd already been on holiday there - that's where I'd met Danny Rampling actually – and thought that'd be a good place for a trip away. There were 200 people that went and it cost £185 and we were away for two weeks. I did the deal with the 18-30 company.

What? It was an 18-30's holiday?

No, we used their hotels and did it out of season. We put on gigs with all the Special Branch DJ's and we found this little place out on it's own called Café Del Mar. No one went up there. We were playing Jazz and Soul and whatever. We were the biggest group out there. They'd never seen anything like it. The following year we did Corfu, and in '88 we did our second Ibiza.

Which is where there was the massive split.

Yes. Half of us started taking pills and checking out the nightlife, listening to Balearic dance music, and there was the break – away from, like, Simon Dunmore, Bob Jones and that crowd – who were saying, "We don't need to take drugs to listen to music," and all that. And they started putting on their own events where I had nothing to do with the organization. They were conflicting with my gigs, so we fell out. I was battling with my own crowd.

I decided to stop the whole Special Branch thing on the way home from there. I'd had enough. We'd all gone in different directions musically and I decided to go the 'House Music' route.

Just previous to the split, the Acid Jazz thing came from one of your events at The Watermans Arts Centre in Brentford.

Yes it did. That was Chris Bangs; well I'm sure you know the story. It was a joke. It was only meant to be a laugh wasn't it.

KEVIN BEADLE

My Mum was into Black music: used to listen to Greg Edwards ' Soul Spectrum' radio show (On Capitol) and she asked me whether I'd go to a concert with her at Fairfield halls in Croydon. It was the Detroit Spinners supported by Brass Construction, this was 76/77. Brass Construction blew me away, you know: 15 piece band, Funky section,. Percussion, that was it for me. Also, I was always into drums and my neighbour used to lend me 40's and 50's Jazz records with people like Gene Krupa and that and I used to tape them. I loved them. I suppose between '77 and 79/80 it all came together in my head: the Funky Soulful thing and the Jazz. I started collecting then.

You lived in Croydon, so what clubs were you going to?

Well, I couldn't get to a lot of the clubs because I couldn't drive then, but there was a DJ who was big in our area called Tony Thorpe and we'd support him. He played a lot of Jazz Funk and Jazz Fusion. He was an influence on me. Then in 1980 I used to go to *Jaffas* at the Horseshoe with Paul Murphy, which was the first Jazz session that I'd gone to. That was amazing. It was very fast and intense. It was my fix.

Where else?

Well I was only about 17 remember, so I couldn't get about. We used to go to local wine bars and pubs that were putting DJ's on that we knew, that were on Pirate radio, like J.F.M. The guy that ran J.F.M – Brian Anthony – used to do his show on Sunday afternoon and would play a lot of Fusion so we'd phone in requests. We used to get a bus to Streatham on a Thursday because he had a residency in a wine bar there. We'd got our fix there.

London is made up of little towns really, isn't it? All these areas had their own scene. How did you start DJ-ing in the scene?

A guy I knew, called Larry, was collecting records and he had a set of decks and asked me if I wanted-ed to be a partner on this Sunday night session in Croydon at a place called *Snifters*. Larry knew Paul Oakenfold and Trevor Fung and actually, later, it was Paul that gave me my break; and Gilles

Bob Jones, Kevin and Sylvester

(Peterson) a break as well. We used to warm up for him – we're all Croydon boys. He (Oakenfold) did Ziggys in Streatham but he did this place called The Royal Oak in Purley and once a month on a Saturday they had guest DJ's like Chris Brown, Pete Tong, Chris Hill, Jeff Young, all that, and I was the warm up DJ and got to know them all.

I'd never associate Oakenfold with anything Jazzy.

No. Trevor played more, but everyone dabbled in those days didn't they? Anyway, at Snifters we played a lot of Soul type stuff and Brit– Funk like Lynx and Shakatak, but I'd always do a solid thir-ty minutes of Jazz. My mates were into it so that's how I got more of a reputation of being a Jazz boy. That's how I met Gilles: Gilles was doing a place in Sutton called *Christies* simultaneously on a Sunday night, and he was on (pirate station) Invicta at the time and I was in to what he was play-ing and he got a tip off about me, so we used to go to each others gigs, and play. This was around 1984.

What else were you up to?

Lots of little places like the Stoned Crow in Streatham, Sherrifs, in Croydon…

By then, did you consider yourself a Jazz DJ or just a Jazz Specialist?

I was Jazz biased. I got bored with the Soul and Funk then. I was playing Soul as well, like Gilles was, but I had a few friends who really liked me to 'let go' with the fast stuff.

(Paul) Murphy told me that at the time, although being the actual pinnacle of the scene he wasn't actually aware of there being a 'scene' as such!

I don't think any of us did. I guess people were just being a bit rebellious. We didn't know we were creating anything. It happened organically.

But there was definitely an explosion. We felt the repercussions of The Electric Ballroom in Essex. The Jazz Dance explosion.

Yeah, and Colin Curtis up North…Nottingham…

You used to DJ on the pirate station KJAZZ.

Yes. I remember we used to broadcast from Chris Phillips shed. And one summer afternoon Baz Fe Jazz and Jez were doing a show together and a bee got in the shed. They were both scared of bees and ran out of there live on air, and all you could hear was this clicking where the record had finished and the needle was in the run-out groove. We used Starpoint's transmitter. They did it in the week and KJAZZ was on air on Sundays. In fact when KJAZZ folded, I carried on DJ-ing at Starpoint.

You did a Jazz show on there?

Yeah. We used to broadcast from some weird places: a council house in Crystal Palace in some lesbians flat in her living room.

Let's talk about The Royal Oak.

Whatever DJ's were doing the main club room downstairs had to do a Jazz set upstairs with us. We had Chris Hill, Pete Tong, Trevor Fung, Chris Brown..... This was in the days when Pete Tong broke the *Quartette Tres Bien* track *Boss Tres Bien*.

Gilles and I got involved with the whole 'Special Branch' thing. That's when the Funkier Soulful nights thought they should have a Jazz room. Most times the Jazz room was the more vibier room. Gilles was pulling me into a lot of gigs. It was me, him and Chris Bangs. I got more and more gigs from playing at the Royal Oak; I didn't have to rely on wine bars anymore.

Were you regular there?

I was Gilles 'warm up' for quite a while. It was Mark Webster and Chris Bangs there originally, then Gilles, then me. Gilles left, then Bob Jones came in, then I left and Danny Rampling came in playing Soul. That Jazz room ended up a Soul room. I would drive Gilles around to other gigs and cover gigs that he couldn't do.

You were everywhere. Didn't you do The Wag?

Yes. Me and Gilles and Bangsy, and later Bob Jones, with Sylvester and Phil Levene upstairs playing the heavy stuff. That's when the whole 'Rare Groove' thing came in and we were playing Funk instrumentals: Funk inc, James Brown instrumentals, *Clarence Wheeler – Right On*, the Prestige records, Johnny Hammond... It was getting a lot funkier in the main room. The latter era of The Wag was around the same time as Dingwalls Monday night -Wag, Friday – Special Branch, Sunday lunchtime – Dingwalls and Sunday night-The Belvedere. Briefly, they were all happening at once.

Chris Bangs was very influential.

Well, he came from that 'West of London' scene, you know - Chris Brown, Sean French. They were always that bit more advanced there. Bangsy really influenced Gilles.

Speaking of Chris Brown, did you ever go to his session at The Belvedere?

Sunday lunchtime? A few times. That area was considered THE area for Jazz and Soul. I suppose that's why I moved more in this direction from South London. To be nearer to it all.

Bangsy was quoted as saying around then 'Putting the fun back into Jazz'. Was it all getting too serious then?

Possibly. To a certain extent. Around that time we thought that if it was going to move on and get bigger we had to open it up, but how could we do that? A lot of people couldn't dance to the 100mph Fusion and Afro Cuban records. We were being looked at as freaks, living in the past. So play the Funk, Jazz Funk, Funky Fusion then full–on Fusion, and there's the link – that's how we worked it. That's how Chris Bangs brought that 'Acid Jazz' thing about; just to bring the fun element in again.

At the end of the day, clubbing's about enjoying yourself and having a laugh but the Jazz Dance scene was too serious and intense and we already had these dancers anyway so how do we make it bigger? The Acid Jazz thing was a joke. Acid House was big and you had our crowd doing the Funky Jazzy thing and that other lot going off and listening to 'Balearic' Housey stuff; there was an 'us and them' situation. I remember at a particular Bournemouth weekender, depending on who was DJ-ing, 100 people going onto the floor and 100 people walking off, no one would mingle. It became bad. Bangsy looked at it and thought: "It's segregated too much and we can't have this" so the only way of bringing it all together was to play something that they could all relate to. The maddest thing I saw was: one night at the Belvedere Arms, Danny (Rampling) had set up *Schoom* (the barrier breaking Acid House night) by then, and his crowd had been out all weekend and they came down on this Sunday night and it was packed solid. Everytime we'd play a Batucada the House crowd would go mad, and one of the biggest cross over tracks for both scenes was *Byron Morris – Kitty Bey*. They loved that. To bring it all back together, Chris Bangs came up with the idea of the whole 'Acid Jazz' thing. It still scares Chris today.

I thought what was even scarier was that people were trying to fucking intellectualize it!

We all took it a bit serious. We made ourselves a bit aloof; I don't know why because it was a joke. We all got into the 'Beat' poetry and all that shit. I look back now and it's quite embarrassing!

The scene had only just built up and recovered after that 'Absolute Beginners' disaster. We all had great expectations for that film.

It wasn't a representation of what we were about.

GILLES PETERSON

There is no point writing an intro about this controversial and maverick DJ, Radio Broadcaster and Record Label-owner. Every person reading this book knows who he is. As with all the main people covered in the book, his interview is much more in depth - learning about his background etc.

I was born in France. My mum is French and my dad is Swiss. He worked for a Swiss engineering firm and was taken to the UK to work for the firm in Brentford. We lived in Sutton (Surrey) on the border of Sutton and Cheam. We spoke French at home and we are completely middle-class. We lived the French life in South London.

I went to the French Lycee – a French school – and had French education in South Kensington until I was 9 years old. My parents thought it would be better for me to have an English education, so it was hard for me to change my hand writing and I had to have extra lessons to get my 11+ exam to get in to grammar school (John Fisher in Purley).

At the age of 13, I made a friend called Andrew Crossley, who introduced me to soul music. His older sister was into jazz-funk and had records like *Bobby Caldwell - What You Won't Do For Love* etc. I was influenced by him. My school was a boys school and the tastes were primarily Punk or rock. There was only three *soul-boys*, and I was one of them! I started going to events like the *Purley All Dayer* and I was hooked.

I started buying records from a shop in Sutton market and, before long, my friend Andrew and I decided to set up a mobile-disco called G and A disco. I housed it in my parents garden shed - which previously housed my train set – and bought it on hire purchase, which my parents weren't too happy about. My Mum was dead against it, and my parents never, not once, contributed any money to my music.

Our first professional gig was an under 14's disco which we earnt £30 each, which meant that I could buy my records without doing a Saturday part-time job (I was working in a green-grocers at the time). We started to do parties all over the place, which messed up my studies as I was too focused on other things. I played rugby for the South of England and went on to play football for Surrey, and I had trials and all that, but the music took over. By the age of 16, I had a residency at The Clarets Wine Bar in Cheam.

I bought a radio transmitter with my neighbour, Ross (who was an addict of alternative radio DJ John Peel). I was into pirate-radio, so we set up one called Civic Radio. He was being 'John Peel' and I was being 'Robbie Vincent', and we recorded in the garden shed. I got my Dad interested and he'd drive us up to Epsom downs where we would hook up the transmitter. We'd wait by a near-by public telephone box, where we'd given out it's number on the broadcast. We got a couple of phone calls, which, of course, spurred us on. Then I got a connection with the pirate station *Radio Invicta*. As small as our station was, we used to attend meetings with all the other pirates and that's where I met Tony Johns - who ran Invicta. I managed to squeeze into that station. I was 17 and had just passed the driving test, and I used borrow my Mums car to drive over to Leyton [East London] at six o'clock in the morning to help put arials up and get *used* by the older guys by running errands for six months. Really, that was my apprenticeship. Eventually, I got a show on that station. That's where I heard proper jazz. There was a DJ on there called *Andy Jackson*, and I heard him play *Herbie Hancock - Shiftless Shuffle* and it blew my mind. He was the man for me: *the don of jazz*. He took it further abstract than Robbie Vincent (Radio London) or Greg Edwards (Capital). It was as important as being on Radio 1 to me. It was cool. So this was running alongside our DJ roadshow. I was also going to the *Caister Soul Weekenders*, seeing *Chris Hill* at *The Goldmine* and going to all-dayers - living the life. A small group of us formed a tribe called *The Sutton Soul Patrol*.

Other than The Claret, did you have any other residencies at the time?

I had *Christies* in Sutton, and then on Sunday I was DJ-ing at a gay club. That was a real education for me, because that was a proper discoteque. They liked me because they must have thought I was young and gay.

You had *Solos* in Croydon and *Frenchies* in Epsom…

I only did those a few times.

What about *The Jazz Junction*?

That was Darren Johnsons residency. It was Saturday lunch times at *Spats* in Oxford Street (started 30/7/83). I did it on rotation originally, and then virtually every week. It wasn't very busy but it was fucking great. Hard jazz and great dancers.

How did you meet Chris Bangs?

I used to get a bus to *Jesters* in Kingston to see him DJ. He was a big influence on me. He introduced me to the deeper side. He used to DJ with this Asian lad called *Tarun*. He had fucking amazing records: *Olli Ahvenlahti – Grandmas Rocking Chair*…….

In those days !

Well (Paul) Murphy was the man for that stuff. I don't remember anyone heavier than him. He and Tarun would be playing records like *John Serry - Just For Kicks* and *Hilary - Amazonas*…..mad Jazz Fusion. That freaked me out, plus seeing the dancers blew my mind. *Jon Lucien - Listen Love* was the anthem. When I heard that in Kingston that was *it*!

I was big into Brit Funk as well and collected all that. I've got it all. I'd go to see all those bands. I'd be one of those sad-bastards trying to shake hands with Mark King (Level 42) in the dressing room (laughs).

As well as seeing the bands and going to the Chris Hill-type gigs, I'd also go to the *Funky Fox* events at The Lyceum Ballroom.

You never saw those events advertised in *Blues And Soul* magazine.

No. Funky Fox you'd see more in *Black Echoes*. Blues And Soul was more of a suburban scene but Echoes was more urban. It was a *Blacker* scene, I was into both sides of the scene. I loved going to Essex because it was less threatening to the white-boy, but Funky Fox events were more hard.

At this point, I was buying records from Groove in Soho and Paladin (Paul Murphys second record shop), below Record Shack in Berwick Street. I was the annoying little bastard that would go in there, and they'd take the piss out of me. I always felt that Murphy wanted me to take over The Electric Ballroom because he thought I'd blow it. I thought there was a bit of "That'll show him!" Maybe not. I know that when I was on the pirate station Horizon (10/4/84), I'd read out their shop chart and half of the records didn't exist. They laughed at me a little bit – *'the over-enthusiastic kid.'*

Did you go to The Ballroom before you started there?

Once. It was a frightening experience. I was the only white person in there. It was hard core. They loved Murphy. When I first started there I was terrible (21/4/84). It was the most daunting and disillusioning DJ night I'd ever had. I was scared shitless. They were looking at me thinking: "Who are you?" Paul Murphy had gone and I'm this little white kid, and they're thinking: "What are you doing, doing 'the big mans' job?" The only reason I survived there and got through it was that the Jazz dancers couldn't get into the *Titanic* on that night - where Paul moved to. They wouldn't let Blacks in, so they came back to me. I had sleepless nights about that night. After a while, I got the tunes....

Did you do the night on your own?

I did the night on my own originally. I got there at 9pm and took my records in and I always started with *Art Blakey - A Night In Tunisia* – the *Philips* label version, which is twenty minutes long and go and get Kentucky Fried Chicken. That was my weekly ritual. There were a couple of lads called Mark and Andy from Bracknell, that were regulars that used to help me later on (19/2/85), because I'd started DJ-ing at Nicky Holloways club *The Royal Oak* once a month on Fridays, and they ended up doing every other week.

Shortly after you started at The Ballroom, you started at The Black Horse in Richmond.

That was very important to me because it was the first time that I realized I had any pull as a DJ. I was doing London gigs and pirate radio and from the first one (3/10/84), the normally empty pub was packed. It was on Sunday nights but only lasted two weeks because there was this huge fight in there, so I found this other pub down the road called *The Belvedere Arms* (8/12/84), and basically, that was a legendary mother-fucking place. It was important for me. Later, a lot of the big players in the Acid-House scene were regulars; even when Schoom (legendary Acid House club) happened. That was where the jazz-heads and the e-heads mixed together.

Why did you stop at The Ballroom?

It wasn't always good – some weeks were better than others. The Special Branch was a more happening spot, I suppose. It was more of a comfort zone too probably; there were girls there! I was doing a lot of things for Nicky Holloway that were beginning to be quite big. Another problem with The Ballroom was that the dancers had too much control. If you played the wrong record, they'd all just get off the floor, and it was just intense and uptempo music. It was pretty heavy in there and there could be violence. It'd gone as far as it could go but it was a good blooding. I got tired of the pressure. I'm a Soul Boy at heart – Caister Boy – which is why I was aligned to the whole Nicky Holloway thing; the whole 'Blues and Soul' thing.

You were doing Mambo Madness events at the same time as the Special Branch events.

These were Chris Bangs ideas. They were something special and alternative to the Special Branch sessions. We kept our independence. They were more 'jazz and jokes'. We wore silly clothes and played records by Joe Loss next to Lee Morgan. Bob Cosby was also DJ-ing on them too. He'd bring a coach from Leighton Buzzard.

When Murphy left The Wag, you DJ'd for Baz Fe Jazz and Andy Mc Connell there (Jan '86).

Sometimes I would play if Baz couldn't make it. Then I started a residency there upstairs from them (Booga Mooga – 15/7/86). Chris Sullivan liked me and wanted me to come in regularly. I brought in a slightly different crowd - more soul-heads would come from out of London I think.

What did you think about Baz? Was there much rivalry? He was very, very active in the scene.

He had very much a different crowd, in a way, didn't he? I think the crowds were quite the same except I brought in that soul boy crowd. Baz was one of my teachers - if there was rivalry, it would have come from him I think. I was just glad to be a part of it. I think Andy McConnell was probably more paranoid of me.

That was the period of the 'Absolute Beginners' film? What was your opinion of it.

I didn't bother going to see it. It meant nothing.

O.K. So your radio career: We're up to Horizon....

My parents retired to Switzerland when I was 18 - obviously, my Dad is Swiss - but they put me through Broadcasting college for a term (in Frith Street, Soho) – which I failed, ironically. I'd just left the pirate station Horizon and had started at another one called Solar. A lot of DJ's left Horizon, but the guy who ran the station – Chris Stewart – was also on the course and one day Horizons transmitter got stolen but Solar's didn't, so Chris and I had a fight over pirate radio at broadcasting college. I fell down the stairs.

The good thing about the college was that I went to Ronnie Scott's jazz club, in Soho, every night, and that was more of an education. I'd see Art Blakey, Arthur Blythe, Sun Ra, Chico Freeman......that's when I discovered jazz in a live sense. I must have seen Blakey forty times!

From doing the pirates, I got a phone call from BBC Radio London (July 86), and they wanted me to do a late night jazz show -10pm-midnight - which was a big step up for me. That was the beginning of Mad On Jazz,, which I did for years.

Didn't Radio London sponsor your original sessions at Dingwalls?

Well, what happened is, I was doing a late-night show on the station and me and two other DJ's had to find way's to fund the show, so I did these big events at The Town And Country Club in Kentish town called Jazz Bops with Chris Bangs. Also, one of the other DJ's at the station, Dave Pearce, got me in at Dingwalls. The first one had Mark Murphy live, I seem to remember. I lost the radio show but I carried on playing there. Bob Jones and Kevin Beadle originally did Dingwalls with me, and, in a rash move - trying to get more people I got Patrick Forge in (October '87), because he was on Kiss FM and had another crowd.

Did it do well straight away?

It never did badly. It went from 150 to 500. There was never a crisis.

Janine Neye was very important at Dingwalls as an....I don't know what....administrator?

A very important part, she was there from the start. I met her one week at The Belvedere in Richmond. She was great with the PR and kept it all rolling. She ran the Jazz 90 events for me too. It was great working with the DJ Sylvester on those, it was hardcore Jazz all the way. We had some great sessions. It was originally a council run-session at The Emerald Centre in Hammersmith. There was a lot going on in that whole period. I'd been doing KJAZZ,

as well as Radio London. KJAZZ was Chris Philips, Jez Nelson, Kev Beadle, Tomek and Rob Galliano. That was the main crew, with support coming from Stuart Lyons the promoter. It didn't broadcast much but it has become rather legendary - especially the day we got busted by another pirate, LWR! After that I was on Jazz FM, plus I was running BGP records with Baz Fe Jazz.

You were also doing your writing for Street Sounds magazine and the legendary Jazz Juice compilations.

They were both ran by Morgan Khan. The column and compilations were just off-beat ideas by Morgan off the back of The Ballroom and the pirate shows I was doing. I compiled the albums all by myself – original GP albums, these. They reflected what was popular on the dancefloor at the time.

What was special about Dingwalls?

We had the Jazz dancers, people from the Soul scene, musicians, post-ravers and the Camden crowd. You'd have musicians like Pharoah Sanders, Airto and Flora and even George Melly checking it out. Plus all the big DJ's would come. It was a hip place for all ages. Live-wise, we had the elements of early 'Acid Jazz'; retro-classics like Roy Ayers; Poncho Sanchez; Dave Valentin; Mongo Santamaria, to Kid Frost and Slim Gaillard and representation from the British Black jazz-scene like Courtney Pine, Julian Joseph and Steve Williamson. Other than the Jazz, Rare Groove, Jazz Funk and Boogie, towards the end we'd play Hip Hop and some Soul and House too. We'd created a scene inspired by what came before it. There were loads of people in it.

Why did Dingwalls finish (March '91)?

Because it closed down.

Did you feel that it was a good place to finish on?

No, I was gutted. I was upset. Dingwalls had an effect globally – *Giant Step* in New York admits that. Things have been different ever since, but brilliant in other ways.

We don't need to keep going on about how 'Acid Jazz' started, as it's covered in Chris Bangs interview, but as Dingwalls was the home of Acid Jazz what did you think about it all?

I loved it really. I just wasn't happy in how it got kidnapped and reinvented! The 'original nutter' was Bangsy; it was his sense of edge that created all this stuff. He also chatted-up John

Dingwalls dancefloor. Photo by Janine Neye

Godfrey at ID magazine to create a sort of 'fake story' on the subject which got printed and, as such, turned the whole movement official. Very clever. Taking a bit of the drug Ecstacy helped too!

The Cock Happy events very much represented 'Acid Jazz' didn't they?

Yes, Chris Bangs and me. They were saturday night rave-ups. The first one was at The Cock Tavern in Spitalfields market (26/3/88), then we moved to the massive Lauderdale House in North London. They were crucial parties for the time. The quintessential 'Acid Jazz' moment. This was our 'Shoom'. Those events were decadent but musical.

Simon Booth got very attached to Acid Jazz initially didn't he, and took it very serious. Was he probably reading too much into it?

Not really. He was coming from a more academic approach, but then again, what made the whole thing interesting was that different people pushed it different ways: Soul Boys/ Mods/ Trendies/ Journalists/ Film Directors. Simon was all good, and both those albums for Polydor - *Acid Jazz And Other Illicit Grooves* (Autumn '88) and *The Freedom Principle* (Spring '89) that he and I produced did really well (especially the first one) and tried to create something new. He was more in touch with the musical progression than Eddie Piller.

Eddie really brought in the 'Mod' side to the scene didn't he, and continued with the Acid Jazz record label – which you started together - after you left. It all changed quite a lot then didn't it.

The 'Acid Jazz' scene, as it had become, would have killed what we already had if it wasn't for the fact that we were so strong musically. It would have gone, because they made it very easy, attack-able music - conservative and retro, and standardized uniform. The whole approach to it was to re-invent *Mod-ism* and it was incredibly limited musically. There was no progressiveness to it.

Well, the Totally Wired compilations were progressive on Acid Jazz.

That's because I was doing them. I came up with the term because it was against *The Wire* magazine, who was always attacking our scene.

Acid Jazz became enormous very quickly.

Not really. It was a marketing term. It was a laugh. Then people started taking it for what they wanted it for. Eddie Piller's an *Ace-Face* from the Mod scene and it inspired him and others for a new beginning, but fundamentally it wasn't coming from them: they were Mods playing Jimmy Smith records. Our only connection with them and Paul Weller and all those, was Gabicci jumpers (sweaters) and Jimmy Smith records. I'm very proud of my Soul Boy background and heritage, and I'd be the first to shout about Chris Hill and Bob Jones and my other influences, and when I finally got into a position where I *could* shout about it and people would listen, the Mod thing came in from nowhere and took Acid Jazz away, and to where it went! Which is where I fucking got out and formed *Talkin' Loud* records in late '89, and made a progressive British Black music label. I love Eddie. He's a charismatic, very charming well-read man, and a friend, but these are the plain facts – black and white. The Mods kidnapped Acid Jazz, and I'm not a Mod. I'm a football-loving Soul Boy – a Casual. The reason I survived Acid Jazz was because I went beyond it. I was moving on all the time.

JANINE NEYE

If you went to any of Gilles' gigs, Janine would be something to do with it. Everyone knows her; and who could forget her with her packet of Rothmans cigarettes and pack of Diet Cokes at Dingwalls? I felt it was important to interview her to get the information from 'inside.'

Bob Jones and Kevin Beadle did Dingwalls with Gilles originally, which was great because we were all like a huge family. We did loads of gigs together and so it felt funny at first when Gilles gradually brought Patrick Forge in, because he was an outsider; which is what I think Gilles wanted – something fresh. Patrick had a show on KISS FM at the time and had his own following; a different one to ours. It was a big risk, but it paid off.

Dingwalls was very anorak-y. The people were well into their music. Gilles and myself had to walk back miles to the car after the session, he used to get such a hard time from some of the regulars: "That record that you played, three from the end – what the hell do you think you were playing that for?" He was always being slated. He was always on the edge and never the purist that they wanted him to be. He was [and still is] into introducing new music – which is a great thing, but some people just don't get it.

Dingwalls wasn't about the jazz-dancers. They made it too intense and people were sometimes too scared to dance near them incase they embarrassed themselves. The dancers were intimidating, and of course, there was always friction between *Brothers In Jazz, IDJ* and other individuals. I remember fights going off a few times, although it never stopped me from putting them on my guest list of 'one hundred'. They were part of my hardcore. Dingwalls was Gilles' first main club that he didn't inherit from *Paul Murphy*, apart from the things that he did with *The Special Branch*, which weren't his own. It was all a major part of my life and my only religion.

It probably wouldn't have existed without you.

I don't know really, it was all a part of BBC Radio London in those days because Gilles had a show on there (July 86). It was the last show of the night on tuesdays before it would switch over to the national BBC radio and there'd be fifteen of us in a deserted studio, being a part of the show and helping. One night, Gilles was playing a track by *The Last Poets* and one of the original members – *Jalal Nuriddin* – happened to be in town and phoned us to say that he was listening. Gilles asked me to run out and meet him somewhere outside Radio London and bring him back to the studio. He became a big part of our lives for the next six months. I remember having to pull Jalal and *Slim Gaillard* apart at The Wag one night. They were having a massive fight, actually over a woman decades ago! They kind of jumped on to what was happening in our scene and it certainly helped revitalize their careers, in a way, like *Roy Ayers*: He was playing at Ronnie Scotts Jazz Club for three weeks and Gilles had interviewed him for his radio show. He said to me: "I wish I'd thought to invite him to Dingwalls." Anyway, I asked Gilles what hotel he was staying at and, without Gilles knowing, I phoned him late Sunday morning and told him that Gilles said I was to pick him up and take him to the club. Because he was a bit dazed and confused from just waking up, he agreed, so I took him, his Sax player and manager there and we did this long walk to the club in this hot sunshine and walked into this dark, smelly, loud, packed and sweaty club, and he just stood there with his mouth open and said: "I've got to play here!" We arranged a secret gig, which seven hundred turned up to, and he played for three hours [and broke his Vibraphone]. It was secret because he was under contract to Ronnie Scotts and was still playing there.

Did he charge much?

More than we were used to, but no. He was just playing in little sit-down clubs in New York then – no one danced. It was a bit like what *Russ Dewbury* did with his *Brighton Jazz Bops*: He brings over these jazz artists and gives them a whole newer, younger audience and gives their career a jump-start. Some had been completely forgotten about in their own countries.

Dingwalls was the template for other clubs that saw how successful we were. We had amazing live acts – which was incredible, as we couldn't afford to pay much. We had Allan Riding selling rare jazz records out of the cloakroom and actually *Soul Jazz* records were next door to the club too.

When Dingwalls closed, you tried to continue down the road at The Underworld.

It wasn't very successful. It was impossible to recreate the vibe, and it was way too soon to recreate something like Dingwalls. It was never the same. It just didn't work.

There were other sessions connected to Dingwalls.

There was *Cock Happy*. The original gigs were at The Cock Tavern in Smithfield Market, and it was there because the licensing laws were different because it was in the Market area. I ran the door and the police tried to stop it because The Cock Tavern didn't have a dance license and you weren't allowed to charge admission either, so we had someone on the door that sent people around the corner where we would sell tickets from my car.

It was Chris Bangs' gig mainly, and it was a club where he and Gilles wouldn't be dictated to about what they had to play - by dancers, or whoever . Because Dingwalls was what it was, I think, in the end, Gilles was pressurized into playing what he did because of the people that were going there. But Cock Happy was a very relaxed gig and he and Chris would play really out-there records at Cock Happy. These gigs happened everywhere after that: From Drinking-Mens clubs in Mayfair to Lauderdale House in Hampstead. That was a beautiful old house backing on to a park. On one floor we had poetry, because people were going through a *Jack Kerouac* stage, and downstairs was Gilles and Chris.

There was also the *Jazz 90* sessions - which was my baby. They were meant to be the jazzier side of Dingwalls, with Gilles and Sylvester and very much a dancers gig.

PATRICK FORGE

For all the achievements Patrick has gone to do, everyone's first encounter of him was as a DJ on Kiss FM and as high-profile support to Gilles Peterson at the barrier-breaking Dingwalls Sunday afternoon sessions .

I'm from Ipswich originally. The first Jazz record I bought was *Tijuana Moods* by Charles Mingus – which was his favourite. I'd never really listened to Jazz before; to be honest, I'd been more into Led Zeppelin, but that album got me hooked into it and I started feeling my way through by buying magazines like Blue and Soul and seeing DJ charts. A lot of that music I knew nothing about. There was no-one to educate me, but I began to piece a collection together. I remember finding four Flora Purim albums in a second hand Fishing-tackle shop in Ipswich!!!

I moved to London, to go to college in Kingston, Surrey, and I was checking out the pirate radios and going to see Paul Murphy a lot, although I never saw him at The Electric Ballroom. I was there when he first brought Tania Maria over to play the Y.M.C.A. I walked over to his record shop (Fusions) in Berwick street [Soho] and as I was going down the stairs, I heard *Janet Lawson – So High*, and went up to the counter and said, "I've got to have this" and I spent £100 that day

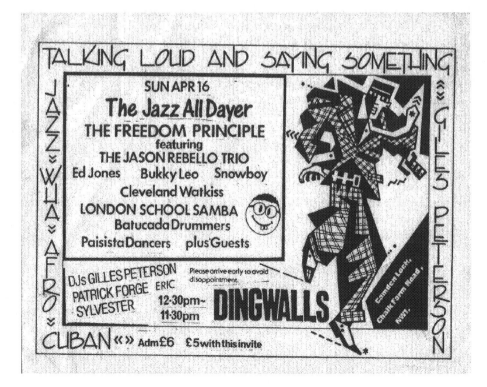

on records. That's when I started to realize that there was a scene that I could access and a shop to buy that music from as well.

When I left college, I got a 'straight job' for a while and it did my head in! I realized by then that I wasn't going to make it as a musician so I started to work in record shops. I had the passion, I had the interest, and I was meeting people and learning -from *rare-groove* to jazz, from a record shop aspect, and what was rare. In 1987 I started working in Reckless in Soho and worked with this wicked guy called Trevor XF who was a pirate DJ on LWR and Jonathon Moore from Coldcut. That's how I harangued my way into DJ-ing. Through Jonathon and Norman Jay I got an interview with Gordon Mac on the pirate station KISS. I'd just been shopping in Record And Tape Exchange and bought *Johnny Hammond - Gears* for £7 and something else and at the interview Gordon wanted to know what I had in the bag. He'd been after Gears so I sold it to him for £10 AND got a show on pirate radio at the same time!

Was your show Jazz?

Yes. I wasn't really connected to the scene and influenced by other DJ's so I was just playing what I liked.

You weren't influenced by a scene?

No. I was just working in a record shop, finding my own records, I was discovering a lot of records that people didn't know, as Reckless had a huge turnover of (second hand) records. That's how I got into DJ-ing. I was passionate about my show and I'd only listened to Gilles' show a few times so I wasn't even influenced by that but I'd stood in for Gilles at *The Royal Oak* a few times whilst he was away but I didn't know him. I'd just bumped into him a few times in record shops and nodded to him. After I'd done my show for a while, he gave me a call and asked whether I wanted to do this club with him at Dingwalls on a Sunday afternoon. Knowing the venue I thought that it wouldn't be any good, but I thought: "Oh whatever. It'll be good to do some DJ-ing. It would be nice to play some of my records", but it wasn't a big thing.

You hadn't done much DJ-ing though had you?

Fuck all. I'd done a couple of parties and a couple of gigs for KISS. But I had fuck all experience in terms of playing in clubs. Prior to Dingwalls I did understand the Jazz dance scene though: I'd seen it and felt it but I had no experience of playing to the Jazz Dancers. It was a 'baptism of fire' in a way. You learn quickly.

You were in a great position in there at Dingwalls because those first couple of hours you did, you could go as hefty as you liked, as self indulgent as you liked. I used to always get there early and I'd stand there and think: "Jesus Christ, this is really heavy" – as heavy as It'd ever been anywhere.

I was carried away with the power (laughs). I was learning, understanding and intensifying my love of jazz on all levels. I was so lucky to be there and I knew I was. I knew that there were a lot of people out there that thought: "Who the fuck are you to suddenly be in this position from nowhere?" I could see how special Dingwalls had become. There was an energy, and it was going somewhere and I don't feel that it was anything to do with me, I just felt lucky to 'get on the train' at the right time. When these things happen, you don't really have any control over it. You just have to ride the wave and I was aware of that, but at the same time, I did think I was bringing something different to this whole thing too. When I met all the people and all the other DJ's, I realized I was coming from somewhere else.

You were thrown in at the deep end with some of the greatest dancers on this planet.

You could say that. Well, at Dingwalls I did it my way, but when I guested at The Wag on a Monday in that small room of Sylvester's it was very intense and very specific – BOOM!!! These are the tunes that work, and if you strayed too far from that: pphhssstt!!!

Yes, they like to know all the breaks. They like to know all the songs and 'take them out.'

Well, I developed relationships with certain dancers at Dingwalls and Wayne James (from the Brothers In Jazz) was my focal point. Fundamentally, I was DJ-ing for him. To me, he was the most graceful, the most interpretive dancer out of all of them.

Gilles could see the potential of what was going on, and I was like that. I didn't want it to be a retro scene, and I was certainly checking out other styles of music such as Hip Hop and House as well. As passionate as I was about Dingwalls, I knew I had to have some kind of contemporary reference, but I didn't want the jazz dance scene to die. The whole *Acid Jazz* thing had eclipsed the whole thing that had led up to it. I mean, if Dingwalls was the birthplace of Acid Jazz and everything sprung up from there, then, what happened to the scene that created that? It wouldn't have happened without the jazz-dance scene; it wouldn't have happened without the dancers that had gone before. I could very much see that.

Other than the Jazz 90 sessions with Gilles and Sylvester, jazz-dance went back to the suburbs.

But the way Dingwalls worked was; that (Jazz Dance) was a big part of it. It was a freestyle session and basically, it was all working there and, if you like 'that was Acid Jazz.' Maybe a lot of people did pass through and see that, but what they went away and did was only ever play funky-Jazz, and *this* 'Acid Jazz' just became this limited funky groove music - you know: 'Student Funk.' There were none of the flavours; none of the intensity; none of the things that made Dingwalls or the jazz-dance scene interesting and so inspiring.

So how did you feel about the Acid Jazz scene?

I've always felt a bit of an outsider; always felt I was observing it a little bit. Even though I was technically in the middle of it at Dingwalls, I was never really involved in the things that were going on. I was literally the spectator to it, to the extent that I was on the roof of Gilles flat in Rotherhithe smoking a cigarette with him and Eddie Piller when they shook hands and parted company with the Acid Jazz record label. I was right in the thick of it, but I knew straight away, as soon as it started appearing in I.D. and other trendy magazines and the media started taking notice, that the music was going to get compromised.

It was a huge explosion though wasn't it?

Yes, but it was horrible going to gigs expected to be an 'Acid Jazz DJ' and not really knowing what *Acid Jazz* was to this promoter or that promoter. If I was going to play *Merry Go Round - Terumasa Hino* to a club crowd in Germany, they're all going to run off, but to me it was the madness of records like that that *was* Acid Jazz.

For all that was good and bad about it: wasn't it odd that the Mods got involved? You even had that 'Nuevo Mod' fashion shoot in The Face magazine....

The Mod scene did get involved through Eddie Piller. I think that was one more confusing factor as well. Obviously, he was bringing that attitude into the Acid Jazz label That did represent a different slant to it as well.

EDDIE PILLER

Already one of the main men from the second-generation Mod movement of the late 70's, he was also a DJ, Record Label owner, Band Manager and promoter before he and his friends discovered the Jazz Dance scene of ours in the mid-80's. He quickly got involved

and soon started the Acid Jazz record label with Gilles Peterson; which Eddie stills runs to date. Not surprising really, he was also one of the main reasons that Mods became such a part of the 'Acid Jazz Scene.' I interviewed ex- Acid Jazz label manager, Music Historian, DJ and Album Compiler Dean Rudland [also from a Mod background] about this, and James Taylor from the James Taylor Quartet. James was managed by Eddie, and from coming from the Mod scene into something quite different, he went on to be, possibly, the first established [and enormous] act in the Acid Jazz scene. His brand of authentic Hammond Organ-led Funk is the sound that most people still associate, world-wide, as Acid Jazz. Finally, I interview Rob Gallagher, who, as Galliano, was the artist on the very first record on Acid Jazz Records. Eddie, how did the Mod element come in to the Jazz Dance scene?

British youth-cultures of the late 1970's – as it turned into the early 1980's, you had Punks, Teddy Boys, Rockabillies, Soul Boys and Mods. By 1983, they'd all hit a brick wall. I don't know why, but there was a certain core of each of these scenes that were into the clothes, the music and the style and I was *that* in the Mod scene. I ran a fanzine, a record label, I was a promoter, I did all-dayers and I was one of the top three DJ's in that scene. I found the scene restrictive; a lot of people with tunnel-vision. I wanted to play different styles of sixties music but the crowd were too selective. I had this club at *Corks* in London called *Voice Your Choice* with a guy called John Cook. We played proper sixties soul and jazz and the Mods hated it. I felt that I'd hit a cul-de-sac because I'd discovered *Miles Davis-Milestones* and realized that *Mod* was more than what was being played on the scene. I made a conscientious effort to leave it and by 1985 I'd started getting into the *Special Branch* at The Royal Oak. Nicky Holloways club had a jazz-room upstairs with Bob Cosby and the other DJ's like Kevin Beadle and Gilles Peterson, and there was great looking women in there! Musically, it was soul music from artists like Tyrone Davis to Miles Davis – what the Mod scene should be all about. Me and about ten friends stepped over into that scene.

Well, they played Latin Boogaloo as well, I guess, but I couldn't imagine you liking Jazz Fusion.

No, I didn't, but I didn't like all the music that was played in the Mod scene either. I was into Jimmy Smith, Jimmy McGriff, Jack McDuff....the Mod organists, and I was hearing all those in the Jazz Room too; songs that I knew, or I felt should be played, in the Mod scene like *Tony Middleton [or Chuito and The Latin Uniques] – Spanish Maiden or Joe Bataan-Subway Joe*.

We'd found ourselves in this scene and there were no Mods in it. The organist – *James Taylor*- was in a big Mod band called *The Prisoners* at the time, and I told him about this scene and suggested that he forms an Organ quartet, and we recorded this record called *Blow Up*. Gilles didn't necessarily like it, but understood it, and gradually, we became a part of the scene and I thought "This is where I belong. I can still be a Mod but still dig this music," and that's how the Mod connection came in. Remember that the 60's *Prestige*-label organ-jazz sound had taken over from the Bop and Bossa in the Jazz Dance scene which coincided with me blundering into it with Gilles and Paul Murphy. It was music for *us*. I'd already seen Murphy from when he was playing jazz at *The Purple Pit* at The Electric Ballroom. The crowd was at least 50% Mod. It was perfect for us.

By 1986, we were a part of the *Special Branch* scene and by '87 I was a DJ on that scene. By the end of that year, Gilles and I started the *Acid Jazz* record label. I already had the know-how because I used to have a record label. Gilles didn't know, but he knew tons of people in the scene. We signed acts individually; rarely together, with the exception of *Bukky Leo*. We were never a team but we were hustling two different sides of the scene together.

The first record released was a 7 inch single by *Galliano – Frederick Lies Still.* Rob (Galliano) just added this ranting *rap* over a break from a *Pucho* record, and it cost us £35 to make. We did a scam where we made out we'd discovered this New York rapper, and it got great reviews. It sold 500 on 7 inch in the first week and 2,000 in the following week on 12inch. It sold about 20,000 altogether.

Not bad for a joke. We can't talk about Acid Jazz without talking about *Dingwalls*.

Well, we talk about Gilles and Murphy, but to me, Nicky Holloway was the main man, because of his Special Branch events at The Royal Oak . You'd have Soul, House, Electro and, of course a jazz room. It was the same at Dingwalls and the other satellite sessions like *Cock Happy* and *Mambo Madness*. Remember, Gilles was one of the Special Branch DJ's and so was Chris Bangs; who was omnipresent and Gilles' guru . Again, it was the same crowd at Chris' *Bournemouth weekenders* as the Special Branch events like the *Do's At The Zoo*. He was very influential.

And he invented the term *Acid Jazz.*

Yes. The first Acid Jazz record was *James Brown - In The Middle*.

No, it was *Mickey and The Soul Generation-Iron Leg.*

Which was a Mod record....

Eh? It's a *rare-groove* record.

Well, o.k. But that's where all these scenes came together in that year: Mod, Rare Groove, Northern and Modern Soul, Boogie and Jazz. They all metamorphasised into *Acid Jazz* by the end of '87 - which was a reaction against House music. All the Black music scenes found themselves disestablished, with nowhere to go. Famous House music DJ's like Judge Jules and Roy The Roach came from the rare-groove scene. It wasn't until our big Special Branch trip out to Ibiza in 1987 that the split came where half the crowd went to *Coup* and got all pilled-up with Ecstacy and came back saying that they'd "seen the future." When we came back, the scene had split in to two. There was House music and there was *us*.

Anyway, back to the record label....

After Gilles left to start *Talkin' Loud* records, I felt that I got a hard time from the Jazz Dance scene. I felt that they were a bit snobby because Gilles wasn't involved anymore and that Acid Jazz was a bad thing – which it may well have been. We did a lot of excellent records that didn't get a lot of reviews, and that was in ten years of being one of the biggest jazz-soul labels in the World. Why that is? I don't know. It may be because people felt that they had to take sides between our labels – which they did, because they thought there was a lot of rivalry between me and Gilles. There wasn't, but people took sides and I found myself – and people associated with me – losing gigs.

I think that the Jazz Dance scene, as I'd originally known it, was over by 1991 and by then the Acid Jazz scene had grown to such an extent that it encompassed so many styles of music that no specific scene felt comfortable within it. Jazz was just 10% of the output. By becoming an umbrella and encompassing anything from De La Soul to Art Blakey, it was too broad a church to keep everybody interested and the jazz scene felt un-catered for and went back underground.

DEAN RUDLAND

I never understood how the Mod's influence came into our scene.

Many ways. The film 'Absolute Beginners' would have attracted some with its Mod imagery, and Paul Murphy's club *The Purple Pussycat* in East Finchley – which was more like a speakeasy – and he played more Mod R&B there. The other club of Paul's at the time was *The Purple Pit* at The Electric Ballroom - but that was very cavernous. We were used to the Mod scene of 'nothing before 1960 or after 67', so this was all very fresh to us. This was a scene in a proper club with a DJ that is *that* good. It was exciting. It let a lot of Mod's into a whole other scene. There was a group of Mod's discovering records there and bringing them back into their scene.

There was definitely a small crowd of Mods that'd always be at clubs like The Wag. You'd see Eddie Piller there or Tommy Chase standing there in his smart three button Italian suit. There were too many conservative people in the Mod scene that wouldn't accept the stuff that we were hearing and bringing back. There was a group determined to get into it (Jazz) and I was one of them.

The beginning of the *Acid Jazz* scene has been well covered here, but, in your opinion, happened to it in the end?

The broadness of the styles of music in the Acid Jazz scene was its downfall in the end. It got too widely spread. What killed it in the end was that it was too big and the people coming in to the scene had no real depth of knowledge. While I knew that sounds elitist, if you have a cultured scene with roots, whether it be from the Jazz scene, Rare Groove, Mod or whatever, it was still roots. To people that got into it through seeing *The Young Disciples, Brand New Heavies* or *The James Taylor Quartet*, they just thought it was good music and a good night out, the scene then just had no foundation.

JAMES TAYLOR of THE JAMES TAYLOR QUARTET

Even at the time when we did the last *Prisoners* album up in Hoxton square, we were listening to a lot of James Brown Hammond Funk Instrumentals, even though we were originally a 'Small Faces' type band – even thy did some funky Hammond instrumentals. When the band died a natural death and split up, it seemed natural to record some Hammond instrumentals. We recorded a *Herbie Hancock* track *Blow Up* and *One Mint Julep* and unwittingly positioned ourselves somewhere that was the coming together of lots of different worlds. It was surprising, we didn't expect anyone to be vaguely interested in it. We did it for ourselves. On the contrary, it got interest from Eddie Piller, and Gilles Peterson but also John Peel – who championed that record. We had Indie/ Alternative music fans to the Jazz Dance crowds to Mods, old Prisoner fans and after struggling for years with the Prisoners, we became successful with the James Taylor Quartet immediately. It reared up and stayed there.

You coincided with our scene, which was playing a lot of Prestige and Blue Note label funky Hammond Jazz.

I had no idea there was a scene for that kind of music. Gilles wasn't into Blow Up at first. He played it on his show but was a bit mocking of it, but when we started playing at The Wag he got into us. He started recommending records to listen to. When we got signed to Polydor he was very much there, at all the meetings. He came along - and Simon Booth of course - when we made the first album.

Our scene must have seemed strange to you at first.

When I heard DJ's playing fast Be-Bop at The Wag, I wondered what the hell I was doing there, as we have nothing to do with that. I don't think that crowd liked us at first but the gigs were packed anyway with our following. After a few more times, we got what they wanted. We were way too 'indie' at first. All our gigs were sold out for a long time, everywhere, and we were getting great press - even in the rock press like NME. I suppose with Paul Weller also on Polydor they were used to punting 60's influenced acts.In terms of fashion, we were in the right place at the right time. People were saying, "This is the next big thing." It was front cover of The Face, front cover of I.D. It was very exciting. We were swept along.

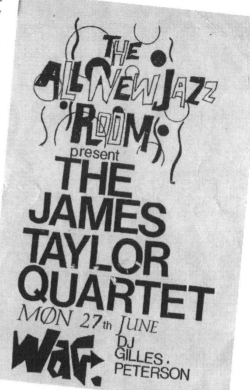

One of the key adventures was a trip we did to Nice Jazz Festival. It was Gilles, me, Eddie Piller, Jez Nelson, Chris Phillips and all that crowd. It crystalised something. That was the coming together of a lot of different worlds. It was a lot of disparate, fragmented things all getting on. Everyone had their own sort of pocket to get on with, and *there* it came together. There Gilles really had ideas for the way forward for J.T.Q – him and Eddie. He convinced me of a way to go forward. They were trying to give me confidence to reach out further. It felt strange but exciting. The result was 'The Theme From Starsky And Hutch.'

How did you feel about the 'Acid Jazz' explosion?

Out of my depth, but ambitious. I did feel though too that something that started out so pure, and organic, ended up in nepotism – friends getting signed to labels. That *Dingwalls* thing really exploded too. That was packed solid, but something happened: With all this coming together of different worlds there was a collision and everything split and fragmented. Within six months no one was speaking to each other and we tried to distance ourselves from that.

Rob and Bob Jones

GALLIANO - ROB GALLAGHER
aka ROBERTO GALLIANO

My poetry all comes from an English teacher at school - Mr Katz. He thought, "How am I going to lure them in?" and he did through lyrics. We'd study Paul Weller lyrics and then we'd study Linton Kwesi-Johnson's, so you've got the Dub-poets, then you've got the Liverpool poets, and suddenly - poetry is cool!! We all started writing lyrics.

I knew you at Dingwalls and all of a sudden one week I saw you up at the decks with Gilles Peterson, kind of ranting over the mic. Was it poetry or narrative?

God knows what it was. I was having lessons with *Jalal* from *The Last Poets*. I was trying to find my own voice. It was a very obscure time. I grew up in the tradition of *Philip Levi* and *Lone Ranger*…

They were (Reggae) Toasters weren't they?

Exactly. I was trying to find a way in and try things. The ranting was probably because I was nervous. Jalal said, "Don't copy. Find your own voice" and I tried not to be American. Find my own style. Some of it sounds terrible. I'm sure, over the mic, it sounded horrific; especially in a club and some people are trying to dance and you're doing a Last Poets impression. But I was learning.

Was Jalal influencing your politics?

No. It was the 80's. It was 'Thatcher - Are you with her or against her?' I was 'left of the left'. At the time of the Miners strike I'd be going to clubs and going from there to strikes. I was just coming off a Sociology Race degree so I was a pain in the arse. You can imagine: Straight from college with all these firmly *left* ideas. It was a magnificently naïve time.

Did Jalal encourage you to take to the mic?

No. I was picking up the mic and doing things way back at *The Belevedere* with Gilles, but I had reams of poetry that I'd show him for his opinion.

How did the first single come about?

I'd been doing my rhymes over tunes at Gilles' gigs, like, by *Funk Inc* and *Pucho* – *Freddies Dead* and Eddie Piller said, "Why don't you record that?" I wasn't embarking on a musical career or anything, Eddie said he knew how to make records, so next thing we're in the studio. It all seemed a laugh at the time. Next thing you know I'm doing an interview for The Face magazine. I was intensely embarrassed by the single: I'm a Soul boy growing up listening to Curtis Mayfield and then I've got to listen to myself ranting on the radio. I was proud of the single and embarrassed by it at the same time.

It was a massive success. Where were you going with it?

There were absolutely no plans at all.

You did a few other tracks as well didn't you? Such as guesting on Six Sharp Fists - The Jazz Renegades and Starsky And Hutch - The James Taylor Quartet and others, but when did 'Galliano - the solo artist' become 'Galliano – the band?'

As far as I remember, when Gilles left Acid Jazz records and started Talkin' Loud at Polygram he just offered me a deal. It dawned on me that we would have to get some sort of a live thing happening.

You got a major record deal and you didn't even have a project!

It didn't occur to me that it was a major deal. It just seemed like Gilles' label and that was it. I didn't really know what I was doing but neither did Gilles at first. It was all new. The drummer Steve White helped put some of the band together. I don't know whether a lot of it worked musically, but creatively it all led to the first album. We thought we'd made a Last Poets album, but in fact we'd made a Pop album.

STEVE BAKER

Not only was (and is) Steve, Simon Booth's manager from Working Week, he also oversaw all the original Acid Jazz projects on Polydor – 'Acid Jazz And Other Illicit Grooves' and 'The Freedom Principle.' He watched it all unfold and develop.

Frederick Lies Still by *Galliano* was obviously the first Acid Jazz single and there was nothing else like it. It was in a zone of it's own and it was from that that the idea of a compilation album on Urban/Polydor came about. It was called *Acid Jazz And Other Illicit Grooves* (1988) - which was a groundbreaking album, and there was obviously a market for it.

The key thing was that it was live musicians and raw talent (like DJ's) that could put a track together; *Chris Bangs* would be at the centre of that. Obviously, I was managing *Working Week* before all this from that 83/84 period, when another wave of bands came through commercially, like *Sade* etc…it was the classic major label requirement of needing a hit. This would have been the case here too, with these bands.

I was attracted to the fresh, almost naïve, approach to the Acid Jazz scene. It was original, a niche, trendy, fashionable scene and pretty unique. Acid Jazz and other Illicit Grooves sold 40,000 in the UK. alone in the first month. It was a completely underground market. It was quickly followed by the album *The Freedom Principle*, and already, between the first and second albums, the music had started to change as the musicians grew and developed and branched off.

Vocalist Cleveland Watkiss' manager, Saxophonist Steve Williamsons manager and me representing Working Week (and I was looking at Galliano too) had an idea of putting together a label, and it would be produced essentially by Gilles Peterson and Simon Booth. It was a naïve idea to take to a label, especially as they had the rights to an album that had just sold 40,000 in a month! We were just trying to keep control, and keep it underground. They obviously thought: "Hang on a minute, why do we need producers and managers when we can just sign them anyway?" They already had the *James Taylor Quartet* anyway, but they signed Cleveland and Steve. They took what was the easiest option, but I felt that the musicians that were the core and the raw talent remained unsigned. Gilles went and formed Acid Jazz label with Eddie Piller and the scene just grew and grew. Gilles took a lot of the talent around him to Polygram with his label *Talkin' Loud*, when he split with Eddie. He signed *Incognito, Young Disciples, Urban Species* and Galliano – who'd probably never even been into a recording studio before. Once they got them, they weren't sure what to do with them. The label had everything: the bands, artwork by *Swifty*; the *Straight No Chaser* magazine behind them but Polygram didn't 'get it.' They thought they could take it and channel it through the system they had in place,

It wasn't even a country-wide scene, it was probably mainly London and home counties.
Exactly. 80% would have just been in London. We couldn't even get acts or agents for a few years. It was always going to be hard taking an underground scene and crossing it over through a major label and a corporate structure that exists there. Gilles did it well because he made that label his rather than it being part of a major label.

JOE DAVIS

Now, the owner of progressive Brazillian record label *Far Out*, Joe came into the London scene at a ridiculously young age in the early 80's. Not only was he an obsessive jazz collector, through his many, many record-finding trips to Brazil, he single-handedly instigated and fuelled a fevered movement within our scene of playing rare 60's and 70's Brazilian music in the late 80's. Of course, Brazilian music was played before in the scene, but nowhere to this level – because of the absurd amount of original [and expensive!] records he was discovering over there.

As a kid I used to listen to Robbie Vincent's radio show from ''77 to '82, or whatever, and I heard Gilles on the pirate station Invicta playing an hour of hard Jazz. It was eye opening.

We had a disco on Wednesdays round our way called Cranford Community Hall, and the music was amazing: *Ingram – Mi Sabrina Tequana, Eddie Russ– Zaius, Manfredo Fest –Jungle Kitten*….. and there was this incredible dancer called Milton McAlpine who I was really close with. It was a teenagers club, I was only 12, and to be exposed to all that music and dancing was incredible. I'd play football in Brentford and we'd all go in there afterwards. A few of the older football players used to go to The Ballroom and that's how I got to know Murphy.

I went to The Horseshoe and The Electric Ballroom a few

Joe with legendary dancer Paul 'Tjader' Haran

times but I shit my trousers; it was very rough. I saw Murphy at *The Wag* and he was playing a different sound than at The Ballroom. It was a cool, trendy, Mod-y, kind of R&B Soul Jazz vibe – a lot of Blue Notes. I was obsessed with that place. I was only 14 and I'd sneak out to go there at 9 o'clock and get a night bus back, I thought: "What the fuck is going on here?"

Cranford was coming to an end and I got to know Gilles. I'd go ice-skating in Richmond on Sundays and that's where his Belvedere residency was, so I'd go there. He played killer stuff. He was doing the Ballroom then, but I still wouldn't go because it was too edgy.

When I was still at school I'd go to Sol Y Sombre on Friday nights. I'd always get there early and I'd stand by Murphy all night, and he'd get me drinks and cigarettes all night, and he was so kind to me. He'd play a lot of Salsa - well whatever he played it would groove.

After Murphy at The Wag, Baz Fe Jazz and Andy McConnell took over with Gilles Peterson upstairs. Andy left so I took his place. Even though I was 15 I'd built up an amazing collection of records from Murphys shop and everywhere. I had big contacts in Brazil too. I was deep into the Fusion and old Blue Note. I lasted seven or eight months but we got kicked out for some reason. I supported it every week still though.

In '86, when I was just 17, I went to Brazil for the first time. There was just tons of records everywhere. I was going there every year and by '89 it was huge over here.

You were the only one bringing it over.

Then yes. The only one for a few years. It was great because in the end I was DJ-ing everywhere and even selling a bag of records while I was there too. From '91 was going there eight or nine times a year. In the end I'd discovered almost everything there was, and by '93 I'd burnt myself out traveling to Brazil and DJ-ing all over the world. Also in '91 I'd just started my record label Far Out', which released House music originally. People just thought of me as a 'record dealer' – which is a poor accolade, as I thought I'd achieved more than that, so I started the label.

Your Brazilian albums didn't make an impression at Dingwalls did they – or perhaps toward the end – because you hadn't started that craze until the late '80's. Dingwalls up to that point, was more Alan Riding and Hugh Albert driven, record-dealer wise.

That's true. My contribution was just that bit after. Dingwalls was so important for shaping the scene then. When it first started, Gilles had me, Sylvester, Bob Jones and Kevin Beadle programmed in to play in rotation and the first four didn't go so well. Just after, they refurbished it and started that session again and that's when it was just Kevin and Bob with Gilles. It was originally intended to be a really heavy Jazz Dance session but developed into something else. It was exciting. Until then, it'd still been that home counties, surburban scene – even *The Special Branch* was like that.

Even Paul Murphy was from Essex.

That's right - *The Don*. But Gilles had a way of pulling it altogether and making it a London thing.

What did you think of Acid Jazz?

I didn't like the new stuff – all this Funky Jazz. I was more into fucking House and Techno by then, to be honest. I found it far more progressive and experimental. It's partly one reason I didn't go to Dingwalls that much – I couldn't stand what was getting played. I found it more exciting going to certain House nights - although still really being into Jazz and Brazilian, and everything, I seriously hooked into New York House music, but it was the same time the Brazilian thing took off for me, so there was a lot of energy flying around.

MARK JONES

Not one of the main sessions, The Shack was running at the same period as Dingwalls (in the evening), and had a loyal following of Jazz dancers. Through working at Percy Prescod's Blue Monk second-hand Jazz shop in North London, Mark amassed an enviable collection and knowledge.

I used to go to Crackers, The Goldmine, Swan And Sugarloaf and all those, and got into Jazz Fusion from there. Although I started to DJ in '82, it wasn't until I read the first issue of Straight No Chaser magazine that I felt it would be possible to play a night of Jazz based music. There came a time when all I wanted to play was just Jazz. I was told this club - *The Shack* nee-Violets in Tisbury Court, Soho, was going to open so I had an interview and got in. I did four days in the week playing Be Bop in between band's that were playing there, and the Sunday night was our straight ahead Jazz Dance night.

Was it a heavy selection?

Totally Latin and Fusion. I remember playing *Trudy Pitts – Love For Sale; Har-You Percussion – Welcome To The Party; Art Farmer – Mau Mau; Ursula Dudziak – Night In Tunisia* for example. Des Antoine, who I DJ'd with, was a real addict, really on top of it. The night wasn't influenced by Dingwalls at all, it was more for the dancers. Gilles used to come in occasionally. There were times when we had thirty five or forty dancers there and you just wished you could have captured it on film. It ran for a year and a half from '88 -'89. I was lucky because I was working at the second hand Jazz shop 'Blue Monk' for Percy Prescod at the time, and had access to so many great Jazz records. Most of the DJ's and dealers used to go there. I used to go over to the US on buying trips with Percy too.

PAUL BRADSHAW – 'STRAIGHT NO CHASER' MAGAZINE

Forming the magazine after the lack of support for the scene from The Wire magazine, where he worked, this magazine immediately became absolutely essential documentation of any-and-all Jazz related, and has always given the most massive support and priority to the Jazz Dance movement. It still runs today.

I was a free-lance writer from as early as 1976. I was predominantly writing about Reggae but I was into Jazz as well; more the Avant-Garde stuff. My Dad was into Jazz as a kid, from pre-war days. He had a very open-minded and open-ended taste, he didn't just stay with Swing all of his life . When I was 17, he was buying John Coltrane albums from *Barrys* in Manchester for peanuts because Trane's albums didn't really sell. They were too far out. He'd listen to everything from *Bob Crosby's Bobcats* to *Dizzy Gillespie* and all those Blue Note and Impulse records: *Ornette Coleman, Coltrane, Cecil Taylor,* everything.

You were brought up in that environment.

Yeah. I went to Art College in 1968 and started hearing about *Sun Ra, Rahsaan Roland Kirk* .....and that kind of spun me round and made me realize what a hip record collection my Dad had. I was into Soul and Funk at the same time and me and my brother, Keith, also used to go to Northern Soul clubs like *The Twisted Wheel* and, later, *Blackpool Mecca* – I'm from just outside Manchester. The early '70's were amazing for music and people were more open-minded: someone who liked Jazz-Fusion would probably like *Parliament* too. Somehow, all these different forms of black music fitted together. *Black Music And Jazz Review* was my Bible and really not that different than *Straight No Chaser*: African music, big articles on Jazz, deep pieces on Fusion, Reggae, Little Beaver next to Bob Marley, and it helped me form my views about music at the time.

When I was at Art College in Cheltenham I was hanging around with people from the Northern Soul scene, traveling to loads of clubs around the country and I was collecting a bit of it as well. When I moved to London, I got deep into Reggae but at the same time I was checking out the Free-Jazz sessions at The Seven Dials in Covent Garden on Thursdays. Towards the end of the 70's I got to know Neil Spencer. He was the editor of NME *(New Musical Express)* which was hugely influential at the time. I started writing a little bit for them. We were both into Reggae, Soul, Jazz, Funk and I was interested in the underground club-culture side of things . You had people getting interested in jazz but it was also to do with the post-Blitz thing (famous New Romantic club) and The Wag, with the zoot-suits and all that, but the first time that I heard of Paul Murphy was seeing a chart for The Electric Ballroom in NME. It was pure jazz and I thought: "Fucking Hell. This is like no club-chart I've ever come across". The place blew me away. It was so intense, I thought "What's going on here?" It was the most important thing happening in London and I started getting more involved with it. I didn't think that the publicity that the scene was getting was good enough for what it was. Murphy was the King-of-the-scene. He was suited up, had the Gerry Mulligan crop and looked the business *and* he was dropping the tunes.

When Murphy left The Ballroom and moved to The Wag (and Sol Y Sombre), the scene moved up a gear. It wasn't musically intense like The Ballroom but everything was in place: he put on live acts like *Tommy Chase* and The Wag was a stylish place that had a lot of media interest. *The Face* magazine took a lot of interest and record companies started paying attention and reissuing the Blue Note catalogue and Murphy was doing some compilations.

Things really started to change.

Yeah. You had the film director Julian Temple checking out The Wag, and hooking that into Colin McInnes' book *Absolute Beginners* was an easy idea, although I don't think it was a great film.

It was terrible.

Whether it was good or not, publicity-wise it did kick it off. It kind of lifted everything up to a different angle: the film premiering in Japan and all the publicity that surrounded it and, live wise, *Working Week* with the IDJ dancers was very potent, and the Be-Bop of Tommy Chase. Slim Gaillard was a regular at The Wag and, infact, around the time of the film I remember seeing *Gil Evans* at the bar there, which blew my mind . Roy Carr at NME was getting us to do free jazz compilations with the paper, with all that stuff from Blues-Honkers and Shouters to Be-Bop and stuff by Babs Gonzales and all that hip stuff which kept The Face interested and reflected a lot of the music playing at The Wag. There was so much going on: the illegal warehouse parties – which was the first time there was a democracy in clubbing here, as there was no door-policy.

And the *Special Branch* scene.

Yes. Anyone that was going to be a key player from that whole suburban soul scene was there. They were *all* there. They all played there.

There was such a merging of so many scenes then. It was all coming together - from Jazz to *Def Jam* Hip Hop, Washington Go-Go, Rare Groove, and from Northern Soul to *Grandmaster Flash*. It was about this time (1986) that I started writing for the jazz magazine The Wire. The editor, Richard Cook, was into Coltrane, free-jazz, and all that type of thing, and I wasn't adverse to that; I was well into all that and wrote about it, but I was given a column where I was writing about the Jazz Dance scene. Basically, I thought it was a waste of time in the end because Richard didn't believe that people should dance to jazz. I told him that he was being ridiculous. What did people do to Duke Ellington at The Savoy Ballroom? Sit down? All the great dance styles came out of jazz. I hung out with Paul Murphy, Gilles Peterson, Baz Fe Jazz and all those people, and I knew what the plan was.

Previously, you had Paul Murphy and Dean Hulme's record shop (Fusions) selling different jazz than you would get in a normal jazz record shop, and I got interested in the Brazilian music through there and I started to listen to Blue Note records in a different way. For me, it was a great education in that period. The Blue Note reissues were causing interest, the 'Absolute Beginners' film was causing another kind of interest, you had the emergence of (saxophonist) Courtney Pine and The Jazz Warriors….but the jazz establishment didn't like what was happening, and to me, that made it *more* exciting .

I always saw Courtney, Jazz Warriors and Steve Williamson as peripheral to our scene at the time. I read about them and was aware of them, but it wasn't until Dingwalls that I saw them all involved.

Of course they got involved. It was what was happening. They were hanging out there to feel the vibes. *You* played Congas on my Straight No Chaser benefit there; you had Jason Robello, Julian Joseph, Ike Leo, Bukky Leo, Courtney, Steve Williamson all playing on that. The live dimension was fucking amazing there: Poncho Sanchez, Roy Ayers, Mongo Santamaria, Dave Valentin – he said that was his best ever gig. It was a complete experience.

When did *Straight No Chaser* start?

Around the summer of 1988. It came out of writing for The Wire and thinking that no-one is representing the Jazz Dance scene. There was not a proper voice. People should read about IDJ and The Jazz Defektors on one hand, and also read about African music and other stuff.

World Jazz-Jive was the style you called it. You also used the (Acid Jazz) slogan The Freedom Principle.

With 'The Freedom Principle,' everything is possible. The first issues of the magazine we put together was in the basement of Sterns (African) record shop in Stuart Lyons office.

I think the pirate radio station KJAZZ was an important coming-together of people. That was when the magazine first started. Gilles was a force on KJAZZ, even though he couldn't be seen to be connected because he had a show on BBC Radio London then. He was a motivator. It brought together Kevin Beadle, Bob Jones, Jez Nelson, Chris Phillips and Wilbur Wilberforce on one side, and on the other you had me and Sue Steward and Simon Emmerson (Simon Booth from Working Week). Every one came from different perspectives, and it was these perspectives that became influential in shaping the magazine. You couldn't do a mag that was about what was going on at Dingwalls and sustain it; you had to make it broader, but at the same time, you could do it so it fed the community. Right from the beginning it had to be a voice for the community. We said, "Fuck The Wire. We're not critics", and they hated that. We were noticing that DJ culture was becoming a serious reality.

I felt awkward around then though, because politics started to come into the scene; not club-politics but World politics.

I felt that. At Dingwalls, as the music policy changed, peoples consciousness was changing. Dingwalls reflected the open door attitude of the warehouse parties, the impact of Rare Groove and of course Rave. You had Gilles and others getting politically aware and then changing the music. It was 60/40 Black to White crowd and a tune like Pharaoh Sanders' You Got To Have Freedom, that was felt by everybody in the club. The politics were organic. I think that there were people in the middle of it all that felt that they had to know about politics, about the Black and White politics in London. Gilles, Galliano, the Young Disciples were hanging around with Jalal from The Last Poets, who was radical. He was very influential.

At Dingwalls, as the crowd changed, the music shifted. You would start to hear Branford Marsalis' Fight The Power and A Tribe Called Quest in the mix – which was right. I remember Sue Steward bringing *Jonathon Rudnick* from New York down there. He couldn't believe what was happening. He was doing a world-music night at S.O.B's in Manhattan and after the Dingwalls experience he decided to set up a night called *Giant Step*.

IDJ's first show at the Camden Jazz Festival 1984. Photo by Nick White

THE DANCERS

Of all the names of the most influential dancers in the 70's, the ones that came up time and time and time again were *Trevor Shakes* and *Paul Anderson*. Trevor told me, that, in order to understand where he comes from, I need to speak to the (main) dancers that influenced him – Travis Edwards, Leon Herbert and Dez Parkes. The reason I have gone into so much depth here is that Trevor and Paul (and of course the multitude of others name-checked) were the inspiration to the dancers that developed the London *Fusion* style of dancing that swept the country in the 80's. Like it or not, the Fusion style was, initially, the most important dance innovation in the UK in the movement that this book is all about – British Jazz Dance.

TRAVIS EDWARDS

Who were the rated dancers when you first started going out?

Firstly, there wasn't any clubs. It was parties or 'blues parties.' All clubs played Rock and I went to one in Goodmayes, Ilford called *The Lacy Lady* around '72, with the DJ called *Gulliver*. Again, it was all Rock. I started bringing some records down by James Brown and some Motown and he'd play them and I'd dance. I started telling my friends and it spread. People were coming from all over London and Southend – everywhere. I'd go and dance there and there'd always be someone there to try and battle me, but I liked it. I'd take care of them.

Who did you see that would influence you?

Those black and white films with Fred Astaire and the Nicholas Brothers, and we'd go to Soho and watch the Kung Fu films and get moves from those. That'd all get incorporated. James Brown too.

Lacy was high fashion. That's where the Punky Soul Boy look came from.

Yes. I used to make all my own clothes, and also for other people to wear on a Saturday. I made quite a bit of money (laughs).

Was there a period when you knew you were rated?

I was a rated dancer from when I first started going out.

What other clubs were you going to?

I went to *A-Train* in Mile End (London), which was a dangerous club. Different areas of London would come in and you knew there'd be a battle. A 'shuffling' battle.....

That's a Reggae dance.

We come from the Reggae. There'd be shuffling and dropping moves and kicking each other, then the loser would get upset and then there's a big fight., then it goes out in the street (laughs)....

LEON HERBERT

When I was 13 or 14 I'd go to reggae clubs like *A-Train* in Mile End Road, East London. I would get involved in 'shuffling' competitions and they could get very rough. People would come from all over London. I would throw my handkerchief into the circle and start battling.

Why do people throw handkerchiefs in?

Because you do things with them, like pick it up with your foot or flip it over your back, In a battle some challengers would get agitated and kick or push or fight. I remember once when someone lost, knives came out, then a machete, a sword. It was dangerous. I'm glad I distanced myself from that scene.

How did you meet Travis Edwards?

I first met him at a house party: we danced against each other all night. He was more of a funk dancer and very acrobatic – somersaults into splits, I was more 'boogie,' I couldn't do what he did but there was a mutual respect. I never saw him again until upstairs at *Ronnie Scotts*, where all the dancers went.

One night I found out I was being searched for all over London by a dancer called *Trevor Shakes*. I was considered the King - although I didn't know it - and many people wanted to battle me, but this guy was persevering. Everywhere I went I heard that he was looking for me and one Tuesday I went to this gay night at the Kennington Oval. I'm not gay, but I liked those clubs: great music, great fashion, great dancers and lots of women. Trevor walked in with his friend Greg Craig (brother of Mikey Craig from the band *Culture Club*) and started dancing. I just sat there and watched it. It was like watching me. He'd studied me so hard, he was good and I told him there was no need to challenge; I like what he does. We became close friends and I took him under my wing and showed him steps: I took him to clubs like *Monkberrys* and *Sombrero*. Quite soon I became in awe of him, He became my equal.

I was the king of Ronnie Scotts, but I had competition there with this White guy called *Mark White* - who was more 'James Brown-style.' No one could take me though, because they couldn't get to me. They'd have to talk to Trevor first who I'd taught all my moves to. There was no club in London that didn't know us.

The dance group 'Torso' has already been covered elsewhere (Trevor Shakes interview), but what was your involvement?

I took care of the 'Mark 2' line up. I'd teach all these young guys my moves, took them under my wing. There was about twenty of them and if we heard that people wanted to challenge us, I'd send the boys to deal with them. They weren't going to get to us.

Like Travis, I started to travel and to model with him and Trevor, and we'd always be bringing back new moves and fashions. We had to be one step ahead. We were so influential that between us three, there wasn't a move in London that didn't come from us at that time.

What did you think of the new *Fusion* style in the early 80's?

I admired all those dancers. I would just watch. That was a whole big movement. That's where Paul Anderson comes in. He was a big influence to those dancers. When our time was up and we moved on, Paul took over as The King.

DEZ PARKES

Being Afro-Carribean, music is our life. We don't discover the music like someone would here in the U.K - get into Motown or something, and progress from there - it's always around from day one. We were doing what they term as Jazz Dance now in the 70's. The rated dancers then were *Travis Edwards, Leon Herbert, Foxy, Lincoln Reiss, Tall Scotty, Donald Peters, Johnny Mitchell, Jabber, Paul Anderson*.... We traveled all over battling. We went to clubs like the Whisky A Go Go, Columbos (In Carnaby St), Upstairs at Ronnie Scotts – which was THE place, and don't let anyone tell you different - Trafalgar (In Kings Rd), all the 'Bird's Nest's: Wanstead, West Kensington, Waterloo, King Georges pub in Harrow, Room At The Top and Lacy Lady in Ilford, The Goldmine, Crackers – which was more underground than those last places, and the music in the Gay clubs was amazing too. We'd go into a club and see who the baddest boy was and watch him, see what he'd got and throw it back at him and more.

We formed a dance group in '75 called *Unknown Quantity* with Greg Craig, Trevor Shakes, Noel Vaughan and Travis Edwards. All those dancers that went on to be in *Hot Gossip* used to come and check us out rehearsing, but we never ended up doing a show believe it or not, after all that. There were a lot of dance groups then though: Greg Craig had one called *Caribbean Showboat*, which had a lot of dancers come from that.

Did you see much of what you were all doing in the Jazz style (Fusion) that came out in the early 80's?

Yes. I could see the boogie in there, and the footwork.

TREVOR SHAKES

I got into dancing from going to upstairs at Ronnie Scotts (1975). I saw dancers like *Leon Herbert, Jeff Davis, Paul Johnson*. That was THE club for the dancers - with the DJ's Barry James and Santi. I got pushed into a dance competition there. I don't know what I did but I got through to the next round so that made me want to start to practice. I eventually got through to the final although I never won.

I saw *Travis Edward*s at the Lacy Lady and that was it. It made me want to be a dancer. He was amazing. He was dynamic. Somersault into splits – he was the best I'd ever seen.

I used to work at Vivienne Westwoods shop called 'Sex' in Kings Road. I met Leon Herbert in there and I respected him because he was the best dancer. I started going around with him and learnt a lot. I never copied his moves but I saw all the dancers and how they used their moves –

or 'colours' as I saw it.

Did you realise you were getting rated as a dancer?

I had no idea. I never thought about it. I just used to like to dance and not be bothered. Every crowd had their own area of a club and *Dez Parkes* was our spokesman. He was known. I would just get on with my business. Eventually, Leon took me under his wing. Its funny because me and a dancer *Greg Craig* always used to go gunning for him; search him out. We never took him on – he was above that – but we let him know that we were there! I moved with him in the end. I had the passion for the dance. I'd practice anywhere: train platforms, the street... just get the moves better, be on top of what you are doing.

How would you describe your style?

I don't know. A lot of urgency and tension. Full on but relaxed, with finesse. That's how me and Leon would destroy people: Take your time, see what they'd got and give it back to them.

Tell me about your dance group 'Torso'. Was it around before 'Hot Gossip'?

Yes. Arlene Phillips (the choreographer and founder) used to come to *Monkberrys* - and most of the other places where I DJ'd - and Hot Gossip did their first show there, Torso was already going. All the guys who were in it used to watch me and one day I said "Stop fucking watching me and come and start learning." So I taught them all I knew, and then I went away modelling. When I came back they were doing shows without me but with my own moves (laughs). Actually, they did do a lot of shows and everything. It hurt me a little bit. Eventually I rejoined them and it all broke up, but I reformed using *Leon, Travis, John Riley* and *Hoyle Baker* with me. We'd go to gay discos too, for inspiration, even though we weren't gay. They had great taste in dancing, fashion and music. When I was a model everybody was gay.

Did you ever encounter *Paul Anderson* as a dancer?

I knew him later on, but not in the 70's. His rise was when I was away in Paris and everywhere.

I'd like to have seen you two battling.

Maybe. He'd have to have been fast on his feet (laughs). You never know (laughs). He'd have to have been quick to get one over on me. I was on my game. It's what I lived for.

Did you know Jerry Barry and all the young ones coming through?

I remember him good. Yeah, I inspired all those guys, and I'm glad I did.

PAUL ANDERSON

This dancer is the same man who is the world-wide famous Soulful Dance music DJ – Paul 'Trouble' Anderson.

I used to live for burn-ups. The preparation I went through...! I'd be at the childrens home practicing all the different styles in front of mirrors, learning peoples moves. Trevor Shakes was my idol, he was a great DJ too. He'd do stuff you couldn't believe. As a DJ, even though I'm straight, like Trevor, I'd go and also DJ in gay clubs too like *Adams* or *Bangs* in the West End. You heard music there that you didn't hear in the regular Jazz Funk clubs. That helped shape me, alongside working with Trevor, *George Power, Chris Hill, Froggy, Tom Holland, Mark Roman*....

One of the original Crackers DJ's.

Around '76. It was more of a white scene then until George Power came in. We'd be dressed in reggae wear like Farrah Stacks and had gold teeth and stuff. There were fabulous dancers. I lived that. And then I got into the punky-soul look - plastic sandals and all that; those clothes from *Sex* (In Kings Road).

Let's go back to the beginning

OK. I used to go to youth discos in '73 when I was in a children's home in Enfield and the first inspiring dancers were *Robert* and *Michael Lopez*. One of them could knock out thirty spins in one go. There was other clubs like *The Newbury* in Edmonton and *The Monster Mash* in Muswell Hill and the best at the time was *The Reservoir* in Oakwood. The dancing there was unbelievable. That was when I started dancing. There was another big dancer known as *Foster*. I still do one of his moves now. He took me under his wing. One guy I used to dance with for years for George Power was *Freddie Johnson*. He was unique. He didn't look like anyone. There was *Bassy* and *Norman Walker*. I became friends with Bassy after burning him up at *The Royalty* in North London, and there was *Bert Francis* – incredible dancer. Everybody knew him. There was *Jabber, Clementine* and *Franklyn. Horace Carter* was the king of Crackers but I took his crown. He was my hero. He put 'Ballet' into his dancing but he was a rude boy. People knew our face-off was coming and George Power would encourage it. I took the crown right up until Crackers closed.

All the main clubs seem to have been in the West end.

Yes, All round there.

Were they attended by the same dancers who would go to The Dun Cow in South London?

No. A different set. These West End dancers would also go to *The Lacy Lady* in Ilford like other dancers *Hoyle Baker, the Walker brothers, Dennis Muttley*, Trevor Shakes, of course, and *Tommy Mac* – who went everywhere, or you had dancers that would follow the DJ Froggy - like *Fitzroy Kelly, Putty, Steve McCaller, Ady Christie* who were famous for their 'shuffling' style.

How did you get established as a DJ?

George Power took me under his wing, first at *The Red Box* in North London, and *Bumbles* in Wood Green, in 1975 - a dancer's club, and I backed up Froggy at The Royalty with Jeff Young – but Crackers was the one that got famous for the Jazz Funk; then the Fusion. Paul Murphy and Dean Hulme DJ'd at Crackers. Paul's THE man for Jazz. When George and me moved to *The Horseshoe* and Paul had the Jazz room, I'd be in there dancing with the IDJ boys.

You started to get all those West London dancers coming through in the early '80's.

That's true. You had the Brown brothers – Michael and Jeff. I schooled them. They were my boys. Their style comes from us. There was *John Riley* - who was one of the kings - Trevor Shakes taught him, there was *Jerry Barry* of course. Fantastic.

So, from The Horseshoe to The Electric Ballroom....

Yes. I went up and had a foot shuffle. It was wonderful. Milton (McAlpine) was the main man there. I was busy downstairs playing Electro. It got too dark up there. It wasn't fun. It became one big battle, and people couldn't take defeat and it got physical. That was the problem for The Royalty too.

MICHAEL BROWN

Unfortunately, I never managed to track down the dancer Richard Baker, but it is considered that, of all the many dancers, it was a mixture of steps and moves from Michael Brown (from the famous group *The Pasadenas*), Kevin Haynes and him, that lay the foundations of what is known country-wide as the 'Fusion' – style of Jazz dancing. Let's not forget Jerry Barry and also the older dancers just interviewed - Trevor Shakes and Paul Anderson - that they mention as influences either.

Influential dancers of the time were *Paul Wing, Mohammed Yermack* and mainly *Jerry Barry*. He was amazing. He stood out. There was *Pinky*, who was a very comedic dancer - he'd try and make people laugh. He'd be cheeky – Mohammed was definitely influenced by him. Watching Jerry made me go and practice. I'd be working on moves all the time. I'd be watching films with Fred Astaire and Gene Kelly, the Berry Brothers and the Nicholas Brothers – especially Fayard. I wanted to incorporate all that in. I'd be constantly watching other musicals too and getting inspired and just remained in the zone. You're doing it because you love it not because you want to be the best. I was never competitive like that, but I practiced and practiced. Actually, I really believe that the best dancers were unemployed. You needed all that time to work on the moves and live it. I was out dancing Sunday to Sunday. I never thought that people would see me as an influence twenty years down the line. I'm surprised.

Paul Anderson felt that he influenced you.

Yes he did. Oh yes. Absolutely. I used to see him at *Crackers* and we'd be in awe of him. He was a massive influence. He had something to aspire to.

The competition that you saw at The Horseshoe would have been healthy wouldn't it?

It was like that in the end. I would be dancing in front of my mirror trying to work out things to beat people in a friendly way. You had to be on your toes. We'd travel though, and then we'd be in a unit. We'd go and smash everybody (laughs).

Did you find much competition on your travels?

Most of the time we knew we were going to smash 'em, but once in a while someone would come through that would hurt us. But we wanted to show what we could do and also represent our area…

And impress the women (laughs)!

Well that's a part of it!

At the end of Crackers and through The Horseshoe there was a 'Punky' look associated

with those clubs.

Yes, I wore all that - the 'James Dean' t-shirts or slashed t-shirts, the studded belts; dying my hair mauve. It was a Punk look, but it was Black people dancing to Jazz. Crackers, before then, we'd wear tight stretch jeans, white socks and ballet slippers – it was an elegant style before the Punk one.

The basic tap rudiment is a time-step, the basic drum rudiment is a paradiddle, and the basic step of the Fusion is Cockroach Stomping or Crushing and it came from you.

I didn't know that. I don't remember naming it either but it's the kind of thing I'd come out with; and members of my family. I used to watch ballet, contemporary – all forms of dance, Kung Fu films – there's so much art and dance in those. I took a move from 'Drunken Master' where I rolled over and over and finished in a sleeping position and people went mad. Later everyone was doing variations of it. That came from me. Late night Kung Fu films were a big thing with the dancers. You'd learn so much from those. That's how it was.

What did you think of The Electric Ballroom?

I didn't go into the Jazz room that much. I went in to look but I got back into the Funk again – where I had started from. I was proud of the Jazz scene; the dance; the integration of all colours; the innovations; the dancing, but that room was too hot and sweaty and too many youngsters, and there were fights up there. It'd changed dramatically. Respect went out the window.

KEVIN HAYNES – THE PENGUIN

I went to Crackers and Spats a few times, but I was only 14. That was the first time I saw dancers doing all different types of freestyle - dancers like *Winston Pitt, Trevor Shakes* and *Paul Anderson*. You started to hear a few Jazz tracks amongst the Funk. Next we went on to Paul Murphy's clubs: *The Green Man* – both of them – and *The Horseshoe*. Everyone was learning quickly: The DJ feeding off the dancers, dancers feeding off the DJ - everyone learning and digging up music. There were people around like a dancer called Lem who'd search for records and he'd turn Murphy onto a few.

I would go out with a crowd of ten from all over West London - half of us dancers, the others just following - and loving the vibe. Some of them were rough boys, getting into this or that or robbing, but this all calmed them down and made them more humane. The dancing was creative - there were about ten main dancers and people would share moves or copy or adapt.

I went to *The Electric Ballroom* for the first year and a half and then stopped going. I got bored. Also, a lot of the individualism had gone. Everyone was copying each other and doing the same style and it was just about the music being as fast as can be.

But you were one of the dancers whose style they defined (laughs)

Maybe. You can borrow a couple of moves but do your own thing. Anyway, I thought it was time to do something else, so from there I actually became a professional dancer. I danced for three companies: Afro International, Rose De Londres: a Samba group - that's how I started learning percussion - and then Dance Company 7. I started playing with flautist Philip Bent and through him, Saxophonist Steve Williamson.

The 'Fusion' style as it came to be know, was a lot to do with the style of you, Richard Baker and Michael Brown: Were you aware of people copying you?

Not at first. But then I did start to realize that people were doing the same moves as myself or Michael. - my side-to-side dancing; the penguin-style (arms right to the sides) and other moves. I always remember people coming up to me and saying: "Yeah that was wicked" or show me respect. I never had any crazy duels or anything like that. I heard all that at The Ballroom people were fighting each other but at The Horseshoe you battled and shook hands.

'Cockroach Stomping' was Michaels move.

Yes it was. And everyone was doing it, even me. But he had lots of moves, he was a 'light.'

You were in The Jazz Warriors. They often get mentioned as part of our scene but I can't see why. The drummer Frank Tontoh got it and you and Orphy Robinson (Vibes player) were dancers of course but....

No, they did what they did but they were learning musicians. The Jazz dance scene was petering out by the time they came along. They missed the heat. A lot of them weren't associated with it or knew about it. It was a different bunch of people. Our musical education from the scene never touched them.

Was Steve Williamson aware of our scene?

Yes. He wasn't a part of it though. Except the Dingwalls period. He did a tour with IDJ around the country for a 6 or 7 months called 'The Fuss Was Us' and the music was tailored for the dancers – fast – just for that tour. It was good for me to see where I came from carrying on. I would get up and dance with them. Fun and excitement.

I bet Steve was shocked seeing you dance.

Yes, they'd say: "Oh, so you're from those times?" It all came together on that tour. I was no longer a dancer, I was now a musician.

I.D.J. – I DANCE JAZZ

This crew is mentioned a thousand times in this book, as you've read. IDJ was comprised of the greatest of the young dancers to come out of The Electric Ballroom, and fully represented the 'Fusion' style of dancing that eventually developed there, and from there sweeping the country's jazz dancefloors creating a whole new movement. After they formed, thing's were never the same again. Here, I interview some of the members: Jerry Barry, Gary Nurse and Steve 'Afro' Edwards, about IDJ and everything surrounding them then.

JERRY BARRY AKA JERRY IDJ

I started going to *The100 Club* in Oxford Street on Saturday afternoons with the DJ Ronnie L, *Spats, Studio 21, Global Village* and *Crackers*. What got me about Crackers is that it was three hours from Midday until 3p.m, but people packed in there early to make the best of the time they had. A lot of people cut school to go. When you saw guys dancing without their shirts in there, it wasn't because they were being macho, it was because they didn't want to get their shirt sweaty because they had to go back to school or work after. This is why the dancers carried beer-towels: to stop the sweat getting on the waist-band of their trousers, and to wipe down before they left. Us youngsters used to come out and just have steam coming off us!

The resident DJ there – George Power – was very jazzy.

He was playing some Fusion, but there were certain tracks that he had that he would goad us with by saying: " I'm not playing this, It's too good for you. You wouldn't understand it." There were some great dancers there: *Clive Clarke; Pinky; Pete Francis* – he was incredible. He was compared to this dancer called *Trevor Shakes*, who was rated. I was never lucky enough to see him. He was a dancer from *The Lacy Lady* in Ilford .

Yes. Crackers had a lot of dancers from The Lacy Lady and also from Froggys under-18's session at Ilford Town Hall, I was told.

The standard of dancing was excellent at The Lacy Lady, but I'd look around the room and choose my spot where I wouldn't be interrupted. What I'd call *the sweet spot*.

Did you just stay in London?

No. I used to travel all over the country. I went to *Cassinellis* in Manchester. The dancing was different up there in the North, and they used to put talcum powder on the floor. The jazz style was very Balletic; flowing. There was a lot of respect between dancers.

When did you start taking your dancing seriously?

Around the time I first befriended the DJ Paul Murphy. It was a club in London near Baker Street called *The Green Man*. It was the first time I really took notice of a DJ. He was just about to start at The Horseshoe. He played really hard Jazz Funk, especially for the dancers, and I picked up on that. Murphy did Saturday and George Power then started a Friday, but George had some fights on his night so the owner stopped both sessions There was a big Jazz Funk club in North London at Southgate called *The Royalty* which closed because of trouble when people left the club, and it was that crowd that then came to Georges night. He then started up at The Electric Ballroom in Camden Town and booked Paul to do upstairs, but we didn't like the room. It was a carpeted floor for a while, and then they pulled up the carpet and we would dance with all that gooey residue from underneath the carpet all over our shoes and trousers.

Was there a lot of competition between dancers?

Yes, but it was often between two friends. There was always two dancers at The 100 Club: one - a friend of Trevor Shakes - called *Ian Baptiste*, and *Pinky*, and I learned from watching them that after a dance-off you would always shake hands. Pinky would joke around, you know, put his arm-pit in the other dancers face or whatever, but it wasn't to be taken seriously. It'd always finish with a shake or a touchdown. I used to dance a lot like that with a friend at The Horseshoe called *Michael Brown*; who went on to be a member of the group *The Pasadenas*. The dance step 'The Cockroach Stomp' (or crushing) came from him.

He was more of a Jazz Funk dancer.

Yes, that was his style. The sound system wasn't loud at The Horseshoe so, when we stepped outside the room, all you could hear was the sound of feet on the dance floor. Michael would say that it sounded like people stomping on cockroaches, and he'd mess around the floor when we'd dance by trying to interrupt our moves by stamping his foot down in front of us – well, it was more of a tap really, and we'd all copy it to continue the laugh. That ended up as *cockroach stomping*.

One of our crowd was a dancer called *Kevin Haynes* – who was known as *The Penguin*. He danced with his hands tight to his sides, like a traditional Irish dancer – hence *the penguin*.

"It is true that I did start to see a few people dancing in my style after a while, but there were so many good moves coming through from so many great dancers that people are bound to influence others. There were these guys from west London that used to mess around imitating. There was one guy called Leman and there was a guy called Leo who also used to find a few records for Murphy here and there. He was talented at watching you and working out the moves that gave you your character and doing them back at you, defining the steps. I think he was very influential."

Kevin Haynes

What happened when Peterson took over from Murphy at The Ballroom?

One day I was taken out to this bar in Croydon called Solos, and my friend pointed out that the DJ. (Gilles) was taking over The Ballroom. He was playing Take 5 by Dave Brubeck at the time, and I thought: " Oh God. No!" but what I didn't realize was that he was just playing to that crowd in the bar, although, when he started at The Ballroom he wasn't quite playing the right selection and occasionally he'd clear the floor. He used to give me a lift home and ask me how I thought the night went, so I got in the habit of finding out reactions from dancers about certain records for him. It took about six weeks but he got it just right.

You know, I remember sitting down with Murphy at The Wag and him telling me that he'd got tired of the music he'd been playing at The Electric Ballroom and, ironically, under a year at The Ballroom, Gilles was saying more-or-less the same thing and that he wanted to play different stuff. You must remember that he was also doing The Special Branch on Fridays and the Belvedere on Sundays, so he had these pockets of playing different stuff and getting a taste for it.

What did you think of his back-up DJ's at The Ballroom – Mark and Andy?

They were hot. You must remember, they had been regulars there before Gilles took over and they knew the stuff Murphy used to play.

How was IDJ formed?

Simon Booth – the band leader of Working Week, said that if the dancers could get something together, he wanted us to perform with them at the first London Jazz Festival. That was something new to us, so we practiced for six weeks and when we performed, the crowd went mad!

I always think of IDJ as having four or five members, but in the Working Week – Venceremos video there are loads.

Yes, ten. That's how many turned up to the first rehearsal in Acton. There was me, Afro, Melvin Obzeracky, Morris Buchanan, Milton McAlpine, Duke (soon to be famous British rapper M.C. Duke), Mark Soynalu, Marshall Smith and a couple of others. The film director, Julian Temple, was directing the video and wanted to use us after seeing us at the festival. There was a long version, which would be shown before the film Absolute Beginners at the cinema, and one for the single promo. The festival was the beginning of IDJ but it nearly all got messed up because there was this guy who was claiming to be our manager and it was causing all kinds of confusion with the company Virgin and Simon. I declined this guys offer but some of the guys wanted to go with him. Luckily they didn't.

I came up with the name of IDJ after a lot of arguing with the other guys. We needed a name for the video. I thought that just using the initials would create some mystique but Simon was having none of that. He told everyone what it stood for - I DANCE JAZZ. Marshall used to joke that it stood for I DANCE WITH JERRY!

We were meant to headline in that film Absolute Beginners, but the songs being 'okayed' by Sade were down tempo, which suited The Jazz Defektors style rather than ours, so that was it - we ended up on the cutting room floor! There was a whole dream sequence that was meant to have featured us but Virgin pulled out half way through the film and a lot of the budget went.

This woman came up to us and said: " Hi. I'm Jean Davenport from The Shaw Theatre. I think you're great and I want to put you on." Her manner was so honest and forthright that it made me want to work for her. Some of the guys didn't want to do it for nothing at first but when they saw the venue they changed their minds. She asked us to do it for free just once and she then booked us loads of times. It was very important for us and put us on the map. With her connections she got us on at important festivals. I wish she'd managed us. At The Shaw, she put us on supporting US Rap acts like Red Alert, DJ Whiz, Afrika Bambaata … …At first I didn't see the connection, but she said that we've got as much right to be out there as they have. We always went down well. She started booking us with artists like Tania Maria too and one day she said that she'd approached Art Blakey to play at The Shaw Theatre and for us to dance with him. There was also to be a documentary made of it, but he wasn't sure of having dancers, so she asked me if I would go and speak to him – he was playing at the nearby Lewisham theatre. When I got there I'd missed the show but managed to get back stage. There was a big entourage there and he was sat in the middle looking tired. Jean introduced me to him, and he said: " You're a dancer? What kind do you do?" so I said: " It may be best if I show you." I went round on the floor, up the wall, swiveled round, spins…… It stopped the entourage dead. When I left, Jean ran after me, almost in tears, and said: " He'll do it!".

There was a documentary being made of that event called *Father Time*, to be directed by Dick Fontaine. I'd already met Dick because he filmed us dancing with Working Week a few weeks earlier. With Blakey would be members of an all-Black London based jazz group called The Jazz Warriors, us and a Jazz Dance crew from Manchester called The Jazz Defektors. At the dress rehearsal, the tempo for the song that we were dancing to was too slow for us but would have suited the more eloquent style of The Jazz Defektors but on the night I asked Blakey to play it fast, so he said: " You want it fast? You're digging your own grave." By the side of the stage we were looking at each other and wondering whether we were perfect enough. We'd had six weeks to rehearse at the venue,but at first, some of the guys were just too relaxed about it. Jean accused them of not taking it seriously and 'read them the riot-act.' They respected that, and we all worked hard.

There wasn't much of a heavy scene left by the late 1980's, so how did you survive?

The original line-up. L to R - Melvin, Milton, Jerry, Marshall, Morris and Afro (with glasses)
Photo by Eric Watson

Well, we got really established and got on to the festival circuit and had Arts funding. We got on to the theatre circuit thanks, really, to Jean and all those Shaw Theatre dates, and we did a video with Chick Corea. We also went to Japan and also did a show with Hip-Hop artist Grandmaster Melle Mel. He said: " I don't know what you are doing here. You should be in the States. They'd love you!" We did a huge concert at Wembley stadium to 'Free Nelson Mandela' and backstage the legendary tap-dancer Gregory Hines also said: " You need to get to the States. You're fresh. There is nothing like you there."

The Mandela gig was an incredible one to get.

Yes. I got that one. I approached the organizer, showed them videos and all that, and they loved it, but they didn't know what to do with us. I told them that I knew all the British jazz musicians like Courtney Pine, Steve Williamson etc and they loved the idea. I was pissed off on the night because we got introduced as 'Courtney Pine and the dancers.' I organized it and we rehearsed hard and didn't even get a name-check. To add further embarrassment, I'd arranged for legendary British jazz-drummer – Robin Jones, to play, and they wouldn't let him in. We went down incredible, even so. Imagine dancing at Wembly Stadium?

What happened to IDJ?

We wanted to form into a band like 'The Pasadenas' and I was talking to the owner of Island Records, Chris Blackwell - who loved us – and he said: "You've got something but you're not a band. How can I use you?" So when he started Island Visual Arts, he wanted to sign us, but there was a bit of trouble within I.D.J. The deal never got signed due to lack of commitment.

Finally, you organized the televised Jazz Dance competition on Channel 4 – 7 Sport

I'd been interviewd by someone who argued that Jazz Dance was a sport and likened it with the Indonesian art form called 'penchaksila' because of the moves on the floor, and that got me thinking. I contacted a woman called Jaswinda Bansell on Channel 4's 7 Sport to put my point forward and she asked me to write down my ideas. I met with her and showed her videos and said that if they based it in a boxing-ring - to represent the battle element and two different styles of dancing - this would be sport and art. She said that she had to use her own researchers but still wanted me involved. Inevitably, it changed from what I wanted. It became a money prize rather than a trophy, and a coach came down from the North of England to support The Brothers In Jazz – who were battling the Back Street Kids (formed by Gary Nurse and Marshall Smith from IDJ). I wanted to bring the scene together, but it just caused animosity. The Back Street Kids were judged to have won – rightly or wrongly, and this caused problems. Of course people blamed me, but by then I didn't have any say in it. I heard that people were after me and wanted to harm me in the North.

I hated the competition. I thought it was pretentious.

If we'd done my original idea, it would have been faked. The dance-off would have been choreographed. It was just meant to show that it (Jazz Dance) was aerobic; it had balance; poise; agility; and is cardiovascular and athletic. That was my original pitch to them.

STEVE 'AFRO' EDWARDS

My first exposure to Jazz on a dancefloor was at The 100 Club on Saturday lunchtimes with the DJ Ronnie L. It blew me away. I was only 15. After a few weeks, I had the courage to dance there and I found I could do it. My style was fast and was better for the Jazz. When my Mum and Dad knew I liked Jazz they played me all this African Jazz they'd bought from as far back as the 50's. They told me that I would dance to it when I was a little boy!

When I knew I was a Jazz man I started going to Crackers with George Power. He played this fast Jazz tune and I was dancing looking down and when I looked up, I saw a big circle of a hundred people watching me and I got shy. People started clapping me and I realized I had a skill. Paul Anderson gave me advice there.

The big Jazz man was Paul Murphy, of course. Going to the Horseshoe I realised that I was an out-and-out Jazz-man. I don't recognize any of the dancers now, from then, they've all disappeared - but they were fantastic. There was less challenging there than at The Electric Ballroom – when it came in there, it was never the same. There were lots of fights, serious fights - I never understood it. I never got involved in challenging. I organized coaches with Marshall Smith to all-dayers, and they all went to challenge, but I wasn't interested. There was violence there too.

How did you start with IDJ?

Simon from Working Week came up to me at the Ballroom and said I should be in a dance group. He pointed to some others as well. We all met in Chiswick, and that was it. There were 15 of us, and we voted who was in or out to get it down to 7. It was hard rehearsing because none of us had done routines before, but we met up twice a week. We were going to perform for Working Week at the Camden Jazz Festival

We did a lot of work at the Shaw Theatre and traveled everywhere. We were tight. We did lots of videos too.

What about the film 'Absolute Beginners?'

A great disappointment. Our biggest scene was a dream sequence where we was dancing and on fire! It got cut. The director – Julien Temple, says that he wished he'd put it in now. It was fantastic.

Of all your shows, what about the Art Blakey one?

Fantastic.

Was there much animosity between IDJ and Jazz Defektors?

I didn't think so. I got on with everyone. My favourite memory is at a rehearsal: The Jazz Defektors and us were all dancing and Blakey just stopped and walked up to me in front of everyone and said: "Man, you keep it up. You're a fantastic dancer and you're right on the rhythm. I've been watching you" – that's the biggest compliment ever.

What about the split when Gary and Marshall formed The Back Street Kids?

I didn't like that name. They asked me to join, but I was just fed up with being in a group. I'm a free spirit and an individual. I wish I could have done the 'Sport 7' Jazz dance battle though. I went. It was good.

GARY NURSE

I started dancing at senior school, about 13 years of age. There were a few guys that were going out to clubs like *Roderick Powell, Paul Shaderai, Paul Da Costa*, and we'd heard of Jerry Barry. We weren't allowed out to clubs so we learnt from them. There wasn't the *Fusion* style of dancing then, the style was much more Jazz Funk. *Milton McAlpine* was a big influence too; we went to school together.

Our first club was *Jesters* in Surrey (with Chris Bangs and Tarun Sen Gupta). There were loads of dancers there, but no one exceptional. From there we started going to The Electric Ballroom. Although The Ballroom is important to me, I still say that the dance experience at school was the most important. We'd practice, whenever, whoever, wherever, however.

What was exciting about The Ballroom was, not only was the club amazing, it was the first time we'd gone to a central London club, so it was a buzz. That's when we started seeing the real dancers. I was about 14. I'd missed the first year of The Ballroom and Milton wasn't there at the time either - he was yet to reign!

How did you feel about battling for the first time?

I feared no one, even at that age. It was nothing. It was fun. I always felt that "I'm going to be as good as that person. I'm going to have my reign." I saw any dancer in front of me as a stepping-stone. All the dancers knew that I had no fear.

What dancers took your eye?

Jerry Barry, of course, he was great. Milton took things to another level – an innovator and inventor. There was a guy we just knew as 'Robert from High Wycombe' and there was Austin. He wasn't the greatest dancer, but he was the funniest character to grace a dancefloor. The dancers weren't all amazing at The Ballroom, but there were a dozen exceptional, innovative talents. A handful. The rest were also-rans.

Were IDJ going by then?

Yes. I wasn't in them to start with. I respected them but they didn't mean much to me. I started coming up and getting known, and one Friday I was dancing to *Eric Kloss-Samba Express* and dealt with the tune. It was my time. That period was my time. I'd taken it to a different level. I'd probably done things that dancers still can't do to this day. Marshall, Melvin and Jerry watched me and asked me to join IDJ.

You wouldn't normally see professionally Jazz Dance crews battling in the Jazz rooms at all-dayers, but IDJ did.

Of course, and I think, in a way, that's why I didn't take IDJ that seriously, because to be honest,

I loved it for the first few years and we had some fun and some amazing shows. It was euphoria sometimes, but what made me get bored of it was that, as soon as we went on stage you lose the root of what it's all about. At The Ballroom it's an individual thing, but you put it on stage and you're sharing it. At the all-dayers, man, I couldn't wait to step in front of someone, what I was doing was revolutionary and dynamic and so I wouldn't have to be in a circle for too long (laughs). Challenging was what it was all about. Like in the martial arts: In order to be the best you have to fight the best. Simple. We'd roam the country and seek out who's worthy of a challenge. Nowadays it's all clean fun but then, if you got burned you'd start wading into someone's face. It wasn't clean - that's what it meant to people back then. London was - in terms of the Fusion dance style - undisputedly the best. It came from London. We were always ahead of the game because we were the pioneers.

Did any of you ever get defeated?

There was great dancer's all over the country, and outside of London, *Lizard* from Birmingham was by far the best. But I didn't know who I was dancing against most of the time. I was just a young cocky kid and when I was reigning, there was nobody going to tear me in a circle.

Any great Jazz artist that came into the country IDJ'd support them, and it was special to dance for Nelson Mandelas 70th birthday at Wembly Stadium – and what was annoying about that was that people talk about that as being us dancing for Courtney Pine (Jazz Saxophonist) but it was *us* being backed by him and all the other musicians. *We* were the headline.

Was there a leader?

Jerry landed himself with that one. I was completely out of control, you couldn't tell me anything. I'd gang up with other guys against Jerry's decisions. He took it very serious. To me it was just a laugh. I was just a silly brat causing problems. It was about having fun, being disruptive and bringing people down to my level (laughs). We wore suits on stage and sometimes I'd just come on in jeans and t-shirts and my 'vans' (Skateboarder shoes). I was proud to be in IDJ though, and I've go to thank Jerry for starting something that will hopefully be a legacy.

Why did you split from IDJ and form *The Back Street Kids*?

Marshall formed the group, not me. There were three of us in it – Marshall, me and a girl dancer called Lynne Page. What an awful name. It was embarrassing. We didn't do loads of work, I mean, it wasn't the next step in my career, but I just got tired of IDJ and arguing with Jerry all the time. I'm the kind of person that moves on. The spirit wasn't there for me in the end. I can't watch the old videos now. It was basic. Also, I started branching out doing other things.

How did you perceive *Brothers In Jazz* who came through quickly and became your rivals?

Others were just also-rans before they came with their flavour. I respected them. They were different. They came along when the scene was dying out and reignited the scene to a certain degree.

How did you feel about the '7 Sport' Jazz Dance competition on Channel 4 against Brothers In Jazz?

I can't watch it. The best parts were edited out. I brought this little furry duck toy and when you clap it walks and you clap again and it stops. The beginning of the second round I put it on the middle of the dancefloor when I was dancing. I stamped, it started, I stamped, it stopped. Wayne from Brothers In Jazz was so annoyed he kicked it out of the ring. I had this phony dog-shit which I brought out and I went into a squat position over it on stage, and the Brothers were left dancing to that! There were a lot of things like that. It all got cut out of the finished broadcast. We won that round. Overall I couldn't care less about that competition. We won, rightly so, but some say that the Brothers should have; I'm really not bothered.

That was the first time The Backstreet Kids appeared.

Yes. Lynne got trained up two weeks before, at Pineapple dance studios. She was just a show dancer.

Jerry continued IDJ. How did you feel about that?

I just wasn't bothered. Honestly, IDJ was a great stepping-stone. I didn't take it seriously.

GARY AND SEYMOUR NURSE - ON 'THE ELECTRIC BALLROOM' ETC

Gary is joined by his twin brother Seymour for important reminiscences.

Gary - We'd dance at school; in the street; outside college. I'd be thinking of moves all the time, like, on a bus or something; how to maim your fellow man on the dancefloor (laughs) - I'd jump off the bus, there and then and start practicing it as soon as the thought hit me, or at a bus stop…

Seymour - You didn't have video games and all those kind of distractions like you have now, so dancing was all we thought about. We weren't rich; we didn't have money, but what we had was our music. I remember when we were dancing to *Norman Connors - Mother Of The Future* in a side street in Hounslow high street and some bloke threw a bucket of water over Milton (laughs), but that's how it was. In the early 80's, the Jazz that was being played – the Brazilian Fusion, predominantly - was dangerous. Where that music went was so extreme and I think the dancing complimented it. As the music got more aggressive and tense, so did the dancing. It was that simple. Milton would be up all night thinking of moves: I remember seeing him on the floor, jump out of his shoes, do these spins, and go straight back into his shoes again (laughs).

There were about 100 to 150 dancers at The Ballroom, and if you'd stop to watch them for 5 minutes you'd see genius. I swear.

Gary - The spirit of The Ballroom was so intense. It was free admission before 9.30, so there was this queue outside and there was such a buzz in there that when the doors opened, it didn't matter whether you were first up the stairs, you were dancing straight away.

Seymour - It was a very dark room with a very Black crowd but it was so intimidating in there because of the music. It was intense, the atmosphere was intense. There'd be Black guys that were too scared to go in there.

I remember Tony Smart telling me that he had to get Rocky Bryan to walk in with him. Having said that, I knew White guys that went in: look at Michael Knott - he's one of the best.

Seymour - That scene was revolutionary…

In my opinion, it was a gradual thing out of the Jazz Funk scene.

Gary - Yeah, but there was no steps before like they danced at The Ballroom. The Soul boys before just used to dance the same way to Soul as they did to Jazz, but faster, but…

That's true. That's how I danced to it – everyone did…

Gary - But certain new standard steps were invented to dance to Fusion at The Ballroom.

You must remember, that almost a whole new generation of people 'started' at The Ballroom who were young and hungry, and a lot of older dancers that came up through the Jazz Funk scene before didn't know what hit them. There was certain records you heard at The Ballroom that were dark, that got you distressed mentally (laughs). Your spirit would be shaken

Seymour - ...but still danceable. Look at *Cecil McBee - Pepis Samba* I mean look where that went. Those dancers were hungry for anything. That's what put Murphy on the map in that sense: anything that man wanted to experiment with, he got away with and he did.

Gary - And Gilles.

Seymour – Yes, and Gilles. That place was monumental. DJ's were discovering 'madness' and playing it, and people were dancing to it. You can understand why battles on the dancefloor happened all the time. The things that used to occurr...stupid.

So what about the battles then?

Seymour - Right, look at Austin. That man was sick.

Gary - He'd throw 'Bangers' (fireworks) at dancers feet.

Seymour - I saw him throw a banger on the floor, and all the knives came out.

There was that amount of people who had knives in there?

Seymour - A fair few, yeah. Quite a lot. That particular night could have got quite ugly. I've seen glasses put into peoples faces. There was a lot of trouble occurring, That was the dark side, which was a shame, with all that talent in there.

Austin came in once in this long coat and bag: he was battling someone and put these pyjamas on while he was dancing (laughs) and slippers and night-hat, set an alarm clock, laid on the floor in a foetal position pretending that he was asleep and people would crowd round him, the alarm would go off while the tune was still playing, he put his shoes on and carried on dancing. No man in his right mind would do this.

Gary - I'm not naming names, but a lot of things went on out there. It was grim. They should have called it the 'Electric Boxing-Ring', not 'Ballroom.' If you got in front of someone, you'd be there to do battle. You're talking about people that have got nothing in their life apart from their dancing you know, so when that was at stake, if you beat him you'd better be prepared to get a slap. You had guys like Milton - he was the best; he was cocky and good looking as well. He used to Break (dance) for the 'London All Star Breakers,' so at all-dayers where you had an Electro room and a Jazz room, he'd go to the Break dance room, beat them, come into the Jazz room and change into his 'spats' and beat everybody in there too. When he'd beaten all the top dancers in the club, that was it. No more challenge. He stopped going to the club after that; stopped Jazz Dancing altogether except later - he appeared a couple of times with I.D.J.

Seymour - There was a period in the early sessions where trouble was a common occurance. It was the 'humiliation factor' that was so strong. When dancers came up to each other, they wanted to humiliate the other person. I've seen people beaten up for beating someone else. I've seen people beaten up by their own crew. I've seen some nasty things. I don't want to blow it out of proportion though, it wasn't all the time.

The last battle I saw was between my brother Gary and Marshall (IDJ). I've seen people take some beatings on the floor, when the battle was so one-sided, but Milton had left the scene to concentrate on his break dancing so Marshall was the top gun. Gary wasn't in IDJ at that point, but everybody used to talk about him. He used to just take everybody apart on the floor, like Milton used to. I remember, it was a Friday night at The Electric Ballroom and Marshall walked in with a woman on each arm and he was all dressed up. It looked like something out of a 'Western'; these girls even took off his coat, honestly - it was out of a film!! Anyway, Gary was dancing and Marshall was dancing and there was tension, and a battle started to occur. Straight away Gilles brought in 'The Bottom End' – that's *the* battle tune - and they got at it. Gary would do a solo and catch a break and so did Milton, and people ran downstairs to the main room shouting: "Gary and Marshall are battling!" It was like a heavyweight fight - move after move after move, in and out, Bang! Bang! Bang! The vocals came in at the end and everyone thought one of the lines in the song was "Get off the floor", which you'd try to catch. They were out of breath, but battling in each other's face and bang! - they both caught the vocal, pointing to the floor - "Get off the floor!" It was a clash of the titans: 'Forman versus Ali' – that kind of a battle.

No-one actually won?

No. It had to be a draw. That was the thing: When you went into a Jazz room your whole reputation went in with you. People like Gary, Marshall, Afro... they didn't speak to each other for years, that's just how it was, you just went in there and did your thing. If there was any tension, you took the man out. Your rep was on the night, you never knew who you might be confronted by. Everything was at stake every time you walked in. Your balls were on the line every single Friday. When we'd be walking home sometimes you had to stop and practice a move you'd seen or you'd go home and immediately practice. You had to take something different to the club every week. (Hypothetically) I would watch you and study your moves and if I saw you about to catch a break on a tune you knew, I'm in there and bump you off so you can't catch it or I'd sweep your legs away. You had to catch the man's best moves. It was like fighting.

You mentioned Gilles: Were people alright about him taking over from Murphy there?

Seymour - Most of the dancers didn't know who he was at the time. He'll admit to you that his first night at the Ballroom was lame. He didn't have the tunes for us until Murphy sold them to him. There were certain tunes that people expected to hear and he didn't have them. Musically or trouble-wise, it wasn't as aggressive. He was so lucky to be given the keys to the kingdom.

When we tried to follow Murphy to The Titanic when he left we couldn't get in, because of the racist door policy, so we had to go back to The Ballroom. Gilles learnt very, very quickly. To me, the boys that did it after the 'Murphy' era were his two back-up DJ's though - *Mark and Andy*. The dancers weren't bothered about the DJ's - the scene was the dancing and the music. There were a lot of dancers at The Ballroom who wouldn't have recognized Murphy in the street - as revered as he was.

Baz Fe Jazz took over the ballroom later on didn't he?

Seymour - Yeah, well what happened is, that they closed the Jazz room to start a Hip Hop room. There was a riot that night and opposite, at this supermarket, it got looted. I don't know whether it was a coincidence…(laughs), but there were a lot of people angry. I went back when the Jazz Room reopened with Baz but it just wasn't the same. A lot of people had the attitude "You shouldn't have taken it away from us, and now you want us back!!"

Did you go to any of Murphy's other clubs?

Seymour - Yeah, I went to the *Rock Garden*. I went to The Wag but it wasn't intense. It was a bigger venue, but to me Murphy was a Guru anyway. The Ballroom was where it was at – not disrespecting anything else he did. He established himself in such a phenomenal way. He'll always be legendary. What he created was very special no matter where he decided to take it, whether for business reasons or personal.

Did you go to any of Gilles' early gigs?

Seymour - Yeah. I went to The Belvedere (1984) It was phenomenal. He played the same stuff that he played at The Ballroom but, of course, there wasn't a dancefloor. It was heavy. It was a pub really, but rammed. I was there.

Did you go to any of the all-dayers?

Seymour - Yeah. I went to The Powerhouse in Birmingham and others. But back then I was into Break dancing as well as the Jazz.

You'd had Electro in the main room, and a Jazz room…

Seymour - It was the best of both worlds. I wasn't too into the Jazz dancing style there: It was a lot more Ballet-style. There was a lot of talent there though obviously. It's funny, it was like 'football violence' at those all-dayers! What I mean is: the crews from different parts of the country would arrange dance battles so that, for example, you knew that Marshall (from IDJ, London) would be battling Bulldog from Birmingham.

Did you see any difference musically from London?

Seymour - No, it was similar, although, I hate to say it: it was much, much harder in London. Heavy, hard Fusion.

Well, Colin Curtis and all the other DJ's played a lot of Fusion up North.

Seymour - The dancing was aggressive to aggressive music in London, and the Balletic-style just didn't fit to something like *Daniel Ponce – Basta De Cuentos*.

Well, I'm sure they'd rip up the Fusion dancers if it was a Be Bop tune.

Seymour - Well, yeah. We're talking about different styles. I saw a lot of people get ripped up on the dancefloor at The Ballroom. I never missed a week. I never danced there but I had a place where I always sat and was known as 'the eyes of the ballroom!' I saw all the battles. Every one.

When I interviewed PC from the Jazz Defektors, he said that, after all the fuss about Fusion dancing, to him, it was nothing new, he saw people dancing similar in Northern Soul clubs..

Seymour - No, no. Well I can see that he draws a comparison with the 'stomping', but with respect, he's wrong. Innacurate. I can see what he's saying though.

That period after The Ballroom closed and *Dingwalls* started, a lot of them stopped going out or whatever. A lot of those dance moves haven't been preserved. That knowledge has gone.

PERRY LOUIS

Perry is really from Luton, not London, but what we talk about deals with London. He is someone that was there at the beginning and lived it. Despite dropping out through some golden years to pursue his athletic ambitions, he came back in to experience Dingwalls and everything that surrounded it, and from there he still dances and leads the Jazz Dance troupe *Jazzcotech*, as well as promotes and DJ's.

Where I'm from in Luton we had some of the top Jazz Funk clubs - *The California Ballroom* (in Dunstable) - artists like James Brown, Roy Ayers and Players Association played there - *Sands, Didos, Devils Den* and *Scamps*. We'd travel everywhere to see Sean French at *Americas* in Hounslow or Chris Brown at *Frenchie's* in Camberley, or *The Goldmine, Global Village* or *Lacy Lady* learning the different styles. We'd go to *The 100 Club, Spats* and *Crackers* - the dancers there were amazing like Pete Francis, Mohammed Yermak, Pinky, Jerry Barry, The Penguin, Trevor Shakes of course and Paul Anderson.

Marshall and Melvin – who went on to be original members of IDJ - used to come and stay at my flat. Marshall wasn't even dancing Jazz then. I'd show him a knee drop and some footsteps.

I went to The Electric Ballroom from day one. It was exciting. The dancers I noticed imme-

'Bubble 'N' Squeak' - Pete Tormey and Perry

diately were *Phil Octane, Richard Baker* and Jerry. After a while, I started to get noticed by the dancers too and I'd get involved in battles. This was before IDJ. I got myself up to being one of the top half dozen. I remember when Milton started to appear: he'd come in and watch and study, go away, come back, watch and study. One day he came in and it was almost like he was 'ready' and he danced against Jerry and I thought "Bloody Hell," and I could sense that I was next. I could do knee spins and favourite moves of the time, like jumping through your leg (right arm holding left leg and jumping through the right leg) and I had a Jazz funk edge, but we battled and it was exciting. All of a sudden he went up a gear and he put his hand on my shoulder and started jumping backwards and forwards through his leg and did three knee drops and it stunned me. And then the battle was over. He showed me where the style was going with all these multiple knee spins and the harder floor work, and I was trying to out dance by the skin of my teeth. I knew that he'd wiped the floor with me.

Right then I'd started getting a little disillusioned with the scene. The numbers at The Electric Ballroom were dwindling – probably because it was summer - and although I was still excited by it, it was time to move on. I thought it was dying down, and also I felt that there was too much 'floorwork' and not enough dancing. I took one last look at the place and as I was leaving - I felt then that whatever I'd built up had probably gone now, with fresh people coming through. I left early that night, because I had a race the next morning - which I won actually – and didn't go to the Jazz club's for a while. I thought I'd give the athletics a go, because I'd really started to let it suffer. The training was severe but I was still going out but not as crazy. I was going to *The Goldmine, Wheelers* (Henley-On-Thames), *Jacksons* in Staines, going to parties, warehouse parties - but not Jazz places. I'd travel to Southend for Gary Dennis' Rare Groove sessions at Chesters / Waves. Because I was traveling with my racing I was going to all the clubs in the local areas. I actually did pop down to The Wag a few times. It was interesting to see that Marshall was dancing jazz now – still pre-IDJ. In fact I heard that they were forming and was encouraged to maybe get involved.

Over a three year period, as well as going to some warehouse parties I went to an event at 'The Steam Museum' - which turned out to be a *Cock Happy* event with Gilles and Chris Bangs. I saw this incedible white dancer there and it was the first time I saw Michael Knott. I found out he was a member of IDJ. Anyway, one day I had a really bad race and so I started going out more. I went to a few more Cock Happy's' and one day I went to a Dingwalls. It was there that I saw *Pete Tormey* from Luton, I hadn't seen him since the old Jazz Funk days and he was dancing brilliantly. We started going around together dancing. We'd come to Southend for your events, as you know, and all over. Pete had this Swing-style mixed with Funk and it was great because I mixed the styles too. Nobody could read us on the floor. We could just change like that'! We had an edge.

What did you think of Dingwalls?
It wasn't The Electric Ballroom; it wasn't The Wag; it wasn't Crackers, but it was special.
The competition was heavy there.
Yes it was. There was a lot of fresh guys that wanted to get involved

By then, the whole 'Acid Jazz' thing was happening and I started dancing for *James Taylor Quartet*. We went to Japan in '89 – and there were loads of things happening. I did a few IDJ dates too - four actually -this was before Marshall and Gary broke off and formed *Back Street Kids*. I was getting asked to dance with both but the IDJ dates happened first. It was Jerry, me, Michael Knott, Melvin and Eyvon Waite. I waited ages. But the shows never happened.

Pete Tormey and I started doing shows under the name *Bubble And Squeak* and we got on this old-boy Jazz network dancing for band leaders Duncan Lamont and Frank Holder, dancing all over. It was hard but we made an impression. We did stuff with the tap dancer Will Gaines, danced at Pizza Express with *Mark Murphy* and others; danced with big bands like Stan Tracey. We were the only ones dancing in that circuit. At the same time we did a Jazz Dance competition in '89 at The Paradiso in Amsterdam. It was organized by Gary and Marshall from IDJ. We came second. We'd go to the Southport Weekender too. You had to prove yourself there. That Jazz room was heavy. Notorious. It was the last person standing'! There were so many different styles but because we're versatile it played into our hands. No one could work out which way we were going. We were trying to break down the barriers. And I'm still doing that. I'm trying to preserve these styles.

BROTHERS IN JAZZ

Again, this influential Jazz Dance group should have been in the Leeds section (even though one of the three dancers, Trevor, is from Bolton). I've put them in the London section (sorry!) purely because they were formed and were based in there.

Brothers In Jazz were absolutely crucial in the development of moves and steps in our scene and offered a complete alternative to the IDJ dancers and their Fusion style. Their influence is to be seen in Bristols *Floor Technicians* and Manchester's *Fusion Beat* crews, amongst others.

Of the three members of Brothers In Jazz: Irven Lewis, Wayne James and Trevor Miller, we hear from Irven and Trevor.

IRVEN LEWIS

I used to go to *The Precinct* and *The* Central in Leeds. The Central played some pretty heavy Jazz. Dancers used to come from Manchester and there were some pretty great battles. Bradford was heavy on a Friday night too. A lot of great jazz was played then. Before those days, the jazz that was played was more 'poppy' like *Weather Report – Birdland* and *Manhattan Transfer* stuff.

Did you go to the all-dayers?

Yes. There was a lot of all-dayers and all-nighters going on then. You could go from Manchester to Bradford to Nottingham. It was great getting on a train to the events: I would get on, say, at Manchester to go to *Clouds* in Preston and the empty train would get fuller and fuller with people going to the all-dayer, and by the time I got off at Preston there'd be a huge queue coming off all the way to the venue. It was very exciting.

What were the best all-dayers?

Nottingham Palais; Birmingham Locarno... it was all about the battling really. I was at The Locarno once and I went into the toilet and some guys said: " Stay off the dance floor tonight," or there was other times that the dancers would stand on my feet or lift me up off the floor. I once had a car waiting for me outside the fire-doors to get away!

Were you one of the dancers other dancers looked out for?

Yes. When I made my way to the top, it got pretty aggressive sometimes. You needed a few guys behind you that could hold a punch, but people just had the admission money and no job, and when the weekend came, that was *all* they had. If they wasn't in the club, they'd be in prison.

A pride thing.

Yes. You'd be battling against each other all week, but at the weekend you'd go to another city and you'd be 'as one' and you'd be battling for your area.

I heard that certain dancers knew who they were going to battle against before the event.

Yes, and I was a messenger. I'd say: "Tell —— that I'm going to battle him next week at Nottingham," and someone will tell someone else, and it passed down the line to that person in 'whatever city.' When you got to the club, you'd be warming up at one end of the full dance floor and him on the other and when it emptied out, you'd battle for an hour sometimes, move-for-move. You'd have someone holding a towel and a drink. In a 'circle' you'd say: "Contact or no contact?" Contact meant *anything*, but if you say 'no contact' and he touches you, there'd be a fight. If you were on the floor near the ' top dog' you'd leave the floor. If you danced next to him, that meant that you wanted a challenge.

It sounds like a bloody school playground, I'm afraid [laughs].

I remember Marshall from IDJ getting in some trouble at Birmingham once and at the next all-dayer, many coaches from London came up and beat everybody up and went home again. It was rough.

Area pride and personal pride.

It was all they had, as I said.

When did you move to London?

1985. I stopped dancing for a few years. I got to the top in the North and I'd battled everyone and there was no one else to beat, so I stopped. Also, the jazz dried up in the North.

The Break dancing; Hip Hop and Electro came in and the jazz dance scene was dying.
Yes, I know a lot of dancers got into Breaking, but I understood that dance floor trouble helped kill it.
Well, it wasn't as bad as that. It was just one city: Birmingham [laughs]. It was Birmingham versus *these*, Birmingham versus *those*...... Leeds, Nottingham, or whatever city, would always take one coach to an all-dayer with a mixture of men and women, but Birmingham had four or five coaches full of men! They were rough and there were lots of them! It wasn't all bad though.
Because of dancers traveling, a lot of the steps spread quickly around the country....
Yes. If you do a step to me, I've got to better it. If you do a step I like, then I'll take it and then do it my way. It was almost like a language. It's all been forgotten now, except IDJ's - steps which are the base of the Fusion style.
    Before I left for London, Colin Curtis used to play a lot of Mambos at *Berlin* [in Manchester] and *The Jazz Defektors* had this style that they did to it. It was a cool style but it didn't fit in London. When I started going to *The Wag* there, people thought me and Wayne James (later of Brothers In Jazz) were trained dancers but we were just doing our

style, which was the Northern (balletic) style mixed with the Mambo.

I saw IDJ dancing with *The Tommy Chase Quartet* at The Astoria in London and I thought: "Fucking hell." I said to Wayne: "That's what I want to do." They were amazing. I wanted to join them! I said to Wayne that we've got to do a new style down here (London) because they don't like ours. Upstairs at The Wag, we used to encourage the DJ - Sylvester – to play more Be Bop and we mixed up the Fusion and Mambo styles and sped the Mambo steps up to fit the Be Bop, and that's how our style 'Be Bop' came about.

We met this Swing dancer called Simon Selman, and he said: " You look like *The Nicholas Brothers*" and we didn't know who he was talking about. He showed us some videos of them and we could see similarities. We thought that what we were doing was fresh but we realized that someone had already done it. We adapted it into our style. We called ourselves - *The Brothers In Jazz*.

There was only two of you?
Yes. We did a show and got so out of breath that we got someone else in called *Trevor Miller*. I knew him from the North. I used to battle him. He's from Bolton. Trevor was at dance college, so we taught him our style. When we got good, we started battling IDJ at The Wag every Monday. Fantastic! Hardcore! We used to get a lot of work from going to The Wag.

The Jazz Defektors did well didn't they, and they remained up North.
Well, Tony Wilson used to manage them. He had The Hacienda and owned Factory records. They got on the TV show - *The Tube*, and were in the film Absolute Beginners. They were top-notch dancers. They wouldn't battle though; they'd say: "You're not good enough. Come back later." They did more *Mambo* and *cool* style. I have seen them battle though; they were rough boys.

What other dancers did you rate in Leeds and elsewhere in the North?
In Leeds, the originals were Oki; Steve Ceaser; Glen Cambell, and then you had Dovel Morten; Sean Adu; Wayne James and White Wayne - who we got our expressive 'hand style' from, in our dancing. In Birmingham you had Rick and Ty – The Twins, Smiler, Gilly, Wrigley and Moron, and there were a couple of girls in Nottingham called Debbie and Sophie. It's endless.

A lot of people have the impression that it was a totally Black scene up North, but it was mixed. Out of the top ten dancers, two were white men and there was a white girl and an Asian guy. Nothing to do with colour; it was all mixed.

What about the competition on TV against the Back Street Kids (see Jerry Barry interview)?
The 'Sport 7' jazz dance battle was fixed because we were from the North. When they screened it they'd edited out two-minutes of one round.

It was awful, in my opinion.
I think the Jazz Dance scene died out after that.

What did you think of Dingwalls?
You got a good hour and a half of heavy jazz - which was great, and then there would be a band and then after, it went all commercial. You got a lot of tourists in there. They had a lot of tourists at The Wag as well. I also had a lot of fights in there!

You had a few fights on the floor at Dingwalls, I heard.
I might have done (laughs). They'd ban me and then let me in again the next week.

TREVOR MILLER

I'm from a Northern Soul background. It was massive in Bolton, where I'm from. My brothers and sisters used to go to The Wigan Casino and both my brothers were brilliant dancers. I'd got them to show me some moves at home – like the 'James Brown' dancing. I was too young to go. I was practicing Northern Soul spins at the age of 11. There was a little gang of us and some would, you know, climb trees, but there were three of us that would dance and we'd swap moves. I'd always be practicing my Northern Soul dancing in youth clubs or wherever. Even when I got older and was working I'd be practicing my spins in the store room. All I thought about was dancing. There was a local disco dancer called *Bevington Williams* who'd be on TV and take over on the dance floors, and I realized that was what I wanted. *Clive Clark* (From London) was influential, who we'd see dancing on TV and (the dance troupe) 'Hot Gossip' were an influence too. There was also one guy called *Sparky* who danced Ballet style that was amazing. I got a little into Jazz Funk and would go to Colin Curtis's club Cassinellis and Greg Wilson's club Wigan Pier. That's where I started to see unusual dancing.

I used to have my hair dyed blonde or like a skunk or in a Mohican, and wear riding boots and a studded belt and an army jacket.

I thought that Black Punky– look was just exclusive to London. Hot Gossip dressed like that too didn't they?

Yes. But look at Bootsy Collins and George Clinton - that P-Funk look was quite 'punky.'

I was getting into challenges at Wigan on a regular basis – particulary with the guys from Huddersfield, and loads of others. The one thing was that we'd never let other dancers come to our area and take over and for about three weeks these four dancers came to our club and they were amazing and getting attention from the ladies. They were very graceful and moving great and were dressed well, so I went over to challenge them and take them off the floor. They were dancing in a square facing each other and I went over to one of them and he just looked over my shoulder and put his nose in the air and carried on with his friends, and that annoyed me.

The Jazz Defektors.

It was the Jazz Defektors (laughs). They were jazz men and they weren't going to waste their time with us, we weren't worthy, so over night I went straight to Manchester and brought stretch jeans, pointed straight shoes and went home, and practiced to Sly – Herbie Hancock. I was wearing out the carpet dancing late at night and my mum would give me a bollocking and send me off to bed sweating, but I did that every night to improve, and I did.

We all got on with the Leeds dancers who were amazing and they come up to us. They could do everything. They were ballet-style but not trained. Irven and Dovel were incredible. They'd been battling for years. They were a super-power at all-dayers and we'd travel with them. I managed to pick off a few dancers, which gave me confidence, and there was an unwritten code of conduct that you abided by whch was never understood in London: The most important Jazz man in that club you didn't go anywhere near unless you were prepared and qualified to challenge him. They earnt their reputation from battling other areas. It was hard fought. It would be 'contact or no contact'. The best dancers had women all over them and had an entourage like they were a Hip Hop star, and they were respected, and I thought that I'd like that.

I was continuously working on my moves but I'd watch this guy called *Dave Angol* at Preston *Clouds* and he'd do all these continuous spins up, down, on the floor, up, and I couldn't work it out. I could watch him for hours.

What did you think about the Fusion dancing?

They got in my way. When they came on I couldn't dance. They'd leg-trap you, jump all over you.

You went to dancing school.

Yes. I did fashion shows for a hair salon in Bolton. The owner Berni Lawrence – wanted the top dancers in the area and we'd choreograph them ourselves. I tried a couple of jazz– ballet classes at Northern Ballet in Manchester too. Berni recommended me to Madge Corr that owned a ballet school and I went there - my mum never wanted me to dance - but after a couple of years in 1984, after a hard audition, I got in at Urdang in London, which was funded by Bolton council. I was all over the local newspapers. I would stay on after classes and practice till midnight and I'd also go to The Electric Ballroom every Friday religiously. Gilles was DJ-ing. I got approached a couple of times by IDJ to join them. I thought they were brilliant. I started to wear jackets or suits there. I wore a blazer in the Northern Soul days - my brother had loads of suits - so it was normal. I was very nearly at the end of my second year when Irven Lewis came to Urdang - which was a dream come true - and next thing I know, Dovel came there as well. Wayne James was at West Street Ballet school and then he came to our school. I went to The Wag with Irven and Wayne: now, Brothers In Jazz were already in existence but it was hard to cover a whole song with just two so they were looking for a third dancer. Those two were amazing! Northern Jazz (ballet-style), fast-footwork and Mambo all rolled in together. I'd been messing around at The Ballroom with an old Northern Soul sequence of steps that I used to use, and that was very Mambo orientated. I would mess around with IDJ with that. I'd heard Jazz Defektors were doing that and wearing those smart suits, so I tried to go that route; anyway that was my style and they liked it. We practiced at the school constantly living and breathing Jazz. We got tighter and tighter and went clothes shopping together. After three years at Urdang our battles with IDJ at The Wag were furious. There was mutual respect but a bit of niggling going on, which made it more exciting. We got our first break from Chris Sullivan from The Wag – he was the epitome of London Soho style: a different suit every day. I wanted to be like that! He took us to Japan to choreograph a fashion show with IDJ and the band A Man Called Adam, and we went again with Gilles Peterson, Working Week and The Jazz Renegades. The crowd were going absolutely mental except for a small group of lads down the front giving that "Yeah, they're alright" kind of attitude.

The Sound Cream Steppers (Japan's original Jazz Dance troupe).

That's exactly who it was. We were being chased down the road by screaming girls there, and doing autographs.

People have said that we copied the Nicholas Brothers, but we'd never seen them before until the Swing dancer Simon Selmon showed us videos. We could see the similarity. We were shocked. We like them and the Berry Brothers, but we're influenced by films like Kiss Me Kate, Seven Brides For Seven Brothers, West Side Story....

Bob Fosse Choreography.

Yes, and Martial Arts films have been an influence as well as a lot of other things.

I wanted us to get pop-star status. Right away we were charging a lot of money - £100 a minute per dancer. We had three solid routines. We demanded the respect to be paid top dollar and we backed it up with a brilliant performance. We've done loads of TV. Chris Sulivan wanted to manage us actually, so did Mark Powell (famous Tailor).

We did a lot of big stuff like pop videos but the big one was to come: We got flown to Japan to film a sequence of five or six adverts for Parco's Christmas campaign. It's considered an honour because they usually use massive American legends to star in them, so this was a massive opportunity. We walked in to the biggest film set in Tokyo – where they filmed the original Godzilla - It was like an aircraft hanger. The ads were shown for two months leading up to Christmas. A couple of months later we went back with Gilles and (the band) Galliano. When we got on the plane we started signing autographs and the rest of the party were wondering what the hell was going on! The shows were incredible.

What did you think of Dingwalls?

Fantastic. Great music. We didn't agree with all the different styles of music being fused together with the word 'Jazz': 'Acid Jazz'? What was that about? Dingwalls had a fantastic dancefloor - you could spin forever. We were still fighting with IDJ - and by this time, with The Floor Technicians as well. When we battled in there it seemed like the whole room wanted to take us on. We got so sick of the battling and the "Brothers in Jazz think they're this or that..." or " They're unfriendly and unsociable." We were so concerned because all we wanted to do was dance amongst ourselves, but we tried to dance with the London dancers and we made a decision to go in and shake everyones hands when we got to the club, and it still made no bloody difference. For us to be at the pinnacle of what we were doing, that says a lot for us. In the end we said, "Fuck them. People can think what they like," and dancefloor etiquette went out the window in London. We'd need space for some of our moves or we could've broken an ankle or something, but people would get in the way and get hit and then the fights would start. We had to put our foot down and not let people in our space. It took fifteen hard years to get to the top and I was going to make it perfectly clear that we were at the top and you need to respect us in that way. We were there to give and share as well.

Why did Brothers In Jazz stop?

We'd done films, adverts, gone all over the world, stage work, festivals. We did everything we wanted to do. I can relax and look back now and know that we took dance to new heights and that, briefly, I was the King of the British dancers, battling from all-dayer to all-dayer, club to club.

JAZZ CHARTS

PAUL MURPHY ELECTRIC BALLROOM – 'JAZZIFUNK' CLASSICS, AS MAINLY REMEMBERED BY SEYMOUR NURSE (WITH ADDITIONS MADE FROM CHARTS AND THE AUTHOR)

Airto – Romance Of Death/ Tomba In 7/4 (Fingers – CTI 73)

Airto – Humble People (Humble People – George Wein 85)

Ariel – The Girl With Three Faces (Ariel – *Pick Up* 80)

David Amram – In Memory Of Chano Pozo (Latin Jazz Celebration – *Elektra* 82)

Monty Alexander 7 – Weekend In LA (Jamento – *Pablo* 78)

Kenny Baron – Bacchanal (*Innocence*)

Various Batucadas

Baaska & Scavelli - Get Off The Ground aka The Bottom End – (*M&K Sound*)

Victor Assis Brasil – Pro Vecha

Babatunde – Levels Of Consciousness (Levels Of Consciousness – *Theresa* 79)

Chet Baker, Jim Hall & Hubert Laws – Malaguena (Studio Trieste – *CTI* 82)

Art Blakey – A Night In Tunisia (A Night In Tunisia –*Phillips* 79)

Art Blakey – Song For A Lonely Woman (Childs Dance - *Prestige* 72)

Art Blakey – Andthenagin' (Andthenagain – *Prestige* 73)

Art Blakey – Mission Eternal (Buhaina – *Prestige* 73)

Chocolate – Trompeta En Cuero (En Sexteto – *Caiman* 83)

Chick Corea – You're My Everything / Captain Marvel (Light As A Feather–*Polydor* 73)

Chick Corea – Fickle Funk / Central Park (Secret Agent – *Polydor* 79)

Chick Corea – Samba L.A./ The Slide (Tap Step – *WB* 80)

Norman Connors & Pharoah Sanders – Beyond A Dream (Beyond A Dream – *Novus* 81)

Richie Cole – Remember Your Day Off (Alto Madness – *Muse* 78)

Richie Cole – Blue Bossa (Cool C – *Muse* 81)

Jayne Cortez And The Firespitters – I See Chano Pozo (There It Is – *Bola Press* 82)

Paquito D' Rivera – On Green Dolphin Street (Blowin' – *Columbia* 81)

Paquito D'Rivera – A Moments Notice (Mariel – *Columbia* 82)

Paulinho Da Costa – Simbora (Agora - *Pablo* 77)

Jorge Dalto – Samba All Day Long (Urban Oasis – *Concorde* 85)

Dirty Dozen Brass Band – Do It Fluid (My Feet Can't Fail Me Now – *Concorde* 84)

Drum Session – Samba Sushi (The Drum Session – *IC* 79)

Dandy's Dandy – April In Paris (A Latin Affair - *LPV* 79)

Ursula Dudziak – Roxanna / Shenkensen (Future Talk – *IC* 79)

Ursula Dudziak – A Night In Tunisia (Midnight Rain – *Arista* 77)

Chico Freeman – Wilpans Walk (Destinys Dance – *Contemporary*)

Chico Freeman – Pepes Samba (Beyond The Rain – *Contemporary* 78)

David Friedman – Rachels Samba (Futures Passed – *Inner City* 76)

Fuse One – In Celebration Of The Human Spirit (Slick – *CTI* 81)

Sonny Fortune – There's Nothing Smart About Being Stupid / Bacchanal (Serengeti Minstrel – *Atlantic* 77)

Sonny Fortune – Revelation (Waves Of Dreams – *Horizon* 76)

Clare Fischer – Descarga Yemaya (Salsa Picante – *MPS* 78)

Jerry Gonzalez and the Fort Apache band – Be Bop/ Parisian Thoroughfare (The River Is Deep – *ENJA* 82)

Jerry Gonzalez and the Fort Apache band – Caravan / Evidence (Ya Yo Me Cure –*American Clave* 80)

Roger Glenn – Rio (Reachin'- *Fantasy* 76)

Grupo Medusa – Ferrovias (Ferrovias -*Som da Gente* 83)

Grupo Medusa – Ponto De Fusao (Grupo Medusa – *Som De Gente* 80)

Patsy Gallant – Te Caliente (Patsy – *Miracle* 79)

Dizzy Gillespie – Caravan (Afro – *Columbia*)

Wlodeck Golgowski – Soundcheck (Soundcheck – *Polydor Pol* 76)

Joanne Grauer – See You Later (Introducing Lorraine Feather – *Pausa* 78)

Herbie Hancock – Sly (Headhunters – *CBS* 73)

Herbie Hancock – Shiftless Shuffle (Mr Hands - *CBS* 80)

Terumasa Hino – Merry Go Round (Double Rainbow – *Columbia* 81)

Terumasa Hino – Samba De La Cruz (City Connection – *IC* 79)

Woody Herman – Third Movement (Chick, Donald, Walter & Woodrow – *Centuary* 78)

Roy Haynes – Quiet Fire (Thank you Thank you – *Galaxy* 77)

Freddie Hubbard – Gilbralter (Born To Be Blue – *Pablo* 82)

Paul Horn – Salvador (Altura Do Sol – *Epic* 76)

Jon Hassel – Voodoo Wind (Earthquake Island – *Tom*

78)

Jay Hoggard – Samba Pa Negra (Days Like These – *GRP* 79)

Dick Hyman – Mas Que Nada (Brazilian Impressions – *Command* 67)

Irakere – Chekere Son (Chekere Son – *Milestone* 81)

Robin Jones – Con Fuego / Denga / Goodbye Batucada (Denga – *Apollo Sound* 71)

Robin Jones – Batucada De Vida (El Maja – *Apollo Sound* 72)

Joachim Kuhn – First Frisco (Hip Elegy – *MPS* 76)

Eric Kloss – The Samba Express (Celebration – *Muse* 80)

Karma – Kwanzaa (Celebration – *A&M* 74)

Fela Kuti – Roforofo Fight (Roforofo Fight – *EMI Nig* 75)

Fela Kuti – Expensive Shit (Expensive Shit – *EMI Nig* 75)

Fela Kuti – Shakara Oloje (Shakara – *EMI Nig* 74)

Azar Lawrence – Forces Of Nature (Bridge Into The New Age – *Prestige* 74)

Pat Longo – I Believe In Love (Chain Reaction – *Town Hall* 79)

Azar Lawrence – Novo Ono (Summer Solstice – *Prestige* 75)

Hubert Laws – Moments Notice/Airegin (In The Beginning – *CTI*)

Ramsey Lewis – Slick (Salongo – *CBS* 76)

Lonnie Liston Smith – Mardi Gras (Rennaisance – *RCA* 76)

Janet Lawson – So High (Janet Lawson – *IC* 81)

David Lahm – Shazam (Real Jazz For The Folks Who Feel Jazz – *PAJ* 82)

Jeff Lorber – Chinese Medicinal Herbs (Jeff Lorber – *IC* 77)

Jeff Lorber – The Samba (Soft Space – *IC* 78)

David Leibman – Loft Dance (Drum Ode – *ECM* 74)

Mike Longo – Gingele (Funkia – *Groove Merchant*)

Jayme Marques – Vera Cruz (So Much Feeling – RCA *Spain* 77)

George Muribus – Brazilian Tapestry (Brazilian Tapestry – *Catalyst* 76)

Cecil McBee – Pepi's Samba (Compassion – *Enja* 77)

Peter Magadini – Samba De Rollins (Polyrhythm – *Briko* 76))

Barry Miles – Magic Theater (Magic Theater – *London* 75)

Barry Miles – Los Viajeros (..and Silverlight – *London* 74)

Alphonse Mouzon – Bakers Daughter (Virtue – *Pausa* 77)

Alphonse Mouzon – Antonia (Essence Of Mouzon)

Idris Muhammed – Rhythm (Peace And Rhythm – *Prestige*)

Idris Muhammed – Sudan (House Of The Rising Sun – *Kudu* 76)

Mat Marucci – Who Do Voo Doo (Who Do Voo Doo – *Marco* 79)

The Byron Morris Unit – Sun Shower (Vibrations, Themes & Serenades – *EPI* 78)

Herbie Mann – Music Is A Game We Play (First Play – *Atlantic* 74)

Herbie Mann – Samba D' Orfeu (Live At Newport – *Atlantic* 63)

Herbie Mann – New York Is A Jungle Festival (Return To The Village Gate – *Atlantic* 63)

Bobby McFerrin – Dance With Me / Jubilee (Bobby McFerrin – *Elektra* 82)

Tania Maria – Mr And Mrs (Live – *Accord* 79)

Tania Maria – Eruption (Taurus – *Concord* 82)

Sergio Mendes – Primitivo (Desafinado – *Contour* 71)

Machito – Macho (Fireworks – *Coco* 77)

Mike Manieri – Bullet Train (Wanderlust – *WB* 81)

Naoya Matsuoka and Wesing – Pao De Acucar (Fiesta Fiesta – *Disco Mate* 79)

Manteca – Batucada (Manteca - *Ready* 82)

Andy Narell – 7 Steps To Heaven (Hidden Treasure – *Inner City* 79)

Opa – Montevideo (Magic Time – *Milestone* 77)

Opa – African Bird (Golden Wings – *Milestone* 76)

The New Dave Pike Sextet feat Grupo Biafro – Samba de Roda (Salomao – *BASF* 73)

Rainer Pusch – Mixing

Pointer Sisters – Salt Peanuts (That's A Plenty – *Blue Thumb* 74)

Dave Pike – Spirits Samba (Let The Minstrels Play On – *Muse* 80)

Dave Pike – Djalma (Times Out Of Mind – *Muse* 76)

Daniel Ponce – Basta De Cuentos (New York Now – *Oao* 83)

Art Pepper – Mambo De La Pinta (No Limit – *Contemporary* 78)

Flora Purim – Moon Dreams (Butterfly Dreams – *Milestone* 73)

Flora Purim – Vera Cruz / Casa Forte (Stories To Tell – *Milestone* 74)

Flora Purim – Bridge - live (500 Mile High – *Milestone* 76)

Paz – AC/DC (Paz Are Back – *Spotlite* 80)

Jaco Pastorious – Used To Be A Cha Cha (Jaco Pastorious – *Epic* 76)

Dewey Redman – Unknown Tongue (Musics)

Reverie – Every Way (Reverie – *Encounter* 80)

Dom Um Romao – Braun Blek Blue (Dom Um Romao – *Muse* 74)

Dom Um Romao – Shake/ Angels/ Highway (Spirit Of The Times – *Muse* 75)

Patrice Rushen – Jubilation (Before The Dawn – *Prestige* 75)

Charlie Rouse – Cinnamon Flower (Cinnamon Flower – *Douglas* 77)

Raices – Lenguas (Raices – *Nemporer* 75)

Rare Silk – Spain (New Weave – *Polygram* 83)

Alfredo Rodriguez & Patato – Dicelo Patato (Patato-Totico – *Disques Esperance* 83)

Lonnie Smith – Apex (When The Night Is Right – *Chiaoscuro* 80)

Lonnie Smith – Straight To The Point (Afro-Desia – *Groove Merchant* 75)

Lonnie Smith – The Call Of The Wild (Think – *Blue Note*)

Finn Savery Trio – Waveform (Waveform – *Metronome* 76)

San Francisco Express- Getting It Together (Getting It Together – *Reynolds* 79)

Semuta – La Fayette / No Face No Name (Semuta – *Lee Lambert* 79)

Harris Simon – Romance Of Death/ North Station (New York Connection – *Teickitu* 78)

Horace Silver – The Gringo (Doin' The Thing – *Blue Note* 61)

Horace Silver – In Pursuit Of The 27th Man (In Pusuit Of The 27th Man - *Blue Note* 73)

Dom Salvador – Passagem (My Family – *Muse* 76)

Mongo Santamaria – Nothing For Nothing (Mongo At The Village Gate – *Riverside*)

David Schnitter – Flying Colours (Thundering – *Muse* 78)

Stone Alliance – Samba De Negra / Vaya Mullato (Stone Alliance -*PM* 76)

Bud Shank – Brasamba (Brasamba! Bossa Nova – *Pacific Jazz* 63)

Bernie Senensky – Free Spirit (Free Spirit – *PM* 81)

Wilfredo Stephenson – Aire Para Respirar/ La Batucomparsa (An Ensemble Of Salsa Percussion – *Amigo* 82)

McCoy Tyner – Love Samba (13th House – *Milestone* 82)

McCoy Tyner – Love Samba – live (Atlantis – *Milestone*)

McCoy Tyner – Samba De Salvador (Fly Like The Wind – *Milestone*)

Cal Tjader – Mama Aguela (Primo – *Fantasy* 73)

Cal Tjader – Tambu in 7/4 (Tambu – *Fantasy*)

Cal Tjader & Carmen McRea – Love (Heatwave – *Concorde* 82)

Cal Tjader – Mambo Mindora (La Onda Va Bien – *Concorde Picante* 79)

Frode Thingnaes Quintet – Around Once More (Direct To Dish -*Talent* 80)

Michael Urbaniak – More Smiles Forever (Smiles Ahead – *MPS* 77)

Nana Vasconcelos – Chega De Corps (Zumbi – *Europa* 83)

James Williams – Flying Colors (Flying Colors – *ZIM* 77)

Bill Watrous – The Tiger Of San Pedro (Tiger Of San Pedro – *Columbia* 75)

Bishop Norman Williams – Billy Ballet (Bishop's Bag – *Theresa* 78)

Working Week – The Bottom End (Venceremos 12" – *Paladin / Virgin* 84)

Sadao Watanabe – Felicadade (Open Road –*Sony Japan* 73)

COLIN CURTIS

A. K. Selim – Drums Origin Africa

Al Jarreau - Take Five

Airto – Tombo In 7/4 / Celebration Suite/ Toque De Cuica

Alive – Skindo Le Le

Art Blakey – A Night In Tunisia

Art Pepper – Besame Mucho / Tin Tin Deo

Art Webb – You Can't Hide Love

Astrud Gilberto – Girl From Ipanema

Azymuth – Aquia Nao Come Mosca

Ben Sidran - Solar

Bobby Lyle – The Genie

Bobby Matos – Tema Da Alma Latina

Byron Morris – Little Sunflower

Cal Tjader And Carmen McRea – Don't You Worry 'Bout A Thing

Cal Tjader – Mambo Inn

Carmen McRea – Take Five

Charlie Rouse – Back To The Tropics

Chet Baker – Do It The Hard Way

Chocolate – Trompeta Brasil

Cocoanuts Crew – On A Clear Day

Carlos Garnett - Various

Dave Brubeck – Take Five

David Lahm – Shazam

David Matthews – Sambafrique

Dee Felice Trio – Crickets Sing For Anamaria

Dianne Schuur – It Don't Mean A Thing

Dirty Dozen Brass Band – Do It Fluid

Dizzy Gillespie – A Night In Tunisia

Dom Um Romao – Spirit Of The Times / Braun Blek Blu

Donald Byrd – Places And Spaces / Dominoes (live) / Jeannine

Duke Pearson – Jeannine

Earl Grant - House Of Bamboo

Ed Lincoln – Miss Balancao / Zum Zum Zum

Eddie Jefferson - Jeannine

Eddie 'Lockjaw' Davis – Afro Jaws

Elbow Bones And The Racketeers – A Night In New York

Ella Fitzgerald – Mack The Knife

Finn Savory Trio – Wave Form

Flora Purim – Casa Forte

Gary Bartz – Music Is My Sanctuary
George Benson – Beyond The Sea
George Muribus – Brasilian Tapestry
Gilberto Gil – Toda Menina Baiana
Grupo Medusa – Various
Guanabara – Brasilian Beat
Himoki Kikuchi – What's Baby Singing
Hugh Masekela – Don't Go Lose It Baby
Ivan 'Boogaloo Joe' Jones – Black Whip
Jackie & Roy – Don't Be Blue
James Mason – Slick City
Janet Lawson – Dindi / So High
Jerry Gonzalez - Various
Jimmy Cobb – So Nobody Else Can Hear
Jimmy Owens – Do It To It
Joanne Grauer & Lorraine Feather – See You Later
Joe Bataan – The Bottle
Johnny Lytle - Selim
John Hendricks – I Bet You Thought I'd Never Find You
Jon Lucien – Listen Love
Judy Roberts – Never Was Love / Rainbow In Your Eyes
Last Poets – It's A Trip
Lee Morgan – The Sidewinder
Lesette Wilson – Caveman Boogie
Lonnie Liston Smith – Never Too Late / Mardi Gras / Expansions (live)
Lonnie Satin - Caravan
Manhattan Transfer – Shaker Song
Marcos Valle – Crickets Sing For Anamaria
Mark Murphy – Two Kites / Rah
Mike Campbell – Soft Strum Blues
Miles Davis - Milestones

Nancy Wilson – Call Me
Nathan Davis - If
Nina Simone – My Baby Just Cares For Me
Nobuo Yagi – Mi Mi Africa
Norman Connors – Mother Of The Future
Opa – Golden Wings
Oscar Brown Jr – Dat Dere / Work Song
Pacific Eardrum – Inner Circles
Pacific Jam – Antes De Me Nada
Pat Longo – I Believe In Love
Peggy Lee - Fever
Pharoah Sanders – You Got To Have Freedom
Pleasure – Glide / 2 For 1
Pointer Sisters – Salt Peanuts
Quartette Tres Bien – Boss Tres Bien / Brasil
Rahmlee - Think
Raices - Various
Ramsey Lewis - Salongo
Reuben Wilson – Got To Get Your Own
Reverie – In Every Way
Rhythm Makers - Zone
Richie Cole – New York Afternoon
Roger Glenn - Rio
Roy Haynes - Vistalite
Sabu – Palo Conga / El Cumbanchero
Sergio Mendes – Mas Que Nada
Sivuca – Ain't No Sunshine
Stone Alliance - Various
Tania Maria – Come With Me / Yatra Ta
Terumasa Hino – Double Rainbow
To Be – Samba De Heino
Victor Feldman - Skippin'
Webster Lewis – El Bobo
Young Holt Trio – Wack Wack

GREG WILSON - WIGAN PIER/LEGENDS

Baya – A Vegas Kind Of Guy
Bobby McFerrin – Dance With Me
Chuck Rainey – Born Again
Cocoanuts Crew – Sambolero
Dom Um Romao – Braun Blek Blu
Gene Harris – Meditation
Gilberto Gil – Palco
Grover Washington Jr – Little Black Samba
Lessette Wilson – Caveman Boogie
Manu Dibango – Waka Juju
Paz – AC/DC
Peter Magadini – Samba De Rollins
Ray Barretto - Pastime Paradise
Studio Trieste – Malaguena
Toki And The Samba Friends – Brasil

Art Blakey – A Night In Tunisia
Art Pepper – Today
Boy Katindig – Midnight Lady
Brazilia – Brazilia
Cayenne – Roberto Who?
Chick Corea – Light As A Feather
Gerry Mulligan – Little Big Horn
Lonnie Liston Smith – Dreams Of Tomorrow
Masura Imada – Andalusian Breeze
Paulinho Da Costa – Agora
Tania Maria – Come With Me
Richie Cole – Return To Alto Acres
Swamp Children – So Hot
Victor Feldman – Secret Of The Andes
War – The Music Band Jazz

DAVID HOLMES - TRACKS REMEMBERED BY A PUNTER, AS PLAYED IN THE NORTH

Terumasa Hino - Samba De La Cruz (City Connection –*Flying Disc*)

Tadao Hayashi - Finger Trip II

Toki & His Samba Friends – Brasil

Genji Sawai & Bacon Egg - Hand & Foot (Skipjack-*Flying Disc*)

Casiopea -Eyes Of The Mind (Original Japanese issue)

Mikio Masuda
- Silver Shadow

Toshiyuki Honda - Coconut Crash

Toshiyuki Honda & Burning Waves – Burning Waves

Nobuo Yagi - Mi Mi Africa (Mi Mi Africa – *Invitation*)

Pacific Jam - Antes De Me Nada/Pao De Acucar (Pacific Jam – *Disco Mate*)

Alphonse Mouzon - By All Means (By All Means – *PAUSA*)

Dave Pike - Swan Lake / Spirit Samba (Lets The Minstrels Play – *Muse*)

David Benoit -Life Is Like Samba (*AVI*)

Richard Evans
- Capricorn Rising

Karma -Kwanzaa (Celebration – *Horizon*)

Barry Miles & Silverlight – Los Viajeros (Barry Miles & Silverlight - *London*)

Neil Larson - Demonette/ Sudden Samba

Ritchie Cole - Back To Bop / Blue Bossa (Cool C – *Muse*)

Richie Cole & Eddie Jefferson – New York Afternoon (Keeper Of The Flame – *Muse*)

Dave Valentin - Land Of The Third Eye/ Fantasy (Land Of The Third eye- *Arista*)

Ray Barretto - Pastime Paradise / The Old Castle (La Cuna – *CTI*)

Chick Corea - The Slide (Tap Step –*WB*)

Chick Corea - Love Castle (My Spanish Heart - *Polydor*)

Carlos Santana - Golden Hours

Raices - Various

Mike Manieri - Bullet Train (Wanderlust)

Al Jarreau - Take Five (live)

Studio Trieste - Malaguena (Studion Trieste – *CTI*)

McCoy Tyner – Love Samba
- Walk Spirit Talk Spirit (Leylanda De La Hora – *Columbia*)
- Rubber Miro (*99*)

Manfredo Fest – Jungle Kitten
- Jungle Kitten (Manifestations – *Tabu*)

Kellis Etheridge - Quickie Nirvana (Tomorrow Sky – *Inner City*)

Clare Fisher - Descarga Yema Ya (Salsa Picante – *Discovery*)

David Sandborn - Lets Just Say Goodbye (Voyeur – *WB*)

Eddie Daniels
- Good Morning Bahia/Carnival Lady (Morning Thunder – *Columbia*)

Jay Hoggard - Sao Paulo (Rain Forest – *Contemporary*)

Tania Maria - Vem P'ra Roda/ Yatra Ta (Piquant – *Concord*)

Judy Roberts - Ole' (Nights In Brazil – *Inner City*)

Boy Katindig - Whatever Happened To The Love / Aqua De Beber (Midnight Lady – *PAUSA*)

Stanley Turrentine - World Chimes (Tender Togetherness – *Elecktra*)

Colliers & Dean - San Juan (Whistling Midgets – *Inner City*)

GRAHAM WARR - A FEW RECORDS PLAYED AT CHAPLINS

Eddie Russ - Tea leaves / Zaius

Dave Benoir - Life Is Like A Samba

Taj Mahal - Salsa De Leventalle

John Gibbs - Trinidad

Renzo Fraize - 12 Engle Street

Johnny Hammond - Los Conquistadores Chocolates

Gary Boyle - Snap Crackle

Doug Richardson - Aphrodesia / On The Prowl

Chick Corea - The Samba

Maynard Ferguson - Soar Like An Eagle

Willie Bobo - Always There

Roy Ayers - Running Away

Lee Ritenour - Fly By Night

John Klemmer - Paradise

CHRIS BANGS CHART FROM 12/3/82

Arild Anderson Quartet - Radkas Samba

Harris Simon - North Station

Roger Glenn - Rio

Opa - African Bird

Pharoah Sanders - Origin

Oli Ahvenlahti - Samba Town

Airto - Romance Of Death

Webster Lewis - Barbara Ann

Last Poets - It's A Trip

Flip Nunez - D'yu Like Me

ALEX LOWES - AS REMEMBERED BY FRIEND GARY ROBSON

Airto - Samba De Flora
Afro Latin Quartet Plus One -Mystic Mambo
Mark Murphy - Brasil Song
Airtio -Toque De Cuica
Herbie Mann And Tamiko Jones - The Sidewinder
Hector Costita -1985
Webster Lewis - El Bobo

Jackie And Roy - Will We Ever Know?
Freddie Hubbard - Gibraltar
Paz - AC/DC
Bucky Leo Quintet - Rejoice In Righteousness
Harris Simon - Factory/Wind Chant
Dianne Reeves -The Lamp Is Low
James Mason - Sweet Power Your Embrace
Lonnie Smith - Raise Your Hand

DJ LUBI - 'WILDSTYLE' JAZZ ROOM 1984

Mongo Santamaria - Cuidado
McCoy Tyner - Love Samba
Herbie Mann - Jungle Fantasy
Charlie Palmieri - Mambo Show
Tania Maria - Sangria
Airto - Celebration Suite
Art Blakey - Night In Tunisia
Batida - Ponteio
Dave Valentin - Enceddido
Poncho Sanchez - Night In Tunisia

Raices - Lenguas
David Amran - En Memoria Do Chano Pozo
Paulinho Da Costa - Ritmo No.1
Chico Freeman - Passin Thru
Jack Costanzo - Taboo
Dizzy Gillespie - Mas Que Nada
Irakere - Chekere Son
Paz - AC/DC
Sergio Mendes Trio - Somewhere In The Hills
Gato Barbieri - Viva Emiliano Zapata

JAZZ PLAYED BY CHRIS HILL AT THE GOLDMINE - CANVEY ISLAND 1973 -1984. TAKEN FROM WWW.SOULPRANOS.CO.UK

Miles Davis - Milestones
Mark Murphy - Milestones
Lee Morgan - Sidewinder
Donald Byrd - Lansanas Priestess
Pat Longo - I Believe In Love
Bobby Humphrey - Harlem River Drive
Don Wilkerson - Dem Tambourines
Grover Washington Jr - Saulsalito
Duke Pearson - Sandalia Lea
Sea Wind - He Loves You
Pacific Eardrum - Inner Circles
Astrud Gilberto - Take Me To Aruanda
Sergio Mendes - Mas Que Nada
Quartette Tres Bien - Boss Tres Bien
Georgie Fame - Little Samba
Mark Murphy - Down St. Thomas Way
Jackie And Roy - Don't Be Blue
Webster Lewis - El Bobo
Richie Cole - New York Afternoon
Jon Hendricks - I Bet You Thought I'd Never Find You
Jimmy Cobb - Pistachio
Paulette Reeves - Jazz Freak
Trudy Pitts - Love For Sale
Barbara Carroll - From The Beginning
Pat Britt - Star Song
Jimmy Smith - Can't Hide Love

Milt Jackson - Soul Fusion
Fela Kuti - Expensive Shit
Lonnie Liston Smith - Mardi Gras
David Sanborn - Love Is Not Enough
McCoy Tyner - Love Samba
Fela Kuti - Roforofo Fight
Freddie Hubbard - Gilbralter
Johnny Guitar Watson - I'll Remember April
Pacific Jam - Antes De Me Nada
Eddie Jefferson - Jeannine
Grover Washington Jr - Little Black Samba
Lonnie Liston Smith - Expansions
Miroslav Vitous - New York City
Alive - Skindo Le Le
Hiroshi Fukumara - Hunt Up Wind
Eydie Gorme - Coffee Song
Earl Grant - House Of Bamboo
Johnny Hammond - Los Conquistadores Chocolates
Donald Byrd - Night Flight
Joanne Grauer - See You Later
Tania Maria - Come With Me
Big John Patton - Latona
David Benoit - Life Is Like A Samba
Nina Simone - My Baby Just Cares For Me
Chick Corea - Central Park
Sonny Stitt - Slick Eddie

Azymuth - Jazz Carnival
Cedar Walton - Latin America
Sivuca - Ain't No Sunshine
George Duke - Brasilian Love Affair
Jimmy McGriff - All About My Girl
Dave Grusin - Mountain Dance
Art Blakey - Moanin'
Jack McDuff - Blue Monsoon
Wes Montgomery - Tequila
Bobby Lyle - The Genie
Mikio Masuda - My Delight
Eddie Russ - Zaius/Tea Leaves
Bob James - Westchester Lady
Webster Lewis - Barbara Ann
Dexter Wansel - Life On Mars
Willie Bobo - Always There
Nancy Wilson - Call Me
Sonny Rollins - Alfies Theme
Wayne Henderson - I'm Staying Forever
Ivan 'Boogaloo Joe' Jones - Black Whip
Joe Sample - There Are Many Stops Along The Way
Massada - Na Na Na Song
Manfredo Fest - Jungle Kitten
Rodney Franklin - The Groove
Gabor Szabo - Keep Smilin'
Eddie Henderson - Prance On
Ed Lincoln - Blues Walk
Jeff Lorber - The Samba
Sea Wind - Free
Brian Auger - In And Out
Young Holt Unlimited - Wack Wack
Walt Wanderley - Cheganca
Sonny Rollins - St. Thomas

Fuse One - Grand Prix
Spyro Gyra - Shaker Song
Manu Dibango - Big Blow
Bobby McFerrin - Dance With Me
John Handy - Carnival
Dee Felice Trio - The Crickets Sing
Urbie Green - Another Star
Neil Larsen - Sudden Samba/Demonette
Lee Ritenour - Fly By Night
Herbie Hancock - I Thought It Was You (Jap version)
Oscar Brown Jr - Mr Kicks
Richie Cole - Hi Fly
Jimmy Smith - The Cat
Ivan 'Boogaloo Joe' Jones - 6-30 Blues
Janet Lawson - So High
Mose Allison - The Seventh Son
Michael Franks - The Lady Wants To Know
Gil Scott Heron - Lady Day And John Coltrane
Mel Torme - Comin' Home Baby
Ray Charles - Hit The Road Jack
Georgie Fame - Yeah Yeah
Richie Cole with Eddie Jefferson - New York Afternoon
Benny Golson - The New Killer Joe
Dianne Reeves - Sky Islands
Jon Lucien - Listen Love
Ella Fitzgerald - Mas Que nada
Chet Baker - Do It The Hard Way
Eddie Jefferson - Take The 'A' Train
Georgie Fame - Moodys Mood For Love
Mose Allison - If You're Going To The City
Gil Scott Heron - The Bottle
George Benson - The World Is A Ghetto

CHRIS HILL - A FEW RHYTHM AND BLUES/SOUL JAZZ TRACKS

Nat Adderley -Work Song
Lee Morgan -The Sidewinder
Freddie Roach - Brown Sugar
Cannonball Adderley - Jeannine
Oscar Brown Jnr - Mr Kicks
Mose Allison - Swingin' Machine
Jimmy Smith - I Got My Mojo Workin'
Don Wilkerson -Dem Tambourines
Ivan "Boogaloo" Jones - 6.30 Blues
Jimmy Mc Griff - All About My Girl
Hank Mobley - The Turnaround

Art Blakey - Moanin'
Rusty Bryant - Friday Night Funk For Saturday Night Brothers
Curtis Amy - Mustang
Big John Patton - Fat Judy
Herbie Hancock - Watermelon Man
Brian Auger - In And Out
Mel Torme -Comin' Home Baby
Willis Jackson - Nuther'n Like Thutherin'n
Hank Jacobs -So Far Away

DR BOB JONES 'JAZZ AND ALL THAT.....'

Jimmy Smith - Back At The Chicken Shack (Blue Note)
John Coltrane - Mr. PC (Atlantic)
Ivan 'Boogaloo Jo' Jones - Black Whip (Prestige)

Miles Davis - Devil May Care (CBS)
Lionel Hampton - A & T (Glad Hamp)
Art Blakey & The Jazz Messangers - Ping Pong (Riverside)

Johnny Lytle - Selim (Tuba)
Fela Kuti & Africa 70 - Roforofo Fight (Editions Makossa Intl)
Gene Ludwig - Sticks & Stones Pts 1 & 2 (Atlantic)
Don Wilkerson - Dem Tambourines (Blue Note)
Dizzy Gillespie - Caravan (Columbia)
Jimmy Smith - The Cat (Verve)
Rusty Bryant - Friday Night Funk For Saturday Night Brothers (Prestige)
Roland Kirk - 3-In-1 Without The Oil (Mercury)
Sahib Shihab - Seeds (YoungBlood)
Lou Donaldson - Rev Moses (Blue Note)
Carlos Franzetti - Cocoa Funk (Guinness)
Julie Kelly - Better Than Anything (Pausa)
Oliver Nelson & Joe Newman - Latino (Prestige)

Stormy Jazzmin - Stormy Jazzmin Pts 1 & 2 (Storm)
Irakere - Chekere Son (JVC)
Lonnie Smith - 3 Blind Mice (Blue Note)
Herbie Mann - New York is A Jungle Festival (Atlantic)
Tito Peunte - Ran Kan Kan (Picante)
Norman Bishop Williams -Billys Ballet (Theresa)
Herbie Hancock - Wiggle Waggle / Fat Mama (Warner Bros)
Horace Silver Quintet - Sayanora Blues (Blue Note)
Freddie McCoy - Spider Man (Prestige)
Sarah Vaughan - Trieste (Verve)
Bill Reddie & Jack Eglash - No Man No (Coral)
Charlie Antolini - Love For Sale (Jazz Power

PHIL LEVENE - WAG CLUB

Live)
Art Blakey - Songs For A Lonely Woman (Child's Dance)
George Benson - Octane (Space)
Ted Curson - Airis Tune (Jubilant Power)
Kenny Clarke / Francy Boland -Wintersong (Off Limits)
Eric Dolphy - Status Seeking (The Quest)
Chico Freeman - Pepis Samba (Beyond The Rain)
Chico Freeman -Wilkins Walk (Destiny's Dance)
Eddie Gomez - Carribean Morning (Mezgo)
Bunky Green - Fast And Foxy (The Latinization Of...)
Louis Gasca - Motherless Child (The Little Giant)

Jerry Gonzalez - Be Bop (The River Is Deep)
Woody Herman - Third Movement (Chick, Donald & Woodrow)
Paul Horn - Dun-Dunnee (Something Blue)
Listen feat. Mel Martin - The Mosquito Steps Out
Yusef Lateef - Drink Water (In Nigeria)
Azar Lawrence - Bridge Into The New Age (same)
Matt Marrucci - Fresh Start (Lifeline)
Lee Morgan - Our Man Higgins (Cornbread)
Emanuel K. Rahim - Spirit Of The Truth (Total Submission)
Louis Ramirez - Rush Hour In Hong Kong (Vibes Galore)

TERRY JONES - 'JAZZ IN THE AFTERNOON' AT NORFOLK VILLAGE

Carmen McRae - More Today Than Yesterday
Doobie Brothers - South Bay Strut
Grover Washington Jnr - Sausalito
Joe Sample - There Are Many Stops Along The Way
Aretha Franklin - April Fools
Peabo Bryson & Roberta Flack - On A Clear Day/Killer Joe (live)
Carmen McRae - Mister Magic
Sivuca - Ain't No Sunshine
Les McCann & Eddie Harris - Compared To What

Roberta Flack - Go Up Moses
MFSB - Lay In Low
Freddie Hubbard - Little Sunflower
Mongo Santamaria - Cloud Nine
Quincy Jones - If I Ever Lose This Heaven
Carmen McRae - Elusive Butterfly
Stanley Turrentine - You'll Never Find Another Love
Nancy Wilson - The End Of Our Love
Herbie Mann - Philly Dog
Ramsey Lewis - Julia
Carmen McRae - Can't Hide Love

DUNCAN UREN - JAPANESE JAZZ CHART

Terruo Nakamura - A Day In The Life Of A Frog/ Snap Crackle
Samba Calioca - Quero De Volta O Meu Pandeiro
Takanaka - Funky Holo Holo Bird
Manhattan Focus - Tara Joe Busco
Kazumi Watanabe- Lonesome Cat
Samurai - Mur'yo
Yutaka Yokokura - Love Light

Takanaka - Sexy Dance
Tomiko Takahashi - Trial Road
Hiroki Miyano - Teou's Dance
Chikara Ueda And The New Herd - Que Lastima
Jun Fukumachi - Sea Horse
Kylyn - Akaska Moon
Yuji Toriyama - Get That Funky Feeling

THE A2 CONNECTION - MAY 84

Batida - Vera Cruz
Sergio Mendes - Fato Consumado
Herbie Hancock - The Eye Of The Hurricane
Betty Carter - Sounds
Julie Kelly - Better Than Anything
Airto - Tombo In 7/4

Robin Jones - Denga
Dizzy Gillespie - Ups 'N Downs
John Coltrane - Impressions
Don Sebetsky - Free As A Bird
Donald Byrd - Dig

MAD MARX / SNOWBOY - THE AUTHORS ALL-TIME FAVOURITE 30

Chick Corea - The Slide
Tico Allegre All Stars - Tito's Odyssey
Airto - The Road Is Hard
Ariel - The Girl With Three Faces
Brand X - Earth Dance
Jon Lucien - Listen Love
Willis Jackson - Nuthern' Like Thuthern'
Lonnie Smith - Call Of The Wild
Bunny Brunel - You
McCoy Tyner - Love Samba
Mike Manieri - Bullet Train
Fela Kuti - Roforofo Fight
Pacific Jam - Antes De Me Nada
George Shearing - Mambo With Me
Working Week - Venceremos

Raices - Whole album
Fuse One - Celebration Of The Human Spirit
Cal Tjader - Tu Crees Que
Barry Miles - Magic Theater
Flora Purim - Moon Dreams
Benny Barth - Caravan
Jon Lucien - A Time For Me To Fly
Eddie Palmieri And Cal Tjader - Bamboleate
Harris Simon - Wind Chant
John Payne - The Razors Edge
Tubby Hayes - Cherokee
Monika Linges - Courage
Mongo Santamaria - Carmela
Tony Bennett - Just One Of Those Things
Walt Dickerson - The Cry

SYLVESTER - FROM AUGUST 1989

Tito Puente - Sax Con Ritmo
Afro Cuban All Stars - Rhythmagic
Bobby Montez - Mambo Caravan
Eddie Palmieri - El Molestaso
Joe Commodore - Latin Dance Party

Vladimir - Mambolito
Ray Barretto - Swing La Moderna
Nina Rivera - Cuban Jam
Bobby Valentin - Rumba Caliente
Machito - Half And Half

'JAZZ NOT JAZZ' CLASSICS

Stetsasonic - Talkin' All That Jazz (Tommy Boy 88)
Soho - Hot Music (USOA 90)
Jazz Not Jazz - Flip And Trip (Eight Ball 91)
Jazz Documents - Scret Code (Nu Groove 91)
Dream Warriors - My Definition Of A Boombastic Jazz Style (Fourth And Broadway 90)

CFM Band - Jazz It Up (Underworld)
Gand Starr - Jazz Thing (CBS 90)
Rebith Of The Cool LP (Fourth And Broadway 93)
Pharcyde - Passin' Me By (Delicious Vinyl 93)
Jean Luc Ponty - In The Fast Lane (Storytelling - Columbia 89)

DINGWALLS CLASSICS BY GILLES PETERSON AND PATRICK FORGE, FROM STRAIGHT NO CHASER MAGAZINE NO. 11 SPRING 1991

Airto And Flora Purim - Samba De Flora
Pharoah Sanders - You've Got To Have Freedom
Gang Starr - Jazz Thing
Soul Tornadoes - Hot Pants Breakdown
Yusef Lateef - Brother John
Jean Luc Ponty - In The Fast Lane

Funk Inc - The Better Half
Willis Jackson - Nuthern' Like Thuthern'
Young Disciples - Step Right On
Jayme Marques - Vera Cruz

There could be millions more..........

DAVID 'TIN TIN' ZEE - ROTTERDAM, HOLLAND TOP 20

Cyriel Jackson - Rumba Abierta
Kenny Dorham - Afrodisia
Art Blakey - The Feast
Airto - Samba de Flora
Rusty Bryant - Cold Duck Time
The Three Souls - Milestones
Big John Patton - Latona
Hank Mobley - Avila And Tequila
Lou Donaldson - Move
Bobby Valentin - Zip Zap
Pucho - Dearly Beloved

Alive - Skindo Le Le
Jon Lucien - Listen Love
Sabu - Cumbanchero
Joe Carroll - Gamblers Blues
Rusty Bryant - Cold Duck Time
Eddie Lockjaw Davis - Wild Rice
Jack Costanzo - Abaniquito
Mongo Santamaria - Nothing For Nothing
Stanley Turrentine - And Satisfy
Willis Jackson - Nuthern' Like Thuthern'

COLIN PARNELL AND BOO 'HORSESHOE' CHART

Louie Bellson and Walfredo De Los Reyes– Para Buenos Bailarines
Carioca – Toru De Samba
Chick Corea – Central Park
Richie Cole – Remember Your Day Off
Caldera – Celebration/ Himilaya
Norman Connors – Mother Of The Future
Eddie Daniels – Good Morning, Bahia
George Duke – Liberated Fantasies
Clare Fischer – Descarga Yema Ya
Clare Fischer – Gentle Breeze
Clare Fischer – African Flutes
Fania All-Stars – Vente Conmigo
Fuse One – In Celebration Of The Human Spirit
Headhunters – Here And Now
Freddie Hubbard – Two Moods For Freddie
Eddie Harris – Commotion
Terumaso Hino – Merry Go Round
Brian Jacks – Home Is Where The Hatred Is
Eric Kloss – The Samba Express
Eric Kloss – Mystique
Joachim Kuhn – Bed Stories
Joachim Kuhn – First Frisco
Joachim Kuhn – Hip Elegy/Kingsize
Janet Lawson – So High
Azar Lawrence – Novo Ono/ Summer Solstice
Ramsey Lewis - Slick
Marcia Montarroyos – Makenna Beach
Peter Magadini – Samba De Rollins

Max Middleton – Theme from A 'B' Movie
Namyslowski – Ladderman
Andy Narell - Stickman
Shunzo Ohno – Antares
Flora Purim – Samba Michel
Flora Purim – Moon Dreams/ Dr Jive
Paz – Yours Is The Light
Paz – AC/DC/ Moonchild
Judy Roberts – Ole/ Country Samba
Emanuel K Rahim – Spirit Of The Truth
Tom Ranier – Sal's Samba
Lee Ritenour – Ipanema Sol
Genji Sawai And Bacon Egg – Hand And Foot
Skyline – La Bufadora
David Schnitter – Flying Colours
Isao Suzuki – Mongolian Chant
Mongo Santamaria - Sambita
Horace Silver - Assimilation
Horace Silver – Time And Effort
Lonnie Smith – Straight To The Point
McCoy Tyner – Love Samba
McCoy Tyner – Fly Like The Wind
McCoy Tyner – Havana Sun
Tarika Blue – Revelation
Michael Urbaniak - Seresta
Roland Vasquez – Some What Others
Al Vizutti – Dragon Fly/ Jami
Kazumi Watanabe – Milestones

SOURCES FOR THE BOOK

All interviews conducted by the Author

Aff Ahmed
Aniff Akimbola
Hugh Albert
Paul Anderson
Tony Ashby
Paul 'Oscar' Anderson
Tony Bains
Steve Baker
Onkar Bancil
Chris Bangs
Richard 'Parrot' Barratt
Jerry 'IDJ' Barry
Zia Basit
Kevin Beadle
'Killer Jim' Bernadini
Berni
Andy Bex
Saranjit 'Sam' Birdi
Dave Bitelli
Simon Booth
Paul Bradshaw
Chris Brown
Michael Brown
Bulldog
Jeff Campbell
Mike Chadwick
Ivan Chandler
Tommy Chase
Paul Clark
De-Napoli Clarke
Hewan Clarke
Bob Cosby
Paul 'PC' Cummings
Colin Curtis
Gip Dammone
Trevor 'Mister T'
Darien
Billy Davidson
Errol Davis
Joe Davis
Gary Dennis
Russ Dewbury
Ian Dewhirst
Peter Duncan
Chris Dinnis
Laurence Dunn
Stewart Dunn

Andy Dyer
Steve 'Afro' Edwards
Travis Edwards
Robert Elms
Hameed Esmaeli
Patrick Forge
Sean French
Rob 'Galliano'
Gallagher
Gilly
Pete Girtley
Peter Haigh
Michael 'Big John' Hall
Rick Hassell
Ty Hassell
Kevin 'The Penguin' Haynes
Winston Hazel
Ronnie 'Fire' Henry
Leon Herbert
Tony 'OBJ'S' Hickmott
Mark Higgins
Chris Hill
Nicky Holloway
David Holmes
Ian Hylton
Rob Hylton
Tony Hylton
Edward Irish
Tony Jacobs
Baz Fe Jazz
Bob Jefferies
Dean Johnson
Patrick 'PJ' Johnson
Robert Johnson
Bobby Johnstone
Bob Jones
Colin Jones
Mark Jones
Robin Jones
Terry Jones
Lubi Jovanovic
Kerrso
Ozzie Lebad
Phil Levene
Paul 'Kermit'
Leveridge

Irven Lewis
Nathan Lewis
Paul Lewis
Lizard
Chris 'Rhythm Doc' Long
Perry Louis
Alex Lowes
Edward Lynch
Trevor M
Kenny MacLeod
Andy McConnell
Manish
Simon Mansell
Toshio Matsuura
Terry 'Maggot' Matthews
Tony 'Maggot' Matthews
Michael McDonach
Michael McFadin
Miller
Eric Miller
Trevor Miller
Tony Minvielle
Roger Mitchell
Tony Monson
Chris 'Chico' Murphy
Paul Murphy
Neil Neale
Jez Nelson
Janine Neye
Gary Nurse
Seymour Nurse
Shuya Okino
David 'Oki' Okonofua
Marvin Ottley
Pablo
Dez Parkes
Nick Peacock
Godfrey Pemberton
Gilles Peterson
Chris Phillips
Eddie Piller
Andrew Pinney
Tony Poole
Michael Powney
George Power

Bruce Q
Anne Quigley
Tony Quigley
Rico
Gary Robson
Dean Rudland
Neil Rushton
Saltz
Dave Samson
Pete Samson
Floyd Scott
Richard Searling
Trevor Shakes
Smiler
Clive 'Jah Burger' Smith
Clive Smith
John Snelling
Spats
Ed Stokes
Stretch
Chris Sullivan
Sylvester
Mark Swaby
Errol T - The Godfather
James Taylor
Linford 'Fanny' Taylor
Mark Taylor
Ralph Tee
Chris Thomas
Tin Tin - Steve Symons
Tin Tin - David Zee
Pete Tong
Duncan Uren
Robbie Vincent
Nic Wakefield
Mike Walwyn
Andy Ward
Graham Warr
Mark Webster
Barrington Wilks
Shaun Williams
Sheldon Willox
Greg Wilson
Jonathon Woodliffe
Eric X

BOOKS
The Family Album - Chris Brown (Music House 1980)

MAGAZINES AND PERIODICALS
Billboard (every edition from 1970 to 1980)
Black Music And Jazz Review (every edition)
Black Echoes (every edition up until 1988)
Blues And Soul (every edition from 1970 to 1988)
The Face (various)
Groove Weekly (all editions)
I.D. (various)
New Musical Express (various)
Record Mirror (all editions from 1988)
Straight No Chaser (all editions up until Winter 1992)
Street Sounds (all editions)

WEBSITES
www.thebottomend.co.uk
www.soulpranos.co.uk
www.soulboys.co.uk

INDEX

SUPPORT YOUR LOCAL JAZZ-JOCKS

THE END